ROYAL HISTORICAL SOCIETY

STUDIES IN HISTORY

New Series

WAR, POLITICS AND FINANCE IN LATE MEDIEVAL ENGLISH TOWNS

BRISTOL, YORK AND THE CROWN, 1350–1400

Letters patent of 30 October 1373 confirming the boundaries of the 'county'
of Bristol [detail showing Edward III dressed as the king of France]:
Bristol Record Office, royal charters and letters patent: 01209.
Reproduced by permission of Bristol Record Office

WAR, POLITICS AND FINANCE IN LATE MEDIEVAL ENGLISH TOWNS

BRISTOL, YORK AND THE CROWN, 1350–1400

Christian D. Liddy

THE ROYAL HISTORICAL SOCIETY
THE BOYDELL PRESS

First published 2005

A Royal Historical Society publication
Published by The Boydell Press
an imprint of Boydell & Brewer Ltd
PO Box 9, Woodbridge, Suffolk IP12 3DF, UK
and of Boydell & Brewer Inc.
668 Mt Hope Avenue, Rochester, NY 14620, USA
website: www.boydellandbrewer.com

ISBN 0 86193 274 9

ISSN 0269–2244

A catalogue record for this book is available
from the British Library

Library of Congress Cataloging-in-Publication Data
applied for

This book is printed on acid-free paper

Printed in Great Britain by
Cromwell Press, Trowbridge, Wiltshire

Contents

List of Tables

Publication of this volume was aided by generous grants from the Isobel Thornley Bequest and from the Scouloudi Foundation, in association with the Institute of Historical Research.

Note on the Text

All unpublished documents cited here are in the The National Archives (Public Record Office), unless otherwise stated. All quotations from original sources have been translated into English.

Acknowledgements

This book began life as a doctoral thesis and I am extremely grateful to those institutions whose financial assistance made my initial research possible, namely the British Academy and the Institute of Historical Research, from whom I held a Yorkist History Trust Fellowship. Mark Ormrod and Sarah Rees Jones supervised the doctoral research and have continued to provide encouragement and inspiration. The book can, and perhaps should, be read as an extended dialogue between a political historian and an urban historian. My examiners, Simon Walker and Jeremy Goldberg, made me think more deeply about the significance of the events in York in 1380–1, which have come to occupy a central place in the book. To Simon, my advisory editor for the Royal Historical Society, who sadly passed away before the book's publication, I owe a particular debt.

Since the completion of my doctorate I have learned a great deal from Caroline Barron, whose undergraduate course on late medieval London first fired my enthusiasm for urban history. Peter Fleming has, in recent years, organised several wonderful one-day conferences on late medieval Bristol. I would like to thank him as well as my fellow speakers on those occasions, including Clive Burgess, Chris Humphrey and James Lee, for providing a friendly and sympathetic environment in which I was able to test out some of my early ideas. Richard Hoyle kindly lent me a transcription of an account in the Public Record Office. Parts of this book were written during my time as a temporary lecturer at the University of St Andrews where Rob Bartlett, both by his example and his friendship, helped enormously in my professional development. The book was completed in the Department of History at the University of Durham, whose research committee, chaired sympathetically by a fellow medievalist, Michael Prestwich, has financed visits to archives and record offices in Manchester, Bristol, York and London. From their different perspectives, two of my Durham colleagues, Len Scales and Richard Britnell, have been a major source of advice, for which I am grateful.

Finally, I would like to thank Lisa who, only a few months after the birth of our son, agreed to read the entire typescript in draft. She has lived with Bristol and York for longer than she would care to remember, and it is to her that the book is dedicated.

Christian D. Liddy

Abbreviations

BIHR	Borthwick Institute of Historical Research, York
BIHR	*Bulletin of the Institute of Historical Research*
BL	British Library
BRO	Bristol Record Office
CChR	*Calendar of charter rolls*
CCR	*Calendar of close rolls*
CFR	*Calendar of fine rolls*
CHJ	*Cambridge Historical Journal*
CPR	*Calendar of patent rolls*
EcHR	*Economic History Review*
EHR	*English Historical Review*
GRB	*The great red book of Bristol*, ed. E. W. W. Veale (Bristol Record Society ii, iv, viii, xvi, xviii, 1931–53)
HJ	*Historical Journal*
HR	*Historical Research*
HT	*History Today*
JBS	*Journal of British Studies*
JEH	*Journal of Ecclesiastical History*
JMH	*Journal of Medieval History*
JRUL	John Rylands University Library, Manchester
LRB	*The little red book of Bristol*, ed. F. B. Bickley, Bristol 1900
NH	*Northern History*
PH	*Parliamentary History*
P&P	*Past & Present*
RP	*Rotuli parliamentorum*, London 1783
RS	Rolls Series
SR	*Statutes of the realm*, London 1810–28
TBGAS	*Transactions of the Bristol and Gloucestershire Archaeological Society*
TRHS	*Transactions of the Royal Historical Society*
UH	*Urban History*
YAJ	*Yorkshire Archaeological Journal*
YCA	York City Archives
YMB	*York memorandum book*, ed. M. Sellers and J. W. Percy (Surtees Society cxx, cxxv, clxxxvi, 1912–69)

Introduction

In a review of Lorraine Attreed's book, *The king's towns: identity and survival in late medieval English boroughs*, Robert Tittler commented that, 'in view of the vast and still growing scholarly literature on the relations between town and crown in late-medieval England, it is odd that we have until now lacked a modern book-length study of the subject'.[1] It is hoped that the reader will not, like the proverbial traveller waiting all day for a bus to arrive only to see two come along at once, find this book equally superfluous.

Relations between towns and the royal government have tended to be located within a particular paradigm based on the interplay between 'finance' and 'privilege'.[2] According to this model, urban relations with the royal government operated within a framework of reciprocity in which the crown sought to exploit urban wealth and resources in return for the confirmation and/or extension of charters of corporate liberties. Thus, Caroline Barron, writing about London and the crown in the mid-fifteenth century, characterised this relationship as an 'equilibrium': though the crown was the dominant partner, its financial need on the one hand was balanced by the city's concern for its privileges on the other.[3] When London stopped lending money to Richard II, the king punished the capital by confiscating its liberties, liberties that were only returned in perpetuity when the city made a loan of 10,000 marks to the crown in 1397.[4] In the 1430s, when the crown's policy of granting monopolies of the offices of wine-gauger, cloth-packer, wine-drawer and garbeller within the city to royal servants infringed the right of the capital to rule itself, the city agreed to make a loan on condition that the grants were revoked.[5] There is no doubt that London was a major royal creditor in the fourteenth and fifteenth centuries and that its loans far outweighed those from provincial towns,[6] but historians have also found a similar pattern of money and charters in the provinces. Lorraine Attreed, in a

---

[1]   R. Tittler, review of L. Attreed, *The king's towns: identity and survival in late medieval English boroughs*, New York 2001, in *Speculum* lxxvii (2002), 1229.
[2]   C. M. Barron, 'London and the crown, 1451–61', in J. R. L. Highfield and R. Jeffs (eds), *The crown and local communities in England and France in the fifteenth century*, Gloucester 1981, 91.
[3]   Ibid. 92.
[4]   Idem, 'The quarrel of Richard II with London, 1392–7', in F. R. H. Du Boulay and C. M. Barron (eds), *The reign of Richard II: essays in honour of May McKisack*, London 1971, 178, 199.
[5]   Idem, 'London and the crown, 1451–61', 91.
[6]   See, for example, A. Steel, *The receipt of the exchequer, 1377–1485*, Cambridge 1954, 465–73.

study of fiscal relations between the crown and York, Norwich, Exeter and Nottingham, described loans as 'another form of urban patronage, more effective than gifts of wine or small pensions in convincing the monarch to extend his favor and grant a desired charter or privilege', while in an essay on the city of York's relations with the crown in the first half of the fourteenth century, W. M. Ormrod posed the question directly and starkly: 'What did the citizens of York have to offer the crown in return for the new jurisdictional privileges they won in the early fourteenth century? The answer, as ever, is money.'[7]

Yet this view of the curial nature of crown–town relations, in which towns acted as royal suitors, seeking favour and reward in return for service, is problematic. A persuasive case can be made for its relevance to the fifteenth century, a period of severe economic and political strain for many English towns and cities, on which much of the research on the subject of relations between towns and the royal government in later medieval England has focused.[8] Indeed, Lorraine Attreed's examination of the city of York's appeals to Richard III and Henry VII for financial relief from its fiscal obligations is, in many ways, a contribution to the debate about fifteenth-century urban decline, one of the major issues in urban history from the late 1970s to the mid-1980s.[9] The experiences of towns in the Wars of the Roses have also been the subject of considerable attention. London's reaction to critical moments in the conflict, especially changes of dynasty, such as the Yorkists' seizure of power in February 1461 and Henry Tudor's accession to the throne in 1485, has been explored thoroughly.[10] Similarly, the cautious response of provincial towns to the Wars of the Roses has been noted, in particular the serious difficulties facing civic rulers who were unsure as to the reception they should provide rival royal and noble protagonists and claimants to the

---

[7] L. Attreed, 'Poverty, payments, and fiscal policies in English provincial towns, in S. K. Cohn, Jr, and S. A. Epstein (eds), *Portraits of medieval and renaissance living: essays in memory of David Herlihy*, Michigan 1996, 336–8; W. M. Ormrod, 'York and the crown under the first three Edwards', in S. Rees Jones (ed.), *The government of medieval York: essays in commemoration of the 1396 royal charter* (Borthwick Studies in History iii, 1997), 28.

[8] See, for example, the doctoral theses of A. P. M. Wright, 'The relations between the king's government and the English cities and boroughs in the fifteenth century', unpubl. DPhil. diss. Oxford 1965, and C. M. Barron, 'The government of London and its relations with the crown, 1400–1450', unpubl. PhD diss. London 1970, as well as Lorraine Attreed's *King's towns*, covering the period 1377–1509.

[9] L. Attreed, 'The king's interest: York's fee farm and the central government, 1482–92', *NH* xvii (1981), 24–43, and 'Poverty, payments, and fiscal policies', 325–48. This debate is summarised most usefully in D. M. Palliser, 'Urban decay revisited', in J. A. F. Thomson (ed.), *Towns and townspeople in the fifteenth century*, Gloucester 1988, 1–21.

[10] Barron, 'London and the crown, 1451–61', 88–109; D. J. Guth, 'Richard III, Henry VII and the city: London politics and the "Dun Cowe" ', in R. A. Griffiths and J. W. Sherborne (eds), *Kings and nobles in the later Middle Ages: a tribute to Charles Ross*, Gloucester 1986, 185–204.

throne.[11] In these straightened circumstances, there can be little doubt that the need for 'good lordship' by towns was compulsive and the quest for patronage more determined.[12]

Towns did seek favour and privilege. Towns also operated within a political system in which patronage relations were important. Throughout the late medieval period and beyond civic officals spent considerable sums on goods and gifts, whose purpose was to raise interest in their affairs among local gentry and nobility, and ultimately, secure access to, and influence with, the crown.[13] Meanwhile, the exercise of patronage through the distribution of titles, offices and privileges was an important aspect of the king's system of governing.[14] None the less, viewing urban relations with the crown in terms of a patron–client nexus reduces the subject to a story of favours bought and gifts given and neglects the public dimension to this interaction. Kingship, as a recent commentator has stressed, was different from lordship, and the king was not simply 'the good lord of all good lords', dispensing patronage to those who gained access to the royal ear.[15] Above all, the king was expected to uphold the common good, a duty which underpinned the rhetoric used by the crown to articulate and to justify its demands on its subjects and from which towns were not immune.

The argument that London's role in national politics was transformed in the course of the fourteenth century so that, 'whereas in the thirteenth century Londoners joined enthusiastically in the martial games of the great magnates, by the fifteenth century they had grown reluctant and stood apart for as long as was consistent with security', is equally reductive.[16] According to Caroline Barron, if London's support was crucial to the success of Simon de Montfort in 1263 and of Isabella and Mortimer in 1326, this sense of growing detachment from 'the magnate-dominated politics of the realm' meant that,

---

11 L. Attreed, 'The politics of welcome: ceremonies and constitutional development in later medieval English towns', in B. A. Hanawalt and K. L. Reyerson (eds), *City and spectacle in medieval Europe*, Minneapolis 1994, 215–16.

12 R. Horrox, 'Urban patronage and patrons in the fifteenth century', in R. A. Griffiths (ed.), *Patronage, the crown and the provinces in later medieval England*, Gloucester 1981, 161.

13 See, for example, the excellent recent study of C. F. Patterson, *Urban patronage in early modern England: corporate boroughs, the landed elite, and the crown, 1580–1640*, Stanford 1999.

14 W. M. Ormrod, *The reign of Edward III: crown and political society in England, 1327–1377*, New Haven 1990, 56–60.

15 C. Carpenter, 'Political and constitutional history: before and after McFarlane', in R. H. Britnell and A. J. Pollard (eds), *The McFarlane legacy: studies in late medieval politics and society*, Stroud 1995, 193; K. B. McFarlane, *The nobility of later medieval England*, Oxford 1973, 119. H. Castor, *The king, the crown, and the duchy of Lancaster: public authority and private power, 1399–1461*, Oxford 2000, ch. i, makes a similar point at greater length.

16 For what follows see C. M. Barron, 'London: the later Middle Ages: 1270–1520', in M. D. Lobel (ed.), *The atlas of historic towns*, London–Oxford 1969–89, iii. 42–3. See also her 'The deposition of Richard II', in J. Taylor and W. Childs (eds), *Politics and crisis in fourteenth-century England*, Gloucester 1990, 132–49.

from the late fourteenth century, London's citizens adopted a more passive role, providing 'money for wars and receptions for conquering heroes'. At times of political crisis, notably Richard II's deposition, Edward IV's seizure of the throne and Henry VII's defeat of Richard III, London pursued a policy of studied neutrality, waiting for the contested throne to be won and then lavishing money on the winner in return for the confirmation and/or extension of the city's liberties.[17] J. L. Bolton's detailed examination of relations between London and the crown in the mid-fifteenth century has provided a valuable corrective to this view.[18] The city corporation, he maintained, could not have remained politically neutral in the 1450s and 1460s because of the role of London's rulers as financial props to the crown and their involvement in the politics of trade as merchants with strong commercial links to Calais and the Netherlands. It was the profound disillusionment of a group of London aldermen and a larger group of the city's merchants, mercers and staplers with Henry VI's commercial policies, according to Bolton, that forced London's leading citizens to take sides and to provide active support for the Yorkist cause in 1460–1.

Yet, with a couple of exceptions,[19] Bolton's suggestive remarks have not been pursued, certainly not in relation to provincial towns and cities. For instance, Lorraine Attreed has perceived a similar dislocation of urban communities from events at the centre, arguing that, during the Wars of the Roses, towns sought survival above all else, literally guarding themselves from external influence and acting only when the outcome of events was already known.[20] R. B. Dobson has commented recently that, during the Wars of the Roses, the mayor and aldermen of York 'were notoriously disinclined to run the risks of being involved in national partisan politics at all'.[21] Towns were apolitical and more interested in their own, private affairs than in issues of wider, public policy. This interpretation has deep roots. According to Alice Stopford Green, writing in the late nineteenth century,

> In those days [the fifteenth century] indeed busy provincials but dimly conscious of national policy found in the confusion of court politics and the distraction of its intrigues, or in the feuds of a divided and bewildered administration, no true call to national service . . . Civil wars which swept over the country at the bidding of a factious group of nobles or of a vain and

---

[17] Guth, 'Richard III, Henry VII and the city', 186–7.

[18] J. L. Bolton, 'The city and the crown, 1456–61', *London Journal* xii (1986), 11–24.

[19] Most notably P. Nightingale, *A medieval mercantile company: the grocers' company and the politics and trade of medieval London, 1000–1485*, London 1995. See also the review of this book by J. L. Bolton, 'Commerce and credit: the grocers' company and the growth of medieval London', *The Ricardian* xi (1997), 25–30 esp. pp. 27–8.

[20] Attreed, *King's towns*, 298–300, and 'Politics of welcome', 215–16.

[21] R. B. Dobson, 'The crown, the charter and the city, 1396–1461', in Rees Jones, *Government of medieval York*, 15.

unscrupulous King-maker left, and justly left, the towns supremely indifferent to any question save that of how to make the best terms for themselves from the winning side, or to use the disasters of warring lords so as to extend their own *privileges*.[22]

The fifteenth-century borough was 'a state within the state', which sought to maintain 'its isolated self-dependent life' through the acquisition of charters of liberties.[23]

In fact, this perception of the insular nature of English towns and cities is grounded not simply in an understanding of the peculiar pressures and challenges confronting urban communities in the fifteenth century. It is also derived from a long-established historiographical tradition. In the late nineteenth and early twentieth centuries urban history was dominated by the pioneering scholarship of historians such as Mary Bateson, F. W. Maitland, James Tait, Adolphus Ballard and Martin Weinbaum, who were interested primarily in the origins and legal and constitutional development of the medieval town. Theirs was the history of the growth of the medieval English town as a corporate personality, with resources and a constitution of its own, told largely through the evidence of urban custumals and royal and seignorial charters issued to individual urban communities.[24] In this respect, their interest in the history of institutions was, of course, shared by a number of their contemporaries such as William Stubbs, writing the history of England, or G. T. Lapsley, studying the rise and fall of the palatinate of Durham.[25] Following the constitutional histories of F. W. Maitland, James Tait and others, there has been a tendency to see the town in its relations with the royal government essentially in institutional terms, as a distinct legal, administrative and physical entity, with its own autonomous personality, detached not just from the kingdom as a whole, but from the individuals who lived in it.[26] Since liberties were seen to define the town and to give it its corporate existence, separating it from the countryside and from the wider realm, it is

[22] A. S. Green, *Town life in the fifteenth century*, London 1894, i. 164. My emphasis.
[23] Ibid. i. 1–2.
[24] F. Pollock and F. W. Maitland, *The history of English law*, 2nd edn, Cambridge 1968, i. 635–88; F. Maitland, *Township and borough*, Cambridge 1898; *Borough customs*, i, ii, ed. M. Bateson (Selden Society xviii, xxi, 1904, 1906); *British borough charters, 1042–1216*, ed. A. Ballard, Cambridge 1913; *British borough charters, 1216–1307*, ed. A. Ballard and J. Tait, Cambridge 1923; J. Tait, *The medieval English borough: studies on its origins and constitutional history*, Manchester 1936; M. Weinbaum, *The incorporation of boroughs*, Manchester 1937; *British borough charters, 1307–1660*, ed. M. Weinbaum, Cambridge 1943.
[25] W. Stubbs, *The constitutional history of England in its origin and development*, 4th edn, Oxford 1906; G. T. Lapsley, *The county palatine of Durham: a study in constitutional history*, London 1900.
[26] For example, L. Attreed, 'Arbitration and the growth of urban liberties in late medieval England', *JBS* xxxi (1992), 205–35, although see her admission (p. 209) that, in the jurisdictional dispute between the city and cathedral church of Exeter, 'each side represented, not just impersonal institutions, but human beings as well'.

scarcely surprising that historians have argued that towns' demands of the crown were limited to the defence and acquisition of urban privileges. Hence Caroline Barron could say of London's role in the parliaments of the first half of the fifteenth century that 'the City was only roused to action in defence of its liberties and privileges'.[27]

Emphasis on the corporate nature of the medieval town also fits nicely with the localist interpretation of English politics in the early modern period, which drew on a sociological rather than a constitutional framework, but which also placed great weight on the collective nature of local society. In the later nineteenth century Ferdinand Tönnies and Max Weber looked back to a pre-industrial and pre-modern world for the ideal community that represented an older way of life that was under threat from the twin forces of industrialisation and the rise of the nation state.[28] They found this community in the town and village of the Middle Ages.[29] Tönnies proposed a transition from *Gemeinschaft* (community), characterised by intimacy, social harmony and isolation from the outside world, to *Gesellschaft* (society), in which people could still share a common habitat, but where social relations were artificial and transitory and people only acted with others out of self-interest. *Gemeinschaft* was an organism with interdependent parts and with a communal life of its own based on common interests.[30] These ideas influenced the work of the Leicester school of local history, notably that of Alan Everitt, who exhorted the local historian to study 'the development of some particular local community *as a whole*, as a complete society or organism, with a more or less distinct and continuous life of its own'.[31] The impact of this approach is to be found in local urban studies such as David Palliser's work on sixteenth-century York, which attempted 'to view an urban community in its totality' and which emphasised, for example, the city's 'very narrow-minded view of parliament', where civic rulers saw local affairs rather than national issues as pre-eminent.[32] In his study of Newcastle-upon-Tyne in the seventeenth century Roger Howell took a similar approach, characterising the town as a 'sub-political society, that is, one in which the conduct of local affairs received the main emphasis, interest in national affairs a secondary one'. Indifferent to national politics, the town's rulers were also extremely suspicious of royal intervention in civic affairs. When war came in the 1640s, according to Howell, there was an 'attitude of drifting with events' among civic corporations. Towns sought neutrality rather than active

---

[27] Barron, 'Government of London', 348.

[28] F. Tönnies, *Community and society: Gemeinschaft und Gesellschaft*, ed. and trans. C. P. Loomis, New York 1963; M. Weber, *The theory of social and economic organization*, trans. A. M. Henderson and T. Parsons, ed. T. Parsons, New York 1964.

[29] Tönnies, *Community and society*, 57.

[30] Ibid. 34–5, 77–8.

[31] A. Everitt, *Ways and means in local history*, London 1971, 6.

[32] D. M. Palliser, *Tudor York*, Oxford 1979, vii. 58.

involvement in any ideological or political conflict;[33] a conclusion which significantly recalls that of Alice Stopford Green and Caroline Barron on the muted response of towns to the Wars of the Roses. To Alan Everitt and others of the county community school, the Civil War itself could be explained from a localist perspective as the consequence of a conflict between the centre and the locality, 'two organisms, each with its own independent existence'.[34] Under severe financial strain from the crown in the seventeenth century, the already fractured polity dissolved into a series of autonomous local communities.

The work of early modern revisionist political historians has cast a long shadow on studies of the medieval gentry.[35] Those arguing for the existence of county communities in late medieval England have concentrated on the leading figures of the shire, the county gentry, whom they contend, over the course of the fourteenth and fifteenth centuries, came to identify themselves increasingly with the shires in which they resided, through marital and kinship ties, and as local landowners and participants in county politics and administration.[36] The concept of the 'county community' has come under sustained attack in recent years from late medievalists and early modernists alike.[37] Several historians have expressed serious reservations about the idea of 'community' underpinning this understanding of county society and politics between the fourteenth and seventeenth centuries. The perceived insularity of the county community has been criticised essentially on structural grounds, both for emphasising the coherence and harmonious nature of social relations within local society at the expense of friction and tension and for presenting the shire as a discrete entity, separate from the wider realm.[38] Reviewing a series of studies of the county community in later medieval England, Rosemary Horrox argued that 'it is important not to see the *communitas* as monolithic, however much it might seek to give that impres-

---

[33] R. Howell, *Newcastle upon Tyne and the Puritan revolution: a study of the civil war in north England*, Oxford 1967, 336, 342.

[34] A. Everitt, *The local community and the great rebellion* (Historical Association, gen. ser. lxx, 1969), 5.

[35] For the origins and development of the historiographical concept of the 'county community' see C. Carpenter, 'Gentry and community in medieval England', *JBS* xxxiii (1994), 341–4.

[36] N. Saul, *Knights and esquires: the Gloucestershire gentry in the fourteenth century*, Oxford 1981, ch. iv, 258–62; M. Bennett, *Community, class and careerism: Cheshire and Lancashire society in the age of Gawain and the green knight*, Cambridge 1983, ch. ii; S. J. Payling, *Political society in Lancastrian England: the greater gentry of Nottinghamshire*, Oxford 1991, esp. pp. 217–19; E. Acheson, *A gentry community: Leicestershire in the fifteenth century, c. 1422– c. 1485*, Cambridge 1992, chs iv–v.

[37] There is an extremely useful discussion of this literature in P. Withington and A. Shephard, 'Introduction: communities in early modern England', in P. Withington and A. Shephard (eds), *Communities in early modern England*, Manchester 2000, 1–15.

[38] The most thorough critique of the late medieval county community school is Carpenter, 'Gentry and community', 340–80.

sion on formal occasions. It consisted of individuals with their own connections and own concerns'. Specifically, she issued a powerful reminder that,
'for contemporaries the word had far more elitist implications than the
modern "community". The *communitas* were the people whose stake in the
region gave them the right to a say in its governance'. She also voiced her
concern about the framework in which relations between the centre and the
locality have been explored in monographs on the late medieval gentry
which, in exploring the social and economic position of landowners in their
shires, have tended to neglect the influence of the crown in the provinces
and to present 'royal government as something distinct from local
concerns'.[39] Similarly, Clive Holmes has questioned the structuralist argument of proponents of the 'county community' school in the seventeenth
century, demonstrating, in particular, that the social experiences of the
gentry stretched beyond the boundaries of their individual shires and that
their involvement in local government as agents of the crown encouraged
their participation 'in a national political culture'.[40]

How do towns fit into the recent critique of localist studies? Only David
Harris Sacks's studies of early modern Bristol have sought to provide a
sustained challenge to the traditional view of English urban political life from
the later Middle Ages. In recent years urban historians have been more interested in placing the medieval town in its social and economic context. In the
process, they have undermined an older view of urban independence,
demonstrating convincingly, for example, the importance of the town's relations with its hinterland and the interconnectedness of town and countryside
in terms of the movement of people and trade.[41] Equally significant, however,
is the comparative neglect, in recent years, of the political history of the
medieval English town.[42] Integrating social and economic with political
history, Sacks's starting-point was the design of Bristol's medieval and early
modern common seal and coat of arms showing a ship entering a gateway:
Bristol, a town dependent on trade for its livelihood, 'was not a closed arena
which drew in upon itself and made of the connections and rivalries of its
inhabitants the sole source of local life', but rather, it was 'an open gate in
which the larger world penetrated into the community and helped shape it'.[43]

---

[39] R. Horrox, 'Local and national politics in fifteenth-century England', *JMH* xviii (1992),
391–403, quotations at pp. 395, 397.
[40] C. Holmes, 'The county community in Stuart historiography', *JBS* xix (1980), 54–73,
quotation at p. 73.
[41] See, for example, A. F. Butcher, 'English urban history and the revolt of 1381', in
R. H. Hilton and T. H. Aston (eds), *The English rising of 1381*, Cambridge 1984, 84–111;
R. H. Hilton, *English and French towns in feudal society: a comparative study*, Cambridge 1992;
and M. Kowaleski, *Local markets and regional trade in medieval Exeter*, Cambridge 1995.
[42] A point noted by D. M. Palliser, 'Towns and the English state, 1066–1500', in J. R.
Maddicott and D. M. Palliser (eds), *The medieval state: essays presented to James Campbell*,
London 2000, 127.
[43] D. H. Sacks, *The widening gate: Bristol and the Atlantic economy, 1450–1700*, Berkeley
1991, 1–4, quotation at p. 4.

In particular, Sacks emphasised the interaction between civic and royal government, highlighting the close ties built up between the crown and members of the civic elite in their capacity as overseas merchants participating in a national economic community and reliant on national economic policy, and as royal agents exercising authority locally on behalf of the central government.[44] Nevertheless, according to Sacks, it was in the late fifteenth and early sixteenth centuries that a combination of social, economic, religious and political changes transformed Bristol's relations with the outside world and with the crown in particular. Where once, in the Middle Ages, Bristol had been characterised by its insular, communal life, the town's rulers in the early modern period became firmly integrated into a national economic and political order and 'now identified themselves with the national regime and took pride in their place in the organization of the state'.[45] In this chronology, then, the fourteenth century remains sadly neglected and the perception of an inward-looking, self-contained medieval urban community persists.

Sacks's work does, though, suggest an alternative direction in which the subject of crown–town relations in late medieval England can be pursued. First is the recognition that, while towns did have a strong corporate character in terms of communal resources, self-government and cultural traditions, they were more than impersonal bodies with a corporate will of their own. They were not simply institutions, as they appear, for example, in the older works of constitutional urban history, but were composed of real people. Just as K. B. McFarlane criticised William Stubbs's institutional approach to parliament, refuting the belief that it was 'possible and desirable to write the history of institutions apart from the men who worked them', so David Palliser has pointed out that 'a city constitution, after all, is nothing without the people who made it work and lived within its constraints'.[46] The second and related point is that townspeople were involved in the business of governing on behalf of the crown. Adapting Pollock and Maitland's familiar description of the medieval town as 'both organ and organism', that is, as both an organism with its own communal life, ruled by its own officials, and an organ of royal government, Sacks argued that 'the work of the town as an organization serving the state was performed by a much narrower group than the community as a whole'. Indeed, his theme was the relation of civic government to the crown rather than the relation of civic community to the royal government.[47]

44 Idem, 'The corporate town and the English state: Bristol's "little businesses", 1625–1641', *P&P* cx (1986), 69–105.
45 This is the theme of his book, *Widening gate*, which is summarised in D. H. Sacks, 'Celebrating authority in Bristol, 1475–1640', in S. Zimmerman and R. F. E. Weissman (eds), *Urban life in the renaissance*, Newark, NJ 1989, 187–223, quotation at p. 215.
46 McFarlane, *Nobility*, 280; D. M. Palliser, 'The birth of York's civic liberties, c. 1200–1354', in Rees Jones, *Government of medieval York*, 105.
47 Pollock and Maitland, *English law*, i. 635–6; Sacks, 'Corporate town', 86.

This book is a comparative study of relations between Bristol, York and the royal government between 1350 and 1400. Fourteenth-century Bristol and York provide a good basis for comparison, despite their contrasting earlier histories. Outsiders assumed that late medieval Bristol was a city and its privileged inhabitants citizens,[48] but in the records produced by their own rulers, the distinction was consistently maintained: Bristol was a town (in Latin *villa*, in French *ville*), whose residents were described as burgesses (*burgenses*, *burgeys*), while York warranted the appellation city (*civitas*, *cite*), whose inhabitants were citizens (*cives*, *citeseyns*). York owed its designation as a city to its status as an ancient (that is, Roman) and cathedral town.[49] York had been a major Roman city between the first and the fourth centuries and was first the location of a bishop's see and then, from the eighth century, the holder of archiepiscopal status.[50] Bristol, in contrast, was never a Roman city or the seat of a bishopric. Compared to York, it was a late urban foundation, whose origins can only be confidently located to the late Anglo-Saxon period, *c.* 1000. Bristol could not boast the rich historical heritage of York. Indeed, while York could advertise its connections with York Minster, the largest Gothic cathedral in England, on its common seal, Bristol had no such glorious associations or distinguished past on which it could draw. Whereas the reverse of York's seal contained the image of St Peter, to whom the cathedral was dedicated, the reverse of Bristol's seal celebrated the town's commercial ties, incorporating the picture of a ship sailing through a gateway, perhaps into the town's port.[51] What Bristol possessed, and what it shared, to an extent, with York, was an excellent geographical position, for the town lay at the confluence of the Bristol Channel and two tributaries, the rivers Severn and Avon.[52] This river network facilitated internal trade up the river Severn into the midlands and encouraged overseas commercial activity out through the Severn estuary, fuelling the town's substantial demographic and economic growth. In the mid-twelfth century the anonymous author of the chronicle, the *Gesta Stephani*, described Bristol as 'almost the richest city of all in the country, receiving merchandise by sailing-ships from lands near and far', with a harbour capable of accommodating 1,000 vessels thanks to the

---

[48] See, for example, the description of Bristol by the commons of York *c.* 1400, noted at p. 208 below.

[49] S. Reynolds, *Kingdoms and communities in western Europe, 900–1300*, 2nd edn, Oxford 1997, 184. Nevertheless, for the sake of convenience, I use the words 'town' and 'city' interchangeably in this study to describe Bristol and York.

[50] For York's early history see D. W. Rollason, *Sources for York history to AD 1100*, York 1998.

[51] For York see R. B. Pugh, 'The seals, insignia, plate, and officers of the city', in VCH, *Yorkshire: York*, Oxford 1961, 544–5. For Bristol see P. D. A. Harvey and A. McGuinness, *A guide to British medieval seals*, London 1996, fig. 107 at p. 109.

[52] York was part of the Ouse/Humber river system: J. Kermode, *Medieval merchants: York, Beverley and Hull in the later Middle Ages*, Cambridge 1998, 7. Bristol's early history and location are best explained in M. D. Lobel and E. M. Carus-Wilson, 'Bristol', in Lobel, *Atlas of historic towns*, ii. 1–2.

strong tide on the river Avon caused by its junction with the Severn estuary.[53]

In the fourteenth century Bristol and York had much in common. They were, after London, the largest and wealthiest towns in England. Measured by the two most commonly used indicators of urban wealth and demography in the late medieval period, the tax returns of 1334 and 1377, Bristol ranked top of the league table of English provincial towns in terms of taxable wealth in 1334, just ahead of York, although York, by 1377, was slightly larger than its south-western rival.[54] If London was in a league of its own, with an estimated population of over 40,000 in 1377, Bristol probably had about 12,000 inhabitants in the same period, compared to York's population of almost 14,000.[55] The two towns sat at the apex of the provincial urban hierarchy.

Bristol and York also possessed fairly sophisticated systems of civic government.[56] Prior to 1373 Bristol was ruled by a mayor, two bailiffs (responsible, among other things, for the payment of the town's financial dues to the crown), two stewards (the town's main internal financial officers), and a common council of forty-eight of the *potentiores* and *discretiores* of the town, who were to act as advisers to the mayor and from whom the leading civic officials of mayor, bailiff and steward were drawn. The city council was brought into existence at the request of Bristol's mayor in 1344 as part of a wide-ranging reform of civic government, in which the town's civic ordinances were examined, amended and, in some cases, created anew by the common council, before being written down in a new civic register, the Little Red Book. Post 1373 Bristol gained a sheriff who discharged many of the duties previously performed by the two bailiffs; the bailiffs acquired new financial functions within the town, replacing the stewards as custodians of the town's treasury; and the common council had a reduced membership of forty. York was ruled through a mayor, two bailiffs (replaced by two sheriffs after 1396) and three chamberlains, the equivalent of Bristol's stewards. Although there is some evidence of a city council as early as 1301, the development of a conciliar system of government only appears to date from the 1370s. Unlike Bristol, though, York had a three-tiered system of government, consisting of the council of twelve aldermen and the council of twenty-four, representing the civic elite of high-ranking officeholders, and the council of forty-eight, representative of the commons of the city, whose members belonged to the civic franchise, but did not occupy the senior offices within the civic hierarchy such as chamberlain, bailiff and mayor. Power lay, in prac-

[53] *Gesta Stephani*, ed. and trans. K. R. Potter, Oxford 1976, 56–7.
[54] A. Dyer, *Decline and growth in English towns, 1400–1640*, Cambridge 1995, 62, 56.
[55] Ibid. 25, 65–6.
[56] For what follows see the introduction to *Bristol charters, 1378–1499*, ed. H. A. Cronne (Bristol Record Society xi, 1945), 73–83; E. Miller, 'Medieval York', in VCH, *Yorkshire: York*, 34–7, 70–9, 80–4; and S. Rees Jones, 'York's civic administration, 1354–1464', in her *Government of medieval York*, 122–3, table 1 at p. 140.

tice, with the two inner councils, which met regularly with the mayor to run the city: the council of forty-eight was expected to add its assent to decisions already made by the other two councils. In both Bristol and York, as in a number of other major English towns and cities, the ruling elite was composed almost exclusively of merchants engaged in overseas trade.[57] York's councils of twelve and twenty-four, for example, were dominated by those involved in the wholesale trade of cloth and wool, while Bristol's common council of forty-eight in the fourteenth century was monopolised by a mercantile elite, especially those participating in the wine import and cloth export trades.[58]

Medieval York has long attracted the interest of historians, drawn by the city's extremely rich civic archive. For the purposes of this book, Edward Miller's wide-ranging and authoritative history of medieval York in the *Victoria county history* series, Jennifer Kermode's work on the social, economic, religious and political interests of York's merchant community, Lorraine Attreed's exploration of York's relationship with the crown from the late fourteenth to the early sixteenth centuries, and the recent studies of R. B. Dobson, David Palliser and Sarah Rees Jones on the political and constitutional development of York, have been most relevant.[59] Bristol suffers in comparison, notwithstanding Clive Burgess's pioneering work on the parish of All Saints' and E. M. Carus-Wilson's detailed examination of the volume and pattern of Bristol's overseas trade.[60] The town has not, until very recently, received the attention it properly deserves.[61] In fact, it may be indicative of the comparative lack of interest in Bristol's late medieval history that some of the best scholarship is by an early modernist, David Harris Sacks, working backwards from the sixteenth and seventeenth centuries, although this, as has been indicated, presents an unduly simplified portrait of

[57] The control of urban government by a small number of merchants was described a long time ago in S. L. Thrupp's seminal study, *The merchant class of medieval London, 1300–1500*, Ann Arbor 1948, ch. ii.

[58] For York see the statistics provided in Kermode, *Medieval merchants*, 39–40. Also revealing is the statistical analysis of Bristol's common council membership in S. A. C. Penn, 'Social and economic aspects of fourteenth-century Bristol', unpubl. PhD diss. Birmingham 1989, ch. iv.

[59] Miller, 'Medieval York', 25–116; Kermode, *Medieval merchants*; Attreed, *King's towns*; and the essays in Rees Jones, *Government of medieval York*, a volume commemorating the six-hundredth anniversary of York's 1396 charter.

[60] C. Burgess, ' "For the increase of divine service": chantries in the parish in late medieval Bristol', *JEH* xxxvi (1985), 46–65, and ' "By quick and by dead": wills and pious provision in late medieval Bristol', *EHR* cii (1987), 837–58; *The overseas trade of Bristol in the later Middle Ages*, ed. E. M. Carus-Wilson (Bristol Record Society vii, 1937), and E. M. Carus-Wilson, 'The overseas trade of Bristol', in her *Medieval merchant venturers: collected studies*, 2nd edn, London 1967, 1–97.

[61] Mention must be made of Peter Fleming who, in his role as co-director of the Regional History Centre at the University of the West of England, has done most to revive interest in late medieval Bristol.

the corporate, self-enclosed nature of the fourteenth- and fifteenth-century town.[62]

The relative neglect of Bristol cannot be explained by a paucity of source material, for while the records of admissions to the freedom of Bristol are not extant, the town is blessed with several medieval civic registers, the most important of which, the Little Red Book and the Great Red Book, begin c. 1344 and c. 1376 respectively.[63] Whatever the reason, this disregard is particularly surprising given Bristol's increasing prominence within the kingdom in the period 1350 to 1400. These years were formative ones in relations between a number of major provincial towns and cities and the outside world: the changes taking place were more important, perhaps, than those identified by David Harris Sacks in Bristol in the late fifteenth and early sixteenth centuries. In 1373 Bristol was the first urban community to become a county in its own right. It was followed by York in 1396, Newcastle-upon-Tyne in 1400, Norwich in 1404 and Lincoln in 1409, and then several other towns and cities including Coventry, Hull and Southampton by the mid-fifteenth century.[64] Although London had been a *de facto* county since the early twelfth century, when its citizens were granted the shrievalty of London and Middlesex, the charters of 1373 and 1396 were the first of their kind issued to English urban communities.[65] A comparison of Bristol and York, both in the vanguard of this wave of royal grants of county status, should open up new possibilities of interpretation in understanding the nature of crown–town relations in later medieval England, permitting the formulation of broader conclusions than can be derived from the detailed study of an individual town or city.

In a recent article G. L. Harriss drew attention to the essential character of the late medieval English polity in which, in the absence of a paid and permanent bureaucracy of its own in the localities, the crown was dependent on local elites in the exercise of royal authority. 'Government', according to Harriss, was not 'arcane or remote, something handed down by officials', but rather, it was 'something in which subjects were involved'.[66] In this respect, he was echoing a much older view of the co-operative nature of medieval English governance expressed in the classic phrase coined by A. B. White: 'self-government at the king's command'. 'One of the most notable things in

62 In addition to the *Widening gate* see his *Trade, society and politics in Bristol, 1500–1640*, New York 1985.

63 *LRB* and *GRB*. This is not to forget the late fifteenth-century civic chronicle, Robert Ricart, *The maire of Bristowe is kalendar*, ed. L. T. Smith (Camden n.s. v, 1872).

64 S. H. Rigby, 'Urban "oligarchy" in late medieval England', in Thomson, *Towns and townspeople*, 80.

65 S. Reynolds, *An introduction to the history of English medieval towns*, Oxford 1977, 113; Palliser, 'Towns and the English state', 133, 140–1.

66 G. L. Harriss, 'Political society and the growth of government in late medieval England', *P&P* cxxxviii (1993), 37.

English constitutional history from the twelfth century to the end of the middle ages', wrote White, 'was that the king was getting his work done largely by the people, and that with little or no compensation'.[67] In fact, as Michael Braddick has recently demonstrated in a series of publications, the involvement of unpaid local elites in the exercise of government in the provinces was a characteristic feature of the early modern state.[68] Developing White's idea of governance as a participatory process, G. L. Harriss argued that the major political development of the fourteenth and fifteenth centuries was the 'emergence of a political society containing the middling landowners' which was deeply involved in 'the activity of governing', serving as sheriffs, parliamentary representatives, justices of the peace, tax collectors, or performing other *ad hoc* services to the crown.[69] 'Government', in Harriss's words, 'was moulded more by pressures from within political society than by the efforts of kings or officials to direct it from above.' In particular, members of political society looked on the crown and the machinery of royal government as an important resource upon which they could draw to protect or promote their interests. In a similar vein, Braddick has viewed the growth of the early modern state as a response to pressure from below. In particular, he has suggested that local elites in the shires sought crown employment in order to both confirm and confer gentry status.[70] In the work of Harriss and Braddick, then, government emerges as a negotiated enterprise between local elites and the crown.

What is missing from their analysis is full consideration of the place of urban elites in English public life. The emerging political society, identified by Harriss, contained urban elites, especially merchants, as well as landed gentry. The participation of leading townsmen in government was not a novelty in the years 1350 to 1400.[71] Indeed, civic officeholders such as the mayor and bailiffs were as much royal officers as urban officials in the sense that they were expected to rule their towns on the king's behalf in matters of finance and law.[72] None the less, the changing strategy by means of which the crown looked to finance the Hundred Years War did have important

---

[67] A. B. White, *Self-government at the king's command: a study in the beginnings of English democracy*, Minneapolis 1933, 2.

[68] See, for example, M. J. Braddick, 'State formation and social change in early modern England: a problem stated and approaches suggested', *Social History* xvi (1991), 1–17, and his *State formation in early modern England, c. 1550–1700*, Cambridge 2000.

[69] For this and what follows see Harriss, 'Growth of government', 33, 35.

[70] Braddick, *State formation*, ch. i.

[71] For the involvement of Southampton burgesses in the service of the king from the late twelfth century see C. Platt, *Medieval Southampton: the port and trading community, A.D. 1000–1600*, London 1973, 14, 60–2.

[72] Palliser, 'Towns and the English state', 135; Rigby, 'Urban "oligarchy" ', 65. Of course, this was only true of royal towns; a significant number were seignorial, held of local lords: M. W. Beresford and H. P. R. Finberg, *English medieval boroughs: a handlist*, Newton Abbot 1973, 40–3.

political consequences. When the onset of war in the 1330s bankrupted the Italian banking firms of Peruzzi and Bardi, Edward III sought credit first from syndicates of English merchants and then, after their collapse, from the wider body of his urban and mercantile subjects.[73] Hitherto, the implications of this fiscal development have only been examined in relation to London. Stephen O'Connor's recent work on the royal service of two London merchants, Adam Fraunceys and John Pyel, has shown, for example, that their close relations with the crown during Edward III's reign were 'founded on their ability to lend the king money', but that they then became involved in other forms of government, acting as diplomats on missions overseas and serving on a range of royal judicial and administrative commissions.[74] Merchants from several English provincial towns and cities including Bristol and York, however, were also drawn further into the world of royal finance, royal government and high politics.

The theme of this book is the increasing participation of urban elites in government between 1350 and 1400. In this period the rulers of Bristol and York were incorporated more fully into the affairs of the kingdom as a whole. In part, then, the book seeks to make a contribution to the debate about the relative strengths and weaknesses of the late medieval English state, in which there has been disagreement about the effects of war on the resources of the crown and on its relations with local elites in the exercise of royal authority in the provinces.[75] In examining the interdependence between royal and civic government, a subsidiary theme is the impact of the crown on the internal politics and governance of Bristol and York. In this respect, the constitutional development of the two towns is not ignored, but rather it is placed primarily within a political context instead of a formal framework of royal charters and grants.

Underpinning the research is an examination of the identity and interests of the individuals from Bristol and York actually involved in the business of governing. In contrast to the numerous county studies of the English gentry, prosopographical analysis has rarely been pursued by historians working on English urban elites, although it has been employed more regularly by urban historians writing about continental towns.[76] Prosopography has been

---

[73] These changes in the structure of royal borrowing are traced in Ormrod, *Edward III*, 183–6.

[74] S. O'Connor, 'Finance, diplomacy and politics: royal service by two London merchants in the reign of Edward III', *HR* lxvii (1994), 18–39, quotation at p. 18. See also C. M. Barron, 'Richard Whittington: the man behind the myth', in A. E. J. Hollaender and W. Kellaway (eds), *Studies in London history presented to Philip Edmund Jones*, London 1969, 197–248.

[75] A debate summarised and addressed in Harriss, 'Growth of government', 28–57, esp. pp. 28–33.

[76] The county community studies include Saul, *Knights and esquires*; S. M. Wright, *The Derbyshire gentry in the fifteenth century* (Derbyshire Record Society viii, 1983); Payling,

defined as 'the investigation of the common background characteristics of a group of actors in history by means of a collective study of their lives'. The assumption behind this collective biography is that it can uncover 'the roots of political action', the underlying reality 'beneath the rhetoric of politics', through 'the exposure of the workings of a political machine and the identification of those who pull the levers'.[77] The methodology is particularly appropriate to this study because it offers a different perspective on urban relations with the crown, providing an important reminder that behind 'Bristol' and 'York' were the small groups who acted in their names. A major criticism of this methodology is that it encourages the equation of politics with self-interest and personal gain to the exclusion of any acknowledgement of the role of ideas or principles from analysis of political behaviour. In fact, it was a sense of dissatisfaction with the equation of politics with patronage and private interest in much writing on the subject of late medieval English politics, which has led to recent calls for a new constitutional history.[78] Edward Powell, for instance, has suggested that more attention should be paid to the language of politics and to 'the values, ideals and conventions governing political life', arguing that the rhetoric of politics, which prosopography sought to penetrate in order to expose the underlying motive of political behaviour, should be taken seriously because political figures had to operate 'within a specific political culture and had to reconcile their actions to its values'. Meanwhile, Christine Carpenter has emphasised the need to 'look at public institutions, and at how private power and private interests focused around them'.[79]

This book examines the interaction of urban elites and royal government within the context of contemporary ideas about government and the institutional framework of parliament. Its focus is what Harriss has termed 'the politics of government'.[80] Urban relations with the crown in later medieval England were conducted through the vocabulary of patronage, metaphors of familial relationships and the rhetoric of the chamber,[81] and there were other

Political society; and Acheson, *Gentry community*. The notable English urban exceptions are Thrupp, *Merchant class*; Kowaleski, *Medieval Exeter*; and Kermode, *Medieval merchants*. For the continent see, for example, F. J. W. van Kan, 'Élite and government in medieval Leiden', *JMH* xxi (1995), 51–75.

[77] L. Stone, 'Prosopography', in his *The past and the present revisited*, London 1987, 45.

[78] For what follows see E. Powell, 'After "after McFarlane": the poverty of patronage and the case for constitutional history', in D. J. Clayton and others (eds), *Trade, devotion and governance: papers in later medieval history*, Stroud 1994, 10, 11. For an example of this new constitutional history see J. Watts, *Henry VI and the politics of kingship*, Cambridge 1996.

[79] Carpenter, 'Political and constitutional history', 175–206, quotation at p. 195.

[80] G. L. Harriss, 'The dimensions of politics', in Britnell and Pollard, *McFarlane legacy*, 10–14.

[81] C. D. Liddy, 'The rhetoric of the royal chamber in late medieval London, York and Coventry', *UH* xxix (2002), 323–49.

channels of communication such as royal visits and noble patrons. Yet it was through the rhetoric of the common good that the crown's demands upon its urban subjects were largely articulated and it was in parliament that urban representatives sat, alongside their colleagues from the shires, to speak for the common good. To Carpenter and others, with an overriding interest in landed rather than urban society, the way forward was the study of the workings of the institution of the law, since 'for landowners the key area of government was the law that defended their property' and it is the law which should be examined for their ideas about governance.[82] Parliament, in contrast, does not appear to have much of a place in this new constitutional history.[83] Parliament, though, was an important public place for debate through which relations between the crown and Bristol and York in the period 1350 to 1400 were mediated, whose significance has also been undervalued by urban historians and whose vocabulary was part of a wider political discourse in which royal and civic government participated. By the late fourteenth century, parliament was 'a regular event'.[84]

The first three chapters of this book explore the urban context of royal military, financial and commercial interests. The opening chapter evaluates the contributions of loans and ships from Bristol and York to the crown's foreign ambitions. Chapter 2 addresses the financial impact of the Hundred Years War in Bristol and York, demonstrating the intimate relationship between national and local politics after the renewal of war in 1369. The third chapter examines the politics of trade, with particular attention to the customs service, the staple and diplomacy. The last two chapters consider, in greater detail, urban aspirations within the polity. Chapter 4 analyses the nature and level of urban interest in meetings of parliament. Chapter 5 reassesses the meaning and significance of the urban liberties enshrined in Bristol's charter of 1373 and York's charters of 1393 and 1396, notably the acquisition, by the towns, of permanent justices of the peace.

Previous studies of urban relations with the crown in later medieval England have emphasised their reciprocal nature, but a reciprocity based on separate interests and different expectations. In fact, it was a form of exchange characteristic of patronage,[85] which some historians have seen as the essence of crown–town relations, one party giving one thing in order to receive something else from the other. Instead of a *quid pro quo* model of crown–town relations, namely a trade-off between royal obligations and urban aspirations, this book argues that there was a partnership in govern-

---

[82] C. Carpenter, *Locality and polity: a study of Warwickshire landed society, 1401–1499*, Cambridge 1992, 2–3, quotation at p. 2.
[83] See the comments of Carpenter in 'Gentry and community', 364 n. 106, and *Locality and polity*, 288 (on the role of the nobility as 'the essential connecting link between centre and locality').
[84] Harriss, 'Dimensions of politics', 10.
[85] Patterson, *Urban patronage*, 2.

ment between the crown and the ruling elites of Bristol and York in the second half of the fourteenth century and that the rulers of Bristol and York had a wider interest, and a wider role to play, in the polity, than has been hitherto acknowledged.

1

The Defence of the Realm

Throughout the later Middle Ages direct taxation, assessed on the value of the goods and chattels of the king's subjects at the rate of a tenth in most towns and in the royal demesne and a fifteenth in the rest of the kingdom, was granted by the parliamentary commons for the king's necessity, usually expressed as a threat to the defence of the realm.[1] However, from 1334, when local communities were allowed to pay a fixed tax quota, towns received a relatively light assessment compared to their total wealth.[2] Instead, the loss of income to the crown was offset to a large extent by the king's dependency on his urban and mercantile subjects for loans. With the opening of the Hundred Years War in 1337, the crown relied increasingly on credit and, in particular, on loans from English merchants, to finance its military operations, since loans, unlike direct taxation, were not fixed, and could be raised much more quickly than the sums due from parliamentary taxation.[3] In addition to loans, the most important contribution made by Bristol and York to the enterprise of war was the supply of ships for the royal navy: the king had a small permanent fleet of his own which, even between 1369 and 1375, a time of intensive naval activity, numbered only forty vessels; by 1380 even this fleet had disbanded.[4] The requisitioning of merchant shipping either as transport vessels or fighting ships was, therefore, essential.

In the absence of both a state bank responsible for a system of public credit and a permanent navy of any significant size, the successful functioning of the state in raising money and making war was dependent on co-operation and partnership between the crown and towns and cities such as Bristol and York. The main theme of this chapter is the nature of this collaboration in the prosecution of war. Upon what kind of reciprocity was the relationship between the crown and Bristol and York in wartime based? How, if at all, did the towns benefit from their service to the royal government as creditors and suppliers of ships? R. W. Kaeuper has argued that the fourteenth century saw the transformation of England from a 'law' state to a 'war' state, in which the concentration of the crown's energies and resources on war weakened the power of the state. War, according to Kaeuper, forced the crown to rely on the wealth,

---

1 G. L. Harriss, 'Theory and practice in royal taxation: some observations', *EHR* xcvii (1982), 811–29.
2 Ormrod, *Edward III*, 179–80.
3 Ibid. 183–6.
4 J. W. Sherborne, 'The Hundred Years' War, the English navy: shipping and manpower, 1369–1389', *P&P* xxxvii (1967), 166.

resources and goodwill of its subjects and to devolve, in return, judicial and administrative powers to the gentry in the localities who then, as justices of the peace, used the law in their own self-interest.[5] In a specifically urban context, a similar argument has been propounded, namely that the crown's fiscal needs led to the granting of charters of self-government and that it was the desire for the acquisition and maintenance of such chartered corporate liberties which largely dictated the urban response to the demands of the crown upon its finances and resources in the pursuit of war.[6] Another theme is the comparative significance of Bristol and York as suppliers of loans and ships to the crown. It has been suggested that the changing military priorities of the royal government in the course of the fourteenth century meant that the city of York, which once had been a seat of royal government and a major source of troops, money and arms in the late thirteenth and early fourteenth centuries, when the crown's attention had been directed towards Scotland, declined in importance to the crown with the beginning of the Hundred Years War.[7]

Loans

Until the later 1330s Edward III, like his predecessors, regularly borrowed enormous sums of money from Italian financiers to meet the crown's financial needs. When the Hundred Years War bankrupted the banking firms of Peruzzi and Bardi, the king turned to successive syndicates of English merchants to provide regular and substantial loans. With the collapse of these companies in the mid-fourteenth century, the crown started to appeal more frequently to the wider body of its subjects for loans.[8] Much is already known about the operation of the wool monopoly companies from the work of E. B. Fryde,[9] but, despite a growing literature on the subject of royal borrowing, the precise nature of the crown's credit arrangements in the second half of the fourteenth century remains complex. If historians are agreed that the English merchant financiers of the 1340s lent money to the crown specifically for financial profit from the farm of the customs duties, there is little consensus about how loans were raised and why creditors lent money in subsequent periods. The chronological bias of existing scholarship is partly to blame for this uncer-

[5] R. W. Kaeuper, *War, justice, and public order: England and France in the later Middle Ages*, Oxford 1988, 1–5, 384–6 and passim. For alternative views on the development of the late medieval English state see Harriss, 'Growth of government', 28–57, and W. M. Ormrod, *Political life in medieval England, 1300–1450*, Basingstoke 1995, 85–6 and passim.

[6] See, for example, Attreed, 'Poverty, payments, and fiscal policies', 336, and *King's towns*, 182.

[7] Miller, 'Medieval York', 54–9; Ormrod, 'York and the crown', 30–1.

[8] Ormrod, *Edward III*, 183–6.

[9] See his collected essays in E. B. Fryde, *Studies in medieval trade and finance*, London 1983, esp. 'The English farmers of the customs in 1343–51'.

tainty, since it has focused almost exclusively on the first half of the fifteenth century, due in no small measure to the greater abundance of relevant extant source material for this period.[10] This study of the loans from Bristol and York begins in 1347, the year in which, 'for the first time', Edward III's ministers 'made a general appeal both to individual merchants and to town governments for loans',[11] and addresses four key issues: the mechanisms through which loans were negotiated and the occasions on which Bristol and York lent money; the question of why the towns lent money to the crown, whether as a duty or in their own interests; the identity of the creditors from Bristol and York and the changing pattern of corporate and individual loans; and the relative fiscal importance of Bristol and York as royal creditors.

How did the crown obtain loans from its subjects and on what conditions did prospective creditors agree to lend money? There has been serious disagreement among historians about the nature of loans to the crown in the later Middle Ages. Although K. B. McFarlane admitted the possibility that 'royal boroughs and other corporations were regarded as having a duty to lend without gain', he preferred to consider loans in terms of a simple dichotomy: 'either these loans were unprofitable and compulsory or they were voluntary and carried with them a guaranteed reward'. Ultimately, he came to the conclusion that creditors received a high rate of interest.[12] In contrast, G. L. Harriss contended that there were two distinct types of loan: the 'state' loan, an obligation imposed on all of the king's subjects to lend money in a national emergency without interest and the opportunity for personal profit; and the large-scale mercantile loan, for which the crown had to pay interest to the 'great merchants (not the ordinary burgesses of the towns)' with whom it negotiated the deal.[13] According to Harriss, the 'state' loan was effectively a form of substitute parliamentary taxation, obligatory in time of necessity, requested on the basis of a fixed roster, and given by magnates, bishops, religious houses, burgesses, gentry and villagers.[14] Several historians, following Harriss's interpretative framework, have characterised the two types of loan as 'forced' and 'voluntary'.[15] To which category of loans did those from Bristol and York belong?

The methods employed by the crown to secure credit in the second half of the fourteenth century varied according to need and opportunity. When

[10] This literature includes K. B. McFarlane, 'Loans to the Lancastrian kings: the problem of inducement', in his *England in the fifteenth century: collected essays*, London 1981, 55–78; G. L. Harriss, 'Aids, loans and benevolences', *HJ* vi (1963), 1–19, and *Cardinal Beaufort: a study of Lancastrian ascendancy and decline*, Oxford 1988; and, most recently, H. Kleineke, 'The commission *de mutuo faciendo* in the reign of Henry VI', *EHR* cxvi (2001), 1–30.

[11] Ormrod, *Edward III*, 184.

[12] McFarlane, 'Problem of inducement', 59, 78.

[13] Harriss, 'Aids', 18–19.

[14] Ibid. 6–11.

[15] See, for example, W. M. Ormrod, 'The west European monarchies in the later Middle Ages', in R. Bonney (ed.), *Economic systems and state finance*, Oxford 1995, 128.

large sums of money were required, the crown did turn to small groups of merchants to finance the war effort. In 1377, for example, the merchants of the Calais staple, including a contingent of York merchants, made a loan of £10,000 to the crown. The arrangement was a straightforward financial one, whereby the merchants were not only vested with control of the wool custom and wool subsidy from which they were to be repaid in full, but, as interest ('in consideration of their good will in the matter of the loan'), were given a monopoly of wool exports.[16] The 1377 deal, namely giving wool merchants a monopoly of the wool trade so that they could lend money to the crown and be repaid from the customs, recalled the practices of the 1340s when a succession of merchant syndicates had lent money to Edward III in return for the farm of the customs.[17] Although the 1377 loan from the merchants of the Calais staple was a one-off credit arrangement and it was not until the fifteenth century that the staplers became a major prop of royal finance,[18] a similar agreement was almost struck with a small group of merchants in the second parliament of 1382. The fact that the negotiations between the merchant community and the crown collapsed is also significant.

In early 1382 the crown summoned a broad-based assembly of merchants drawn from the whole country to meet in London at Easter in order to negotiate a loan for Richard II's expedition to France, his first in person as king and therefore of considerable symbolic importance.[19] As the chancellor, Richard Lord Scrope, explained in the opening address to the parliament which met in the immediate aftermath of the failure of the negotiations with the merchants, this gathering before the king's council had consisted of certain London merchants as well as two or three of the wealthier merchants ('de pluis suffisantz') from each town and city within the realm.[20] The merchants turned down the king's request, claiming that only parliament rather than the king's council could provide suitable surety to guarantee repayment of 'so great a sum of money'. Potential lenders were always anxious to acquire adequate security, but it was especially wise in this instance given the large sums of money involved. Accordingly, the king summoned parliament, seeking authorisation from the parliamentary commons for the making of a loan on the security of its grant of direct taxation. In this respect, the approach to the commons in 1382 was highly unusual, foreshadowing a practice that would become increasingly common in the first half of the fifteenth century, whereby the commons in parliament agreed that general loans could

---

[16] CCR, 1377–81, 30–1; CFR, 1377–83, 41–2, quotation at p. 42. The loan is discussed briefly in J. L. Bolton, *The medieval English economy, 1150–1500*, London 1980, 295–6.
[17] For the relations between Edward III and the farmers of the customs in the 1340s see Fryde, 'English farmers of the customs', 1–17.
[18] See, for example, G. L. Harriss, 'The struggle for Calais: an aspect of the rivalry between Lancaster and York', *EHR* lxxv (1960), 30–53.
[19] See the summonses to 'various merchants in all the counties of England' to attend this assembly recorded in the issue rolls of the royal exchequer: E 403/487, 14 Mar.
[20] *RP* iii. 122.

be raised on the security of its tax grants.[21] Armed with such a guarantee, the crown perhaps anticipated that the merchants, who previously had been reluctant to lend, would now be more forthcoming in their financial support.

Yet it is clear that the crown was now negotiating with a much smaller group of merchant financiers than had met in the merchant assembly prior to the summoning of parliament. After the commons had discussed among themselves the crown's request for £60,000, the knights of the shire approached the lords and informed them of 'a matter well known to all' ('notoire chose est a toutes gentz'). Since, in the making and organising of such a loan, the merchants would provide the main source of help ('le principal confort et aide'), 'the merchants now present in this parliament had been specially entrusted with the charge because they knew more about such business and know better how to handle it than any other estate of the realm'.[22] The lords then appointed fourteen merchants – Thomas Beaupyne of Bristol, John de Gysburn of York, John Polymond of Southampton, Robert de Sutton of Lincoln, William Spaigne of Boston, Stephen Haym of Winchester, seven Londoners and William Greville, a Gloucestershire wool merchant, but also a non-resident London freeman – to meet separately from the knights of the shire and the remaining parliamentary burgesses so as to negotiate the loan among themselves.[23] The merchants, however, refused to make the anticipated loan, fearful of lending for profit and recalling the fate of Sir William de la Pole, John de Wesenham, John Malewayn and Walter Chiriton, who had contracted loans with the crown for interest ('pur un poy de gain') and who had been impeached for taking advantage of the king. Some of the merchants, though, the shire knights reported to the lords, said that if the lords and other knights and esquires would lend a considerable sum of money freely without interest ('franchement sanz gain reprendre aucune notable somme'), then they would do so on similar terms, on condition of adequate security. The spectre of the wool monopoly companies of the 1340s, whose restrictive activities generated so much hostility within parliament, continued to haunt the crown's large-scale credit dealings,[24] forcing it to contract loans through other methods.

The two main ways in which Bristol and York were approached for loans were first, through the summons of individual merchants from the two towns to merchant assemblies, and secondly, through royal agents carrying letters of privy seal to the towns themselves. Merchant assemblies, as the work of George Unwin has shown, were summoned regularly by the crown in the first

---

21 Kleineke, 'Commission de mutuo faciendo', 7.
22 For this and what follows see RP iii. 123.
23 For Greville see Saul, Knights and esquires, 231, and Calendar of letter-books . . . of the city of London, ed. R. R. Sharpe, London 1899–1912, Letter-book H, 146.
24 In 1369, when Edward III returned to the monopolistic practices of the 1340s and relied increasingly on a small group of London merchants for loans, this activity came under serious attack in parliament: G. Holmes, The Good Parliament, Oxford 1975, 102–3, 108–13.

Table 1
Bristol's loans to the crown, 1347–1401

Date	Purpose	Lender	Amount	Reference
June–Sept. 1347	'the defence and safety of England'	individual	£293 6s. 8d.	E 401/388; CCR, 1346–9, 360
Aug.–Sept. 1351	'the defence of the realm'	individual	£495	E 401/407; CCR, 1354–60, 573
Aug. 1356	Poitiers campaign	individual	£50	E 401/434
May 1370	resumption of Hundred Years War	corporate	£500	E 401/501
June 1370	resumption of Hundred Years War	corporate	£333 6s. 8d.	E 401/501
Sept. 1370	wages of soldiers accompanying Guy Lord Brian 'beyond the sea'	individual	£33 2s. 2d.	E 401/501; *Issue roll of Thomas de Brantingham*, 258
Sept. 1377	'the expedition over sea'	individual	£45	E 401/527; CPR, 1377–81, 29
Oct. 1377	'the expedition over sea'	corporate	£621 13s. 4d.	E 401/528; CPR, 1377–81, 29
May 1379	'for certain business concerning war'	corporate	£666 13s. 4d.	E 401/535; E 364/22, rot. 4r
Dec. 1381	expedition to France	corporate	£400	E 401/544
Oct. 1386	threat of Franco-Scottish invasion	corporate	£200	E 401/566
Dec. 1394	king's expedition to Ireland	individual	£100	E 401/596
Oct. 1396	Anglo-French peace conference	individual	£200	E 401/604
Dec. 1397	unknown	corporate	£800	E 401/608
July 1400	'the king's journey to Scotland'	individual individual	£50 £66 13s. 4d.	E 401/619 E 401/619
Aug. 1400	the king's 'journey to Scotland'	individual individual individual	£26 13s. 4d. £40 £80	E 401/619 E 404/17/385 E 401/619 E 404/17/385
March 1401	'expenses of the king's chamber' for Scottish campaign	corporate	£333 6s. 8d.	E 401/621
May 1401	Scottish campaign	corporate	£162 17s. 10½d.	E 401/622

half of the fourteenth century to negotiate wool subsidies and loans and to discuss wider issues relating to trade.[25] In 1347 a succession of merchants from several English urban communities including Bristol and York were summoned to appear before the king's council 'to treat with him [the king] upon things touching the war of France and the defence and safety of England', and as a result twenty-five Bristol merchants and twenty-seven York merchants made loans.[26] In 1351, although there is no evidence of a formal summons of a merchant assembly, 'a deal' involving repayment from the wool subsidy seems to have been struck between the crown and individual export merchants, and seventeen merchants from Bristol and York lent money to the crown.[27] Similarly, in August 1356, six Bristol merchants summoned to a merchant assembly in June agreed a joint loan.[28]

Thereafter, the policy of negotiating and contracting loans through merchant assemblies was abandoned, although it was revived briefly in 1382. W. M. Ormrod has argued that the actions of the wool monopoly companies of the 1340s alienated a wide cross-section of the mercantile community, which turned to the parliamentary commons to articulate its concerns and to protect its interests. Henceforth, the commons became the 'mouth-piece of the business classes'.[29] In this context, it is little wonder that Richard II's attempt to reconstitute a separate estate of merchants for the purposes of organising a loan was a signal failure. Instead, from about 1370, just after the renewal of the Hundred Years War following a decade of uneasy peace between England and France, there appears to have been a shift in the way that Bristol and York were approached for loans, as the crown appealed to the town governments rather than to individual merchants.

G. L. Harriss was especially interested in the 'state' loan made through letters of privy seal or itinerant commissioners for loans.[30] These loans were obtained in two ways: either commissioners sent letters of privy seal directly to individuals or corporations whom they already knew would lend money, or else they summoned a meeting of the county or town so that the inhabitants could hear the king's request, thus allowing the crown's agents to identify prospective creditors whom they could persuade to provide loans on the grounds of the king's necessity. Once a loan was agreed upon, an indenture

---

[25] G. Unwin, 'The estate of merchants, 1336–1365', in G. Unwin (ed.), *Finance and trade under Edward III*, Manchester 1918, repr. 1962, 179–255.

[26] The writs of summons are in *Report from the lords' committees . . . for all matters touching the dignity of a peer*, London 1820–9, iv. 565–71. The quotation is from *CCR, 1346–9*, 360. See tables 1 and 2 for all future references to the loans from Bristol and York.

[27] Unwin, 'Estate of merchants', 225.

[28] For the writ of summons see *Dignity of a peer*, iv. 609–10.

[29] Ormrod, *Edward III*, 189–90, 194–6, quotation at p. 196.

[30] For what follows see Harriss, 'Aids', 13–14. The process by which royal commissioners approached potential lenders is explained in greater detail in Kleineke, 'Commission *de mutuo faciendo*', 1–30.

Table 2
York's loans to the crown, 1347–1401

Date	Purpose	Lender	Amount	Reference
Aug.– Oct. 1347	'the defence and safety of England'	individual	£450	E 401/388, 391; CCR, 1346–9, 360
Sept.– Nov. 1351	'the defence of the realm'	individual	£585	E 401/407, 410; CCR, 1349–54, 436
Aug. 1359	Rheims campaign	individual	£666 13s. 4d.	E 401/447
May 1370	resumption of Hundred Years War	corporate	£600	E 401/501
June 1370	resumption of Hundred Years War	corporate	£300	E 401/501
April 1372	'in support of the war at sea'	corporate	£66 13s. 4d.	E 401/508
Sept. 1377	the king's 'great need'	Calais staple	£10,000 (total)	CCR, 1377–81, 30–1; CFR, 1377–83, 41–2
Aug. 1385	Richard II's expedition to Scotland	corporate corporate individual	£120 £16 £27 12s. 4d.	E 401/561 E 401/561 E 401/561
Oct. 1386	'safekeeping of Carlisle'	corporate	£100	E 401/566
Nov. 1386	threat of Franco-Scottish invasion	corporate	£100	E 401/566
Dec. 1397	unknown	corporate	£200	E 401/608
1399	the king's 'necessity before he undertook the governance of the realm'	corporate	£333 6s. 8d.	CPR, 1399–1401, 354
1400	'expenses of his [the king's] household in his present journey to Scotland'	corporate	£666 13s. 4d.	CPR, 1399–1401, 354

was then drawn up containing the amount to be advanced and a date and a promise of repayment by the crown.

'The commission *de mutuo faciendo*' was, according to Harriss, 'a well-tried instrument of royal government' from the fourteenth to the sixteenth centuries.[31] In 1370, for example, the issue rolls of the royal exchequer record payments to certain royal agents sent out from Westminster into the provinces carrying letters of privy seal addressed to the mayors and bailiffs of the

31 Harriss, 'Aids', 3.

towns and cities of Boston, Barton-upon-Humber, Beverley, Lincoln, Hull, York and Newcastle-upon-Tyne, and to the mayor and bailiffs of Winchester and the bailiffs of the town of Bristol 'to borrow and contract for money for the King's use'.[32] The letters sent to Bristol and York have not survived, but the letters of privy seal sent to the mayor, recorder, sheriffs, aldermen and citizens of London on 8 June 1370 reveal more precisely both the nature of the king's need and the manner in which it was articulated. They informed the Londoners of the 'King's present need of a sum of 100,000 marks on behalf of his son the Duke of Lancaster and Robert de Knolles, who were about to go abroad in the King's service, and also for the defence of the realm' and asked that, by 24 June 1370, the city lend him £5,000 by way of a contribution.[33] In 1379 various towns and cities including Bristol received visits from crown agents seeking loans.[34] One Richard Hembrigg, a king's sergeant-at-arms, was paid for his journey to Bristol in February and March 1379 on the instructions of the king's council to ask for loans for certain business relating to the war with France.[35] A few months later, during parliament, Bristol lent over £600 to the crown; presumably, the town's MPs paid the money directly into the royal exchequer. James Sherborne's study of the preparations for war in 1386 suggests that the loans made by Bristol and York and other towns and cities during the October parliament were also preceded by the distribution of signet and privy seals requesting loans.[36] Moreover, in 1400, Richard Kyngeston, the dean of the royal chapel, seems to have been especially active as a royal commissioner for loans, visiting Bristol among other places.[37]

What was the nature of the loans from Bristol and York? Were they voluntary or compulsory? Although the specific circumstances preceding each of their loans is not always clear, only the 1377 loan from the York staplers can be seen to fit into the category of a large mercantile loan which entirely freely given and made for personal financial profit. Otherwise, the process of negotiating loans was characterised by a degree of coercion: this was true of loans made by merchants from Bristol and York meeting in a national merchant assembly or by creditors from the two towns approached locally by royal agents. In March 1347 a merchant assembly was summoned to convene the following month for the purpose of raising loans. Writs were sent to seventy-nine named merchants, including three from Bristol and nine from

[32] *Issue roll of Thomas de Brantingham . . . 44 Edward III*, ed. and trans. F. Devon, London 1835, 129–30, 138.
[33] *Letter-book* G, 263.
[34] For the arrival of crown officials at Norwich in 1379 see *The records of the city of Norwich*, ed. W. Hudson and J. C. Tingey, Norwich 1906–10, ii. 45.
[35] E 364/22, rot. 4r.
[36] J. W. Sherborne, 'The defence of the realm and the impeachment of Michael de la Pole in 1386', in Taylor and Childs, *Politics and crisis*, 105; CPR, 1385–9, 216.
[37] E 401/621, 27 Mar.; Harriss, 'Aids', 14.

York.[38] Some did not lend money, while others agreed to lend but then did not, forcing the king to threaten them with the forfeiture of their goods.[39] At the end of June, having found it very difficult to secure the necessary loans, the king summoned 186 merchants, including sixteen Bristol merchants and twenty-four York merchants, to appear before the king's council at various times throughout the summer of 1347.[40] Nevertheless, in July, there were still some merchants, such as Roger Turtle of Bristol and William Graa of York, who had ignored the king's summons on two occasions, compelling him to order the sheriffs to attach the merchants or threaten them with the penalty of forfeiture in order to secure their presence before the king's council.[41] Similarly, in 1352 pressure was imposed on prospective creditors to ensure that loans were forthcoming.[42] Nicholas Fouk and 'certain other men of the city' of York agreed to lend money 'before certain lieges sent to that city', and in order that 'the sum might be paid more readily the king sent lieges to receive that sum there', but the crown's agents did not receive the loan. Fouk was ordered, under pain of forfeiture, to make the agreed loan and to appear before the king's council to explain his conduct, while the mayor and bailiffs were instructed to distrain those who refused to pay. In fact, the loans from Bristol and York were neither entirely voluntary nor compulsory.

G. L. Harriss saw the 'state' loan raised from all of the king's subjects contracted under letters of privy seal or through commissioners for loans as an obligation. Given in time of urgent need and for the common profit, the loan, like royal taxation, was impossible to refuse. Although a potential lender could try to avoid making a loan by arguing that security for repayment was inadequate or by claiming a plea of poverty, 'having been asked – under the appropriate safeguards – it could not be refused'.[43] The evidence from Bristol and York suggests that the process of lending was far more sensitive to a town's needs and the level of negotiation with the crown much greater than has been previously argued. It is certainly evident that royal demands could be reduced. In 1397, for example, the abbot of Rievaulx pleaded that he could not lend the 'considerable sum' ('une somme notable') requested by the king, but that he could give twenty marks instead.[44] Similarly, Caroline Barron's work on the pattern of corporate London loans between 1416 and 1438 (using the records of the city's common council) has shown that, while 'the citizens very rarely refused to lend', it was also true that 'on no occasion did they lend as much as the king requested'. 'This was a custom', according to Barron, 'which both parties probably well under-

38 *Dignity of a peer*, iv. 563–5.
39 F. R. Barnes, 'The taxation of wool, 1327–1348', in Unwin, *Finance and trade*, 169.
40 *Dignity of a peer*, iv. 567–71.
41 CCR, 1346–9, 360.
42 For what follows see CCR, 1349–54, 336–7.
43 Harriss, 'Aids', 5–6, 16–17, quotation at p. 6.
44 E 34/1B/30.

stood.'[45] There is indirect evidence to suggest that the loans raised from Bristol and York were also the subject of intense negotiation and bargaining. It was G. L. Harriss's view that loans were requested from an individual or community according to their 'known circumstances or degree', so that these amounts would become stereotyped and 'larger cities, like York and Bristol, were usually asked to loan not less than 500 marks and often more'.[46] Measured by the 1334 subsidy and the 1377 poll tax, Bristol and York were the largest and wealthiest provincial urban communities in the fourteenth century: similar in size and wealth, they should have lent comparable amounts when they were both asked to make loans.[47] In 1386 Bristol and York each lent £200, but just over ten years later in 1397, Bristol lent £800 while £200 came from York. There was clearly some flexibility in the system of negotiating loans.

In fact, there is evidence, albeit circumstantial, of outright refusal. In 1393, for example, a royal messenger, Nicholas Inglefield, was paid for his journeys to London and Bristol to request money to pay for the expenses of the royal household.[48] There is, however, no record of a subsequent loan from Bristol in either the exchequer receipt or issue rolls.[49] In short, it is important to acknowledge the fact that the refusal of a loan was a distinct possibility. The city of London may have been the exception to the rule, for it is apparent that the crown was very reluctant to accept any excuses from what was, by far and away, its most important royal creditor, whose loans greatly outweighed those from provincial towns and cities. In 1370, for example, after London's rulers had received letters of privy seal seeking a corporate loan of £5,000, a deputation was sent from the capital to see the king in order 'to ask that the City might be excused in consideration of the heavy burdens it had already been called upon to bear'. The king refused to accept London's apology, and the city's rulers eventually obliged.[50] None the less, it is worth asking: what could a king do to force prospective creditors to lend money if they proved recalcitrant? To individual lenders, there was always the threat of an appearance before the king's council, but this practice was not always successful. In 1398 Richard II commissioned various local royal officials including the mayor and sheriffs of York to secure loans totalling over £2,000 from a group of prominent York citizens who 'are indebted in divers sums of money to the king by their letters obligatory'. If the creditors refused to lend the money, they were to appear before the king's council, but despite

---

45 Barron, 'London and the crown, 1451–61', 92.
46 Harriss, 'Aids', 11. A similar argument was made in Steel, *Receipt of the exchequer*, 146.
47 Dyer, *Decline and growth*, 56, 62.
48 E 101/403/22, fo. 17r; N. Saul, *Richard II*, New Haven 1997, 331.
49 Although the wardrobe could receive loans directly, repayment was dependent on the exchequer. For the relationship between the two institutions see G. L. Harriss, *King, parliament, and public finance in medieval England to 1369*, Oxford 1975, 208–28.
50 *Letter-book G*, 263.

continual pressure, there is no evidence that the crown ever received the money it demanded.[51] Moreover, it was even more difficult for the crown to deal with towns and cities in their corporate capacity. As Caroline Barron's study of Richard II's seizure of London's liberties in 1392 suggests, a king could remove a town's powers of self-government if it were not providing the loans which were expected by the crown, but he could not do this without other justification, in this case a perceived breakdown of law and order within the capital.[52]

Without the possibility of refusal, it is very difficult to explain the fact that, with the exception of the 1377 loan from the merchants of the Calais staple to which a small group of York merchants contributed, the citizens of York, whether corporately or individually, did not make a loan to Richard II until 1385. In the same period the town of Bristol lent over £1,700. How can York's omission as a creditor be explained? The records of meetings of York's city council in the later 1370s indicate that the city was experiencing some serious financial problems at this time, notably the high cost of maintaining the city's barges which had been built at the city's expense in 1373 and 1377 for the defence of the realm.[53] The subject of York's barges will be discussed in more detail in the second section of this chapter. Certainly, though, if the claim of the citizens of York in 1378 that they had built 'previously a large barge and recently a large barge and a small balinger, which are all at sea, at greater expense than any other city in the kingdom with the exception of London' can be believed, then the outlay made by York must have been considerable.[54] London's barge, the *Paul*, constructed in 1373, cost £621.[55] It may indeed be the case that in 1379 the city's governors not only made a plea of poverty, but drew attention to the city's loyal service to the crown as a supplier of vessels for the war effort, which more than compensated for the lack of direct financial support: it is otherwise difficult to account for the conspicuous absence of the city of York from a list of more than 150 creditors in 1379.[56]

There were also political reasons for refusal to pay, which were unrelated to the financial incapacity of a potential lender to provide a loan. In 1375 the king wrote letters under the privy seal to the mayor and sheriff of Bristol and four other provincial towns and cities asking for loans. The letter described, somewhat dramatically, recent rumours of an imminent French invasion and spoke of the urgent need to resist the enemy 'for the protection of ourselves,

[51] CPR, 1396–9, 363–4, 368; CCR, 1396–9, 425. Anthony Steel's work on the exchequer receipt rolls confirms this point: *Receipt of the exchequer*, 118.
[52] Barron, 'The quarrel of Richard II', 173–201, esp. pp. 178–81, although for a more recent reassessment see her 'Richard II and London', in A. Goodman and J. Gillespie (eds), *Richard II: the art of kingship*, Oxford 1999, 136–7, 144–8.
[53] Rees Jones, 'York's civic administration', 129–30.
[54] SC 8/216/10758.
[55] *Letter-book G*, 304.
[56] The list of creditors is in CPR, 1377–81, 635–8.

yourselves and our whole kingdom' ('in salvacionem nostri ac vostri et tocius regni nostri').[57] There is no evidence, however, that Bristol or the other urban communities made a loan. It has been suggested that there was a loss of faith among prospective creditors because of the crown's failure to repay many of the debts incurred on the renewal of war in 1369–70.[58] This was certainly not true of Bristol, for the town's corporate loans totalling over £800 in 1370 had been repaid from the Bristol customs in the same year.[59] Although the precise reasons for Bristol's refusal are not stated, it is plausible that the negative response of the town expressed discontent towards the conduct of the royal government and, in particular, hostility towards a government that was dominated by a small clique of courtiers who were perceived to have taken advantage of the king in his increasing infirmity to profit financially.

This kind of disenchantment came to a head in the Good Parliament of 1376 when, in the context of a series of military reverses, continuing royal demands for financial aid and the king's ill health, the parliamentary commons accused some of the king's prominent ministers and advisers of a series of financial offences which they had committed, in the wording of the parliament roll, 'for personal profit and advantage' ('pur singuler profit et avantage'). These included the sale of licences to merchants to avoid the wool monopoly of the Calais staple, the purchase of royal debts at less than their face value and the provision of loans to the crown at an extortionate rate of interest.[60] The theme of the accusations against the king's chamberlain, William Lord Latimer, was his embezzlement of the king's money through his control of the king's chamber, thereby defrauding the king of revenue that should have gone towards the costs of war. According to Thomas Walsingham in the Chronicon Angliae, one of the charges levelled against Latimer was that Bristol had paid £10,000 for the charter granting the town county status, of which the king only received £2,000, while the chamberlain dishonestly pocketed the rest for his own use.[61] The accusation is only found in this one source and, although Walsingham seems to have been well informed of events at parliament, his own highly critical attitude towards the royal court and to John of Gaunt, in particular, means that it must be treated with extreme caution.[62] Yet there was evidently something amiss with the

---

57 SC 1/55/84(i).

58 Ormrod, Edward III, 185.

59 E 401/501, 10 May, 22 June.

60 RP ii. 323. The best account of the context and events of this parliament remains Holmes, Good Parliament, esp. ch. v, but see also C. Given-Wilson, The royal household and the king's affinity: service, politics and finance in England, 1360–1413, New Haven 1986, 146–60.

61 Chronicon Angliae, 1328–1388, ed. E. M. Thompson (RS, 1874), 78. For further discussion see Holmes, Good Parliament, 133–4.

62 J. Taylor, 'The Good Parliament and its sources', in Taylor and Childs, Politics and crisis, 85–7.

circumstances surrounding the grant of the charter for it to attract the chronicler's attention, and there was an element of truth to the charge in the sense
that Bristol paid 600 marks (£400) into the king's chamber for the charter.[63]
This practice was normal since every charter was purchased by a payment
into either the chamber as a fine for the concessions contained within it or
the king's hanaper for the sealing of the document.[64] However, £400 was an
extraordinarily large sum. Edward III's 'declining health' in the early 1370s, as
W. M. Ormrod has shown, 'allowed his courtiers even greater influence', so
much so that, 'Lord Latimer now virtually dictated who might have access to
the monarch.'[65] It looks suspiciously as if Bristol's rulers had been forced to
pay £400 merely in order to secure the royal ear. It is no wonder that the town
did not respond favourably to the king's letter requesting further financial
assistance two years later.

The making of a loan, then, rested upon a unity of interest between the
crown and the creditor. G. L. Harriss's seminal work on royal borrowing set
out explicitly to counter the argument that the crown's dependence on its
subjects was 'both a sign and a cause' of royal weakness because it forced the
king to rely on the generosity of his subjects who, finding themselves in a
position of strength, were able to profit from his need for revenue.[66] The
evidence of the loans from Bristol and York presents a different picture. As
Harriss himself later argued in relation to the development of the system of
public finance in later medieval England, 'in the last analysis the King's interpretation [of the common good] could not conflict with the political interests
of his subjects. Specifically, he could not devote the resources of the realm to
his personal profit or that of a group of intimates'.[67] Loans were not a
knee-jerk reaction to royal pressure; in the cases of Bristol and York they
expressed urban as well as royal interests.

For what purposes did the crown ask for loans and for what reasons did
Bristol and York agree to lend money? Virtually all the loans coincided with
periods of intensive military activity by the royal government and, in particular, with phases of the Hundred Years War.[68] In the general absence of
extant letters of privy seal requesting loans from Bristol and York,[69] the
purposes of the loans from the two towns have been established directly from
references in the exchequer receipt and issue rolls, warrants for issues and
letters patent (enrolled as surety for creditors to ensure repayment), and indirectly from comparison between the timing of loans and known military

---

[63] *Bristol charters, 1155–1373*, ed. N. Dermott Harding (Bristol Record Society i, 1930),
118–21.
[64] H. C. Maxwell-Lyte, *Historical notes on the use of the great seal of England*, London 1926,
332, 342.
[65] Ormrod, *Edward III*, 117.
[66] Harriss, 'Aids', 1.
[67] Idem, *King, parliament, and public finance*, 228.
[68] See tables 1 and 2.
[69] The exceptions are SC 1/55/84(i), 88.

campaigns. With the notable exception of the loans of 1397, the purpose of which remains a source of disagreement among historians, and York's loan of 500 marks in 1399 to Henry Bolingbroke before he became king,[70] all the loans were for military expenditure often expressed in terms of the 'defence of the realm'.[71] The loans from Bristol and York should be seen primarily, in the context of war, as a committed response by the king's subjects to the need to assist in the defence of the realm. This was one aspect of the common good and it was part of a morality of government which united the king and his subjects.[72]

It has been argued that the key to understanding the relationship between London and the crown in the Lancastrian period was the 'the interplay of finance and privilege'.[73] Studying the pattern of London loans to the crown between 1400 and 1450, for example, Caroline Barron suggested that the city lent money out of a sense of duty, but hoped that the loans would act 'as oil to lubricate the machinery of royal favour and privilege'.[74] In short, in return for loans London expected the confirmation and extension of its charters of corporate liberties. This pattern has also been found among the provincial towns and cities, where loans have been viewed as 'another form of urban patronage', and where, according to Anthony Steel, 'a large town like Coventry', for example, 'might buy (in effect) a new charter with a loan'.[75] The problems with this approach are both evidential and conceptual. First, a comparison between the timing of loans from Bristol and York and the occasions on which the towns were granted new charters or had their existing charters confirmed, indicates that if their civic rulers hoped to secure chartered privileges through the extension of credit, then it was not a particularly successful strategy.[76] Indeed, the town of Bristol lent far more money to the crown after its acquisition of the 1373 charter than it had previously. Secondly, it was customary for charters to be granted in return for a payment into the king's hanaper or chamber.[77] The amount Bristol paid in 1373 into the king's chamber was highly unusual, but even it serves as a reminder that a town's money did not secure a charter outright and was not the reason it was

---

[70] For different interpretations of these loans see, for example, C. M. Barron, 'The tyranny of Richard II', *BIHR* xli (1968), 17–18, and Saul, *Richard II*, 441. For the purpose of York's loan in 1399 see *CPR, 1399–1401*, 354.

[71] For the loans of 1347, for example, see *CCR, 1346–9*, 360.

[72] The literature on the common good is enormous. A useful summary is in A. Black, *Political thought in Europe, 1250–1450*, Cambridge 1992, 24–8. For a discussion of its relationship to late medieval kingship see Watts, *Henry VI*, 18–80.

[73] Barron, 'London and the crown, 1451–61', 91.

[74] Idem, 'Government of London', 423.

[75] Attreed, 'Poverty, payments, and fiscal policies', 336; A. Steel, 'English government finance, 1377–1413', *EHR* li (1936), 46.

[76] Compare the information in tables 1 and 2 above and *British borough charters, 1307–1660*, 38–9, 132.

[77] See p. 32 above.

granted, but merely gained valuable access to the monarch. Moreover, there were other forms of urban patronage much more profitable to town and king than a loan which, after all, had to be repaid. In 1396, when York's rulers took advantage of the king's presence in the north to petition for a charter elevating the city to county status, Richard II was courted with hospitality, entertainment and various gifts, including the presentation of £200 in silver gilt basins ('in presentacione facta domino regi in duabus pelvibus argenti deauratis CC li.').[78] Loans were part of a wider public discourse of politics based on the common good.

The crown was not averse to manipulating the language of the common profit to appeal to more narrow interests among the prospective creditors: in the case of towns the sectional interests of the merchants who dominated civic government. A letter from the duke of Gloucester in 1424 on behalf of the king asking for a loan from the city of Coventry to finance the duke's planned expedition to the Low Countries illustrates this point well, for it reminded Coventry's rulers that 'the well of us and of this our viage is lyke to turne to ryght great ese of the people, and specially of thies merchauntis of this Realme'.[79] An undated royal letter, probably of 1371, addressed to the citizens and burgesses of various unnamed cities and towns within the kingdom, asked for a gift of money and chose to emphasise the particular need at that time to defend shipping and overseas trade. The letter reminded the urban communities to respond positively 'as you desire the protection of our said realm and shipping and of merchandise, especially' ('come vous desirez la salvacion de noz ditz roialme et navye et par especial de marchandises').[80] Admittedly, the request was made to accompany a grant of tonnage and poundage and to contribute to the equipping of an armed fleet that had been assembled in the first place for the protection of shipping, but the appeal to the commercial interests of the towns was persuasive. Merchants had a vested interest in keeping the seas free from the predatory attacks of enemy vessels. The city of York responded with a gift of 100 marks; London gave £1,000.[81]

The crown also recognised that some threats to the safety of the realm affected certain areas of the kingdom more than others. In April 1403 Henry IV wrote to a number of prospective creditors seeking loans in order to resist 'the wickedness of our Welsh rebels and enemies of Scotland'. Given their close geographical proximity to Wales and Scotland respectively, it is perhaps no surprise that the only urban communities to receive letters of

---

[78] *York city chamberlains' account rolls, 1396–1500*, ed. R. B. Dobson (Surtees Society cxcii, 1978–9), 4–8, esp. p. 5.
[79] *The Coventry leet book*, ed. M. D. Harris (Early English Text Society o.s. cxxxiv, cxxxv, cxxxviii, cxl, 1907–13), i. 83–4.
[80] SC 1/55/88. For the meaning of the free gift which, unlike the loan, was not repaid see Harriss, 'Aids', 8–11.
[81] E 401/508, 29 Apr., 24 July.

privy seal were Bristol and York.[82] The rulers of Bristol and York did not need reminding of the interrelationship of local and national politics. In July 1377, in the context of another invasion scare, the royal keeper of a local forest was ordered by the crown to deliver a consignment of oak to the mayor of Bristol in order 'to make barriers and other things needful for the defence of the town'.[83] Within the next three months a total of 1,000 marks was lent by Bristol to the crown to finance a military expedition overseas. The defence of the town and the defence of the realm were, in this case, inseparable. In June 1385 the French sent an army to Scotland and in the summer of 1386 there were real fears that the Scots would co-operate with the French to invade England's northern border.[84] Some of these concerns were expressed by the commons in the parliaments of 1385 and 1386.[85] In 1385 the parliamentary commons petitioned the crown that the marcher lords should stay in the northern marches until the next parliament, where they should protect and defend the same marches and help to resist the enemy. A similar request, with equal urgency, was made in 1386 when the commons petitioned, on behalf of the counties of Yorkshire, Northumberland, Cumberland and Westmorland, that all the lords of these counties should remain there to withstand the imminent incursions and raids of the men of France and Scotland who were assembling daily along the northern border. It can be no coincidence that the city lent over £350 to the crown between August 1385 and November 1386. In fact, some of this revenue was earmarked specifically by the crown to meet the combined Franco-Scottish threat: York's loan of £100 in October 1386 was assigned to Ralph Lord Neville and Thomas Lord Clifford, the keepers of the castle and the town of Carlisle, for the safekeeping of the garrison, thereby making explicit the connection between the loan and the defence of the north.[86]

There could also be financial inducements to encourage lending, although, with the exception of the 1377 loan from the Calais staplers, these were not a source of direct financial profit to the creditor in the form of an interest payment. K. B. McFarlane's argument that the interest was disguised in the exchequer receipt and issue rolls by recording a fictional total of the amount lent, inclusive of interest, is, in a sense, an argument from silence and is impossible to prove.[87] Instead of the prospect of the payment of interest, there is more persuasive evidence that trading privileges occasionally accompanied requests for loans. In 1353 Edward III banned wool exports by native merchants and, in return for special trading licences, English merchants

---

[82] *Proceedings and ordinances of the privy council of England*, ed. N. H. Nicolas, London 1834–7, i. 199–203, quotation at p. 200.
[83] *CCR, 1377–81*, 8.
[84] Sherborne, 'Defence of the realm', 99–106.
[85] For what follows see *RP* iii. 213, 223.
[86] E 401/566, 27 Oct. For the appointment of Neville and Clifford see *CPR, 1385–9*, 42.
[87] McFarlane, 'Problem of inducement', 76–8.

provided loans to the crown.[88] Although it was mainly Londoners who took advantage of the licences, a loan of £50 from a group of Bristol merchants in 1356 might have been made under similar circumstances. Moreover, the corporate loans from Bristol and York in 1370 totalling over £1,700 could well have been part of a trading agreement between the English merchant community and the crown, in which the ban on foreign exports imposed in the summer of 1369 was lifted only when substantial loans were forth-coming.[89]

Considering the motives behind the involvement of the London merchant, Richard Whittington, in royal finance, Caroline Barron has suggested that, 'in advancing money to the crown, he must have been informed, and probably consulted, about matters of high policy', and that, 'it was Whittington's intention, in lending money to the crown, to buy the royal ear and the public eye'.[90] In other words, Whittington's participation in royal finance was predicated on his personal ambition to be at the centre of events. A similar argument has been advanced by Stephen O'Connor, in work on the public and private lives of two London merchants active in Edward III's reign, Adam Fraunceys and John Pyel, whose regular financial assistance to the crown led to other forms of public service for the king as well as for the city of London and helped to secure the social status and prestige to which they aspired.[91] The question of the personal benefits accruing from royal service will be examined in more detail in chapter 5. Here it is important to note that, while neither Bristol nor York produced a royal creditor on the scale of a Whittington, a Fraunceys or a Pyel, its leading burgesses and citizens were drawn into the web of royal finance and administration. Those individuals from Bristol and York who lent money on a personal basis were deeply involved, directly and indirectly, in the pursuit of the crown's military ambitions. Walter de Derby of Bristol, for example,[92] who lent just over £30 in 1370 to pay the wages of men-at-arms, archers and mariners preparing to sail from Plymouth to France in a ship that he had also supplied to a royal fleet, went on to farm the profits of Bristol for the crown and to serve in the customs service in the port of Bristol. Thomas Beaupyne of Bristol,[93] who

---

[88] Ormrod, *Edward III*, 185; Unwin, 'Estate of merchants', 218.
[89] Ormrod, *Edward III*, 185; T. H. Lloyd, *The English wool trade in the Middle Ages*, Cambridge 1977, 217.
[90] Barron, 'Richard Whittington', 204.
[91] O'Connor, 'Finance, diplomacy and politics', 18–39.
[92] See *CPR, 1367–70*, 389, and appendix below for what follows.
[93] See appendix below. For his service on the tax commission see *CFR, 1377–83*, 164; for his role as a diplomat to treat for peace with the representatives of the count of Flanders and of the towns of Ghent, Ypres and Bruges see *Foedera, conventiones, literae, et . . . acta publica*, ed. T. Rymer, The Hague 1745, republ. 1967, iii/4, 23–4. Beaupyne received more in wages and expenses than the other London merchants on the commission, perhaps a reflection of his greater experience in royal service: E 364/22, rot. 2d; E 403/519, 14, 16 May; E 403/521, 24 Feb.

lent £100 in 1394 for Richard II's expedition to Ireland, had served previously in the customs service in Bristol, helped to collect the town's 1379 poll tax and travelled to Calais in 1388 as the leading mercantile member of a royal diplomatic mission. Similarly, William Graa of York, who contributed to a loan of more than £600 with several of the 'good men' ('probi homines') of the city in 1359, was especially active in the royal war effort at this time. Along with John de Sevenhous, another York merchant, and a group of London merchants, Graa appears to have been paid £400 by the crown in 1358 for his services 'either in assisting with wages or, more likely, in supplying military equipment to the Wardrobe'.[94] In many respects, then, the likes of Derby, Beaupyne and Graa were 'as much royal servants as traders'.[95]

In fact, there is no single reason why leading townsmen from Bristol and York or the towns in their corporate capacity lent money to the crown. Instead, a more complex picture has emerged, which considers the interplay of private and public interests. Government in later medieval England, as W. M. Ormrod has argued, functioned 'with the consent and active co-operation of the elite', and there were 'vested interests bound up in the mechanisms of the state – and the mechanisms of state finance in particular'.[96] In 1400 the city of York acted as a collecting point for loans for Henry IV's expedition to Scotland, and the mayor of York, William Frost, and Thomas Graa, twice former mayor of the city, were appointed to 'receive all such sums and treat about their repayment and bring them to the king in person'.[97] A year later, Frost was re-elected mayor of York and was rewarded by the city for his exertions ('pro magno labore') on its behalf to secure the repayment of £1,000 which York had lent to the new regime in 1399 and 1400 with a grant of 6d. of every pound repaid by the crown.[98] In order to raise loans, the crown required the consent and co-operation of its subjects. The potential consequences that could result when this consensus was undermined are evident from the city of York's reaction to the arrival of Henry Bolingbroke in England in 1399. In 1398 Richard II forced two York citizens and former mayors of the city, Thomas de Howom and William de Helmeslay, to sue for fines of pardon.[99] He also tried to exact (in addition to a corporate loan of £200 already raised from the city in 1397 which remained unpaid) over £2,000 from a number of prominent York citizens including Robert Warde, Thomas del Gare and four former mayors of York, William and Robert Savage, Simon de Quixlay and John de Howeden, with no apparent promise

94 The payments totalling £400 are recorded in E 403/388, 24 Feb., and E 403/394, 15 Nov. See also E 401/447, 28 Apr., and E 401/449, 5 Feb. 1359. The quotation is from O'Connor, 'Finance, diplomacy and politics', 25.
95 Platt, Medieval Southampton, 124–5.
96 Ormrod, 'West European monarchies', 157–8.
97 CPR, 1399–1401, 356. Their account is E 101/42/36.
98 YCA, Freemen's roll, D1, fo. 10r.
99 C 67/31, mem. 12; C 67/30, mem. 28. For the background to the events of 1398 see pp. 151–2 below.

of repayment.[100] It is scarcely surprising that, when Henry Bolingbroke travelled through Yorkshire on his arrival in England in 1399 to claim the throne, the city's rulers lent him 500 marks 'in his necessity before he undertook the governance of the realm'.[101]

Before considering the pattern of personal and corporate loans, it is necessary to establish the identity of the individuals who made personal loans to the crown. Very few of them were regular royal creditors. Only a small number of individuals from Bristol and York lent money on more than once occasion, the most notable being Robert de Howom of York and Richard le Spicer of Bristol who each provided three loans to the crown. Indeed, Robert de Howom also supplied credit to John of Gaunt, duke of Lancaster, for his military exploits on behalf of the crown. In 1375 he lent £200 to Gaunt at Bruges, where the duke was negotiating a truce between England and France.[102] The vast majority of creditors from Bristol and York were already politically active in their towns when they first made loans to the crown. Of the fifty-four lenders from Bristol, forty-five (83 per cent) had held high civic office in their town, whether as mayor, bailiff, sheriff, steward and/or common councillor. Of York's forty-eight creditors, thirty-five (73 per cent) had occupied similar positions in their city. In other words, the individual creditors from Bristol and York were drawn almost exclusively from the governing elite of the towns.

None the less, the second half of the fourteenth century saw a significant shift in the way loans from Bristol and York were contracted as urban lending on a corporate basis became much more common. Until 1370 all the loans from Bristol and York were from individual burgesses and citizens.[103] The 1359 loan from seven York citizens 'and their colleagues, the good men (*probi homines*) of the city of York' could be described as semi-corporate, since the men were part of the governing group within the city, yet given that the creditors were named individually, it would appear that the loan came directly from their own pockets and was a personal arrangement with the crown. From the reopening of the Hundred Years War in 1369 until 1401, ten out of twelve loans from the city of York and nine out of eighteen Bristol loans were levied on a corporate basis. A possible reason for this trend has already been suggested, namely the decline, from the mid-fourteenth century, of a separate 'estate of merchants' meeting in merchant assemblies. Perhaps the most

---

100 CPR, 1396–9, 363–4, 368; CCR, 1396–9, 425; Barron, 'Tyranny', 5–6.
101 CPR, 1399–1401, 354. For Henry's movements in the summer of 1399 see Saul, *Richard II*, 408–11.
102 *John of Gaunt's register, 1372–1376*, ed. S. Armitage-Smith (Camden 3rd ser. xx–xxi, 1911), ii. 343–4; A. Goodman, *John of Gaunt: the exercise of princely power in fourteenth-century Europe*, London 1992, 53–4.
103 See tables 1 and 2 above for what follows. Note that no loans were made in the 1360s, reflecting the formal peace between England and France.

important factor lay in the development of civic government in the second half of the fourteenth century.

On the one hand, the very reason the crown began to contract loans with Bristol and York in their corporate capacity lay in their ability to organise their own affairs and to raise money for their own purposes. This was a crucial point of difference between urban and county communities. Despite the existence of the institution of the county court, and the shire's function as a unit of royal government for the purposes of royal taxation, counties did not raise taxes outside of parliament.[104] Indeed, W. N. Bryant has shown that Edward III's attempts to secure grants of money from the counties without parliamentary authority led to resistance among their inhabitants who denied the 'taxative competence' of the county community.[105] Consequently, loans were raised from individual members of the gentry within the shires rather than from the counties in their corporate capacity.[106] Just like the arrangements for the payment of royal taxation after 1334, which were organised on a fixed quota system, the crown's policy of communicating directly with the civic governments of Bristol and York to secure loans meant that negotiation would take place within the towns themselves rather than between the crown and individual burgesses and citizens. In a similar vein, a writ of privy seal addressed to the mayor, recorder and aldermen of the city of London in 1374 enclosed 'a list of names of the wealthier citizens' and asked that London's rulers 'use their best endeavours to prevail upon those named to advance money to the King, who was in great need'.[107] On the other hand, and more importantly, the demands for loans after the renewal of war in 1369 placed new strains on the system of civic government in several English towns and cities, including Bristol and York, requiring new administrative measures.[108]

It is very difficult to determine how the corporate loans were levied within the communities of Bristol and York because of the lack of evidence among their civic records. In the receipt rolls of the royal exchequer the corporate loans from York were described variously as from the 'men' ('homines'), 'citizens' ('cives'), 'mayor and citizens' ('maior et cives') and 'mayor and good men' ('maior et probi homines') of the city, while those from Bristol were expressed as from the 'men' ('homines'), 'good men' ('probi homines'), 'mayor and good men' ('maior et probi homines') and 'mayor and community' ('maior et communitas') of the town.[109] In York's case one loan was also

104 Pollock and Maitland, *English law*, i. 555.
105 W. N. Bryant, 'The financial dealings of Edward III with the county communities, 1330–1360', *EHR* lxxxiii (1968), 760–71, esp. p. 765.
106 Steel, *Receipt of the exchequer*, 190–4, 259–61.
107 *Letter-book* G, 330–1.
108 These political tensions are the subject of ch. 2 below.
109 York: table 2, drawing on E 401/501 (*homines*), 566 (*cives*), 501, and *CPR, 1399–1401*, 354 (*maior et cives*), and E 401/561, 608 (*maior et probi homines*); Bristol: table 1, based on E

in the name of the bailiffs of the city.[110] In Bristol the *probi homines* referred specifically to members of the common council of forty-eight (reduced to forty after 1373), while in York, the *probi homines* were members of the councils of twelve and twenty-four.[111] The problem is that, as James Tait has shown, the term *probi homines* continued to be used indiscriminately by the royal chancery, despite its more precise local usage, as a synonym for *homines*, *cives* or *burgenses*, which, like the word *communitas*, meant the corporate body of burgesses or citizens.[112] Evidence from London suggests that corporate loans could be raised from general levies on all of the citizens based on the usual system of collecting parliamentary taxation, namely fixed quotas from each of the wards.[113] A corporate civic loan was a loan negotiated by a civic government on behalf of the whole civic body, whatever the ultimate identity of the actual lenders within the town. The difficulty for towns was that sometimes there could be serious disagreement about the right of their governors to speak in the name of the community to sanction a loan. Thus, in 1351, when London's mayor, four aldermen and eleven members of the common council visited Edward III to 'signify the City's assent' to lend him 20,000 marks, the king later discovered that the loan was not forthcoming because 'some of the community of the city, scheming to deprive the king of that loan and to move the people against him' had asserted that 'the loan was made without the consent of the community'.[114]

In the case of York the crown's regular requests for loans and other financial aid after 1369 led to the development of new institutions of civic government. The 1370s saw the emergence of a conciliar and centralised system of government in York in which political authority was divided between three councils: the councils of twelve and twenty-four, representing the civic elite of high-ranking officeholders, and the council of forty-eight, the bottom tier of civic government, representing the commons.[115] York's rulers could have negotiated a corporate loan with the crown on behalf of all of their urban subjects without consultation, but it can hardly be doubted that they recognised the need to consult widely to authorise a loan and other fiscal payments owing to the crown,[116] especially when large amounts of money were at stake.

401/501, 622 (*homines*), 501, 535, 544, 566, 621 (*probi homines*), 608 (*maior et probi homines*), and 528 (*maior et communitas*).
[110] E 401/561, 19 Aug.
[111] *Bristol charters, 1155–1373*, 137; YMB i, pp. iv–v.
[112] Tait, *Medieval English borough*, 244.
[113] E. J. Davis and M. I. Peake, 'Loans from the city of London to Henry VI, 1431–49', *BIHR* iv (1926), 166–7.
[114] *Letter-book F*, 235; *CCR, 1349–54*, 394.
[115] Rees Jones, 'York's civic administration', 122–3.
[116] For example, the considerable sums spent on the building of barges and balingers in 1372 and 1377, discussed below at pp. 80–1, 85. See also Susan Reynolds's suggestive comment in *English medieval towns*, 173, that a conciliar structure emerged in many towns and cities in the fourteenth century 'to answer the need for wider consultation'.

The commons of York were summoned on important occasions to participate in the system of civic governance and although their role was fairly limited in as much as they were expected to give their assent to decisions already taken by the councils of twelve and twenty-four, they were part of the political process and needed to be informed of the king's necessity.

How important were Bristol and York as royal creditors in the second half of the fourteenth century? With the collapse of the Italian banking firms and the English wool monopoly companies, the crown, from the mid-fourteenth century, turned to the wide body of its own subjects for credit. In this respect, the loans from Bristol and York, whether contracted by individual burgesses or citizens, or by the towns in their corporate capacity, acquired a greater significance to the crown than they would have done prior to 1350. But how much did Bristol and York lend to the crown? Which urban community was more valuable as a source of credit, and how did the amounts given by Bristol and York compare to the figures for other towns and cities?

At the beginning of the period the men of York lent considerably larger sums of money than their counterparts in Bristol. In 1347 and 1351 York merchants lent more than £1,000, while just over £500 was forthcoming from Bristol. When it is remembered that, in the same period, a group of York merchants led by John Goldbeter lent about £20,000 to the crown through the Chiriton company, York's pre-eminence as a centre of royal credit in the mid-fourteenth century can be appreciated more fully.[117] From the accession of Richard II Bristol succeeded York as the largest lender among the provincial towns and cities. Although it is impossible to determine exactly how much of the 1377 staplers' loan was provided by York merchants and, as Caroline Barron has argued in relation to London, 'a large advance by the Staplers or by a group of prominent citizens might well make it difficult for the city to raise a corporate loan if it were asked for one soon afterwards',[118] the contrast between the amounts raised from Bristol and York in Richard II's reign is striking. Between 1377 and 1399 Bristol's corporate and individual loans totalled more than £3,000 compared to just over £500 from York. Anthony Steel's analysis of the sources of royal credit in the reign of Richard II enables Bristol's loans to be placed in a wider urban context. Between 1377 and 1399 the total loans from all English provincial towns and cities amounted to just over £12,000, of which Bristol alone contributed a quarter.[119] In the same period Norwich made corporate loans adding up to just over £850, considerably more than those from York, but still only a quarter of Bristol's total.[120] Although Bristol was not in the same league as

---

[117] E. B. Fryde, 'Some business transactions of York merchants: John Goldbeter, William Acastre and partners, 1336–1349', in his *Medieval trade and finance*, 6.

[118] Barron, 'London and the crown, 1451–61', 91.

[119] Steel, *Receipt of the exchequer*, 144.

[120] Norwich's total was actually £866 13s. 4d., a calculation based on the figures in Attreed, *King's towns*, table 9 at p. 159.

London, which lent £66,000 under Richard II, the town was 'easily pre-eminent' among the list of provincial urban lenders.[121]

There are several reasons for the relative decline of York and simultaneous rise in prominence of Bristol within the crown's credit dealings. Certainly, the answer is not to be found in their comparative wealth, for the second half of the fourteenth century was a period of sustained economic growth for both urban communities, especially their merchants. In the case of York it has been calculated that, by the end of the fourteenth century, the city's merchants 'handled over half the wool and cloth exports of Hull and a third of her imports of wine and miscellaneous imports and exports', while Bristol too became a major cloth manufacturing town, whose merchants were engaged in the export of cloth and the import of wine.[122] Throughout the 1350s and 1360s, for example, the port of Bristol received 'some half or more of all England's shipments of cloth', while by the early fifteenth century, for which yearly figures are available, Bristol was the largest importer of wine among the provincial towns and cities, with 'up to 24 per cent of England's wine' passing through the town.[123] The participation of a prominent group of York merchants in the disgraced wool monopoly companies of the 1340s might have been a factor. When the Chiriton company went bankrupt in 1349, the crown initiated legal proceedings against the company's debtors in order to recover some of its losses, and litigation continued into the 1350s and 1360s against some York merchants, the most important of whom was John Goldbeter.[124] Two of Goldbeter's named associates, William de Skelton and Roger de Hovyngham, did provide loans to the crown after the collapse of the Chiriton company, but it is possible that their involvement in various legal suits 'much reduced their confidence in Edward III's ability to pay his debts',[125] a loss of faith which may have been compounded when the royal exchequer was unable to honour its commitments to repay loans contracted in the years 1369 to 1370. Complaints from the parliamentary commons about non-payment continued into the reign of Richard II,[126] and the city of York was one of the unfortunate creditors, for although the city was assigned repayment (on the Hull customs in 1370) of loans totalling £900, the assignment was subsequently cancelled.[127] Nevertheless, it is perhaps more signifi-

---

[121] Steel, *Receipt of the exchequer*, 141, 144, quotation at p. 144.

[122] J. N. Bartlett, 'The expansion and decline of York in the later Middle Ages', *EcHR* 2nd ser. xii (1959), 26; Lobel and Carus-Wilson, 'Bristol', 10–11.

[123] E. M. Carus-Wilson, 'Trends in the export of English woollens', in her *Medieval merchant venturers*, 248; M. Horton, 'Bristol and its international position', in L. Keen (ed.), '*Almost the richest city*': *Bristol in the Middle Ages* (British Archaeological Association Conference Transactions xix, 1997), 13.

[124] Fryde, 'Business transactions', 3–27.

[125] For Skelton and Hovyngham see ibid. 4–5, and appendix below. The quotation is from Ormrod, 'York and the crown', 31.

[126] *RP* ii. 347, 370; iii. 64, 70.

[127] For this and what follows see E 401/501, 11 May, 3 July; E 401/515, 3 Aug.

cant that in 1374, when £500 of the £900 owing York was eventually repaid, the remaining £400 was remitted to the crown in an act of extraordinary generosity on the part of York's civic elite. Up until this point, York gave its full financial support to the war effort.

The main reason for York's slide down the list of provincial urban lenders from the mid-1370s lies in the city's complex internal politics of this decade, which will be explored in the next chapter and which revolved around the interrelated issues of civic and royal finance. Here it is important to note that the financial demands of the crown in the 1370s led to debate and negotiation between the *probi homines* and the commons of the city about the costs of civic and royal government and, ultimately, to serious disturbances in York in 1380–1 involving an armed siege of the city's guildhall, the forced exile of the mayor and a bitter factional struggle between two members of York's council of twelve. Under pressure from the urban commons, there was a significant scaling down of York's financial commitments to the crown in the later fourteenth century by the city's rulers, so that on those rare occasions when the city did lend money to Richard II, it was for military ventures close to home, namely the defence of the north, an issue with which more urban subjects could identify. Thus, the city lent just over £160 for the king's expedition to Scotland in 1385 and £200 in 1386 to combat the threat of a Franco-Scottish invasion of the northern border.[128] Equally, it is likely that the fine of 1,000 marks imposed on the city of York by the crown in 1382 as the cost of a charter of pardon for the tumultuous events of 1380 and 1381 greatly reduced the city's ability to provide loans.[129] In Bristol, a town whose livelihood was based largely on the exchange of English cloth for French wine at the port of Bordeaux, there was a more extensive interest in the fate of the duchy of Gascony.[130] As a consequence, Bristol's status as the most important royal creditor among the provincial towns and cities in the later fourteenth century continued under the Lancastrians.[131]

Shipping

English towns and cities, particularly coastal communities, also supplied ships to the royal war effort. This naval service was especially significant in the conduct of war because the crown only possessed a small permanent navy in the fourteenth century. The urban contribution to shipping in the second half of the fourteenth century essentially took two forms.[132] First, and most

128 E 401/561, 19 Aug.; E 401/566, 27 Oct., 3 Nov.
129 *RP* iii. 135–6.
130 For the deleterious impact of the loss of Bordeaux to the French in 1453 on the economic well-being of the town of Bristol see Sacks, *Widening gate*, 20–4.
131 Steel, *Receipt of the exchequer*, 196.
132 For what follows see Sherborne, 'Shipping and manpower', 164–9.

important, urban communities supplied privately-owned merchant vessels, which were requisitioned either by royal agents as they travelled from port to port under royal commission or by a town's civic officials under royal command. These merchant ships generally needed to be adapted for the purposes of war, both to accommodate the transport of soldiers, horses and supplies, and to equip them in case of naval conflict with defensive structures consisting of raised platforms on the bow and stern and attached to the mast. Secondly, alongside the ancient royal right of impressment, the crown asked a number of towns, in 1372 and 1377, to construct purpose-built fighting vessels known as barges and balingers – types of oared vessels with masts – at their own cost for service at sea.[133] This second form of naval employment was much more unusual than the first. Individual maritime communities had been asked to build ships at their own expense before the 1370s. In 1356, for example, both the burgesses of Great Yarmouth and the citizens of London had been instructed to pay for the construction of sailing ships 'for the King's use',[134] but the general orders of 1372 and 1377 to a large number of towns and cities recalled Edward I's decision in the autumn of 1294, at the outbreak of war with France, to order the building of thirty galleys from various seaport towns, including London, Newcastle-upon-Tyne, Southampton, Grimsby, Lynn, Great Yarmouth, Bristol and York.[135] What was even more extraordinary about the crown's demands in 1372 and 1377 was that they were issued so close together. Thus, on the one hand there was the government's wartime deployment of existing merchant shipping; on the other hand there was the requirement that towns build new ships specifically for the defence of the realm.

This discussion explores the nature of the partnership between the crown and Bristol and York in the conduct of its naval operations and concentrates on three areas: the level of their naval contributions in quantitative and qualitative terms; the identity of the shipowners from Bristol and York whose ships were arrested for naval service; and the issue of reciprocity. How, and to what extent, did Bristol and York benefit from their role as suppliers of ships to the crown? Were they rewarded with grants of chartered civic privileges? How much consideration should be paid to the purpose for which ships were arrested and constructed anew, namely the 'defence of the realm', an aspect of the common good which the king's subjects expected their ruler to uphold?

The significance of Bristol and York vessels to royal fleets can be measured both quantitatively and qualitatively because of the survival of the royal

---

[133] Idem, 'English barges and balingers of the late fourteenth century', *Mariner's Mirror* lxiii (1977), 109–14.

[134] A. Saul, 'Great Yarmouth and the Hundred Years War in the fourteenth century', *BIHR* lii (1979), 111; *Letter-book* G, 57. For examples from the 1330s see A. E. Prince, 'The army and the navy', in J. F. Willard and others (eds), *The English government at work, 1327–1336*, Cambridge, Mass. 1940–50, i. 384–5.

[135] M. Prestwich, *War, politics and finance under Edward I*, London 1972, 138–9.

naval accounts recording the payment of the wages of shipmasters and their crews and, less frequently, the disbursement of a sum called 'tontyght' to the shipowners,[136] a form of compensation for loss and damage to ships incurred while they were in royal employment. None the less, although they contain a wealth of information about the size, number and type of vessels engaged in royal naval activity, interpretation of the records is problematic for a number of reasons. First, it is very difficult to reconstruct the overall numbers of particular fleets because of the dispersed nature of the accounts of the royal sergeants-at-arms who seized ships for service. Secondly, dating can be hazardous because several of the accounts are in a highly fragmentary condition. Thirdly, and more fundamentally, the accurate counting of ships is an impossible exercise given the tendency for ships to share the same names.[137] With these *caveats*, however, it is possible to measure the numerical significance of Bristol and York vessels to the crown's war effort in a meaningful way.

In her study of Devon's shipping fleet in the fourteenth century Maryanne Kowaleski calculated the number of ships from each incidence of service,[138] a methodology which has also been employed for the purposes of this study, not least because it allows for comparison between Bristol and York and other towns and cities. Table 3 is based on a systematic trawl of all the extant naval accounts in the period 1350 to 1400 for which precise dating is possible,[139] and shows the number of Bristol and York ships in royal employment with each incidence of service counted once. The figures include ships for the war against France as well as for expeditions to Ireland and Scotland, and the table is divided into five-year periods to highlight the fluctuating levels of naval activity by the two towns. The table demonstrates plainly that Bristol ships were in royal service three times as often as those from York. When the figures are placed alongside Kowaleski's statistics for the Devon ports, a more telling comparison can be made. Between 1324 and 1402, a longer period than this study, Plymouth and Dartmouth supplied ships to the crown on 137 and 213 occasions respectively.[140]

The number of Bristol ships in particular royal fleets was substantial. In 1381, for example, the naval force that transported the earl of Cambridge to Portugal consisted of forty-one vessels, of which eight came from the south-west town. Only Dartmouth, which contributed eleven ships, supplied more.[141] Similarly, in 1386, when John of Gaunt and his army were taken to Spain by a fleet of 117 ships, twelve each came from Bristol and Plymouth

136 Sherborne, 'Shipping and manpower', 165.
137 T. J. Runyan, 'Ships and fleets in Anglo-French warfare, 1337–1360', *American Neptune* xlvi (1986), 92–3 n. 10.
138 Kowaleski, *Medieval Exeter*, table 1.3 at p. 29.
139 The following accounts are excluded for this reason: E 101/36/11, 13; E 101/42/22.
140 Kowaleski, *Medieval Exeter*, 29.
141 E 101/39/17.

Table 3
Bristol and York ships in royal service, 1350–1400*

	Bristol	York
1350–5	0	0
1355–60	5	7
1360–5	17	4
1365–70	11	5
1370–5	39	4
1375–80	40	25
1380–5	8	8
1385–90	27	8
1390–5	21	0
1395–1400	28	1
Total	196	62

* This table is based upon the following accounts, in chronological order:
E 101/36/20, 27/5, 27/22–4, 28/21, 28/24, 29/1–2, 29/36, 36/14, 30/29, 32/7, 32/22;
BL, MS Add. 37494, fos. 36r–v; E 101/33/12, 33/31, 34/7, 34/21, 34/25, 37/7,
37/13–15, 37/18–20, 37/23, 37/25, 38/19, 38/30, 39/1–3, 39/17, 40/8–9, 40/19,
42/18, 40/20–1, 40/36, 40/40, 41/31, 42/8, 531/31, 42/3, 42/5.

and sixteen were from Dartmouth.[142] Bristol ships were also numerous in transport fleets to Ireland. In 1394 the naval force that accompanied Richard II to Ireland included twenty-one Bristol vessels.[143] Anthony Saul has argued that the Hundred Years War and the crown's naval demands, in particular, meant that, although naval activity increased generally after 1370, the contribution of the East Anglian town of Great Yarmouth was small, if not negligible.[144] In contrast, Bristol's role as a supplier of vessels to the crown did not diminish in the later fourteenth century. Indeed, in 1400 twenty-two of the seventy-seven ships ordered to assemble at Sandwich for naval service to Scotland were from Bristol.[145] If Dartmouth provided more ships for the Hundred Years War than any other port in England,[146] Bristol, too, was a major supplier of ships for the war effort against the French.

Despite the numerical superiority of Bristol's merchant shipping, the city of York's contribution to the crown's naval policies should not be overlooked. One of the city's two vessels built in 1373, appropriately named the *Peter*

[142] E 101/40/19–20.
[143] E 101/41/31.
[144] Saul, 'Great Yarmouth', 109–12.
[145] E 101/42/5.
[146] For Dartmouth's naval importance see Kowaleski, *Medieval Exeter*, 29–30.

(given the dedication of York Minster), was particularly active in royal employment in the 1370s: it served twice in 1373 and was at sea almost continuously between May 1377 and January 1379.[147] In 1378 alone the barge spent thirty-two weeks away. The effectiveness of the vessel is difficult to gauge, but the military exploits of the barge, employed specifically as a fighting ship to defend the English coast rather than as a transport vessel, captured the attention of the chronicler, Thomas Walsingham, who described the seizure, by 'a multitude of galleys', of the 'noble' barge of York, which then sank with all of its crew and all of its captors on board in 1379.[148] Yet in qualitative terms, too, Bristol's vessels were much larger than those from York, which meant that they could carry more soldiers both for expeditions overseas and for war at sea. The carrying capacity of a ship was measured in tons and the calculation of the average size of the vessels from the two towns has been based on the tonnage figures provided in the naval accounts.[149] The mean tonnage of Bristol's ships was 134, almost double the average seventy-two tons of York's ships,[150] a discrepancy which is probably explained as a consequence of York's geographical position on the river Ouse, many miles inland, which meant that it was very difficult for large ocean-going vessels to reach the city.[151] The Bristol figures are even more impressive when they are compared to the average of eighty-one tons of the merchant vessels impressed for royal service in the reigns of Henry IV and Henry V, a period notable for the construction of considerably larger ships than in the previous century.[152] However it is measured, Bristol's contribution to the war at sea was more distinguished than that of York.

Who were the shipowners from Bristol and York whose vessels were arrested by royal officials? The question is important because naval employment set Bristol apart from York. That York's merchants should have had so few ships in royal service is hardly surprising given their dependency on the shipping and port facilities of Hull for overseas trade; recent work has revealed that shipownership was not a characteristic of York's merchants in the fourteenth and fifteenth centuries.[153] Indeed, ships owned by members of

147 E 101/31/29, 34/25, 37/7, 37/13–15, 37/17–18, 37/25, 38/18. The vessel was referred to as a 'balinger' at a meeting of the *probi homines* of York in 1376, where it was decided to repair the vessel: YMB i. 32–3. A balinger was a small barge, but the terms were interchangeable: Sherborne, 'Barges and balingers', 109.
148 *Chronicon Angliae, 1328–1388*, 233.
149 D. Burwash, *English merchant shipping, 1460–1540*, Newton Abbot 1969, 88–93.
150 Statistics are based on the sources in table 3 above, as well as E 101/36/11, 36/13, 42/22.
151 J. N. Bartlett, 'Some aspects of the economy of York in the later Middle Ages, 1300–1550', unpubl. PhD diss. London 1958, 95–8.
152 Burwash, *Merchant shipping*, 96; I. Friel, 'Winds of change? Ships and the Hundred Years War', in A. Curry and M. Hughes (eds), *Arms, armies and fortifications in the Hundred Years War*, Woodbridge 1994, 189–90.
153 W. R. Childs, *The trade and shipping of Hull, 1300–1500* (East Yorkshire Local History Society xliii, 1990), 22–7; Kermode, *Medieval merchants*, 213–14.

York's merchant community and employed at sea on behalf of the crown tended to be sailed by shipmasters from Hull, John Benetson, a parish constable in York in 1380 and also a mariner from the waterside parish of St John at Ouse Bridge End, being one exception.[154] In fact, the city could not even rely on its own mariners to sail the barge built in 1373 from corporate funds for the defence of the realm. The record of forty mariners paid for service in York's barge listed them according to their place of residence, and the majority came from towns south of the city such as Selby and Doncaster and from as far away as Gainsborough in Lincolnshire and Faxfleet in the East Riding of Yorkshire. Only ten were from the city of York.[155]

In contrast, Bristol was a major shipowning centre. A key theme of the overseas trade of Bristol in the fifteenth century was the full emergence in the town of the 'specialised shipowner', who made his fortune not through his own trade, but through the charging of freightage on the merchandise of other merchants that he transported.[156] This development represented a natural progression from the investment in ships, by many of the town's merchants, in the late fourteenth century. A comprehensive analysis of the Bristol and York shipowners whose vessels were lent to the crown is impossible given that the naval accounts are primarily a record of the payment of the wages of shipmasters and that it only became essential for the royal clerks to note the names of shipowners after 1380 when they were paid 'tontyght', and even then, the compensation was intermittent.[157] Although there are occasional references to the arrest of ships for naval service in other records,[158] the following analysis is based on seven naval accounts from the last three decades of the fourteenth century, a chronological span which should provide a representative sample.[159]

In the case of York the sample is very small. All four of the York shipowners, Thomas Smyth, John de Gysburn, William Fyssh and William de Cawod, held high civic office in the city as mayor, bailiff and/or chamberlain before their ships entered royal employment, and William de Cawod and John de Gysburn also served the crown in other ways, lending money, and, in the case of the latter, holding the post of tax collector of the ordinary

---

[154] See, for example, William Dudeley and Hugh Pogger, identified in Hull's 1377 poll tax return (E 179/206/45, rot. 3r) and in E 101/37/25, 39/2. For Benetson see YMB i. 154, 'The lay poll tax returns for the city of York in 1381', ed. J. N. Bartlett, *Transactions of the East Riding Antiquarian Society* xxx (1953), 23, and E 101/34/25, 37/15.

[155] E 101/37/26, no. 3.

[156] Carus-Wilson, 'Overseas trade', 86–7.

[157] Sherborne, 'Shipping and manpower', 165.

[158] See, for example, CCR, 1349–54, 76; CPR, 1367–70, 389.

[159] E 101/32/7 (1372); BL, MS Add. 37494 (1373); E 101/33/31 (1374–5); E 101/42/22 (pre-1375); E 101/40/21 (1386); E 101/41/31 (1394); E 101/42/5 (1400). It should be noted that although E 101/42/22 is undated, William de Cawod, one of the York shipowners, died in 1375: YMB iii. 7.

fifteenths and tenths as well as of the poll taxes.[160] The extent of Gysburn's shipping interests is not known, but the use of his ship for the war against France gave him a personal stake in the conduct of war and in the success of the crown's naval policy. When in 1373, in the context of growing royal concern about the danger to merchant shipping posed by French naval attack, the parliamentary writ of summons required the urban representatives to be more knowledgeable in shipping and the conduct of trade ('ac in navigio ac in exercicio mercandisarum noticiam habent meliorem'), Gysburn was one of York's MPs elected to the parliament.[161] He was obviously a man experienced in naval and mercantile matters.

The sample for Bristol consists of sixty-four shipowners whose vessels were used for service overseas. Among this group was a handful of men who monopolised all the main civic offices in Bristol in the second half of the fourteenth century and whose ships served the crown on several occasions. They included Walter de Derby, Thomas de Knappe, Walter de Frompton, Ellis Spelly, Richard le Spicer and William Canynges, who between them occupied the mayor's office for twenty-five years between 1354 and 1403.[162] Bristol's mayoralty, like that of Dartmouth, was characterised by shipownership.[163] Shipownership was based on the 'share system' whereby, in order to share the risks of shipwreck and piracy, individuals had shares in ships which could be bequeathed in wills as a valuable source of income in the same way as movable property and land.[164] William Canynges, for example, left to his son, Simon, 'all my share' of the ship which he owned jointly with Ellis Spelly, while Walter de Derby left the fourth part of his ship called the *Mary* and one half of the balinger called the *Trinity* to John Stevenes, possibly his apprentice, who later became bailiff, sheriff and mayor of Bristol.[165] Examples of shipping partnerships included Walter de Frompton and Ellis Spelly, Ellis Spelly and William Canynges, and William de Somerwell and Thomas Knappe.[166] The share system bound the political elite of Bristol together and incorporated them into a wider, national 'community of shipowners' which extended beyond the town to form an interest

[160] See appendix below. For Gysburn's appointment to royal tax commissions see *CFR, 1368–77*, 230, 269, and *CFR, 1377–83*, 150.

[161] *Dignity of a peer*, iv. 661, and appendix below. For the military background see J. W. Sherborne, 'The battle of La Rochelle and the war at sea, 1372–5', *BIHR* xlii (1969), 21–6.

[162] See appendix below.

[163] Kowaleski, *Medieval Exeter*, 30, 257.

[164] J. Schildhauer, *The Hansa: history and culture*, trans. K. Vanovitch, Leipzig 1985, 150; G. V. Scammell, 'Shipowning in England, c. 1450–1550', *TRHS* 5th ser. xii (1962), 114–16.

[165] T. P. Wadley, *Notes or abstracts of the wills contained in . . . the great orphan book and book of wills* (Bristol and Gloucestershire Archaeological Society, 1886), 48, 16.

[166] BL, MS Add. 37494, fo. 36r; *CPR, 1367–70*, 212; E 101/42/22.

group in parliament whose concerns about the state of English shipping found frequent expression in the commons.[167]

To men such as William Canynges, Walter de Derby, Richard le Spicer, Walter de Frompton and Thomas Knappe, lending ships for the war effort was another service that they performed for the crown. Four of them lent money to the royal government, three on more than one occasion, all served as royal tax collectors, and four were involved in the administration of the poll taxes.[168] Royal service at sea tied these men, already dominant locally in their town, even more closely into the apparatus of royal government. Thomas Knappe, Walter de Frompton and Ellis Spelly were also masters of their own ships and were involved in the transport of John of Gaunt and his army to France in 1373.[169] Indeed, for Bristol, in contrast to York, royal naval service went beyond the supplying of ships. Several Bristol merchants were appointed in the place of royal sergeants-at-arms to arrest ships for the crown. Thomas Beaupyne requisitioned vessels for John of Gaunt's expedition to Gascony in 1370, while Walter de Derby helped to assemble a fleet in 1383 for the passage to Ireland of Sir Philip de Courtenay, the king's lieutenant in Ireland.[170] Thomas Norton, who had been a bailiff and sheriff of Bristol and who would later become mayor, came close to developing a full-time naval career when, having lent ships to the crown in 1394 and 1400, he was appointed captain of a royal fleet which disembarked from Bristol, Dartmouth and Plymouth in 1403.[171]

In his work on the east coast town of Great Yarmouth in the fourteenth century Anthony Saul has argued similarly that a few prominent Yarmouth men became deeply involved in royal naval service as masters of royal ships and as admirals. Yet he has also demonstrated convincingly that the town suffered serious economic decline because of the dislocation of trade arising from royal naval demands. Ships were lost at sea during royal employment, while the long periods of arrest before active service limited the participation of Yarmouth's vessels in the town's important herring trade. In short, although a few burgesses benefited from piracy and others pursued prestigious naval careers, in the last quarter of the fourteenth century 'the town was in decline and the war was substantially to blame'. According to Saul, Yarmouth's economic fortunes 'suggest that far from stimulating England's merchant marine the war caused profound disruption of trade and shipping'.[172] Saul's picture of urban decline fits into a broader debate about the impact of the Hundred Years War on English society and economy, with

---

[167] The expression belongs to Schildhauer, *Hansa*, 150. For the operation of this interest group see pp. 52–3 below.
[168] See appendix. For their service as royal tax collectors see CFR, *1347–56*, 268; CFR, *1368–77*, 390; CFR, *1377–83*, 52, 150, 164, 189, 228, 231, 341.
[169] BL, MS Add. 37494, fo. 36r–v.
[170] *Issue roll of Thomas de Brantingham*, 124; CPR, *1381–5*, 288.
[171] CPR, *1401–5*, 363.
[172] Saul, 'Great Yarmouth', 105–15, esp. p. 106.

which this study is not specifically concerned.[173] Yet there is good reason to question the prevailing view, to be found in the work of Saul and others,[174] that the crown's naval policies were inimical to the interests of merchants engaged in overseas commerce. In the words of James Sherborne, merchants and shipowners 'favoured strong naval policies, for government neglect of the seas exposed their trading ventures to serious hazards'.[175]

The crown presented the Hundred Years War to its urban and mercantile subjects as a war for the defence of trade and shipping, an issue with which they were encouraged to identify. On 26 October 1369, for example, a council was summoned to meet at Westminster in November to discuss how best to protect English merchant shipping from French naval attack in the wake of the resumption of the Hundred Years War. Thirty towns and cities, including Bristol and York, were ordered to send representatives with 'the best knowledge of foreign parts and skill in the guiding of shipping, merchants and merchandise' to provide advice and information to the crown on maritime matters.[176] In 1373 the parliamentary writs requesting the election of parliamentary burgesses experienced in shipping and commerce suggest that the crown was once more interested in securing the advice of the towns on naval issues.[177] The defence of the realm was specifically the defence of overseas trade, and through such consultation royal naval policy became, in effect, a joint-stock enterprise between the crown and the ruling elites of provincial towns and cities such as Bristol and York. The city of London was consulted separately on maritime issues relating to the war with France. In December 1369, for instance, the mayor and sheriff of London received instructions to elect four citizens 'experienced in naval and mercantile matters' to attend a meeting of the king's council in January 1370 'to consult about measures to be taken against France'.[178] At the beginning of Richard II's reign London's rulers were given similar orders to send four of the 'wisest citizens' to attend a council at Westminster in August 1377 assembled to discuss 'the war and the protection of commerce on the sea'.[179] This special treatment was undoubtedly a reflection of London's singular importance to the crown as a source of loans; by seeking the active participation of prominent Londoners in royal policy-making and encouraging their identification

---

173 For this debate see M. M. Postan, 'Some social consequences of the Hundred Years' War', *EcHR* xii (1942), 1–12, and 'The costs of the Hundred Years' War', *P&P* xxvii (1964), 34–53; K. B. McFarlane, 'War, the economy and social change: England and the Hundred Years War', *P&P* xxii (1962), 3–13; and A. R. Bridbury, 'The Hundred Years' War: costs and profits', in D. C. Coleman and A. H. John (eds), *Trade, government and economy in pre-industrial England: essays presented to F. J. Fisher*, London 1976, 80–95.
174 For example, Runyan, 'Ships and fleets', 96–9.
175 Sherborne, 'Shipping and manpower, 1369–1389', 169.
176 CCR, 1369–74, 109–10.
177 *Dignity of a peer*, iv. 661.
178 *Letter-book G*, 256.
179 *Letter-book H*, 73.

with the naval policies of the crown, the crown hoped that the capital would provide the necessary financial support for the war.

Yet the civic elites of Bristol and York and other towns and cities were not just the passive recipients of royal instructions on issues of defence and maritime protection. The crown was made acutely aware of its obligation to safeguard the seas and protect England's merchant fleet through increasing parliamentary pressure during the 1370s. In 1371, 1372, 1373, 1379 and 1380 the parliamentary commons drew to the king's attention the decay of English shipping and its causes.[180] In 1372 the commons petitioned on behalf of 'the merchants and mariners of England', providing a painful reminder to the crown of the contrast between the ignoble present and a previous golden age when English shipping had been plentiful and so renowned that Edward III had been commonly known as 'the king of the sea' and other nations had been afraid to make war on him because of the strength and reputation of the English merchant fleet.[181] There were two main points of friction between the commons and the crown regarding the service of merchant vessels in war. The first was the long periods of inactivity: ships requisitioned for royal service could remain in harbour for several months before they eventually sailed. The 1372 petition from 'the merchants and mariners of England' complained that ships were arrested for three months or more before departure from port, while in 1373 a petition from the parliamentary commons on behalf of 'the shipowners throughout England' alleged that the arrests could be as long as six months.[182] Secondly, shipowners often demanded compensation for the expenses incurred in equipping their ships for war and for the damage and loss suffered by their vessels in royal employment. In 1379 and 1380 the commons petitioned on behalf of shipowners, asking for payment to cover maintenance costs, and in 1380 the crown granted a payment of 3s. 4d. for each ton of carrying capacity ('tontyght'). Five years later shipowners were allowed 2s., and in 1386 the commons petitioned once more for the shipowners, asking that payment be increased to the earlier assessment.[183] In short, there was a vociferous and critical shipowning interest group within parliament that was concerned with the damage to English trade and shipping posed by certain aspects of naval service.

It can hardly be doubted that Bristol's MPs, many of whom were shipowners, were active members of this pressure group.[184] Although the

---

[180] *RP* ii. 306–7, 311, 320; iii. 66, 86.

[181] *RP* ii. 311. Such rhetoric seemed designed to inflict the maximum embarrassment on the pretensions of the king who, in the mid-1330s, claimed to be 'lord of the sea': Prince, 'Army and navy', 386.

[182] *RP* ii. 311, 320.

[183] *RP* iii. 66, 86, 212, 223.

[184] Bristol shipowners suffered, like those of other towns and cities, from the deleterious effect of prolonged arrest of their vessels: SC 8/335/15828. The maritime legal code known as the 'laws of Oléron' was copied into the town's fourteenth-century civic register, The Little Red Book, and upheld in the mayor's court. It is calendared in *LRB* i. 88. For a full

names of Bristol's parliamentary representatives in 1379 and 1380 are not known because of the absence of the town's parliamentary returns, Walter de Derby was an MP in both 1372 and 1373, while Thomas Knappe, Ellis Spelly and William Canynges represented the town in 1385 and 1386.[185] Crucially, while there were tensions arising from the arrest of merchant ships for service at sea, the crown became increasingly sensitive to the wider issue of naval defence. In 1372, at the same parliament which heard a complaint from English merchants and mariners about the impact of war on English shipping, the crown ordered the urban representatives to remain behind after the knights of the shire had departed. Although they hardly needed reminding of the 'perils and hardships which could befall their ships and merchandise' from enemy attack, the parliamentary representatives of the towns and cities were asked to grant a subsidy of tonnage and poundage for the following year, which they duly did.[186] In the autumn of 1372 a convoy of twenty vessels, funded by a parliamentary grant of tonnage and poundage, was appointed to safeguard the wine fleet on its annual journey to and from Gascony.[187] The revenue was used to array the vessels for war and covered the cost of wages of the additional mariners who were needed to man the armed ships.[188] Walter de Derby, a prominent Bristol burgess, was the owner of one of the ships, the *Gracedieu*,[189] and he must have been greatly involved in the planning of this mission, for he had been one of Bristol's MPs at the 1372 parliament which had granted the subsidy of tonnage and poundage and he was a collector of the subsidy in the port of Bristol in the same year.[190] Such close personal involvement guaranteed that the crown would not misapply the tax earmarked specifically for the protection of trade and shipping and would spend it on the purposes for which it was authorised. Significantly, in 1385, when the commons petitioned the crown on behalf of the shipowning community to ask for the renewal of 'tontyght', they described the need to equip ships in terms of 'the protection of merchants, and in defence of the realm'.[191] This was the order of their priorities.

A similar agenda can be found in the response of the city of York to its obligation to provide barges and balingers for naval service, which is recorded in the city's civic register, the York Memorandum Book. In the parliament of

text of the laws with translation see *The black book of the admiralty*, ed. T. Twiss (RS, 1871–6), iii. 4–33.

185 See appendix below.

186 *RP* ii. 310.

187 For the 'periodic discussions on how to regulate and protect the Gascon wine fleet' in parliament see, with accompanying references, Ormrod, *Edward III*, 196.

188 M. K. James, 'The fluctuations of the Anglo-Gascon wine trade during the fourteenth century', in her *Studies in the medieval wine trade*, ed. E. M. Veale, Oxford 1971, 25–6 and n. 1.

189 His account for expenses is E 101/32/7.

190 See appendix below.

191 *RP* iii. 212.

November 1372 Edward III's government ordered several port towns and cities including Bristol and York to build barges at their own expense explicitly for the defence of the realm.[192] Five years later, in October 1377, the crown, responding to parliamentary complaints from urban representatives about the neglect of the defence of the sea, ordered the construction of a total of thirty-two balingers from Bristol and York and other urban communities.[193] The city of York was expected, therefore, to deliver a total of two vessels for royal naval service. Significantly, York financed the construction of another vessel in addition to what was required of it by the crown. Despite the commons' formal role in governing the city from the early 1370s, York's civic elite retained a dominant position in civic government, and in the first few years after the renewal of war in 1369, the city's rulers gave their whole-hearted support to the crown's military ambitions. Bad debts amounting to £400 were written off, while the city funded the building of two fighting ships in 1373 when it was only obliged to provide one.[194] Such actions went far beyond the obligatory duty of the king's subjects to assist in the defence of the realm at times of urgent need and should be viewed as evidence of the commitment of York's civic elite of overseas merchants to the defence and maintenance of trade and shipping.

The crown, too, recognised the value of trade as an incentive with which to make its naval demands on towns and cities more palatable. For example, Richard II's instruction to certain towns in 1377 to build a balinger for service at sea contained a promise that, once the voyage was over, the vessel was to be delivered 'to them who have built in this time of need to dispose of it to their advantage'.[195] Yet York's rulers did not need to be told. One of the city's ships, built in 1373, had already been used for commercial purposes when it was not required by the crown: in 1374, for example, the vessel was in Bordeaux purchasing wine.[196] In 1379, when the civic elite decided to sell the much travelled vessel, the *Peter*, it was agreed that the ship should first be freighted to Calais for one final journey 'with wool of the men of the said city', a decision which would have appealed to the city's wool merchants who dominated York's civic government and who were already deeply involved in the operation of the Calais staple. The voyage, however, brought no reward as the vessel was captured by enemy ships in the very same year.[197]

What did Bristol and York gain in return for their role as a supplier of ships to the crown? There is little evidence that piracy was especially profitable. Indeed, in the mid-1370s York's barge, *en route* to Bordeaux to collect wine,

---

[192] E 403/447, 27 Nov. See also Sherborne, 'Shipping and manpower', 169.
[193] *RP* iii. 5–6; *CCR, 1377–81*, 32–3, 51.
[194] E 401/515, 3 Aug.; *YMB* i. 32–3.
[195] *CCR, 1377–81*, 32.
[196] SC 8/103/5133, 5137; SC 8/170/8457. This vessel seems to have been the barge that was eventually sold off by the city in 1376: *YMB* i. 33.
[197] *YMB* i. 32; *Chronicon Angliae, 1328–1388*, 233.

captured a French ship on its way to La Rochelle carrying wheat, wine and peas. The enemy vessel was taken to Bordeaux where, it was alleged, the constable of Bordeaux, Robert de Wykford, presumably enforcing his rights to forfeiture, seized the goods it was transporting as his own, much to the displeasure of York's mayor, who petitioned the crown on several occasions demanding redress.[198] Privateering was a potentially more profitable enterprise in which a few Bristol merchants sometimes participated. In 1403, for example, John Stevenes, the mayor of Bristol, was commissioned by the crown to array the town's ships 'to make war on the men of Brittany' who had broken the terms of a truce recently concluded between England and France.[199] More significantly, Bristol and York did receive charters of civic liberties from the crown in return for their naval service. In 1378 and 1379 the rulers of Bristol and York, as well as of the other towns and cities such as Norwich, Nottingham, Exeter, Ipswich, Lincoln, Coventry and Grimsby which had built vessels at their own expense 'for the defence of the realm' in response to the crown's order of October 1377, negotiated the confirmation of their civic charters. Such negotiation was traditional on the accession of a new monarch, but, on this occasion, it was completed without the usual cash payment into the hanaper or chamber, the subsequent royal grants referring instead to the vast sums of money already spent on the construction of balingers for service at sea.[200]

In the case of Bristol, however, attention must be drawn to the terms on which the town's 1373 charter was granted. The charter, elevating the town of Bristol to the status of a county, was made, according to its preamble, 'in consideration of the good behaviour of the said burgesses towards us and of their good service given us in times past by their shipping'.[201] Interestingly, while the crown readily acknowledged Bristol's maritime importance, the town's rulers chose not to refer to Bristol's essential role as a supplier of ships in the petition that preceded the charter and did not use it as a bargaining tool with which to extract chartered civic privileges from an unwilling royal government.[202] Rather, in the illuminations adorning the royal grants of county status in 1373, Bristol's civic elite sought to articulate in visually resonant terms the interdependence between urban and royal government in the prosecution of war. Bristol's transformation into a county in its own right was

---

198 SC 8/103/5133, 5137; SC 8/170/8457. Although undated, the petitions refer to the title of Robert de Wykford as, successively, constable of Bordeaux and then archbishop of Dublin, an appointment made in 1375: cf. E. B. Fryde and others (eds), *Handbook of British chronology*, 3rd edn, London 1986, 351.

199 *CPR, 1399–1401*, 298. For the background to this commission see C. J. Ford, 'Piracy or policy: the crisis in the Channel, 1400–1403', *TRHS* 5th ser. xxix (1979), 163–78.

200 SC 8/216/10758 and *CChR, 1341–1417*, 248 (York); *CPR, 1377–81*, 150, 153 (Bristol); Attreed, *King's towns*, 36 (Norwich, Nottingham, Exeter); *CChR, 1341–1417*, 249 (Ipswich), 240 (Lincoln), 243 (Coventry); *CPR, 1377–81*, 317 (Grimsby).

201 *Bristol charters, 1155–1373*, 118–21.

202 A copy of Bristol's petition is in *LRB* i. 115–26.

proclaimed in three documents: a charter of 8 August 1373, separating Bristol from the neighbouring counties of Gloucestershire and Somerset; letters patent of 30 October 1373, confirming the perambulation of the new county's boundaries; and letters patent of 20 December 1373, confirming the previous two grants with the authorisation of parliament.[203] All three documents are richly illuminated,[204] containing images of Edward III in the initial 'E' of the king's name, to the right of the arms of both Bristol and the king, yet it is the illuminations of the first two grants, the most important in the process of charter acquisition in 1373, which are the most interesting. In the charter of 8 August Edward is crowned, holding a sceptre and sword and, crucially, wearing armour bearing the quartered arms of England and France underneath a blue, ermine-lined cloak.[205] The armour is suggestive of the role of the king as warrior, prepared for battle, fulfilling his duty to defend the realm.[206] In the letters patent of 30 October confirming Bristol's boundaries the portrait of Edward III is even more evocative, for the monarch appears as the king of France, a title he had formally assumed in January 1340, bearing a crown of *fleurs de lis*, wearing the royal robes of France over a scarlet gown and holding a sceptre in his left hand, symbolising wisdom and the king's responsibility to provide justice.[207]

Charters and other royal documents were not routinely illuminated in this period because of the expense it entailed, so why were the grants of county status to Bristol illustrated? Elizabeth Danbury has argued that the decoration of the letters patent of 30 October 1373 representing Edward III's pretensions to the French throne should be viewed as an aspect of the propaganda of the Hundred Years War,[208] but this is to miss its essential meaning and to ignore the most important aspect of the illumination, namely its audience. Such illumination depicting the majesty of the king was usually paid for by the recipient of royal favour,[209] and the document itself is likely to have been preserved in the town's guildhall for the eyes of Bristol's civic elite.[210] The illumination was a visual expression by, and for, the town's rulers, of their

[203] *Bristol charters, 1155–1373*, 118–41, 168–73.
[204] The three documents are in BRO, royal charters and letters patent: 01208, 01209, 01210.
[205] Ibid. 01208.
[206] On the visual imagery of kingship see, for example, Watts, *Henry VI*, 21 and n. 38.
[207] BRO, 01209. See frontispiece.
[208] E. Danbury, 'English and French artistic propaganda during the period of the Hundred Years War: some evidence from royal charters', in C. Allmand (ed.), *Power, culture, and religion in France, c. 1350–c. 1550*, Woodbridge 1989, 79–80.
[209] Ibid. 75.
[210] The 1373 charter was commemorated more publicly by the construction of a cross – the High Cross – which was erected in the centre of Bristol at the crossroads of the four main streets into the town. The cross is the centrepiece of the famous drawing of Bristol in Ricart, *Maire of Bristowe is kalendar*, which is reproduced, with discussion, in E. Ralph, 'Bristol *circa* 1480', in R. A. Skelton and P. D. A. Harvey (eds), *Local maps and plans from medieval England*, Oxford 1988, 309–16.

collaboration with the crown in the prosecution of war against the French and of the pride they derived from their material and fiscal as well as personal support of Edward III's claims to the throne of France.

In some ways Bristol was not typical of England's urban communities in the way in which it responded so vigorously to the crown's demands for credit and shipping in the second half of the fourteenth century. First, the town's economic fortunes were linked more closely than those of any other English town or city to the fate of Gascony.[211] Secondly, there is evidence that Bristol received preferential treatment from the crown in the repayment of loans. In 1370 the town of Bristol was repaid its two corporate loans totalling over £800 from the Bristol customs,[212] a form of repayment that was of particular importance at this time. Chris Given-Wilson has argued that, 'apart from the Earl [of Arundel] and the Londoners, no lender to the crown in the period October 1369–March 1371 – and there were hundreds of them – was allowed repayment from the customs, although this was almost certainly regarded as the best type of Crown security'.[213] That Bristol too should be reimbursed from the customs was surely a sign of the crown's awareness of the town's importance to the war effort and of the need to maintain the trust and commitment of the town's rulers in the conduct of war. In contrast, the town of Lynn was still seeking repayment of a loan of 500 marks made to the crown in 1370, seven years and one king later.[214]

Yet the rulers of both Bristol and York were involved in the financing of war, in the supply of ships, even in the formulation of naval policy. The crown could coerce where it could not command but, ultimately, it was dependent on the willing collaboration of urban elites in the prosecution of war. Although the supply of ships to the crown differed from the provision of loans because it could be less easily negotiated, the way in which the crown appealed to York and Bristol and other towns and cities for advice on maritime matters is significant. One of the consequences of this co-operation was that the crown had to respond to parliamentary pressure from urban representatives about the need to defend trade and shipping from enemy attack and began, therefore, to develop commercial policies and to act in defence of economic interests. As the following chapters will reveal, many of the economic policies of Edward IV, described by Charles Ross as 'the first "merchant king" in English history', were anticipated in the reigns of Edward III and, more particularly, Richard II.[215]

211 J. W. Sherborne, *The port of Bristol in the Middle Ages* (Bristol Branch of the Historical Association, 1965).
212 E 401/501, 10 May, 25 Oct.
213 C. Given-Wilson, 'Wealth and credit, public and private: the earls of Arundel, 1306–1397', *EHR* cvi (1991), 11.
214 Ormrod, *Edward III*, 186.
215 C. Ross, *Edward IV*, London 1974, 351–70, quotation at p. 351.

2

The Financial Costs of Royal Government

In her seminal study, *Kingdoms and communities in western Europe, 900–1300*, Susan Reynolds drew attention to a familiar paradox of English urban growth that, 'while one imagines that in Italy, for instance, municipal institutions profited from the weakness of the monarchy, in England they were developed partly because town officials, however appointed, were kept busy raising royal taxes'.[1] The work of an older generation of urban historians, most notably James Tait, whose interest in medieval English towns was prompted by the question of the origins of urban constitutions, made clear that the first steps towards urban self-government could be found in the royal grants to towns and cities of the *firma burgi* ('farm of the borough'), by which urban communities, rather than the sheriffs of the counties in which they were located, became responsible for paying the annual dues owed to the crown at the royal exchequer. Since the need to collect money on behalf of the crown required a measure of self-determination, so the right of townsmen to pay their own farm was often accompanied by the privilege of electing their own officials.[2] It was argued in the previous chapter that, in the case of York, the crown's fiscal demands arising from the reopening of the Hundred Years War in 1369 stimulated the further development of the structure of civic administration, incorporating a wider element of consultation in the process of government. The following discussion seeks to develop this argument and to explore the impact of the crown's financial policies on the politics and governance of Bristol and York, concentrating largely on the period 1369 to 1381. The years after 1369 saw regular and heavy grants of royal taxation to finance the war against France, including the traditional lay subsidies known as fifteenths and tenths as well as novel forms of taxation in the parish subsidy and the poll taxes. It has been calculated that over one million pounds was spent by the English crown on the war effort between 1369 and 1381.[3]

What follows is not an attempt to assess the precise fiscal burden of the crown's financial demands either on the taxpayers of Bristol and York or – as Lorraine Attreed has done so expertly in the context of an analysis of the nature, causes and extent of urban decline in fifteenth-century England – the

---

[1] Reynolds, *Kingdoms and communities*, 180.
[2] Tait, *Medieval English borough*, ch. vii.
[3] J. W. Sherborne, 'The cost of English warfare with France in the later fourteenth century', *BIHR* 1 (1977), 136.

finances of the two towns in their corporate capacity.[4] The relative paucity of the financial records for both Bristol and York in the second half of the four-teenth century precludes such a fiscal approach. Neither town has, for the period of this study, evidence within its own civic archives of what Chris Dyer has described as 'actual tax-paying practice' in the form of 'records of assessments for the royal subsidies . . . and of levies for loans to the crown',[5] although there are nominative tax returns for the distribution of the poll taxes of 1377 and 1380 in the city of York.[6] Meanwhile, the extant records of the financial officials of Bristol and York are such that a detailed examination of the receipts and expenses of civic government in the second half of the fourteenth century is impossible. In the case of Bristol the records of civic finance do not survive until the sixteenth century,[7] while, apart from an incomplete chamberlains' account roll of 1396–7 and an early sixteenth-century extract of the chamberlains' receipts for the year 1391–2,[8] the internal financial records of York are equally meagre until the fifteenth century.

Instead, the focus of this study is the politics of finance, the evidence for which is comparatively rich in both the civic and royal archives. It is well known that the period 1369 to 1381 was dominated, at the national level, by debate about the cost and conduct of royal government.[9] Yet the same years also saw questions raised in a number of towns and cities including Bristol and York about how, by whom and in whose interest they should be governed, questions which were provoked, in the first instance, by the inter-related costs of royal and civic government. A detailed examination of the effects of the crown's financial demands on the internal politics of Bristol and York should provide a new opportunity to explore the intimate relationship between local and national politics in the years that followed the renewal of war in 1369. Existing work on this subject has focused almost exclusively on issues of personality and personal connections. The existence of a court party among London's mercantile elite, whose direct links with the royal court intensified a factional struggle within the city in the 1370s, is well docu-mented.[10] Anthony Saul's equally intricate study of an urban conflict in East

4   Attreed, *King's towns*, ch. v.
5   C. Dyer, 'Taxation and communities in late medieval England', in R. H. Britnell and J. Hatcher (eds), *Progress and problems in medieval England: essays in honour of Edward Miller*, Cambridge 1996, 175.
6   'The 1377 poll tax return for the city of York', ed. J. I. Leggett, YAJ xliii (1971), 128–46; 'Lay poll tax returns for the city of York in 1381', 1–91.
7   *City chamberlains' accounts in the sixteenth and seventeenth centuries*, ed. D. M. Livock (Bristol Record Society xxiv, 1965).
8   *York city chamberlains' account rolls*; R. W. Hoyle, 'Urban decay and civic lobbying: the crisis in York's finances, 1525–1536', NH xxxiv (1998), 91, drawing on E 163/12/1.
9   Holmes, *Good Parliament*, passim; J. S. Roskell, *The impeachment of Michael de la Pole, earl of Suffolk in 1386*, Manchester 1984, chs i–ii.
10 C. M. Barron, *Revolt in London 11th to 15th June 1381*, London 1981, 13–14; P. Nightin-

Anglia in the 1370s has elucidated the provincial base of this court party, demonstrating how the close ties between a dominant grouping at court and two prominent burgesses of Great Yarmouth, William Elys and Hugh Fastolf, enabled the lesser burgesses of the town to take advantage of the attack on Elys and Fastolf in the Good Parliament of 1376.[11] This chapter suggests that greater attention needs to be paid to the broader debate about governance at both the local and national level, which revolved around issues of private interest and public duty. Before considering the extent to which the experiences of Bristol and York were part of a wider picture, however, it is important to acknowledge the basic differences between the crown's fiscal relations with the two towns, notably the position Bristol occupied within the queen's finances.

Bristol: the 'queen's chamber'?

The fee farm was a fixed annual sum payable by urban communities in place of individual payments owing to the crown from feudal revenues such as court profits, tolls, rents and escheats. The sum arose from the landed resources of the crown because certain towns and cities, including Bristol and York, were part of the royal domain.[12] The late twelfth and early thirteenth centuries saw the permanent acquisition by many towns of the privilege of farming the revenues which were due to the crown in return for a lump sum payable annually at the exchequer. Previously the crown had leased the farming privilege to towns on a temporary basis, but the financial needs of Richard I and King John encouraged the crown to grant the farm to particular towns permanently for a fixed annual payment.[13] For example, in 1212 the citizens of York were granted their city to farm for a yearly sum of £160 in perpetuity, an amount that they continued to render at the exchequer until their pleas for a partial remission of the fee farm were conceded in the 1480s and 1490s.[14] In contrast, the revenues of the town of Bristol were farmed by various individuals including the constables of Bristol castle, as well as by the

gale, 'Capitalists, crafts and constitutional change in late fourteenth-century London', *P&P* cxxiv (1989), 3–35.

[11] A. Saul, 'Local politics and the Good Parliament', in A. J. Pollard (ed.), *Property and politics: essays in later medieval English history*, Gloucester 1984, 156–71.

[12] The best introduction to the subject remains Tait, *Medieval English borough*, ch. vii. For the crown's landed revenues see B. P. Wolffe, *The royal demesne in English history: the crown estate in the governance of the realm from the conquest to 1509*, London 1971.

[13] Within the secondary literature, the permanent, hereditary grant of the farm is known as the fee farm so as to distinguish it from the temporary lease: T. Madox, *Firma burgi*, London 1726, 3–4. To hold at fee farm meant 'to hold heritably, perpetually, at a rent; the fee, the inheritance, is let to farm': Pollock and Maitland, *English law*, i. 293. But I use the words fee farm and farm interchangeably for the sake of convenience.

[14] Attreed, 'The king's interest', 24–43.

town's burgesses collectively. When the burgesses did farm the feudal profits of Bristol, they did so on a number of short-term leases, and it was only in 1462 that Edward IV ended this practice in favour of a permanent grant.[15]

It was common practice for very little of the revenue owing from a town's fee farm that could have been paid directly to the king's exchequer to reach the crown.[16] Instead, assignment meant that potential income was paid in advance to a combination of crown servants, members of the royal family and religious institutions, leaving only a residual and occasional profit to the royal government. York's fee farm amounted to £160, on which there were three permanent assignments. The oldest was the £7 12s. 1d. paid annually to the family of David le Lardener, whose hereditary function since the twelfth century had been to stock the king's larder in York with the accompanying right of keeping the forest gaol.[17] The largest assignment was £100 (originally £120) granted to the Roos family of Helmsley in 1318 in return for the castle of Wark-on-Tweed, which lay on the Scottish border and which Edward II had taken in order to improve border defences.[18] Finally, in 1351, £35 14s. 7d. was alienated perpetually to the royal foundation of St Stephen's chapel, Westminster, originally built by Henry III, in return for alms.[19] In permanent assignments alone, therefore, £143 6s. 8d. of York's £160 fee farm was not received by the crown.[20] In addition, there was money regularly awarded to royal servants as pensions, such as the £10 per annum granted to Robert de Swylington and the five marks per annum paid to Walter Whithors, one of Edward III's esquires.[21] The cumulative effect of these assignments was that usually less than £10 was paid to the crown directly each year.[22] In fact, it was not unusual for York's fee farm to be overburdened with assignments. Table 4, drawn from a sample of exchequer pipe rolls at ten-year intervals, shows the value of the assignments made on York's fee farm between 1350 and 1400.

One of the consequences of assignment was intense competition between the various recipients of the revenues from York's fee farm to secure payment,[23] and the crown was just one recipient among many. Thus, in 1358, in response to a complaint from Thomas de Roos, the king ordered the

15 For the complex history of Bristol's fee farm between the thirteenth and fifteenth centuries see the editor's introduction to Bristol charters, 1378–1499, 41–56.
16 For the figures see Attreed, King's towns, 145.
17 R. B. Pugh, 'Prisons and gallows', in VCH, Yorkshire: York, 494–5.
18 CCR, 1318–23, 18, 609.
19 CPR, 1350–4, 190.
20 See, for example, E 372/246, rot. 7r.
21 For example, E 372/196, rot. 9r; E 372/193, rot. 5d.
22 E 372/206, rot. 8r, contains a reference to £9 15d. 'which the bailiffs and citizens of the said city were accustomed to render annually at the exchequer over and above all the assignments'.
23 For the problems facing the royal creditor who sought payment from a source of royal revenue see A. Steel, 'The practice of assignment in the later fourteenth century', EHR xliii (1928), 172–80, and G. L. Harriss, 'Preference at the medieval exchequer', BIHR xxx (1957), 17–40.

Table 4
Assignments on York's fee farm, 1350–1400*

	Assignments	Fee farm	Difference
1350–1	£150 18s. 9d.	£160	+ £9 1s. 3d.
1360–1	£160	£160	even
1370–1	£153 6s. 8d.	£160	+ £6 13s. 4d.
1380–1	£176 13s. 4d.	£160	− £16 13s. 4d.
1390–1	£153 6s. 8d.	£160	+ £6 13s. 4d.
1400–1	£178 7s. 4d.	£160	− £18 7s. 4d.

* The figures are drawn from E 372/196, rot. 9r; E 372/206, rot. 8r; E 372/216, rot. 9r; E 372/226, rot. 8r; E 372/236, rot. 14d; E 372/246, rot. 7r. Note that in the pipe rolls, the value of York's annual fee farm is occasionally recorded as £152 7s. 11d., but with the £7 12s. 1d. assignment of the le Lardener family, the total is £160.

exchequer to deliver £10 to the petitioner since he 'has learned that the treasurer and barons of the exchequer . . . have arrested and caused to be paid for the king's use . . . £10 which the bailiffs of York ought to have paid to him'.[24] That York's fee farm was extremely valuable to the crown is evident from the way in which its revenues were on occasion over-assigned. Although the crown did not receive any significant direct financial benefit, York's fee farm was an important source of patronage with which to reward royal servants.

From 1275 Bristol's fee farm was assigned in its entirety to successive queens as part of the landed estate that comprised their dower. In 1275 Edward I assigned the profits of the town and castle of Bristol with the neighbouring royal manor of Barton to his wife, Eleanor of Castile, for the term of her life, to supplement her existing dower assignments.[25] Throughout the later Middle Ages and into the seventeenth century the town of Bristol was granted to the queen consort when the king provided her with a landed income of her own,[26] and it became customary for the queen to grant the farm of the town to the burgesses at a fixed sum for a period of years. In 1330 the town, castle and manor of Barton were assigned to the dower of Edward III's wife, Queen Philippa.[27] In April 1332 the queen's steward and constable of Bristol castle, John de Heigham, granted the town to the mayor to farm for ten years at £140 *per annum*, with an agreement that after the ten years had

[24] CCR, *1354–60*, 483.
[25] CChR, *1257–1300*, 193.
[26] CPR, *1317–21*, 115–16; CPR, *1330–4*, 55–6; CPR, *1381–5*, 125–6; CPR, *1401–5*, 234–5, 271–2; CPR, *1461–7*, 430; CPR, *1485–94*, 75–7; *Letters and papers, foreign and domestic, of the reign of Henry VIII*, 2nd edn, London 1864–1932, i/1, 48–50, vii. 176; Ricart, *Maire of Bristowe is kalendar*, 113–14.
[27] CPR, *1330–4*, 55–6.

passed the farm of the town should be devised to the mayor and commonalty of Bristol for the term of the queen's life if it pleased the queen and her council.[28] From this date until Queen Philippa's death, Bristol remained part of the queen's landed endowment and continued to pay its £140 annual fee farm to the queen's receivers and to be administered by the queen's ministers and estate officials.[29] Bristol's civic officials also owed an oath of loyalty to the queen as the lord from whom they immediately held the town. The mayor's oath to be faithful and loyal to the king and his heirs included a declaration that he would keep and guard the town of Bristol for the king and for 'my lady Queen Philippa, to whom the said town was granted for the term of my said lady's life'; the entry in the town's civic register was subsequently erased, presumably on her death in 1369.[30]

Only on the death of a queen consort did the king receive the profits of Bristol's fee farm, which otherwise belonged to his wife. In the fifteenth century the queen's dower lands were so substantial as to attract the attention of Sir John Fortescue who saw them as lost revenue for the crown.[31] Valued at £140 *per annum* in 1332, Bristol's fee farm amounted to almost one-thirtieth of Queen Philippa's original dower assignment of £4,500 and it was the largest contribution of any urban community. This and the longevity of its financial association with the queen consort were the basis of Bristol's claims to be the 'queen's chamber'. In August 1535 Henry VIII and Anne Boleyn resided at the neighbouring royal manor of Thornbury in Gloucestershire, where, concerned about an outbreak of plague in Bristol, they received instead a civic delegation including the town's chamberlain, who presented the king with cattle and sheep for the sustenance of the royal household and delivered to the queen a silver-gilt cup containing one hundred marks. These items, according to the record of the visit in Robert Ricart's *Kalendar*, were 'a gifte of this the kynges Town and hir Chambre of Bristowe'.[32] In 1612 James I's wife, Anne of Denmark, deigned to visit Bristol, 'being called and accompted her Majestes Chamber', whereupon she was met on the eastern outskirts of the town by Bristol's ruling elite, one of whom, the recorder, presented her with a satin purse bearing her initials containing the equivalent of £110.[33] The most emphatic declaration of Bristol's status as the 'queen's chamber' was made in 1628 when Bristol's rulers petitioned Henrietta, Charles I's queen, asking for her intercession with the king in order to annex Bristol castle and its precincts to the town under the mayor's authority.[34] The castle had been a jurisdictional minefield for Bristol

---

28 C 47/9/58, rot. 1r.
29 In chronological order, the relevant accounts are SC 6/1091/1, rots 1d–4d; E 101/389/2, mem. 2; E 101/389/7, mem. 1; SC 6/1091/5, mem. 1; E 36/205, fo. 3r; SC 6/1092/3, mem. 3. This last record is dated 1365.
30 *LRB* i. 46.
31 John Fortescue, *The governance of England*, ed. C. Plummer, London 1885, 131.
32 Ricart, *Maire of Bristowe is kalendar*, 54.
33 Ibid. 65.
34 For what follows see ibid. 113–18, esp. pp. 113–14.

for a long time: the castle precincts lay outside the boundaries of civic jurisdiction and, therefore, offered a safe haven for criminals. In the petition Bristol's mayor appealed to the queen as the town's most important patron,
reminding her that:

> the Cittie of Bristoll hath aunciently bene reputed and called the Chamber of
> the Queenes of England, as London is called the Kinges Chamber, and it hath
> pleased the Queenes of England, your most noble predecessors . . . soe to
> esteeme thereof as to receive and take the same unto her especiall favour and
> protection whiles she lived. And bycause the same Citty is parcell of your Maj-
> esties joincture wee most humbly pray your Majestie to receive it into your
> Highnes favour.

The rhetoric of the royal chamber was one to which several towns and cities,
from the early fourteenth century, had recourse on occasion in order to negotiate their relations with royal authority at certain critical moments.[35] The
seizure of London's liberties and the removal of the organs of royal government to York in 1392, prompted York to claim the distinction of being the
'king's chamber' in imitation of London. Meanwhile, Coventry's rulers chose
to refer to their city as the 'prince's chamber' on the occasion of royal visits
during the Wars of the Roses, in reference to the fact that the city, from 1358,
was traditionally part of the patrimony of the king's eldest son, the prince of
Wales, whose fee farm contributed to his landed income. The rhetoric had
several connotations. First, just as the king's chamber was, in essence, the
king's privy purse, a financial office with responsibility for the payment of the
king's personal expenses,[36] so a town's status as a royal chamber had a financial significance. Secondly, in the same way that the chamber was an intimate and private physical space within the royal household – the king's
bedchamber – where the king was surrounded by 'a small inner circle of
friends and counsellors',[37] so there was a sense in which the rhetoric of the
royal chamber implied a close personal relationship between a town and the
royal government based on physical proximity. Thirdly, and more generally,
the deployment of the rhetoric of the chamber by towns and cities such as
Bristol, York, Coventry and London in connection to the king, queen or heir
to the throne invoked a special relationship with the figure of royal authority.
In what sense did Bristol enjoy a special relationship with the queens consort
in the second half of the fourteenth century?

Evidence of the visits of the queens consort to Bristol in the period 1350 to
1400 is slim, largely because the most detailed sources which can be used to
reconstruct a royal itinerary – the wardrobe books (the annual accounts of

---

[35] Liddy, 'Rhetoric of the chamber', 323–49.
[36] Given-Wilson, *Royal household*, 5.
[37] Ibid.

the expenditure of the royal household) – are almost wholly lacking.[38] There is no evidence of correspondence between Bristol and Edward III's queen, Philippa of Hainault, or Richard II's first wife, Anne of Bohemia, while the few extant financial records of the two queens relate, instead, the more prosaic details of estate administration.[39] Similarly, Bristol's internal financial records, precisely the place where the expenses associated with gift giving and hospitality to royal visitors would be recorded, have not survived.[40] Contemporary chronicles are a potentially more rewarding source, but they tend to be more interested in the movements of the king than the queen unless they travelled together. For instance, Froissart's account of the plans of Robert de Vere (recently created marquess of Dublin) to lead an expedition to Ireland in the summer of 1386 reveals that de Vere established his base at Bristol, from where the expeditionary force was to set sail. At Bristol, described by Froissart as 'a handsome and strong town', Richard II joined de Vere, fixing 'his residence in the castle'. Almost as an afterthought Froissart concludes his account of these events by mentioning that the king left his queen at Bristol before setting out to return to London.[41]

The presence in Bristol of the king and queen for a tournament on New Year's Day 1358 is better documented, due in no small measure to the 1357–8 household account of Queen Philippa's cofferer.[42] The Bristol tournament was part of a cycle of festivities between autumn 1357 and spring 1358 intended to celebrate the victory of Edward III's eldest son, the Black Prince, at the Battle of Poitiers in 1356, in which John II of France and other members of the French nobility had been taken prisoner.[43] The cycle began with jousts at Smithfield in the presence of Edward III and the captive kings of France and Scotland, included a major royal feast at Marlborough on Christmas Day, and culminated in a feast of the knights of the Order of the Garter at Windsor on St George's Day attended by the French king as well as other foreign dignitaries, followed by jousts 'not seen since the time of king

[38] For the usefulness of such records in relation to the king's itinerary see N. Saul, 'Richard II and the city of York', in Rees Jones, Government of medieval York, 5.
[39] The extant sources are referenced in H. Johnstone, 'The queen's household', in T. F. Tout, Chapters in the administrative history of medieval England, Manchester 1920–33, v. 250–60.
[40] In contrast, the chamberlains' accounts of Lynn reveal much about this town's relations with the queen dowager, Isabella, during her periods of residence at nearby Castle Rising: H. Harrod, Report on the deeds and records of the borough of King's Lynn, King's Lynn 1874, 68–71.
[41] John Froissart, Chronicles, trans. T. Johnes, London 1839, ii. 269, 271, 281, quotation at p. 281. Froissart's chronological framework for the years 1386–8 is, however, 'muddled': J. W. Sherborne, 'Charles VI and Richard II', in J. J. N. Palmer (ed.), Froissart: historian, Woodbridge 1981, 59. For the precise timing of Richard II's visit see Saul, Richard II, 155.
[42] JRUL, MS Latin 236.
[43] R. Barber and J. Barker, Tournaments: jousts, chivalry and pageants in the Middle Ages, Woodbridge 1989, 34–5.

Arthur', according to one chronicle.[44] The tournament at Bristol is famous because it marked the first time that nocturnal jousts ('hastiludia nocturna') had been fought in England, an event of cultural significance which moved the author of the *Eulogium historiarum*, writing nearby at Malmesbury abbey, to comment that 'the like of which had not been seen before in dignity and splendour' ('qualia non sunt ante visa prae nimio honore et magnificentia').[45]

Edward III's visit to Bristol was also his first in over thirty years as king.[46] After celebrating Christmas with the queen at Marlborough, Edward seems to have been in Bristol for about a week, arriving on 1 January 1358, when his court celebrated the feast of the Circumcision with the night-time jousting. He continued to reside in the town until about 6 January, when he attended the great mass held in the queen's chapel at Bristol castle to celebrate the feast of the Epiphany with a royal party including the queen and their son, Thomas of Woodstock, two daughters, Mary and Margaret, and daughter-in-law, Elizabeth countess of Ulster.[47] The fortunate survival of the queen's household account for 1357–8 reveals that the queen and her children, however, spent considerably longer in Bristol than the king and that careful preparations were made in readiness for a prolonged visit. Over £13, for example, was spent on various unspecified works undertaken at Bristol castle presumably to improve the accommodation for the queen and members of the royal family.[48] The queen's son and daughters were certainly at Bristol from as early as 5 December 1357, when they heard children singing the motet *sospitati dedit*, part of the liturgy of St Nicholas.[49] In fact, payments to certain of the queen's officials 'sent from the court at Bristol' to London on the queen's business suggest that the queen's household was in residence in Bristol from late October 1357 to early February 1358.[50] The queen, the prince and the two princesses were definitely in Bristol on the feast of the Purification of the Blessed Virgin Mary (2 February) 1358, when they

---

[44] M. Bennett, 'Isabelle of France, Anglo-French diplomacy and cultural exchange in the late 1350s', in J. S. Bothwell (ed.), *The age of Edward III*, York 2001, 215–25. The quotation is from *Eulogium historiarum sive temporis*, ed. F. S. Haydon (RS, 1858–63), iii. 227.

[45] J. Vale, *Edward III and chivalry: chivalric society and its context, 1270–1350*, Woodbridge 1982, appendix 12 at p. 174 (although mistakenly dated to 1 Jan. 1357); *Eulogium*, iii. 227.

[46] Evidence from the place-dates in published chancery enrolments indicates a royal presence in Bristol from around 14 to 20 August 1347, but this itinerary was that of Prince Lionel, the king's second son, in his capacity as keeper of the realm, while the king was engaged in the siege of Calais: CCR, 1346–9, 307, 311, 313, 370, 373, 375; CPR, 1345–8, 365, 367, 368, 369. I would like to thank W. M. Ormrod for his help in clarifying the identity of this royal visitor.

[47] JRUL, MS Latin 236, fo. 2v; E. A. Bond, 'Chaucer as page in the household of the countess of Ulster', in *Life-records of Chaucer*, ed. W. D. Selby and others (Chaucer Society 2nd ser. xxi, 1886), 112.

[48] JRUL, MS Latin 236, fo. 9r.

[49] Ibid. fo. 3r. The account records a payment to four 'parvis cantantibus sospitati in presencia librorum Regis apud Bristoll' on the eve of St Nicholas.

[50] Ibid. fo. 5v.

attended a great mass in her chapel at the castle.[51] Philippa's lengthy sojourn in Bristol in the winter of 1357–8, for which even the queen's household account only provides a bare outline, offers a tantalising picture of what might have been a close relationship between the queen and the town of Bristol that otherwise is difficult to recapture from the extant sources.

Such a relationship helps to explain the protracted nature of the conflict between Bristol and Queen Philippa over the issue of queen's gold, which was provoked in the 1330s in the context of the town's financial negotiations with the crown over the form of its contribution to royal taxation. The late thirteenth and early fourteenth centuries saw the emergence of a new fiscal obligation in the form of direct taxation. Compared to the fee farm, this was a different kind of obligation because it arose not from the feudal rights of the crown, but from the Romano-canonical doctrine of necessity, according to which it was the obligation of a ruler's subjects to help the ruler in time of emergency.[52] There were, however, similarities between the way in which towns and cities paid direct taxation and the fee farm. Until 1332 the lay subsidy was levied directly on townspeople by royal tax collectors. In 1334 the system of direct taxation was reorganised so that it was assessed on the communities of town and vill rather than on individual taxpayers.[53] Royal tax collectors negotiated with local communities to agree on a lump sum payable to the king that had to be equal to, or greater than, the amount paid in 1332. In 1334 Bristol's tax quota stood at £220 compared to York's quota of £162.[54] York's sum was certainly a preferential rate because the crown had instructed the tax collectors to negotiate a sum that was not less than the amount paid in 1332. In 1332 York had paid £166 to the king, so the figure of £162 was a small, but none the less significant reduction of £4. It is likely that York's generous assessment by the crown in 1334 reflected the city's importance as the second seat of royal government in the early fourteenth century.[55] It may also be the case that the city's officials used the opportunity provided by the presence of the royal government in the 1330s to press for a reduction. After all, the 1334 parliament which fixed the level of tax quotas was held at York.[56] In the same period Bristol's tax quota increased from £200

---

51 Ibid. fo. 2v.
52 Harriss, *King, parliament, and public finance*, 3–48.
53 For the history of the lay subsidy before 1334 see J. F. Willard, *Parliamentary taxes on personal property, 1290 to 1334: a study in mediaeval English financial administration*, Cambridge, Mass. 1934. For the arrangements in 1334 see *The lay subsidy of 1334*, ed. R. E. Glasscock (British Academy Records of Social and Economic History n.s. ii, 1975), pp. xiv–xvii.
54 J. F. Hadwin, 'The medieval lay subsidies and economic history', *EcHR*, 2nd ser. xxxvi (1983), table 3 at p. 217.
55 D. M. Broome, 'Exchequer migrations to York in the thirteenth and fourteenth centuries', in A. G. Little and F. M. Powicke (eds), *Essays in medieval history presented to T. F. Tout*, Manchester 1925, 291–300.
56 Fryde and others, *Handbook of British chronology*, 557.

to £220.[57] In 1334, too, responsibility for the actual valuation and collection of the tax within their communities was entrusted to the villages and towns themselves, although there was still an element of royal supervision inasmuch as tax commissioners continued to be appointed by the crown to collect the tax quotas assessed internally within each town and vill, to pay the sums to the crown, and to account directly to the king's exchequer for whatever shortfalls might arise in the taxes levied. This quota system remained in force, albeit with successive revision, from 1334 until the seventeenth century. Thus, in the same way that towns were allowed to farm the feudal revenues owing to the crown, paying a fixed annual lump sum to the king instead of the individual revenues from court profits, tolls and rents, so from 1334 it was also the right of local communities to pay a fixed tax quota.

Yet even before 1334, when the responsibility for the assessment and collection of royal taxation passed into the hands of local communities, the town of Bristol sought to free itself entirely from 'the inconvenience of assessment' by royal officials.[58] In 1332 the mayor of Bristol, Hugh de Langebrigge, fined for £200 so that the 'goods within the town and suburbs' of Bristol 'shall not be taxed for this turn for the fifteenth and tenth granted to the king by the commonalty of the realm'. Two years later the mayor, Roger Turtle, acquired the same exemption for the town in return for £220, and similar grants were made to Bristol in 1336 and 1337.[59] Other urban communities had previously fined for exemption from royal taxation in exchange for an agreed sum of money,[60] so the practice of fining by Bristol was in no sense unique. In many ways Bristol's fine in 1332 for a fixed sum of money was an important antecedent to the general reorganisation of the system of taxation in 1334. As to why Bristol's rulers should continue to seek immunity from royal tax officials after 1334, it is important to note that Bristol only received its own specially appointed royal tax collectors in 1373 with the acquisition of county status.[61] Before this date Bristol, like the vast majority of English towns and cities with one or two notable exceptions including the city of York, was not classed as a county in its own right for the purposes of royal taxation and was expected instead to pay its lay subsidy to county officials drawn from outside the town, who then delivered the revenue to the king's exchequer.[62] By fining for exemption from the normal structure of royal taxation, Bristol became corporately responsible for the process by which the sum of £220 was to be raised within the town and directly accountable to the

---

[57] Hadwin, 'Medieval lay subsidies', table 3 at p. 217.
[58] The quotation belongs to C. Johnson, 'The collectors of lay taxes', in Willard and others, *English government at work*, ii. 211.
[59] CPR, 1330–4, 337; CFR, 1327–37, 428, 486, 506.
[60] Johnson, 'Collectors of lay taxes', 211.
[61] CFR, 1368–77, 230.
[62] York ranked as a county in fiscal terms from 1319: Johnson, 'Collectors of lay taxes', 203.

crown in fiscal matters, entirely free from the intrusion and interference of external tax collectors.

The problem for Bristol was that the town became embroiled in a conflict with Queen Philippa over Philippa's claims to queen's gold from Bristol's fine for £220 in place of direct taxation. The dispute began in the 1330s, but the issue re-emerged in 1353 when Philippa and her officials tried to exploit more fully her customary sources of revenue in the context of declining income and increasing expenses. Queens consort enjoyed two main sources of revenue: prerogative income, which belonged to the queen as queen; and lands assigned by the king to the queen in dower.[63] Queen's gold occupied the former category: it was a traditional prerogative of the queen by which she could claim a tenth of the value of a voluntary offering of more than ten marks made to the king.[64] This offering was known as a fine, but this was not a fine in the sense of a punishment for a criminal offence imposed by a court, but rather a fee paid on the acquisition of a royal grant, licence, pardon or exemption. The sum was payable in addition to the money received by the king, and in Bristol's case, Queen Philippa claimed £22 as queen's gold from the fine of £220. Queen's gold could be paid by an individual or a corporate body such as an urban community, irrespective of whether they formed part of the queen's landed estate, but the conflict is instructive because the determined attempt by Philippa to assert her claims in Bristol reflected a pre-existing financial relationship between the queen and the town.

Although in theory the king's rights over the payment of queen's gold were minimal so that he could not, for example, remit or even reduce the amount payable to the queen without her consent,[65] in 1336 and 1338, in response to petitions from Bristol, Edward III issued writs of *supersedeas* to the exchequer to cancel its demands for queen's gold.[66] The reason for Edward's action is not clear, but it is likely that the king recognised the need for domestic peace at the outset of the French war and sought, in particular, to ensure Bristol's financial support.[67] None the less, while the king was sympathetic to Bristol's requests, queen's gold remained the prerogative of the queen and in the mid-fourteenth century, the queen, like other landowners in the aftermath of the Black Death, was experiencing diminishing landed revenue.[68] It is in this

[63] J. C. Parsons, 'Eleanor of Castile (1241–1290): legend and reality through seven centuries', in D. Parsons (ed.), *Eleanor of Castile, 1290–1990*, Stamford 1991, 30.
[64] There is a brief discussion of queen's gold in H. Johnstone, 'The queen's household', in Willard and others, *English government at work*, i. 263–4.
[65] *Dialogus de scaccario: the course of the exchequer by Richard, son of Nigel*, ed. and trans. C. Johnson, London 1950, 122.
[66] CCR, 1333–7, 689; CCR, 1337–9, 231.
[67] For the political and fiscal background to the late 1330s see E. B. Fryde, 'Parliament and the French war, 1336–40', in his *Medieval trade and finance* . For the cancelling of demands for queen's gold from the city of London in the same period see CCR, 1333–7, 689.
[68] M. K. McIntosh, *Autonomy and community: the royal manor of Havering, 1200–1500*, Cambridge 1986, 58.

context that, fifteen years after the king's grant of immunity to Bristol, Philippa decided to assert her right to queen's gold on Bristol's fine in 1338 for exemption from the first year of a triennial subsidy. The legal proceedings resulting from Bristol's opposition to this belated claim are recorded in the exchequer plea roll of 1353 (Easter term).[69]

On 24 February 1353 a writ was issued to the sheriff of Gloucestershire to distrain Eborard le Frensshe (mayor of Bristol in 1338) and the burgesses of the town and to deliver to the exchequer the £22 owing to the queen.[70] The sheriff delivered the writ to Bristol's bailiffs, Walter de Derby and Robert de Cheddre, because Eborard's goods and chattels were in the liberty of the town, but the bailiffs refused to co-operate with the king's sheriff, denying that they had received the writ in the first place. Shortly afterwards Walter de Derby appeared in the court of the exchequer to argue against the principle of queen's gold in relation to Bristol's fine for £220.[71] Derby claimed that Eborard's payment of £220 in 1338 was a recognizance rather than a fine and since a recognizance was not a voluntary offering, it was therefore not liable to queen's gold.[72] It is certainly true that Eborard le Frensshe had entered into a recognizance in chancery for the £220 and that a recognizance was an obligation rather than a voluntary offering.[73] Nevertheless, on the basis that queen's gold was, according to the late twelfth-century *Dialogue of the exchequer* (a manual on the operation of the king's exchequer and the contemporary authority on the subject of queen's gold), payable on any offering which bestowed honour and dignity to the donor, the queen's attorney argued that the recognizance was made to free the inhabitants of the town of Bristol from the interference of royal tax collectors, 'which tended to the profit and honour of the same men' ('quod cecidit in proficuum et honorem eorundem hominum').[74]

In 1354 Bristol's former bailiff, Walter de Derby, acknowledged that he had not answered the writ sent to him by the sheriff of Gloucestershire and he fined for contempt and paid damages of 100s. to the queen.[75] In contrast, it would appear that Philippa's claims to queen's gold in respect of Bristol's fine for exemption in 1338 were never settled and the record of the case in the plea roll trails off without the judgement of the barons of the exchequer.[76] William Prynne, the antiquary who transcribed the court case in the seventeenth century, believed that Philippa 'recovered her gold',[77] but the absence of Philippa's financial records for this period makes this conclusion impos-

---

[69] All references to this exchequer plea roll are from W. Prynne, *Aurum reginae*, London 1668, 37–8, 112–14.
[70] Ibid. 37.
[71] Ibid. 112–14.
[72] Ibid. 113.
[73] *CPR, 1334–8*, 564–5.
[74] Prynne, *Aurum reginae*, 114.
[75] Ibid. 38.
[76] Ibid. 114.
[77] Ibid.

sible to verify. In fact, there are good reasons for thinking that the case was terminated on the crown's orders.

What was at stake in this quarrel between Bristol and the queen over queen's gold? After all, £22 was not an enormous sum of money. From the queen's perspective, the attempt to enforce her financial rights in Bristol can be seen as part of a more general policy pursued by her ministers to collect aggressively as much revenue as possible from all potential sources of income, particularly from properties which belonged to her as her landed endowment. It is no coincidence that in the early 1350s and in 1353, in particular, the queen's officials also launched inquiries into lands and rights that they believed had been withheld from the queen in her manor of Havering in Essex.[78] There might also have been an element of principle at stake, for although queen's gold was in theory payable by anyone who made a fine with the king, the queen sought to enforce her rights more vigorously in communities such as Bristol and Havering that were part of the queen's dower. Equally interesting is the role of the king as a mediator between local communities and the queen's fiscal demands. When the queen's finances became a parliamentary issue in the 1350s, prompted in part by the actions of her officials, the king responded to the concerns of his subjects. In 1353, for example, when the representatives of the shires and towns, meeting in a great council at Westminster, complained about the fines and amercements exacted by John de Molyns, the queen's steward, Edward III promised redress if Molyns was found guilty of such offences.[79] Similarly, it can be no coincidence that it was at the parliament of 1357, the first to grant direct taxation since the beginning of the legal proceedings between Bristol and Queen Philippa, that the king assured his subjects that queen's gold would not be claimed for the fifteenth and tenth just approved by the commons, thus releasing his subjects from the threat of queen's gold on parliamentary taxation.[80] Bristol's MPs must have made their displeasure known to the king.[81]

The town of Bristol was, then, an important part of Philippa's landed resources. Indeed, when the town and castle of Bristol and the neighbouring royal manor of Barton were granted to Philippa in 1330, the three properties were valued at a total of £210, exclusive of customary payments. Two years later, when the queen's officials made separate provision for the profits of the town of Bristol and the manor of Barton, Barton alone was farmed for £160, while Bristol, exclusive of the castle, was farmed for £140.[82] The queen had increased her potential income by nearly 50 per cent. Such financial measures did nothing, however, to alleviate the queen's growing debts in the

78 McIntosh, *Autonomy and community*, 50–63.
79 *RP* ii. 253.
80 *SR* i. 352.
81 Unfortunately, there is no extant roll of the 1357 parliament to confirm this supposition.
82 *CPR, 1330–4*, 55–6; C 47/9/58, rot. 1r.

mid-fourteenth century. Thus, in 1360, in the face of mounting debts, as Chris Given-Wilson has shown, Edward III decided to create a joint royal household, absorbing the queen's household into his own.[83] The extent of this merger, nevertheless, is difficult to gauge, for while the queen's household officials came to live with those of the king and a significant proportion of the queen's annual income was channelled by the king to pay off her debts, Philippa's lands, including Bristol,[84] continued to be administered by her own officials, and 4,000 marks arising from the profits of her landed estate were reserved for her own personal expenses separate from those of the royal household. It was only on Queen Philippa's death in 1369 that the town of Bristol reverted to the crown, as was customary when a queen died.

Philippa died in August 1369, only three months after Edward III had announced his resumption of the title of king of France and his intention to recover his rights to the French crown after a decade of formal peace. The town of Bristol, along with Philippa's other dower properties, returned to the king's hands, and the king sought to exploit to the full his newly acquired revenue in order to help finance the war against the French. Between 1369 and 1382 the profits of Bristol went directly and in full to the crown and were free from the types of assignments that were charged against, for example, York's fee farm.[85] The crown's treatment of Bristol's fee farm, the ensuing conflict which arose between Bristol's rulers and the royal government, and the manner in which the dispute was settled, not only help to illuminate more clearly the precise context in which the town's 1373 charter was granted, but raise wider questions about the political impact of the crown's fiscal demands on English towns and cities after the renewal of war in 1369.

On 6 November 1369 Edward III's treasurer, Thomas de Brantingham, appointed William de Somerwell collector of all rents, customs, tolls, perquisites of court, chattels of felons and fugitives and other profits of the town of Bristol for the current financial year.[86] Why was Somerwell appointed to collect the feudal profits of the town? Why was the town not farmed, and why were the burgesses not corporately responsible for the profits of Bristol, as York's citizens were for the revenues of their city? The answer lies in the crown's financial situation. As a collector of the individual revenues owing to

---

[83] C. Given-Wilson, 'The merger of Edward III's and Queen Philippa's households, 1360–9', *BIHR* li (1978), 183–7.

[84] See, for example, SC 6/1092/3, mem. 3.

[85] E 372/214, rot. 16d; 215, rot. 33d; 216, rot. 37d; 217, rot. 36d; 218, rot. 27d; 219, rot. 1r; 220, rot. 2r; 221, rot. 2r; 222, rot. 2r; 223, rot. 2r; 224, rot. 2r; 225, rot. 2r; 226, rot. 2r; 227, rot. 1r. There were several customary payments associated with Bristol's fee farm, such as the wages of the officials of Bristol castle and tithes to Tewkesbury abbey, but these were paid in addition to, rather than from, the profits of the town. By the early fifteenth century, they amounted to close to £60.

[86] The writ ordering Bristol's mayor and bailiffs to be intendant to Somerwell as the collector of the town's issues is in E 368/142, *adhuc commissiones et littere patentes*, Michaelmas.

the king from rents, court profits and tolls, Somerwell was a *custos* in all but name. As a *custos* or keeper, rather than a farmer, Somerwell was appointed to collect as much revenue as possible from the various sources of income pertaining to the crown.[87] In contrast to the fee farm, which was a fixed payment, there was, in theory, no limit as to the amount of money that could be paid to the king from Bristol.

William de Somerwell had been elected to Bristol's common council in 1350 and he had served as a bailiff of the town between 1367 and 1368. Thus, he not only held a position of civic authority in Bristol, but he was also a trusted royal servant.[88] In the circumstances, his appointment was a sensible move by the crown, since Bristol's burgesses had a longstanding enmity towards the appointment of outsiders to collect and pay the town's fee farm, who were suspected of seeking to profit personally from their commission. In the late thirteenth and early fourteenth centuries Bristol was in the custody of a series of constables of Bristol castle who paid a fixed sum of £210 to the queen for the town and castle of Bristol and manor of Barton.[89] In 1283 the burgesses of Bristol petitioned Edward I, requesting that they be given collective responsibility for the payment of the farm of the town rather than 'an outsider', since he 'would not seek it except for his own personal gain', while 'none can know so well as those whose work is concerned with merchandise, and who earn their living by it, how to regulate the affairs of merchants properly and honestly'.[90] In 1312 and 1313 serious disturbances in Bristol, involving an attack on the constable of the castle, Bartholomew de Badlesmere, and his men by the town's burgesses, came to the crown's attention. Among the charges levelled against the constable was that he had tried to make a profit from his appointment as farmer of the town.[91]

If the crown had been expecting a financial bonanza from Somerwell's appointment, however, it was to be disappointed. The particulars of Somerwell's account show that a total of nearly £160 was received from nine sources of income in the town (*see* table 5), the most important of which – comprising 44 per cent of the total revenue – was a local customs tax consisting of an import and export duty levied on boats freighted with all kinds of merchandise entering and leaving the port. The discharge of customary payments, including the wages of the constable of Bristol castle and the keeper of Kingswood forest, tithes to Tewkesbury abbey, as well as Somerwell's fee of £10, meant that the king's exchequer only received £83 8s. 10d. in overall profit.[92] The amount was almost half what Philippa had received when the town of Bristol had been farmed by the

---

87 For a definition of the *custos* see Tait, *Medieval English borough*, 151.
88 See appendix below.
89 *Bristol charters, 1378–1499*, 49–50.
90 *Rotuli parliamentorum Anglie hactenus inediti*, ed. H. G. Richardson and G. O. Sayles (Camden 3rd ser. li, 1935), 18, translated in *Bristol charters, 1378–1499*, 42–3.
91 E. A. Fuller, 'The tallage of 6 Edward II (December 16, 1312) and the Bristol rebellion', *TBGAS* xix (1894–5), 174–8.
92 Compare SC 6/851/13; E 364/4, rot. 2d; E 372/214, rot. 16d.

Table 5
Particulars of account of William de Somerwell, collector of the profits of Bristol, Michaelmas 1369–Michaelmas 1370*

Source of revenue	Amount
Assessed rent: Fixed and leased rent from tenants, langable within and without the town walls, and rents from 2 capons, 2 pairs of gilded spurs and 1lb. of cumin	£22 10s. 3d.
Customary dues ('consuetudines'): Customary dues from 53 weavers, 10 bakers, 24 cobblers and 10 regrators selling fish and vegetables	49s. 2d.
Customs ('custuma'): Customs from ships and boats carrying wine, iron and other merchandise	£70 15s. 9¾d.
Court pleas and profits: Court pleas and profits during the fairs and the Tolzey Court together with fines for suit of court and amercements of butchers, bakers and other regrators who did not sell their victuals at the old market as was customary during the fairs	£35 19s. 7d.
Farm of the mill: Farm of the castle mill	£20
Tyna Castri: Custom called 'Tyna Castri' (a prise of ale payable to the constable of Bristol castle for the maintenance of the castle) from 4 brewers	56s.
Wood-silver: Rent called 'wood-silver' (a customary payment from the king's forest beyond the Avon)	32s.
Escheats: Farm of 5 tenements	31s. 11d.
Chattels of felons and fugitives: Goods and chattels of felons and fugitives	12s. 8d.
Total	£158 7s. 2¾d.

* SC 6/851/13.

burgesses from 1332. The following financial year, from Michaelmas 1370 to Michaelmas 1371, saw the crown's profits decline even further and £67 17s. 3d. was eventually rendered to the king after the customary obligations had been paid.[93] Potentially even more damaging to the crown was a protracted legal case in the court of exchequer involving Somerwell, Bristol's mayor and bailiffs and the king, which arose from the auditing of Somerwell's account for 1370–1, most of which was copied into the Great Red Book, and which had not been resolved by the time of Henry IV's accession to the throne in 1399.[94]

The case revolved around the crown's demands for an additional £132 from the profits of Bristol,[95] including £20 from the profits of waif and stray, £40 of goods and chattels from wreck, an extra £20 of chattels of felons and fugitives and, most controversially for the town, £20 of fines from bakers who broke the assize of bread and £40 of fines from those entering the freedom of the town. Somerwell said that he could not collect the profits of these last two sources of revenue because they belonged to the mayor and bailiffs of Bristol ('huiusmodi proficua pertinent ad Maiorem et Balliuos dicte ville Bristoll') as important components of the town's internal income.[96] Bristol's mayor and bailiffs appeared by their attorney to defend the town's claims to its own sources of revenue, deliberately choosing to base their defence on the terms of royal charters, which they were able to produce in court as incontrovertible evidence of rights formally authorised by the crown. However, it is interesting to note that Bristol's attorney first grounded the town's defence in something far less tangible than written documentation: memory. Regarding fines for admission to the freedom of Bristol, the town's attorney argued that 'the town of Bristol is an ancient borough and a mayor, bailiffs and community have existed in the same borough from time out of mind'. This was essentially an argument derived from tradition, in which antiquity was seen to confer legitimacy on Bristol's urban status and the town's origins were located in the distant past.[97]

Searching for precedents for the town's right to collect payments from those entering the franchise, Bristol's attorney argued that the mayor and bailiffs and their predecessors had had a guild merchant in the town from time immemorial by which they were accustomed to take 'a certain payment for their own uses' ('quandam prestacionem ad vsus suos proprios') from all

---

93 E 372/217, rot. 10d; E 372/218, rot. 27d.
94 The case is recorded in E 368/144, *adhuc recorda*, Michaelmas. A copy of the majority of the legal proceedings is to be found in *GRB* ii. 165–72. The case, however, continued beyond the entry in the civic record. The following account relies on the copy in the Great Red Book and Veale's transcription of the case from the exchequer memoranda roll after the point where the town's record ends: *GRB* ii. 257–8.
95 This calculation is my own.
96 All of the following references to the case are taken from *GRB* ii. 165–72.
97 It may also be the case that the word 'borough' was used here with the specific meaning of a privileged place: Reynolds, *English medieval towns*, 112.

those who were admitted into the freedom of the guild. Despite the fact that Bristol's system of admissions into the civic franchise seems to have absorbed the town's much older institution of the guild merchant by the fourteenth century,[98] the important point was that the early existence of a guild merchant in Bristol (a similar kind of organisation to the system of freedom admissions, in which individuals received certain economic privileges in return for a fine) could be supported by the crown's own documents. Thus, Bristol's attorney recited the 1188 charter to the burgesses according to which 'they shall have all their reasonable guilds (*racionabiles gildas*) as they best had them in the time of Robert and William, his son, Earls of Gloucester'.[99] Similarly, the town's attorney contended that the mayor and bailiffs were accustomed to fine bakers for breaking the assize of bread and to levy amercements 'for their own uses' ('ad vsus suos proprios') because of their view of frankpledge, a traditional right which had existed 'from time out of mind', and which been confirmed in Edward III's *inspeximus* of October 1331 to Bristol and amplified by the charter of 1347 authorising the mayor and bailiffs to punish bakers breaking the assize by drawing them on hurdles through the town.[100] By not granting the profits of Bristol to the town's burgesses to farm, the crown had interfered with the way in which the town's rulers fulfilled their customary fiscal obligation to the queen, claiming income as its own which had previously belonged to the town's rulers and thereby violating the principle of 'self-government at the king's command'.[101] The crown's policy towards Bristol's fee farm had raised fundamental questions about the financial basis of the town's government, and the court case and the ensuing search through the town's archive for documentary evidence of the town's chartered rights, can only have encouraged the town's rulers to think more widely about the nature of Bristol's corporate status and of the town's relations with the crown.

On 31 October 1371 the crown granted the profits of Bristol to two burgesses, Walter de Derby and Henry Derneford, to farm for £100 *per annum*. In addition, they were expected to discharge the customary obligations traditionally associated with the farm, including the wages of the constable, porter and watchmen of the castle, which amounted to just over £58. The grant marked the beginning of a policy of farming the town of Bristol which continued up to 1382 when the castle and town, still valued at a yearly figure of £100, were given to Queen Anne as a dower assignment.[102] Three issues arise from the appoint-

---

[98] For a discussion of the relationship between the earlier guild merchant and the later urban franchise in medieval English towns see the seminal work by C. Gross, *The gild merchant*, Oxford 1890, i, ch. v, 158–61, and Tait, *Medieval English borough*, 222–34. I have found no references to the operation of the guild merchant in Bristol in either of the town's main civic registers, the Little Red Book and the Great Red Book.

[99] *British borough charters, 1042–1216*, 206.

[100] The charters are published and translated in *Bristol charters, 1155–1373*, 78–83, 108–11.

[101] This concept is discussed at pp. 13–14 above.

[102] For the successive grants see *CFR, 1368–77*, 137–8, 254–5, 287, 365.

ment of Derby and Derneford: the first relates to the nature of their commission; the second concerns their identity; and the third relates to the amount of the fee farm. As farmers rather than *custodes*, Derby and Derneford were expected to make a lump sum payment of £100 to the king's exchequer from the issues of rents, tolls, court profits and customs, over and above the discharge of the customary obligations attached to the fee farm. From the crown's point of view, this meant that the king was guaranteed a fixed sum of money and the opportunity for further conflict over the nature of the king's financial rights in the town was reduced.

It is also interesting to note that the grant to the two farmers was accompanied by an order to the mayor and bailiffs of the town to allow Derby and Derneford 'to make their profit thereof' from Bristol's farm.[103] Any money that they made in addition to the £100 due to the crown (and nearly £60 in customary payments) was theirs as profit. The grant was a form of royal patronage with which the crown could reward its servants,[104] and in the person of Walter de Derby, in particular, the crown had identified one of its most able and experienced administrators in the town of Bristol. Walter de Derby had been elected to the town's common council in 1350 and had already served twice as mayor and five times as bailiff of the town. Yet it was really from the renewal of the Hundred Years War in 1369 that his career in royal employment began in earnest, as he served the crown in a variety of roles, lending his ship and money to pay the wages of men-at-arms and archers accompanying the Gloucestershire knight, Guy Lord Brian, on a military expedition overseas in 1370, and acting as a collector of the wool and petty customs and of the subsidy of tonnage and poundage in the port of Bristol over many years in the 1370s and 1380s.[105] Between 1371 and 1372 Walter de Derby farmed the town jointly with Henry Derneford, a merchant of the Bristol staple who was named, alongside Derby, as an elector of the mayor and constables of the Bristol staple in 1356 and 1359. From 1372 to 1376 Derby farmed the town of Bristol on his own, until he was replaced by John de Woderoue, a deputy controller of the customs in the port of Bristol from 1368 to 1382, who also seems to have been – from testamentary evidence – a close associate of Walter de Derby and other prominent civic officials such as William Canynges and John de Stoke.[106]

Despite the terms of the grants to Derby and his associates, it is significant that the interests of the town and its civic officials were not prejudiced. Notwithstanding the possibility of personal financial gain from the arrange-

103 Ibid. 138.
104 For the use of Philippa's lands to reward crown servants see Ormrod, *Edward III*, 118–19.
105 See appendix below.
106 For Derneford see C 47/33/5, nos 1, 4. For Woderoue's involvement in the customs service see E 356/5, rot. 22d; 13, rot. 107r. Woderoue was remembered in John de Stoke's will: Wadley, *Great orphan book*, 5–7.

ments of Bristol's fee farm, Derby, as a prominent member of Bristol's civic hierarchy, seems to have taken his civic responsibilities very seriously. Evidence from the lord treasurer's memoranda rolls suggests that Derby, perhaps using his royal connections to the town's advantage, was able to negotiate a reduction of £20 in the amount of Bristol's fee farm from the previous year. Certainly, he appeared in person at the exchequer at Michaelmas 1373, claiming that the treasurer, Richard Lord Scrope, had granted him the farm for one year from Michaelmas 1372 for the reduced sum of £80.[107] Evidence from the pipe rolls, moreover, suggests that it was not long before the town in its corporate capacity was able to take over the payment of the fee farm in an unofficial but none the less significant way. Between 1378 and 1380, for instance, the 'men of the town of Bristol' paid into the exchequer half of the farm owing by John de Woderoue.[108] In the process, of course, the town of Bristol benefited from a greatly reduced fee farm – £40 less than when Philippa had received the profits of the town – and it may be that the crown was willing to tolerate this reduction because it was offset by the substantial contributions in loans and shipping that the town was already making to the war effort. In 1370 alone, for example, Bristol made two corporate loans totalling almost £850.[109]

The conflict over Bristol's fee farm had two main effects on the broader framework of the town's relations with the crown. On the one hand, once the level of Bristol's fee farm was fixed at a reduced rate by the crown in 1371, it was very difficult to increase it. Richard II's wife, Anne of Bohemia, inherited the arrangement, so that the farm of the town and castle of Bristol was granted to her as a dower assignment, valued at £100 *per annum*.[110] The paucity of Anne's estate records means that there is no precise way of knowing how much the farm of the town on its own was worth, whether the burgesses farmed the town separately from the castle, or whether the queen increased her revenue from Bristol from the initial dower assignment.[111] However, when, on Anne's death in 1395, the farm of the town alone was granted to Bristol's burgesses on a twelve-year lease, it was valued at £100 *per annum*.[112] It is, therefore, doubtful whether Anne benefited financially from Bristol's farm to the same extent as her predecessor. If Bristol's fee farm was an important source of revenue to the queen in the period 1350 to 1400, it was the king who set the financial parameters within which the queen had to operate.

[107] E 368/146, *adhuc recorda*, Michaelmas.
[108] E 372/224, rot. 2r; 225, rot. 2r.
[109] See table 1 above.
[110] CPR, 1381–5, 125–6.
[111] For the manuscript references to the few extant records see Johnstone, 'Queen's household', 260. None, unfortunately, relates to the town of Bristol.
[112] CFR, 1391–9, 137.

On the other hand, it would appear that the crown's attempt between 1369 and 1371 to exploit all possible sources of revenue from Bristol provides the immediate background to the town's petition for a new charter in 1373 separating Bristol from the neighbouring counties of Gloucestershire and Somerset and elevating it to the status of a county in its own right.[113] In particular, the dispute over the respective financial rights of royal and civic government in Bristol had threatened to undermine the town's existence as a corporate body with its own sources of income. The final request in Bristol's petition was that the mayor, bailiffs and common council of the town be allowed, through 'their common assent', to raise taxes from the town's burgesses 'for the necessities and utilities of the said town' and to appoint two good men ('prodeshomies') of the town 'elected for that purpose by their common assent' to collect such levies and account for them before the mayor and bailiffs and others specially elected by the community. The subsequent royal charter granted the substance of this request practically verbatim.[114]

Although unusual, rulers of other towns and cities had sought on occasion to acquire royal authorisation to raise taxes for their own purposes, a right which they had previously exercised by prescription. A 1305 charter to Norwich, for example, permitted the city's bailiffs to assess civic taxes, with common assent, 'for the protection and common benefit of the city, as often as need be'.[115] Similarly, the 1312 charter to the city of York stated that everyone living and trading in the city should be in 'lot and scot' with the citizens of York, that is, that they should take up the franchise of the city, paying the tallages and other royal charges on the city as well as civic taxes that were incumbent on them as freemen.[116] As David Palliser has argued, the clause was to the mutual interest of the crown and York's governors, increasing the number of people liable to pay civic and royal taxes.[117] In the case of Bristol the town's rulers had levied their own taxes before 1373 without royal chartered approval as and when they were required, most notably in the 1330s when they had fined for exemption from the interference of royal tax collectors in order to organise their own fiscal payments to the crown.[118] Yet the financial pressures on Bristol immediately preceding the grant of the 1373 charter were of a different magnitude. The need to raise civic taxes was greater than it had ever been in Bristol in the years following the onset of war in 1369, for it was precisely from this period that the town was approached in its corporate capacity to raise loans for the war effort and to build barges and balingers at its own corporate expense for royal naval

---

113 A copy of the petition is in *LRB* i. 115–26; the charter is in *Bristol charters, 1155–1373*, 118–41.
114 *LRB* i. 125; *Bristol charters, 1155–1373*, 136–7.
115 *British borough charters, 1216–1307*, 344–5.
116 *CChR, 1300–26*, 185–6.
117 Palliser, 'York's civic liberties', 103–4.
118 See pp. 68–9 above.

service.[119] In these circumstances Bristol's rulers sought royal authority to buttress their intensifying demands on their subjects.

In some ways Bristol's particular experiences with its fee farm were not typical, inasmuch as the town did not gain a perpetual grant of the farm until 1462.[120] Short-term leases provided the town with the opportunity to negotiate the amount of the fee farm, an opportunity that did not exist for York until the crown responded to the city's urgent pleas for a reduction of its fee farm in the later fifteenth century. While York's fee farm remained fixed at £160 *per annum* from the thirteenth century to the end of the fifteenth, the value of Bristol's fee farm fluctuated considerably. In contrast to York, where the fee farm was a fiscal obligation which had become fossilised and which did not reflect the true level of urban wealth, the value of Bristol's fee farm in the second half of the fourteenth century was linked intimately to the crown's ability to exploit the town's wealth in other ways, primarily through loans. The level of Bristol's fee farm at the end of the fourteenth century was almost identical to the amount recorded in the Domesday survey of 1086 when the town of Bristol was farmed with the royal manor of Barton for just over £100.[121]

Yet the consequences of Bristol's position within the landed estate of the queen consort should not be overstated. Certainly, the extant sources, extremely limited though they are, do not suggest that the queen was an important patron to the town in the period 1350 to 1400, whom Bristol's rulers relied on to forward their interests at court. Despite the assertion in 1628 of the antiquity of Bristol's distinctive claims to be the 'queen's chamber', there is little evidence that the metaphor of the chamber, in the case of Bristol, was anything more than an occasional and fairly recent rhetorical device to which the town's rulers had recourse in the early modern period. As to Bristol's special relationship, it is perhaps significant that the town gained the charter elevating it to the status of county corporate four years after Queen Philippa died. The town paid 600 marks to the king's chamberlain, William Lord Latimer, for the privilege.[122] If Bristol's rulers had wished to employ the metaphor of the chamber in the second half of the fourteenth century, they could have claimed, with some justification, that the town was the 'king's chamber'. It was the king and his officials who were the recipients of Bristol's generosity.

The November 1380 uprising in York

After the recommencement of the Hundred Years War in 1369 Bristol was not the only town to experience the financial stresses of war. A major charge on civic income in this period was the expense of building, equipping and

---

[119] See pp. 38–40, 44 above.
[120] *RP* v. 626.
[121] *Bristol charters, 1378–1499*, 21 and n. 4.
[122] *Bristol charters, 1155–1373*, 118–21.

maintaining the vessels assembled at the crown's instruction in 1372 and 1377. In response to a royal order for naval service in March 1376, the *probi homines* of York decided, with the approval of the commons, to sell one of the city's ships and to repair the other. In the three years since the city had financed the building of two vessels, one had seen such frequent service in the king's navy that it had become, according to the council minutes, 'worn out, weakened and damaged at sea'.[123] The fiscal burden arising from such naval service was not peculiar to York.[124] The chamberlains' accounts of Lynn show that a total of over £250 was spent on the building of the town's barge in 1373 and that a further £46 was laid out the following year, presumably in maintenance costs.[125] Norwich's city assembly met regularly to discuss the crown's demands for barges and balingers in the 1370s.[126] In Norwich nearly £400 was raised from the citizens to fund the construction of a barge, but even this did not cover the total expenses of the vessel, leaving the city in debt.[127] In the case of London, although the city was ordered to build two barges in November 1372, only one vessel was ever constructed, possibly because of the financial outlay involved, and this ship, the *Paul*, proved more expensive to build than the city had envisaged.[128]

How did civic rulers respond to the crown's demands for military and financial aid? What was the administrative framework within which they operated? In the case of York it was provided by the system of royal taxation known as the fifteenth and tenth. In February 1378 the crown ordered the city's mayor and bailiffs to repair one of the city's two remaining vessels (the *Peter*) for service at sea; the ship had been away at sea throughout 1377 and was evidently in a state of disrepair.[129] York's inner councils of twelve and twenty-four decided, with the assent of the commons, that the cost should be met by a levy on the city's citizens of a quarter of York's parliamentary tenth ('de hominibus civitatis quartam partem decime domini Regis').[130] Else-where, the same mechanism for raising royal subsidies was used to assess civic taxes, further evidence, in fact, of the fiscal interdependence of civic and royal government. In 1372 and 1373 Norwich financed the construction of the city's barge through the levy of four parliamentary tenths, while the rulers of the town of Lynn in 1386 agreed to a tax of £100 'for the defence of the

---

123 *YMB* i. 32–3.
124 In early 1373 the crown intervened to empower the civic officials of the towns and cities of Salisbury, Boston, Lincoln and Beverley to distrain those individuals who refused to contribute their share of taxation towards the cost of the corporately funded vessels: *CPR, 1370–4*, 245.
125 Harrod, *Deeds and records of King's Lynn*, 82–3.
126 *Records of the city of Norwich*, i. 79–83.
127 Ibid. i. 80–2.
128 *Letter-book G*, 302–4.
129 For its record of naval service see pp. 44–7 above.
130 *YMB* i. 30. 'Men' seems to have been a synonym for citizens: Reynolds, *Kingdoms and communities*, 184.

town to be assessed in the same way as the tenths'.[131] London's mayor and aldermen also met royal demands on the city for corporate loans and shipping through its traditional mechanism, based on wards, for paying its contribution to the fifteenth and tenth.[132]

The advantage of this system of general levies was that, from 1334, when towns and cities were expected to make a lump sum payment to the crown, their contribution was attuned to the differences in wealth within each community. For example, Bristol paid its parliamentary tenth of £220 on the basis of fixed quotas from each of the five quarters or wards of the town: All Saints', St Ewen's, Mary-le-Port, Holy Trinity and Redcliffe.[133] The first four wards reflected the ancient division of the walled town by the four main streets of Corn Street, Wine Street, High Street and Broad Street and were named after the churches of All Saints', St Ewen's, St Mary-le-Port and Christ Church.[134] Redcliffe ward was on the southern side of the Avon and its status as the fifth ward reflected enormous suburban growth in this part of Bristol during the twelfth and thirteenth centuries. In the 1230s Bristol's walls were extended to incorporate the wealthy suburban areas of Redcliffe and Temple, marked by a concentration of cloth workers and traders from whom most of the town's growing prosperity was derived, and from the early fourteenth century the town was able to tap the wealth of these areas for the purposes of royal taxation.[135] In 1373 Redcliffe ward contributed £80 of the town's total of £220 to a recently granted fifteenth and tenth.[136] In the case of York the unit of taxation was the parish, on which both the standard fifteenths and tenths and poll taxes were assessed. The copy of the parish quota inserted in the York Memorandum Book in 1419–20 indicates that a similar attempt was made in York to ensure that a significant proportion of the tax burden was met by the city's richer parishes.[137] Thus, for example, the largest quotas of £10 and more were from central parishes including those of St John at Ouse Bridge End and St Michael at Ouse Bridge End (facing each other on either side of the river Ouse and dominated by members of York's mercantile community), St Crux in Fossgate, another equally prosperous

---

[131] *Records of the city of Norwich*, i. 80–2; D. M. Owen, *The making of King's Lynn: a documentary survey* (British Academy Records of Social and Economic History n.s. ix, 1984), 390.

[132] *Letter-book G*, 58–62, 251–3.

[133] For the particulars of account of the lay subsidy levied in 1373 and 1395 see E 179/113/27, 16, 42. In contrast, the poll taxes were levied in the town's eighteen parishes: E 359, rot. 9r; *CFR, 1377–83*, 228.

[134] For the layout of medieval Bristol see Lobel and Carus-Wilson, 'Bristol', maps 3, 7.

[135] For the incorporation of Redcliffe and Temple see R. H. Leech, 'The medieval defences of Bristol revisited', in Keen, '*Almost the richest city*', 18–30.

[136] E 179/113/27.

[137] *YMB* i. 178–9. Although undated, the list of parish tax quotas can be dated to 1419–20 on the basis of the mayoralty of Thomas del Gare, who was named as mayor: YCA, D1, fo. 12v.

parish populated by merchants, and Holy Trinity, King's Court, where York's wealthy butchers lived and worked.[138]

Chris Dyer has argued that, although the tax burden was spread more widely after 1334, the redistribution of taxation in villages continued to reflect 'a web of neighbourly co-operation, and a belief that the better off should help the poor'.[139] In contrast, he suggested that in urban communities 'the burden was shifted from the wealthy to the less affluent, causing friction'.[140] In York, however, it would appear that the tax burden was spread more widely and, therefore, more thinly in the later fourteenth century. Indeed, it has long been noted that the number of freemen in York rose dramatically in this period as the cost of entering the franchise became cheaper and that the increase in admissions to the franchise was due to the manipulation of the franchise by the civic authorities, who saw it as financially advantageous to have a large freedom membership.[141] Yet what is less understood is why the city's rulers required a greater income in the second half of the fourteenth century. The broadening of the civic franchise increased the city's internal revenue two-fold. First, the city's chamberlains profited directly from the payments made by those willing to purchase the franchise. In 1391–2, for example, the greatest source of income to the city – 40 per cent of the chamberlains' annual receipts – was the revenue from entry fines charged on new freemen.[142] It is instructive here to compare York's freedom system with that which operated in the city of Exeter, where Maryanne Kowaleski has found that 'when the city needed to raise funds to meet extraordinary circumstances . . . it suddenly allowed large numbers of men to enter in order to collect the admission fees'.[143] Secondly, and perhaps more important, a large pool of freemen meant that there were more people among whom the financial costs of government within the city could be shared. Why were the expenses of local government increasing? Sarah Rees Jones has suggested that the 'general inflation of the later fourteenth century' was partially responsible and that, in consequence, there was 'growing concern over the cost of the mayor's office' within York between 1370 and 1400.[144]

The key to the expansion of York's franchise in the later fourteenth century lies in the crown's increasing financial demands on the city, as York made corporate loans and built ships at its own expense for the war at sea, in

---

138 For the occupational topography of York see P. J. P. Goldberg, *Women, work, and life cycle in a medieval economy: women in York and Yorkshire, c. 1300–1520*, Oxford 1992, 66–7.
139 Dyer, 'Taxation and communities', 190.
140 Ibid. 188–9.
141 R. B. Dobson, 'Admissions to the freedom of the city of York in the later Middle Ages', *EcHR* 2nd ser. xxvi (1973), 1–22.
142 Hoyle, 'Crisis', 91. I would like to thank Richard Hoyle for providing me with a transcript of the itemised account of the city's income (E 163/12/1).
143 Kowaleski, *Medieval Exeter*, 98–9.
144 Rees Jones, 'York's civic administration', 133.

addition to contributing to the standard fifteenths and tenths and the poll taxes. York's rulers sought to spread more widely the costs of government by tapping the real growth in prosperity that the city's craftsmen were experiencing in the 1360s and 1370s.[145] In York, as in other towns and cities, admission to the freedom brought with it certain rights and responsibilities.[146] On the one hand, it became essential for all those wishing to engage in the retail trade, while also exempting them from the payment of toll both within York and in other towns throughout the kingdom. On the other hand, those who entered the franchise were expected to contribute to taxation imposed on the city – both by civic and royal government – and were liable to hold civic office.[147]

Similar policies regarding the franchise were adopted by London's rulers at times of urgent need for money engendered by the crown's demands. In the 1370s, in particular, the city cast its fiscal net widely in order to share the financial burden of government among all those liable to taxation. In 1373, for example, the king was forced to intervene in the collection of taxation in London, sending a writ to the collectors of the parliamentary fifteenth and tenth and of the subsidy levied to finance the building of the city's barge, ordering them not to exact payment from one of the king's officials in the Tower of London mint, who was traditionally exempt from taxation as one of the privileges of office. The London tax collectors replied bluntly that the individual in question lived in one of the city's wards, traded in the city and held a free tenement there. He had, therefore, been assessed to make a contribution to the royal and civic taxes just 'like other citizens' and been distrained for his share, presumably when he refused to pay.[148] Under severe financial strain, London's tax collectors applied a more fluid and much older concept of citizenship, in which living, trading and owning property in the city was enough for an individual to be counted as a London citizen for the purposes of taxation.[149] There was also a concerted attempt to ensure that non-resident London citizens who enjoyed the privileges of citizenship also bore the burden of public finance.[150] In 1378 each of the aldermen was instructed to make inquiries in his ward 'as to the number of freemen not residing within the franchise' and to submit his return to the guildhall for examination. Two years later, on 30 April 1380, the mayor and aldermen of London issued an ordinance declaring that from henceforth non-resident freemen, like resident citizens, were to pay their share of taxes – 'for the King or the common advantage of the City' – and warning, in the starkest terms

---

[145] For the growth of York's economy after the Black Death see Goldberg, *Women, work, and life cycle*, ch. ii.

[146] For what follows see Dobson, 'Admissions', 15.

[147] This was the meaning of the obligation to be in 'scot and lot' with the citizens.

[148] *Letter-book* G, 308–9.

[149] Reynolds, *English medieval towns*, 123–4.

[150] For what follows see *Letter-book* H, 84, 146.

possible, that 'if any freeman fail to pay his assessment on the day appointed he shall lose his freedom'.

In York the consequence of this fiscal strategy employed by the civic authorities was that there was a relatively large enfranchised community of citizens entitled to play a part, however small, in the government of the city. When the crown began to approach the city of York for corporate loans and corporately financed ships after 1369, York's rulers needed to consult and negotiate more widely with the citizens as whole. The basic distinction between York's citizens was, as elsewhere, between the commons and the *probi homines*, between the larger group of ordinary citizens and the civic elite.[151] From the 1370s, as was demonstrated in the previous chapter, the commons were represented on the council of forty-eight, while the councils of twelve and twenty-four represented the civic elite of high-ranking officeholders.[152] The commons were part of the political process and while they were only summoned on important occasions essentially to approve the decisions of the councils of twelve and twenty-four, there was the opportunity for the commons to use their formal position in civic government to develop an independent political voice, which could provide either a critique or an endorsement of the policies of the civic elite.[153]

The three councils were summoned regularly in the mid- to late 1370s to debate and negotiate the cost of maintaining York's ships for royal naval service.[154] By 1379, two years after the city had been instructed to build a new balinger for the war at sea, York's civic elite realised that the cost of maintaining two ships had become too much for the citizens to bear. Assembled before the commons of the city in the guildhall, the mayor and *probi homines*, seeing 'that a great burden and great expense would come to the community in future from keeping and maintaining the two barges', resolved to sell one of the two remaining ships, the *Peter*, to pay off the city's debts.[155] As they became party to discussions about the expense of the war effort, the commons of York extended a critical eye over the state of the city's finances. Their aim was to make civic government more accountable and efficient. The volume of the York Memorandum Book now known as A/Y, begun in January 1377, was one of the results: the first few folios of the civic register are essentially a record of various aspects of the city's financial business, beginning with the opening entry listing the rents issuing from the city's corporate property.[156]

There was also an increasing insistence on the need for the civic elite to uphold the common good, witnessed, for example, in the concern about the

151 H. Swanson, *Medieval artisans: an urban class in late medieval England*, Oxford 1989, 120.
152 See pp. 40–1 above.
153 For example, the commons were able to petition the civic elite on issues of common concern: Rees Jones, 'York's civic administration', 123.
154 YMB i. 30–3.
155 YMB i. 32.
156 YMB i. 1–12.

activities of York's three chamberlains, the city's main internal financial officials. On 3 February 1375 it was agreed, before the commons assembled in the guildhall for the mayoral election, that the chamberlains' annual election would now take place on 3 February rather than (as had been the case) on 21 September. This ordinance aimed to improve the city's internal accounting procedures, so that the mayor and chamberlains would enter and leave office at the same time and conduct their business 'relating to receipts, costs and expenses of the said city' together.[157] In the context of continuing anxiety about the conduct of the chamberlains, all three of the city councils met on 4 July 1379 and decided that the chamberlains must sit with the mayor to oversee the city's finances rather than withdraw themselves to pursue their own personal business at the expense of the whole community. Furthermore, at least one of the chamberlains was to work alongside the mayor on a daily basis and was to pay a daily fine of 6d. 'for the benefit of the community' if he neglected this duty.[158] Here, then, was an attempt to make civic government more open and accessible, to ensure that it took place in a public rather than private space, and to prevent the abuse of public office for individual gain.

Another target for the commons was the common clerk, John de Rufford, one of whose key responsibilities was the writing and preservation of the city's records in the civic archive. Rufford was the subject of repeated criticism throughout the 1370s, as a 1379 petition from the commons of York to the mayor and his council makes clear.[159] The petition recounted that Rufford had been common clerk during John de Langton's tenure of the mayoralty, but had been found guilty of several deceits and removed from office. Despite his dismissal, Rufford was once more common clerk during Thomas de Howom's mayoralty in the mid-1370s, only to be attainted for similar offences and removed from office for a second time. In 1379 Rufford was again retained as common clerk, but on this occasion, having committed further duplicitous acts, he was expelled from office 'forever'. Rufford's crime was abuse of office for personal financial gain, and in 1379 the commons of York reiterated their desire for fiscal accountability: they asked that the mayor and council elect, with their assent, fourteen 'good and loyal men' to examine 'all the [money] bags together with the rolls of the bridgemasters and all other financial records and things pertaining to the commonalty from the time of John de Rufford'. The most remarkable aspect of this episode is that John de Rufford continued to be appointed to office despite his history of embezzlement. The fact that Rufford's behaviour was tolerated for so long by the city's rulers can only have led to growing suspicion among the commons of York that civic government was acting in the narrow interests of the urban elite. Thus, the allegations against Rufford, like the continued unease about

---

[157] YMB i. 16–17.
[158] YMB i. 33–4.
[159] There are two copies of the petition: SC 8/212/10596 and SC 8/213/10637.

the performance of the chamberlains, provide clear evidence of a loss of confidence among the commons of York towards the city's political elite by the end of the 1370s.

The figure of John de Gysburn exacerbated tensions between the commons and the *probi homines* of the city. Gysburn had entered the freedom of the city of York as a mercer in 1347 and was an overseas merchant specialising in the export of wool and cloth through the port of Hull like many members of York's civic elite at the time,[160] but he was perhaps, of all his mercantile contemporaries, the most experienced in royal service: he was a royal cred‑ itor, a member of the Calais staple, a collector of royal taxation (both the lay subsidy and the 1379 poll tax) and an adviser to the crown on maritime and commercial affairs.[161] He was also the most dominant in civic government, occupying the mayoralty two years running in the early 1370s.[162] Like London's 'élite merchant class' of the later fourteenth century, whom Caroline Barron has described as 'clever, successful, ruthless, and opportun‑ ist',[163] Gysburn was able to use his position in government to his own personal advantage, as his participation in the organisation of the city's annual Corpus Christi play suggests. The third station on the procession route for the performance of the individual pageants was immediately outside Gysburn's large residence on Micklegate, the main street into York from the south.[164] The benefits to Gysburn were clearly financial, for it was the prac‑ tice for stationholders to charge the audience to view the pageants at each of the stopping places, either by renting out rooms in their houses or by providing seating in the form of scaffolding in front of their houses in return for payment.[165] The Corpus Christi play cycle, then, provided commercial opportunities, which Gysburn was quick to seize. Such actions aroused suspi‑ cions that he was profiting at the city's expense, at a time when the citizens as a whole were under intense financial pressure from royal and civic govern‑ ment. Indeed, one of the charges levelled at Gysburn by York jurors before a commission of the peace in the summer of 1381 was that on 11 January 1381 he broke into ('fregit et intravit sine licencia et voluntate civium') the mayor's chamber on Ouse Bridge, where the chamberlains kept the city's

---

160 *Register of the freemen of the city of York*, ed. F. Collins (Surtees Society xcvi, cii, 1896–9), i. 39. For the large-scale nature of Gisburn's involvement in foreign trade see, for example, E 122/59/5 (wool) and E 122/59/1 (cloth).

161 For Gysburn's involvement in royal finance as a creditor see appendix below; his service as a tax collector can be found in *CFR, 1368–77*, 230, 269, and *CFR, 1377–83*, 150. His participation in the Calais staple is discussed at pp. 110–11, 130 below, while his role as a royal adviser is explored at pp. 179–80 below.

162 See appendix below.

163 Barron, 'Richard II and London', 135.

164 See the complaint in 1399 that the pageants should be performed at their customary locations, the third of which was 'ad ostium Johannis de Gyseburne': *YMB* i. 51.

165 D. J. F. Crouch, 'A medieval paying audience: the stationholders on the route of the York Corpus Christi play in the fifteenth century', unpubl. MA diss. York 1990, esp. pp. 12–14.

financial records and receipts, and took £54 belonging to the citizens.[166] Whether strictly true or not,[167] the charge revealed, in a very direct way, the keen sense of financial insecurity felt by the commons of York.

The emergence of a specific issue – a tax known as schamel toll – helped to crystallise existing fiscal discontents from 1379. On this occasion it was specifically the butchers among the city's commons who felt most aggrieved. The butchers were unhappy with what they perceived to be the extortionate practices of the city's bailiffs who, it was alleged, were taking a weekly penny from each of them. John de Westiby, a York butcher, would later protest in the court of exchequer in May 1381 that on every Sunday from 2 October 1379 to 18 February 1380 the bailiffs unjustly entered his house in the parish of Holy Trinity, King's Court, and took 1d., claiming it as a custom, when, in fact, it was not a customary payment at all.[168] This tax of a weekly penny was known in York as schamel toll or stallage, the schamel being the stall on which the meat was placed for sale.[169] Other towns and cities had a similar sales tax and in Exeter, for example, the 'most universal toll' was 'that paid by sellers for the privilege of selling (or even exposing for sale) goods in the town's marketplaces' either at a daily rate or as an annual rent.[170] Although the butchers believed the tax to be a new imposition, it was, as a search of the exchequer pipe rolls revealed, far from novel. The right to take a weekly penny from each butcher for selling meat had long belonged to the city's bailiffs as an integral part of the city's contribution to its annual fee farm of £160 owed to the crown.[171] The butchers, however, refused to accept the evidence presented to them, and by September 1381, on the election of new bailiffs, fourteen butchers each owed 35d., totalling just over £2. The bailiffs tried to collect the arrears by distraint, but the butchers forcibly resisted the bailiffs' attempts ('vi et armis – scilicet securibus, gladiis, baculis'), thus bringing the case before a commission of oyer and terminer appointed by the crown in 1382, which found against the obdurate butchers.[172]

If schamel toll was, then, a customary payment, why did the butchers complain about the tax specifically in the late 1370s and early 1380s? More particularly, why did they allege that it was a new imposition? The butchers were certainly reluctant to pay the tax: when the city's bailiffs tried to distrain

---

[166] KB 27/482, mem. 35v.

[167] The accusations were made by a presentment jury before a commission of the peace headed by Gysburn's then rival for the mayoralty, Simon de Quixlay, the significance of which is discussed in C. D. Liddy, 'Urban conflict in late fourteenth-century England: the case of York in 1380–1', *EHR* cxviii (2003), 19–20.

[168] YMB i. 121.

[169] A. Raine, *Mediaeval York*, London 1955, 185.

[170] Kowaleski, *Medieval Exeter*, 193–4.

[171] YMB i. 121–5.

[172] For the original record of the 1382 commission appointed to Yorkshire in August 1382 see JUST 1/1138, mem. 3r–v, a copy of which was made by the city in YMB i. 125–31.

their goods, they resisted with axes and swords.[173] Financial and political issues were at stake in the conflict between them and the city's bailiffs. The tax was not particularly onerous, especially given that the butchers were a prosperous craft. There might have been a feeling that the butchers were being singled out to pay a civic tax and a resentment towards what they perceived as an attempt to tax their new wealth, for the second half of the fourteenth century saw a major growth in local consumption of fresh meat, symptomatic of a general rise in the standard of living.[174] Most of all, however, the butchers' hostility sprang from a profound distrust of York's civic elite and of the behaviour of the city's financial officials in particular. John de Westiby's complaint was as much to do with the manner in which the tax was raised – what he saw as the intrusive entry of public officials into his private residence – as with the burden of taxation itself. The butchers' grievance was symptomatic of a widespread suspicion of York's rulers among the commons of the city occasioned by the rising costs of civic and royal government which, as the schamel toll itself demonstrated, were interrelated. This distrust had manifested itself earlier in the desire for greater financial accountability from the city chamberlains and in the repeated complaints against the city's common clerk, John de Rufford, and, on this occasion, was expressed in the armed opposition to the extortionate practices of the city's bailiffs.

On 26 November 1380 the tensions evident in York during the 1370s erupted into a violent uprising against the mayor, John de Gysburn. According to the parliamentary petition presented to the king at Northampton,[175] Gysburn was attacked by 'various malefactors among the commons of the city', who drove him out of York. Armed with axes and other weapons, the rebels then laid siege to York's guildhall, smashing down the doors and windows to gain entry. Once inside, they found a certain Simon de Quixlay, compelled him ('against his will') to swear to be their mayor, and made all the *probi homines* of York ('against their will and for fear of death') swear an oath of loyalty to the new mayor. It is no coincidence that the uprising occurred at the same time that parliament was meeting in Northampton to discuss the crown's demand for financial aid for the war effort. This was no ordinary demand. When parliament assembled at the beginning of November, in direct contravention of the crown's promise in January 1380 that it would not be summoned for another eighteen months, the atmosphere was understandably strained.[176] The parliamentary commons requested that they be told exactly how much money was required so that they could concede only what was absolutely necessary, and

---

173 YMB i. 127.
174 Swanson, *Medieval artisans*, 14. For the wider context see C. Dyer, *Standards of living in the later Middle Ages: social change in England*, c. 1200–1520, Cambridge 1989, 199–202.
175 *RP* iii. 96.
176 For this and what follows see *RP* iii. 88–90, and M. Jurkowski and others, *Lay taxes in England and Wales, 1188–1688*, Kew 1998, 60–2.

the crown presented the commons with an itemised account of expenses amounting to £160,000, roughly four times the total expected from the usual form of lay taxation, the fifteenth and tenth. The commons considered the demand 'outrageous' and said that they would grant a more 'tolerable sum', which, after lengthy debate, amounted to 100,000 marks, to be paid by a poll tax.

One of the main reasons for the protracted nature of the parliamentary negotiations was the fear of popular reaction to new taxation. Although the grant of the poll tax was finally made on 6 December, over a week after the York uprising, news of the crown's demand for £160,000 would have been explosive in an urban context where there were already serious tensions arising from the impact of civic and royal taxation. While there is no conclusive evidence that the commons of York knew about the discussions at parliament, there was clearly a considerable amount of communication between parliament and the city and keen interest in York in what happened at parliament.[177] The financial policies of the crown provided the spark for the uprising in York in November 1380, as they would for the Peasants' Revolt six months later.

Yet although the rebellion was, in large part, a spontaneous reaction to news of events in parliament, it also betrayed signs of premeditation.[178] After Gysburn's expulsion from the city, the rebels overwhelmed the guildhall, the main centre of York's civic government, where the mayor and other civic officials were elected each year. Engineering their own mayoral appointment, the rebels then issued a new ordinance that whenever the bells on Ouse Bridge were rung 'aukeward', all the commons of York should rise together for the proclamation of various ordinances which they had recently composed. 'Aukeward', in this instance, seems to have meant that the bells were rung 'in reverse order', in contrast to customary practice.[179] Ouse Bridge was the site of the council chamber where the civic elite met on a regular basis and the bells were the official form of summons used to assemble the citizens of York to hear royal and parliamentary proclamations. By their actions on 26 November 1380, then, the rebels were appropriating and subverting the usual mechanisms of civic and royal government to their own ends. But what were these ends?

Satisfactory answers to this question are elusive as the only extant account of the uprising is the parliamentary petition, the author of which is

---

[177] An excellent example of both the speed with which news travelled between the city of York and parliament and the informal channels of communication between centre and locality is provided by the petitions delivered in person by five of Gysburn's supporters in the 1381 parliament. All five petitioners claimed that Simon de Quixlay and his faction had accused them of being the authors of a commons petition presented in the same parliament which successfully sought the annulment of bonds and recognizances made under compulsion during the recent troubles: SC 8/103/5140–4; RP iii. 114.

[178] For the following see RP iii. 96.

[179] Middle English dictionary, Ann Arbor 1956– , 'auk-ward' (adv.), (b).

unknown.[180] The first objective of the uprising was clearly the removal of Gysburn: he was forced into exile before the rebels launched their assault on the guildhall. Yet as mayor he was only the most visible member of the civic elite in whom the commons of the city had lost their trust. While the butchers were the major interest group involved in the uprising and, as the conflict over schamel toll showed, had their own particular complaints about taxation, the twenty-two leading rebels who forced John de Gysburn from York and besieged the guildhall represented a cross-section of the commons of the city. Freemen of York, they included a shipman, a baker, a carpenter, a sheather, two tailors, four weavers and six butchers, as well as one mercer and three drapers, only one of whom, William Redhode, had held high civic office.[181] Indeed, their actions become more explicable when placed in the context of the increasingly strained relationship between the commons and the civic elite of York in the 1370s.

The new appointment as mayor of another York merchant, Simon de Quixlay, could be interpreted as evidence of the fundamentally conservative nature of the rebellion, which was 'more preoccupied with replacing old men than with introducing new measures'.[182] Yet there are strong indications that the rebels did seek structural change in York's system of government, such that the commons would play a larger role in the political life of the city. On the one hand, if Quixlay's frustrated personal ambitions for the mayoralty and antipathy towards Gysburn made him an obvious alternative,[183] the significant aspect of his appointment is that the rebels 'made' him 'their' mayor. One of the main issues for the commons throughout the 1370s had been the accountability of York's civic officials, and it was surely this concern that explains why the rebels themselves appointed York's mayor directly in November 1380. On the other hand, it is clear that the commons sought a greater legislative function in York than they had hitherto enjoyed, so that they would not just assent to decisions already made by the civic elite, but could issue ordinances in their own right. The parliamentary petition referred to 'several ordinances newly composed' by the commons, which were to be proclaimed whenever the bells on Ouse Bridge sounded in a particular way. Unfortunately, none of these ordinances is extant, but the royal writ that was issued to the mayor and bailiffs of York at the end of the Northampton

180 The absence of both an extant election return and writs de expensis means that York's MPs at the November 1380 parliament cannot be identified.
181 CCR, 1377–81, 421; Register of freemen of York, i, passim.
182 R. B. Dobson, 'The risings in York, Beverley and Scarborough, 1380–1381', in Hilton and Aston, English rising, 139. For a similar view see Kermode, Medieval merchants, 57.
183 Gysburn's successive elections to the mayor's office in November 1379 and February 1380 provoked the rivalry between Gysburn and Quixlay, breaking the terms of a 1372 civic ordinance according to which no one was to be elected mayor in two consecutive years. See appendix below and YMB i. 16.

parliament, ordering them to prohibit the collection of the tax that the rebels had recently imposed, suggests that one of them was financial.[184]

Despite the efforts of York's rulers to reduce the fiscal burden on the city in the years after 1369 by broadening the franchise and thereby increasing the number of people expected to contribute to the financial charges on York, the policy could not prevent the uprising of November 1380 and the serious disturbances within the city which followed.[185] In one sense, there was little, ultimately, the civic elite could do to reduce the sheer weight of royal and civic taxation which, from the beginning of Richard II's reign, included the two fifteenths and tenths granted by parliament in November 1377, an additional quarter of the city's tenth granted by the city's *probi homines* in February 1378 to finance repairs to the city's barge, as well as the poll taxes of 1377, 1379 and 1380. The poll taxes were a new form of direct taxation that, unlike the fifteenth and tenth, were assessed on individuals rather than on every household's movable property.[186] The 1377 poll tax was a standard rate of 4*d.* per head charged on every adult over the age of fourteen, except the poor. The 1379 poll tax was a graduated tax based on social status, in which the minimum rate was 4*d.* and the wealthy were expected to pay more according to a sliding scale fixed by parliament. The third poll tax was a combination of the first two taxes. Although the precise reasons behind the introduction of the poll taxes remain unknown, there is no doubt that that they represented an attempt to obtain more revenue than the regular system of lay taxation – the block quotas for fifteenths and tenths – was accustomed to produce, in order to meet the crown's urgent financial and military requirements.[187] The 1377 poll tax, for instance, was granted to fund a naval expedition to defend the realm against imminent attack from a Franco-Castilian naval fleet.[188] Crucially, the poll taxes, which set no fixed figure on the total amount of tax to be raised from each community, were a particular challenge to the tax collectors, who sought to balance royal obligations with local needs.

Underpinning the growing unrest in York, however, was the perception that the city's rulers were not governing on behalf of the common good, as they were supposed to. Perhaps the key issue relating to the cost of the barges and balingers in York and elsewhere was not their expense as such, increasingly burdensome though that was, but an awareness that, while the responsibility of financing the ships was shared widely within the city, the benefits seemed to be confined to the few who were engaged in overseas trade. As was

---

[184] SC 8/103/5139.

[185] For the situation in York after the uprising see Liddy, 'York in 1380–1', 29–30.

[186] For the following see *The peasants' revolt of 1381*, ed. R. B. Dobson, London 1970, 103–18. Under the traditional lay subsidy, as W. M. Ormrod has pointed out, 'the household, rather than the individual, provided the basic taxable unit': 'The politics of pestilence: government in England after the Black Death', in W. M. Ormrod and P. G. Lindley (eds), *The Black Death in England*, Stamford 1996, 161.

[187] The fiscal and diplomatic background is provided in Saul, *Richard II*, 31–55.

[188] *RP* ii. 362–4; Sherborne, 'Cost of English warfare', 146.

discussed in the previous chapter, York's ships, built explicitly for the defence of the realm, were also employed for commercial purposes when they were not required by the crown.[189] Similarly, John de Gysburn, the most prominent member of the civic hierarchy in the 1370s, exploited his privileged political position for personal financial gain.[190] Exacerbated by the financial pressures of war, this tension – between the pursuit of private interests and the maintenance of public responsibilities and duties – helps to explain the tumultuous nature of York's internal politics after 1369.

When the crown demanded further financial aid from the city after November 1380, York's civic elite were acutely aware of the potential for further unrest arising from the burden of taxation. The survival of York's 1381 poll tax return means that it is possible to examine the way in which the third poll tax was redistributed within the city. Unlike the previous poll taxes, neither of which, in theory, 'gave much scope for the local elites to exercise any power or influence over the assessment', the third poll tax gave tax collectors more freedom to decide how the tax was to be levied within their communities.[191] The collectors were to ensure that each village and town paid an average of 1s. per person, with every person charged 'according to his means', so that 'the sufficient' should 'aid the lesser'.[192] The 1381 parish assessments for York were, as Neville Bartlett first noted, based on the parish quotas of the 1374 subsidy, which in turn were related to those of 1334.[193] Bartlett believed that the York returns of 1381 were the result, therefore, of widespread tax 'evasion' in the city. In contrast, P. J. P. Goldberg has argued convincingly that there was no deliberate attempt to defraud the crown and has suggested instead that, faced with the problem of having to produce an average assessment of 1s. per taxpayer throughout the whole city despite the wide differences in wealth between the parishes, the tax assessors and collectors in 1381 adhered closely to the parish quotas of the traditional lay subsidy which were 'more sensitive to economic realities and variation between parishes'.[194] At the same time, within the richer parishes, the fiscal burden was borne largely by a small group of wealthy taxpayers who subsidised the poorer taxpayers, while the very poor north-eastern and south-eastern parishes were simply 'excluded' on the basis that 'the political and social implications of burdening poor taxpayers, who could not be effectively subsidized, outweighed the fiscal

---

189 See pp. 54–5 above.
190 See p. 87 above.
191 The comparison between the 1380 tax and the earlier poll taxes is drawn by Dyer in 'Taxation and communities', 174.
192 *RP* iii. 90, translated in *Peasants' revolt*, 117.
193 'Lay poll tax returns for the city of York in 1381', 6–7, and table 1 at p. 12.
194 Compare ibid. 7 ('the failure of the intentionally heavy 1381 Poll Tax to increase the amount raised by the 1334 Lay Subsidy by even a third is striking evidence of the scale of tax evasion in the city'), and P. J. P. Goldberg, 'Urban identity and the poll taxes of 1377, 1379, and 1381', *EcHR* 2nd ser. xliii (1990), 205.

Table 6
Poll tax contributions of York's tax officials in 1381*

Name	Office	Tax**	Parish+
John de Santon	royal assessor and collector	17s. 4d.	St Crux
William de Burton	royal assessor and collector	20s.	St Saviour
John de Rypon	royal surveyor	6s.	St Helen, Stonegate
John de Brathwayt	royal surveyor	8s. 4d.	St Michael, Spurriergate
William Fyssh	constable of St Mary, Bishophill Senior and Junior	6s. 4d.	St Mary, Bishophill Senior
William de Clapham	constable of St Mary, Bishophill Senior and Junior	3s. 4d.	St Mary, Bishophill Junior
John de Cottyngham	constable of St Michael, Spurriergate	4s. 4d.	St Michael, Spurriergate
John de Ceszay	constable of St Michael, Spurriergate	3s. 8d.	St Michael, Spurriergate
John de Askham	subconstable of St Martin and St Gregory, and Holy Trinity, Micklegate	3s. 4d.	St Martin and St Gregory, Micklegate
Robert Tothe	subconstable of St Martin and St Gregory, and Holy Trinity, Micklegate	4s.	St Martin and St Gregory, Micklegate
Simon de Quixlay	constable of St John at Ouse Bridge End	13s. 4d.	St John at Ouse Bridge End
John de Kenley	constable of All Saints' Pavement and St Peter the Little	3s.	All Saints' Pavement
William Redhode	constable of All Saints' Pavement and St Peter the Little	6s.	All Saints' Pavement
William del Pountfrayt	constable of All Saints' Pavement and St Peter the Little	8s. 2d.	All Saints' Pavement
Roger de Moreton, Sr	subconstable of St Martin, Coney Street	7s. 4d.	St Martin, Coney Street
Adam de Misterton	subconstable of St Martin, Coney Street	6s.	St Martin, Coney Street
Robert del Gare	constable of St Michael le Belfrey	9s. 8d.	St Michael le Belfrey
William de Leuesham	constable of St Helen, Stonegate and St Wilfrid	3s.	St Helen, Stonegate
Thomas de Kilburn	constable of St Helen, Stonegate and St Wilfrid	3s.	St Helen, Stonegate
Richard de Soureby	subconstable of Holy Trinity, Goodramgate and St John del Pyke	2s. 4d.	Holy Trinity, Goodramgate

94

Hugh del Chartres	constable of St Sampson, St Andrew, and St Helen in the Walls	4s.	St Sampson
John de Howeden	constable of Holy Trinity, King's Court	9s. 4d.	Holy Trinity, King's Court
Walter de Frothyngham	constable of Holy Trinity, King's Court	1s. 4d.	Holy Trinity, King's Court
Roger de Moreton, Jr	constable of St Saviour and St Cuthbert	20s.	St Saviour
John de Barden	constable of St Crux	18s.	St Crux
John de Pathorne	subconstable of St Crux	9s.	St Crux

* Statistics are drawn from 'Lay poll tax returns for the city of York in 1381', 18–79.
** All the figures given are for married couples, with the exception of Thomas de Kilburn, who was assessed as a single person.
+ The parishes are those in which they were taxed in 1381.

benefits'.[195] This fiscal strategy explains the reduction in the number of taxpayers in York from 7,248 in 1377 to 4,015 in 1381.[196]

York's tax collectors tried to ensure the equitable distribution of the poll tax. Royally appointed assessors and collectors, supervised by surveyors, administered the poll tax, below whom the subtaxers, as with the previous poll taxes and the traditional lay subsidy, made the 'door-to-door visits' necessary to collect taxation from each household.[197] There is a list in the York Memorandum Book of the names of the parish constables and subconstables who were appointed on 10 August 1380 to keep the peace,[198] and it is almost certain that it was these parish officials who acted as subtaxers in 1381 since the parish was the main unit of taxation in the city.[199] The incomplete nature of York's 1381 poll tax returns means that there is firm statistical data about only four of the assessors, collectors and surveyors and twenty-two of the fifty-one parish officials.[200] With the exception of Thomas de Kilburn, one of the constables of the parishes of St Helen, Stonegate and St Wilfrid, who paid 3s. as a single person, all the taxers were assessed as married

[195] Goldberg, 'Urban identity', 206.
[196] E 359/8B, rots 9r, 12d.
[197] The poll taxes of 1377, 1379 and 1381, ed. C. C. Fenwick (British Academy Social and Economic n.s. xxvii, 1997), p. xix.
[198] YMB i. 151–4.
[199] Miller, 'Medieval York', 67, also draws attention to the role of the parish constable in assisting with the collection of royal taxes.
[200] The absence of complete data does not mean that the others escaped payment: see Bartlett's comments on the nature of the extant returns in 'Lay poll tax returns for the city of York in 1381', 2–3.

couples. York's royal taxers paid an average of almost 13s. for themselves and their wives, compared to a mean rate of nearly 7s. for the subtaxers (*see* table 6).

Since the mean rate for a married couple agreed on in parliament was to be 2s.,[201] it is clear that York's taxers were paying three to six times the required amount. No married couple was to pay more than 20s. according to the guidelines drawn up in parliament, and some York citizens such as William de Burton and Roger de Moreton, Jr, were taxed at the maximum rate, while others such as John de Santon and John de Barden paid the maximum of 20s. by paying for their wives and household servants.[202] There is also evidence to suggest that there was an attempt among the taxers themselves to redistribute the tax equitably. Thus, in the affluent parish of St Crux, for example, one of the constables paid 18s., while his junior in the civic hierarchy, the subconstable, contributed 9s. In York in 1381 the tax collectors, drawn predominantly from the civic elite, did not seek to evade assessment, but to fulfil their responsibilities as good citizens.

In Bristol, too, the ruling elite demonstrated a renewed interest in ideals of active citizenship based on the common good. Here, news of the Peasants' Revolt was probably the catalyst. On 26 June 1381, less than two weeks after the rebels' march on London, Bristol's mayor, Walter de Derby, with the assent of the members of the common council and of the commons of the town, issued a series of civic ordinances for the safekeeping of the town's records and the proper auditing of civic taxation.[203] The burning of documents was a pronounced and recurrent feature of the Peasants' Revolt, as the rebels carefully targeted those forms of written record, including royal tax receipts and manorial accounts, which oppressed them.[204] Equally, as Steven Justice has shown, the rebels wanted to preserve certain documents which could be of use to them: in Bury St Edmunds, a monastic borough, the rebels 'demanded that the monks produce "in the sight of the commons" the charters of liberty for the vill "which Cnut, the founder of the monastery, once granted" '. The first of the ordinances produced by Bristol's civic elite towards the end of June 1381 sought to make civic government more accessible to the commons of the town. Although 'all the records, papers and muniments touching the Commons' were to be preserved 'within the Guildhall or in some other privy place under lock' ('ou en aultre place prevee sur serure'),[205] two or three of the commons, in addition to the mayor, were now to be given their own keys in order that 'every man can have copies or the

---

[201] 2s. per married couple, or 1s. per person: *RP* iii. 90; Goldberg, 'Urban identity', 207.
[202] For Santon and Barden see 'Lay poll tax returns for the city of York in 1381', 29, 32.
[203] *LRB* i. 110-13.
[204] The following draws on S. Justice, *Writing and rebellion: England in 1381*, Berkeley 1994, 40-8, quotation at p. 47.
[205] Jack Trewman's claim in the Peasants' Revolt that 'trewþe. hat bene sette under a lokke' would have struck a chord with the commons of Bristol. For a brilliant analysis of the cultural significance of this image see ibid. 67-73.

records when need be'.[206] The town's civic archive was to be available for public consideration: no longer was government to be carried out in private beyond the scrutiny of the commons. The revolt of 1381 had underlined for Bristol's rulers the need to be more sensitive to pressure from below and to adopt a more consultative style of civic government.

Yet why did the commons of Bristol seek greater access to civic business and increased participation in government? The Peasants' Revolt was not simply the trigger for the civic ordinances of 1381: the wider political issue which lay behind it, namely the deleterious impact of royal government in the localities,[207] seems to have been the subject of serious debate within Bristol long before the outbreak of the rebellion. It is difficult otherwise to explain the decision in June 1381 that the receivers of civic taxation, whose existence had been formally acknowledged and sanctioned by the 1373 charter, should be subject to an annual audit, at which they would present their account before the mayor and 'others of whom four or six elected by assent of the commons yearly be then present'.[208] The 1373 charter was partially responsible, for it both reduced the size of the common council from forty-eight to forty and transferred the power of election to the mayor and sheriff rather than through 'common assent'.[209] These were constitutional changes which can only have led to suspicion that the common council was no longer – if, indeed, it ever was – representative of the wider interests of the freemen at large. None the less, the 1381 ordinances had a strongly financial slant and in their concern that the town's financial officials be subject to more rigorous accounting procedures, can be seen as a response to the escalating financial costs of government in the 1370s. After all, only two years earlier, in May 1379, the town had made a corporate loan of £666 13s. 4d., and just six months later Bristol's rulers would agree to another substantial corporate loan of £400 for the war.[210]

But for the 'vagaries of record survival', R. B. Dobson has suggested, 'it could well be the case that few English boroughs of substantial size were entirely unaffected by the turbulence of the "hurlyng time" ' in the summer of 1381.[211] It has been argued that the civic disturbances in 1381 'can all be explained largely in terms of local issues and local factions' rather than 'the more general political grievances that precipitated the simultaneous rural revolts'.[212] Yet this chapter has shown otherwise: towns and cities such as Bristol and York were not immune to the 'deep-seated political malaise' from

[206] *LRB* i. 110–11.
[207] See Ormrod, 'Politics of pestilence', 147–77, esp. p. 167.
[208] *LRB* i. 112.
[209] *Bristol charters, 1155–1373*, 136–7. The quotation comes from the election of the common council in 1344: *LRB* i. 25.
[210] See table 1 at p. 24 above.
[211] Dobson, 'Risings', 112–13.
[212] Ormrod, *Political life*, 45.

which England was suffering in the years before the Peasants' Revolt.[213] In Bristol and York, just as elsewhere in the kingdom, not least Westminster, there was, in this period, a growing concern with the common good provoked by the stresses of war and the growth of government.

The crown's financial demands on the city of York arising from the Hundred Years War prompted discussion in York about the nature of civic government and the conduct of the civic elite in the period after 1369, the main aim of which was the greater accountability of the civic elite to the citizens as a whole. Similar anxieties were expressed by the parliamentary commons about royal government in the face of continuing royal demands for financial aid. It is hard to believe that events in parliament were not influenced by political debate within the city of York. When the parliamentary commons sought greater accountability from the crown, parliamentary committees were appointed to oversee the expenses not only of the royal household, but also of the royal government generally, one of which, in January 1380, included Thomas Graa, a member of York's council of twelve and a former mayor of the city.[214]

Equally, national political tensions evident in parliament in the 1370s directly affected the local political agenda in York. Richard Britnell's work on the town of Colchester has shown that in the early 1370s the town's government was transformed with the creation of a town council and appointment of new financial officials, a constitutional change which was influenced by 'a revival of public concern about the accountability of financial officers', one of the main themes of national politics in the 1370s and 1380s.[215] The emerging structure of civic government in York in the 1370s was, as Sarah Rees Jones has noted, 'similar to that of a contemporary Parliament',[216] and the commons of York enjoyed similar powers to those of the parliamentary commons inasmuch as they could petition the *probi homines* for redress of common grievances. In exactly the same way that the commons in parliament voiced their dissatisfaction with the state of royal government and criticised the expense, corruption and malpractices of its officials, so too did the commons of the city of York begin in the 1370s to express their unease about the cost of civic government, the disbursement of civic finances, and the corruption of the city's civic officials who were seen to be profiting financially from office.

Indeed, fiscal awareness and knowledge of parliamentary procedure had filtered down to the commons of York to such an extent by the close of the fourteenth century that around 1400 they presented a petition to the councils of twelve and twenty-four, asking that henceforth civic taxes would only

[213] M. McKisack, *The fourteenth century, 1307–1399*, Oxford 1959, 422.

[214] *RP* iii. 73–4; appendix below. The significance of this committee is discussed at pp. 175–7 below.

[215] R. H. Britnell, *Growth and decline in Colchester, 1300–1525*, Cambridge 1986, 115–20, quotation at p. 116.

[216] Rees Jones, 'York's civic administration', 123.

be raised with the prior consent rather than assent of the council of forty-eight.[217] By this date, the council of forty-eight was composed of craft searchers representative specifically of the city's crafts.[218] In the event of future taxation, the searchers were to be summoned before the mayor and aldermen in the guildhall and informed of the reason for the tax demand; the searchers would then consult with each of the members of their craft before returning to the guildhall with their response. In this way, the searchers would not be forced to levy civic taxes against their will. At stake were principles of consent, accountability and consultation, in which a statement of necessity was required and taxation had to be freely given, all part of the dialogue made familiar by G. L. Harriss through which the parliamentary commons granted taxation to the crown.[219]

[217] YCA, D1, fo. 348r.
[218] Rees Jones, 'York's civic administration', 122–3.
[219] Harriss, *King, parliament, and public finance*, passim, esp. pp. 509–17.

3

Commercial Policy

The king's obligation to defend the realm from external attack was one aspect of his duty to pursue the common good. Thomas Aquinas outlined a more positive view of the functions of government whereby the ruler was to ensure that the realm was provided with what was necessary for its sustenance, an idea underpinning the increasingly interventionist nature of government in economic matters in the later Middle Ages.[1] Examining the interaction of political ideas about the king's responsibilities in economic affairs and practical politics, one of the key issues of this chapter is the extent to which the crown's commercial policies were the product of its fiscal, political and diplomatic interests rather than of any particular concern with trade and with ideas about the promotion of commerce and the common good. In fact, it can be doubted whether the crown's policies towards trade were indeed solely the product of direction and instruction from the centre. In his most recent book on the process of state formation in sixteenth- and seventeenth-century England, Michael Braddick has emphasised the multiplicity of pressures influencing state growth, arguing persuasively that there was 'no single will' consciously ordering affairs, that the institutions, policies and resources of the state developed in response to local initiative as much as central directive, and that observed as a whole the process was, in many ways, 'undirected'.[2] The following discussion explores the commercial aspects of relations between the royal government and Bristol and York in the second half of the fourteenth century and concentrates on three aspects of the crown's policy towards trade: the customs service, the staple and diplomacy.[3] What is evident is that the civic elites of Bristol and York were greatly involved in the formulation as well as implementation of the commercial policies of the royal government. The theme of the chapter, then, is the nature of this collaboration between urban elites and the crown.

[1] E. Miller, 'The economic policies of governments', in M. M. Postan and others (eds), *The Cambridge economic history of Europe*, Cambridge 1963, iii. 285; Bolton, *Medieval English economy*, 328.
[2] Braddick, *State formation*, 7, and passim.
[3] Other aspects of the crown's commercial policies, dealing notably with ideas of balance of trade and bullionism, are examined at pp. 177–88 below.

The customs

Bristol, unlike York, was a head port for the collection of customs. Briefly, in 1333, 1339 and 1341, York was appointed the centre of a customs administration,[4] but thereafter the city's merchants were dependent on the port facilities at Hull. The reason lay in York's unsuitability as an international port because, although the river Ouse was tidal as far as York, some thirty miles inland, the water was too shallow for large vessels of the kind engaged in overseas trade to reach the city. The crown was aware of this problem and the 1339 grant authorising York to act as a customs port made an allowance: in the event that 'great ships' were unable to reach the city to collect sacks of wool and other merchandise for export because of the shallow depths of the river Ouse, these commodities could instead, once they had been assessed for customs duties in York, be loaded on to 'small ships or boats' to Selby, about fifteen miles downstream, or to Faxfleet, over thirty miles away from York at the junction of the river Trent and the Humber, from whence they were to be transported overseas.[5] In contrast, although Bristol was not strictly a coastal port, the town was able to serve as a port for the collection of customs because of the 'exceptionally high tides' on the river Avon where it met the Severn.[6] Bristol's status as a customs head port was also the result of a series of building projects undertaken in the town in the 1240s, including the construction of a new deeper harbour on the river Frome for the mooring of large ocean-going vessels.[7] The crown played a crucial role in this process, for it was in 1240 that Henry III ordered the men of Redcliffe who lived in the area south of the river to assist the burgesses of Bristol in the digging and financing of a new channel for the river Frome, diverting it through St Augustine's Marsh to meet the river Avon. This new dock became known as The Key and was used for overseas trade, while the smaller vessels involved in coastal and inland trade were able to unload at The Back.[8] Equipped with these harbour facilities, the town became the centre of a customs jurisdiction stretching from Chepstow in the north to Bridgwater in the south.[9]

This examination of the customs administration will focus on two subjects: the identity of the personnel of the customs service and the issue of reciprocity. Royal service in the customs distinguished the civic elite of Bristol from that of York. With the exception of John de Barden, who served as a collector of the wool and the petty customs in the port of Hull between 1390 and 1391, no other York citizen was appointed to the customs service in

---

4   Miller, 'Medieval York', 98; Bartlett, 'Economy of York', 95–7.
5   *CPR, 1338–40*, 393.
6   For Bristol's geographical position see Lobel and Carus-Wilson, 'Bristol', 1–7, esp. p. 3.
7   For what follows see *Bristol charters, 1378–1499*, 37–8.
8   See Lobel and Carus-Wilson, 'Bristol', map 3.
9   E. M. Carus-Wilson and O. Coleman, *England's export trade, 1275–1547*, Oxford 1963, 8.

the second half of the fourteenth century.[10] In contrast, up to the early 1390s, the offices of collector of the wool and the petty customs and collector of tonnage and poundage in the port of Bristol were monopolised by a very small group of the town's burgesses.[11] Previous studies of the local administration of the customs have tended to be preoccupied with the question of the fiscal efficiency of the customs service and, by extension, that of the royal government. R. L. Baker, in particular, has cast doubt on the efficacy of the system of 'self-government at the king's command' represented by the customs service, viewing the collection of customs and subsidies as evidence of the weakness of late medieval English government, which was reliant on local elites.[12] Specifically, he argued that local sentiment was more powerful than attachment to the royal government and that it was inevitable that customs officials would collude with their friends and neighbours to evade or reduce the payment of customs duties. Indeed, according to Baker, the crown acknowledged the complete failure of the customs system by appointing successive companies of English wool merchants in the 1340s to farm the customs.[13]

The issue here is not the success of the customs system in maximising revenue for the crown. There is no doubt that there were suspected cases of bribery and fraud within the Bristol customs service as there were at other customs ports.[14] None the less, interest in the efficiency of the customs administration does draw attention to the central issue about the customs system: its purpose. As W. M. Ormrod has pointed out, 'the English customs system differed fundamentally from those of most other western European monarchies in that it was intended as a means of profit rather than of protectionism'.[15] Yet the customs service did not operate in the financial interests of the crown alone. Rather, the administration of the customs was an integral part of the system of public credit, in which the repayment of loans from royal creditors was assigned to various sources of crown revenue, most notably the customs. Meanwhile, up to 1386 the subsidy of tonnage and poundage was not 'a regular element within the wider customs system', and its revenue was devoted specifically to the protection of trade and merchant shipping.[16] There is a good case for believing that Bristol's customs officials, the majority of whom were overseas merchants and/or shipowners, had a real stake in the collection of the subsidy of tonnage and poundage for the defence of their

[10] *CFR, 1383–91*, 344.
[11] See appendix below. The change in the early 1390s is discussed at pp. 106–9 below.
[12] R. L. Baker, *The English customs service, 1307–1343: a study of medieval administration* (Transactions of the American Philosophical Society n.s. li, 1961), 9, 50–1.
[13] Ibid. 48.
[14] See, for example, *CPR, 1354–8*, 41; *LRB* i. 129–32; *CFR, 1399–1405*, 95–6.
[15] W. M. Ormrod, 'Finance and trade under Richard II', in Goodman and Gillespie, *Richard II*, 158.
[16] Ibid. 172–3.

commercial interests and those of their friends and neighbours within the town of Bristol.

This study of the customs personnel at the port of Bristol will examine two sets of officials: the collectors of the wool and the petty customs, and the collectors of tonnage and poundage. Although there were other customs officials at the port, most notably the controller, whose responsibility it was to oversee the work of the collectors, it was the collectors who were the most important individuals within the operation of the customs system, receiving all of the money collected in the head port and outlying ports under their jurisdiction and then accounting for it at the exchequer.[17] In London there were separate officials for the wool customs (comprising the ancient custom of 1275 paid by all merchants, native and alien, on exports of wool, and the wool subsidy, imposed at first only during periods of war but levied also in peacetime from 1362); the cloth and petty customs (consisting of the new custom of 1303 paid only by alien merchants on wool exports, wine imports and the import and export of general merchandise such as fish, wax and spices, and the cloth custom of 1347 levied on the cloth exports of native and alien merchants); and the subsidy of tonnage and poundage (a customs duty on native and alien imports of wine and imports and exports of general merchandise including cloth for the protection of English shipping and trade from attack at sea). In Bristol, as in other provincial ports such as Boston, however, two collectors were appointed to collect the wool and the petty customs, and two to collect tonnage and poundage.[18]

From November 1351, immediately after the assumption of direct responsibility for the customs service by the crown, to December 1391, the office of collector of the wool and the petty customs in Bristol was held by sixteen individuals, but it was monopolised by eight men who each occupied the position for five or more years.[19] Of the latter, with one exception,[20] all had held high-ranking civic office in the town before their first appointment and four, Walter de Frompton, John de Stoke, Thomas Beaupyne and Walter de Derby, between them held the office of mayor of Bristol a total of thirteen times. Similarly, between 1351 and 1391, the office of collector of tonnage and poundage was dominated by four individuals, Walter de Derby, John Candever, Ellis Spelly and Thomas Beaupyne. Candever was a sheriff of the town before his appointment, while the other three, between them, occupied the mayoralty for a total of eleven years. A total of five men, Walter de

[17] For a description of the operation of the customs system and of the hierarchy of customs officials see Baker, *English customs service*, 6–12, and M. H. Mills, 'The collectors of customs', in Willard and others, *English government at work*, ii. 168–200.

[18] S. H. Rigby, 'The customs administration at Boston in the reign of Richard II', *BIHR* lviii (1985), 12.

[19] See appendix below for what follows.

[20] William de Cheddre was none the less a prominent burgess of Bristol and the brother of Robert de Cheddre, twice mayor of the town: see appendix below. Together, they founded a perpetual chantry in Cheddar (Somerset): *GRB* iii. 195–200.

Frompton, Thomas Beaupyne, William de Combe, Walter de Derby and John Candever, all of whom were drawn from the political elite of Bristol, held both offices. Thus, the evidence from Bristol supports Maryanne Kowaleski's conclusions about late medieval Exeter, in which she found that royal appointments to the customs service were made to citizens of the highest political rank within the city.[21]

According to Kowaleski, these appointments not only enhanced the social and political status of members of the civic elite of Exeter, but also presented officeholders with 'additional opportunities for financial gain (either legal or illegal)'. Several mayors of Exeter were found guilty of fraud in the collection of the customs, but the crown generally tolerated such corruption because it expected that appointments to the customs service would reap political rewards, allowing it to build up 'a strong political base that often bore fruit' when members of Exeter's political elite participated in military expeditions overseas or else lent money to the royal government.[22] The customs administration, in short, was designed not simply to provide revenue to the king, but to provide a source of patronage to urban elites, tying them more closely to the maintenance of the broader interests of the crown. It would be hard to disagree with the main thrust of Kowaleski's argument that appointment to the customs service was a form of royal patronage. This sort of royal employment was a source of prestige to the individuals involved, bolstering the authority they already enjoyed through civic officeholding.[23] For John de Stoke, for example, the Bristol customs service presented an opportunity of future royal employment: he was a deputy controller of the customs between 1361 and 1362 before his appointment, three years later, as a collector of the wool and the petty customs and then as a diplomat to Calais in 1372.[24]

The opportunities for personal financial gain, however, should not be exaggerated. In her study of London's customs collectors in the reign of Richard II, O. Coleman argued that the reason for the monopoly of the office of collector by certain individuals lay in 'their personal and corporate financial relationships with the crown'.[25] Londoners either lent money to the crown once they had the security of a position as a customs collector in the London customs or else they tried to secure a customs appointment for themselves or their associates in order to gain repayment of a loan. In Bristol there is scant evidence of a similar pattern in terms of individual lenders. Indeed, the only example is Walter de Frompton, who lent money to the crown in

[21] M. Kowaleski, 'The commercial dominance of a medieval provincial oligarchy: Exeter in the late fourteenth century', in R. Holt and G. Rosser (eds), *The English medieval town: a reader in English urban history, 1200–1540*, London 1990, 193–5.
[22] Ibid. 195.
[23] This issue is examined in detail at pp. 203–7 below.
[24] E 356/5, rot. 19r (deputy controller); appendix below.
[25] For what follows see O. Coleman, 'The collectors of customs in London under Richard II', in Hollaender and Kellaway, *Studies in London history*, 184–7, quotation at p. 184.

August 1351 and who was then assigned repayment of the loan in 1352 and 1353 from the wool and the petty customs of which he was also a collector.[26] None the less, it is clear that loans to the crown made by Bristol in its corporate capacity tended to be repaid from the port's customs, whether the wool and the petty customs or the subsidy of tonnage and poundage. The corporate loans of May and June 1370, October 1377, December 1381 and October 1386, totalling over £2,000, were all repaid, in part or in full, from Bristol's customs.[27] The process by which repayment of Bristol's loans was assigned to the customs of the port of Bristol meant that the town, in effect, paid itself. The security of the customs, coupled with the occupation of key customs offices by members of Bristol's political elite, meant that the town's rulers could be confident of making loans. Both of these facts may help to explain further why Bristol lent far more money to the crown than the city of York, whose loans tended to be repaid from the Hull customs and whose rulers had to compete with other creditors seeking refunding.[28] In 1370 the city of York made two corporate loans to the crown totalling £900, for which it was agreed that repayment would come from the Hull customs. The initial assignment, however, was cancelled, presumably because of over-assignment, and it was 1374 before York was eventually reimbursed, although even this was a partial repayment since the city's rulers cancelled the remaining debt of £400 owed to the city.[29]

As Coleman realised, if a customs collector contributed to the making of a corporate civic loan, he would be able to ensure that the city was first in the queue for repayment.[30] A similar pattern is discernible in Edward III's reign. In June 1370, for example, London's rulers were approached for a corporate loan of £5,000. Their first reaction was refusal, but after negotiation with the crown a deputation from the city agreed to lend the money 'on the security of the custom and subsidy of wool, woolfells, and leather in the Port of London', a condition of lending that the crown conceded and that was noted with particular interest (and approval) in the city's records.[31] One of London's two collectors of the wool customs was John Bernes, who had been reappointed to the office on 10 August 1370 after occupying the position the previous year.[32] Is it a coincidence that Bernes was elected mayor of London on 13 October 1370 and that it was during his tenure in office, in the autumn of 1370, that

---

[26] CCR, 1349–54, 344, 573; appendix below.
[27] E 401/501, 10 May, 22 June (1370); E 401/528, 26 Oct. (1377); E 401/544, 16 Dec. (1381); E 401/566, 28 Feb. (1387).
[28] York's corporate loans of 1385, 1386, 1399 and 1400 were repaid, in part or in full, from the Hull customs: E 401/563, 9 Dec. (1385); E 401/566, 14 Feb. (1387); CPR, 1399–1401, 354 (1399, 1400).
[29] E 401/501, 11 May, 3 July (1370); E 401/515, 3 Aug. (1374).
[30] Coleman, 'Collectors of customs', 190.
[31] Letter-book G, 263.
[32] CFR, 1368–77, 92, 28.

the city's loan of £5,000 was repaid?[33] It is tempting to think that Bernes owed his election to the London mayoralty primarily to his position within the city's customs service, whence, presumably, London's ruling elite hoped that he would secure repayment of the loan. Certainly, once in the mayoral office, when London made a corporate loan of more than £4,500 on 1 February 1371, Bernes, contributing £200, headed the list of London creditors, while the loan was repaid from the wool customs five days later, on 6 February 1371, during which period he remained in office as a collector of the wool customs.[34] Vested interests were bound up with the administration of the customs, but these were not so much opportunities for financial profit as a guarantee that loans would be repaid. Moreover, given the integration of the customs in the system of public credit, it could well be the case that the appointment of Bristol men to the local customs administration acted as a major stimulus to the collection of customs duties in the port and as a spur to greater efficiency. Baker's argument about the failure of the customs service before 1343 may be correct, but when the wool monopoly companies of the 1340s collapsed and the crown was reliant on the wider body of its subjects for loans, the customs service became part of a system of public finance in which the crown and local elites had a shared fiscal interest.[35]

Given the effectiveness of the customs system, then, it is worth exploring the reasons for the general reform of the customs administration in the early 1390s when royal clerks and local gentry were appointed as collectors of the customs. Anthony Steel first noticed this change in the port of Newcastle-upon-Tyne, arguing that royal policy was a reflection of the exchequer's view that 'the well-known and widespread laxity, not to say corruption, of the burgess class as a whole in all customs administration could no longer be endured'.[36] Coleman also identified a 'definite change in the character of London wool collectors' in the same period, and in a general survey of the composition of the customs service in the reign of Richard II, Steel found the pattern in Newcastle repeated everywhere, concluding that in the years 1391 to 1392 'the exchequer became so dissatisfied with leakages in the collection of the customs' that the crown 'decided either to get rid of merchant princes entirely in favour of clerks and special agents or at least to place them under strict supervision'.[37]

In a more recent study, however, S. H. Rigby has argued persuasively that the introduction of royal clerks into the customs ports in December 1391 was

---

[33] *Letter-book* G, 267, 266.

[34] Ibid. 275–7, 281–2.

[35] Harriss, 'Growth of government', 35–6.

[36] A. Steel, 'The collectors of the customs at Newcastle upon Tyne in the reign of Richard II', in J. C. Davies (ed.), *Studies presented to Sir Hilary Jenkinson*, London 1957, 390–413, quotation at p. 413.

[37] Coleman, 'Collectors of customs', 193; A. Steel, 'The collectors of customs in the reign of Richard II', in H. Hearder and H. R. Loyn (eds), *British government and administration: studies presented to S. B. Chrimes*, Cardiff 1974, 38.

the consequence of new bullion legislation which the collectors were to enforce. In short, increased central control of the local customs administration was the result of 'changes in royal commercial policy' rather than 'an attack on a corrupt customs system'.[38] In Bristol Richard des Armes, a king's clerk, held the offices of collector of the wool and the petty customs and of tonnage and poundage by joint commission from 1391 to 1395, and Richard Mawardyn, a king's esquire and sheriff of Wiltshire (1389–90, 1393–4 and 1396–9), held the two offices simultaneously between 1395 and 1397.[39] Nevertheless, Thomas Knappe, Thomas Beaupyne and John Stevenes, all mayors of Bristol, served alongside these men, and in 1397 Armes and Mawardyn had been replaced. This is not to underestimate the significance of the changing royal policy towards the customs administration, but to support Rigby's point that what happened in the early 1390s was not the result of the crown's perception of wholesale corruption among the customs officials. In fact, what is more significant about the changes in the customs personnel is that they were, in part, the consequence of parliamentary pressure. Rigby may be right to associate the development with the new bullion legislation, but there was a political as well as an economic reason behind the reorganisation of the customs administration.

In the parliament of November 1390 the commons expressed their unease about the nature of the customs personnel.[40] They asked first that the collectors should be among 'les plus sufficeantz' in the port or the neighbouring area, articulating a sentiment also familiar in urban political discourse concerning the necessary qualifications of those entitled to hold civic office, namely that officials have sufficient wealth to render them more impervious to bribery and corruption than the less affluent.[41] Secondly, the parliamentary commons requested that the customs collectors should not be residents of the same town, fearing that they would co-operate ('pur doute de covyne'), presumably to show favour to local merchants in the assessment of customs duties to the detriment of the king's finances. It was to prevent a similar kind of corruption that the king was also asked that the customs collectors should neither be shipowners nor merchants, occupations that would blur the distinction between public office and private, commercial interests. It was not the first time that the parliamentary commons had been concerned about the types of people appointed to the customs administration. In the last

---

[38] Rigby, 'Customs administration at Boston', 17–18, quotation at p. 18.

[39] Richard des Armes was a king's yeoman of Edward III whose receipt of an annuity at the exchequer was confirmed by Richard II: CPR, 1374–7, 370; CPR, 1377–81, 146. For Mawardyn see Given-Wilson, *Royal household*, 250.

[40] RP iii. 281.

[41] For the urban picture see, for example, S. Reynolds, 'Medieval urban history and the history of political thought', *Urban History Yearbook* (1982), 21, citing Brunetto Latini's twelve qualities required of a good ruler in *Li livres dou tresor*, which was copied into London's *Liber custumarum* in the early fourteenth century. For subsequent parliamentary concern about the financial standing of customs officials see RP iii. 625–6.

parliament of Edward III's reign, in January 1377, the commons petitioned that, 'for the advantage of the king and the benefit and profit of all the merchants of the realm and the whole community', no wool merchant or shipowner be appointed to the offices of collector of customs or weigher of wool.[42] In 1379 the parliamentary commons asked that, 'for the profit of our said lord the king and the common profit of the realm', all the customs officials and controllers, like the sheriffs, be appointed annually,[43] rather than serve at the king's pleasure, as was normally the case.

It is possible to see in these petitions the vested interests of merchants who were concerned about their treatment by customs officials, who showed favour to some and not to others and who monopolised office for long periods. Equally, the petitions articulated a wider political morality about the need to uphold the common good, on which there was increasing insistence in the later fourteenth century, as the parliamentary commons became disturbed by the level of the crown's income and expenditure, anxious 'that the taxes that they granted should be properly spent' and critical of 'the extravagance of the royal household and the administration'.[44] The 1379 petition, for example, aimed to improve the collection of the royal customs duties on wool which formed, the commons reminded the crown, 'a large part of the profit of the realm belonging to our said lord the king'.[45] It can be no coincidence that one of the proposals drawn up by the commission, appointed by the commons in the parliament of October 1385 to investigate the state of the royal finances, was that the profits of the customs would be greatly increased if the customs collectors were both 'bons et loyalx gentz' (men most likely to be able to resist the temptations of office to defraud the king of customs revenue) and permanently resident within the customs ports to which they had been appointed, carrying out their duties in person rather than through deputies or attorneys.[46] In 1377 and 1379 the crown rejected the requests of the parliamentary commons, wanting to preserve its freedom to appoint as customs collectors as it pleased.[47] The years immediately following Richard II's assumption of personal responsibility for the governance of the realm in 1389 saw the king show 'greater sensitivity to his subjects' feelings than he had in his youth'.[48] One aspect of this 'more conciliatory style' of kingship was a greater readiness to listen to, and act upon, his subjects' concerns in parliament.[49] In 1390 the king agreed to implement the

[42] *RP* ii. 371.
[43] *RP* iii. 62.
[44] Harriss, 'Growth of government', 45.
[45] *RP* iii. 62.
[46] A transcription of the reforming ordinance drawn up by the commission is provided in J. J. N. Palmer, 'The impeachment of Michael de la Pole in 1386', *BIHR* xlii (1969), 100–1, quotation at p. 100. The political background is traced in Saul, *Richard II*, 146–7.
[47] *RP* ii. 371; iii. 62.
[48] Saul, *Richard II*, 235.
[49] Ibid. 236, 256.

commons' petition and outsiders were appointed in several ports.[50] One year later the crown appointed royal clerks. The fiscal potential of the customs was, therefore, a shared concern of the king and his subjects, even though each might have different views about, and different interests in, the best way to maximise this revenue.

The collection of the subsidy of tonnage and poundage operated under a different series of constraints. Although the customs system was geared primarily to the fiscal needs of the crown and its subjects, it is also the case that, before 1386, the subsidy of tonnage and poundage was designed specifically to finance armed convoys of ships for the protection of mercantile shipping and for the defence of the seas from piracy and enemy attack. It was introduced by the king and council in 1347 as an occasional tax on wine and general merchandise, but from the 1370s, with the resumption of the Hundred Years War, the subsidy was granted by the commons in parliament and became a more regular levy.[51] With the exception of Richard des Armes and Richard Mawardyn, Bristol's collectors of tonnage and poundage were characterised by their commercial and maritime interests.[52] The collectors would have had a vested interest in the collection of a subsidy earmarked specifically for the protection of overseas trade. In fact, if the collectors did not appreciate this point, it would have been impressed on them by the local communities from which they were drawn. In an undated petition, probably of 1382, Robert de Selby, a collector of tonnage and poundage in the port of Hull, petitioned the king's council in parliament to inform it that he had been forced to arm two ships and one balinger with 200 men and victuals for six weeks at his own expense to protect the coast from enemy attack.[53] Between Easter and Pentecost, in 'parts of the north', several enemy vessels had seized and burned a great number of ships, 'whereupon the whole country (la pais) complained most grievously to the said Robert because he was a collector of the custom of poundage, which had been granted for the keeping of the sea, on which nothing was done' ('a quele garde rien estoit fait'). Although, in this instance, the collection of tonnage and poundage had proved inadequate, the collector had been forced to provide personally the naval defence for which the subsidy had been originally awarded.

Within parliament, too, there was a particular concern among the commons to ensure that the revenue from the subsidy of tonnage and poundage was spent solely to protect maritime interests. In the parliament of

---

[50] Rigby, 'Customs administration at Boston', 16.

[51] The best introduction to the subsidy of tonnage and poundage remains Harriss, *King, parliament, and public finance*, 459–65, although see also J. S. Roskell, 'Introductory survey', in J. S. Roskell and others (eds), *The history of parliament: the House of Commons, 1386–1421*, Stroud 1993, i. 122–4, 130–4.

[52] See, for example, the biographies of Thomas Beaupyne, Robert Gardener, Thomas Knappe, Ellis Spelly and John Stevenes in Roskell and others, *House of Commons, 1386–1421*, ii. 164–6; iii. 156, 525–6; iv. 414–17, 474–5.

[53] SC 8/139/6911. For Selby's appointment as a customs collector see *CFR, 1377–83*, 300.

May 1382 'the mariners of the west' offered to equip 'an army at sea' for two years, and the commons made a grant of tonnage and poundage to finance the naval force during its period of service.[54] To ensure that the taxes would be 'used wholly on the safeguarding of the sea and nowhere else', the crown, at the request of the commons, appointed three parliamentary burgesses to act as receivers of the subsidy: John Philipot, a London MP; John Polymond, MP for Southampton; and Thomas Beaupyne, Bristol's MP and a former collector of tonnage and poundage in the port of Bristol. These appointments recalled the commission, in Richard II's first parliament in October 1377, of two prominent London merchants, William Walworth and John Philipot, to act as guardians of the royal taxes and to account to parliament for the receipts and issues of this revenue.[55]

At the Wonderful Parliament of 1386 the commons granted a subsidy of tonnage and poundage for an unlimited period, and thereafter the subsidy was collected continuously like other customs duties. It was in 1386 that tonnage and poundage 'was symbolically upgraded from a modest tax in aid of local defence to a national subsidy paid into the royal treasury and available for the general expenses of the Crown'.[56] In other words, tonnage and poundage, rather than a tax levied specifically for the defence of trade and the commercial interests of the crown's subjects, now became another source of royal revenue. None the less, the circumstances in which the concession was made are also significant, for the subsidy was conditional on the king's willingness to allow a commission of government, appointed at the request of the commons to implement a series of financial reforms, to do its work without hindrance.[57] The customs service was part of a wider system of public finance in which the crown and its urban and mercantile subjects, in particular, had a shared interest.

The staple

In essence, the staple was 'a fixed point through which all wool (and sometimes other goods) intended for the foreign market had to pass'.[58] In 1353 the ordinance of the staple fixed domestic staples at fifteen towns and cities in England, Wales and Ireland, including Bristol and York.[59] Ten years later a staple was established at Calais, and of the twenty-six merchants appointed by the king and council to govern the town, two were Bristol merchants, Reginald le Frensshe and Walter de Frompton, and two were York merchants,

---

[54] For what follows see *RP* iii. 124.
[55] *RP* iii. 7; *CPR, 1377–81*, 99.
[56] Ormrod, 'Finance and trade under Richard II', 173.
[57] *RP* iii. 220–1.
[58] Ormrod, *Edward III*, 190.
[59] *SR* i. 332.

John de Gysburn and Roger de Hovyngham.[60] The following discussion of the staple examines three topics: the reasoning behind the creation of the series of domestic staples in 1353; the purpose of the staples and their relations with the towns and cities in which they were located; and the role of merchants from Bristol and York in the establishment of the Calais staple in 1363. The key point is that the staple system was not imposed on Bristol and York by the crown primarily as an expression of royal interests, but that, both in its inception and operation, it was based on collaboration and negotiation between the crown and the ruling elites of the two towns.

How and why was royal policy towards the staple devised in 1353, and why were Bristol and York chosen as the location of staples? The reasons for the establishment of home staples in 1353, and for the ban on wool exports by native merchants which accompanied their creation, have been keenly debated by several historians.[61] To George Unwin, the abandonment of the Bruges staple in 1352, the creation of home staples and the prohibition of wool exports by English merchants in the 1353 ordinance of the staple, could all be explained by a parliamentary alliance between the lesser merchants and the wool-growers in the commons, who were hostile towards the wool monopoly companies associated with the Bruges staple. This alliance of wool-growers and lesser merchants petitioned repeatedly in parliament about the monopolists. When the last monopoly company went bankrupt in 1351, the crown was forced to listen to their complaints and responded with the ordinance of the staple, which reflected their interests as much as those of the king and which prevented future export monopolies by English merchants in order to guarantee 'the freedom of trade'.[62] T. H. Lloyd offered an alternative interpretation of the ordinance of the staple. He believed that the initiative lay with the king and that the reason for the policy of domestic staples was to be found in the crown's diplomatic interests and, in particular, in 'the state of relations between England and Flanders'.[63] With Louis de Mâle, the new count of Flanders, increasingly hostile to England, and Bruges too dangerous to be the location of the staple for English overseas trade, Edward III established domestic staples and placed a ban on native wool exports so that 'any losses at sea or in the Low Countries would cost England nothing and the government would not be embarrassed by the demand of its own subjects for reprisals'.[64] At the same time, Lloyd questioned Unwin's view of the 'anti-monopolist nature' of the 1353 ordinance, arguing that the officials of the Westminster staple and the provincial staples were either 'colleagues of

---

[60] *Foedera, conventiones, litterae et . . . acta publica*, ed. T. Rymer, London 1816–69, iii/2, 690–1.

[61] The ordinance of the staple is in *SR* i. 332–43.

[62] Unwin, 'Estate of merchants', 227–33, quotation at p. 232.

[63] Lloyd, *English wool trade*, 206.

[64] Ibid. 207.

the so-called monopolists' or else 'prominent wool exporters'.[65] Thus, to Lloyd, though the 1353 ordinance reflected essentially the interests of the crown, it did not entirely preclude those of the greater merchants. More recently, W. M. Ormrod has emphasised that the ordinance of the staple was part of a wide-ranging programme of reform of the regulation of trade in the early 1350s that was 'instigated by the government in its own specific interests'. The crown granted a monopoly of the wool trade to alien merchants in order to benefit from the increased rates of customs duties paid by foreign merchants, while the purpose of the home staples was to prevent fraud and loss of revenue from the customs system.[66]

Why were Bristol and York appointed as staple towns in 1353? One of the king's avowed aims with the 1353 staple system was the prevention of future wool monopolies by a small group of English merchant financiers. As Sir William Shareshull, the king's chief justice, explained at the opening of the 1353 great council, when the staple had been overseas 'the profit which ought to have come into his realm to the common people by the sale of their wool had been usurped for the benefit of individuals (*singuleres persones*) of the same realm to the great damage and impoverishment of the community of the same realm'.[67] The crown's adoption of the morality of the common good was in stark contrast to Edward III's earlier support of the wool monopoly companies of the 1340s, and the institution of domestic staples can be seen, in part at least, as an attempt to conciliate the commons in parliament. From this perspective Bristol made an ideal choice as a staple town: the town's merchants were engaged primarily in the export of cloth rather than wool and Bristol was not a wool town, geographically distant as it was from the Flemish markets, so the likelihood that English merchants would monopolise wool exports from the town was minimal.[68] A similar concern on the part of the crown about the future development of monopolies may help to explain the selection of York rather than Hull as a staple town, for the staples were located not at the major east-coast wool ports of Hull, Lynn, Boston and London, but at inland ports. York was different from Bristol in that many of the city's merchants were wool exporters and a number of them had been engaged in the wool monopoly schemes of the late 1330s and 1340s.[69] Yet, with a couple of exceptions,[70] the officials of the York staple were not associ-

[65] Ibid. 206.

[66] W. M. Ormrod, 'The English crown and the customs, 1349–63', *EcHR* 2nd ser. xl (1987), 27–40, esp. pp. 28–9.

[67] *RP* ii. 246.

[68] Carus-Wilson, 'Trends', 239–64; P. Nightingale, 'Knights and merchants: trade, politics and the gentry in late medieval England', *P&P* clxix (2000), 42.

[69] See, for example, Kermode, *Medieval merchants*, appendix 2 at pp. 330–1.

[70] Most notably, Walter de Kelstern, a wool merchant involved in the wool monopoly deal of 1337 and a member of Thomas Melchbourn's company in 1344, who served as a constable of the York staple in 1355 and 1356 and was mayor of the staple in 1357, and Roger de Hovyngham, one of the York merchants whose participation in the wool

ates of the wool monopolists. They represented a new generation of York merchants.

It may also be significant that both Bristol and York had been appointed as staples before 1353. In 1326 staples were fixed at Bristol and York and seven other English towns – London, Newcastle, Lincoln, Norwich, Winchester, Exeter and Shrewsbury – as well as at a number of towns and cities in Wales and Ireland.[71] Among the English towns, only London and Shrewsbury did not become staples again in 1353. If the choice of Bristol as a staple town in 1326 was, as Pamela Nightingale has recently argued, 'a political rather than a commercial decision', reflecting the interests of Hugh le Despenser the younger, the keeper of Bristol castle,[72] the merchants of Bristol and York were also strongly in favour of the home staples. When the status of domestic staples was reviewed at a merchant assembly held in York in 1328,[73] a series of letters was exchanged between the cities of London and York which suggest that neither York's civic government nor its merchants wanted the staple to be transferred overseas.[74] On 29 January 1328 York's mayor wrote to the mayor, sheriffs and aldermen of London to complain about the misconduct of Richard de Betoyne, a London merchant who had proposed the removal of the domestic staples and whose actions, they believed, did not meet 'with the approval of the City [of London], since they found John de Grantham and John Priour [the official representatives of London's merchants] of a different opinion'. Indeed, according to Grantham and Priour, writing to the city of London on 30 January 1328, they, as the representatives of London, along with the representatives of York, Lincoln, Winchester and Bristol, were all opposed to the removal of the staple.[75]

The ordinance of the staple issued in the great council of September–October 1353 was preceded, as George Unwin noted, by two assemblies in August 1352 and July 1353 at which it is likely that the subject of home staples was discussed, although no records of either meeting are extant.[76] Five of the towns and cities represented in 1352, including Bristol and York, became staple towns one year later.[77] In July 1353 a merchant assembly was convened, composed of seventy-one English merchants from twenty-three

---

monopoly companies led to litigation with the crown in the early 1350s and whose election as mayor of the York staple in 1354 was overturned by the crown. For Kelstern see the biography in J. Kermode, 'The merchants of York, Beverley and Hull in the fourteenth and fifteenth centuries', unpubl. PhD diss. Sheffield 1990, ii, appendix 4 (York). For Hovyngham see Fryde, 'Business transactions', 4–5; C 267/8/83; C 67/22, mem. 18.

[71] CPR, 1324–7, 269, 274.
[72] Nightingale, 'Knights and merchants', 44.
[73] For the background to this dispute see Lloyd, English wool trade, 117–20.
[74] The correspondence is in Calendar of plea and memoranda rolls of the city of London, 1323–1482, ed. A. H. Thomas and P. E. Jones, Cambridge 1926–61, i. 52–9.
[75] Ibid. i. 53–4.
[76] Unwin, 'Estate of merchants', 228–9.
[77] Compare Dignity of a peer, iv. 593–5, and SR i. 332.

towns and twelve foreign merchants. Four merchants each from Bristol and York were summoned to attend and, with one exception, all the towns represented in July 1353 were made staple towns one month later.[78] Unwin thought that 'the scheme [for home staples] in its main features was drawn up by this purely mercantile body and was afterwards submitted to the more parliamentary assembly of September'.[79] More conclusive evidence that this was indeed the case is provided by a comparison of the names of those summoned on 1 July 1353 with the names of the staple officials appointed by the king and council on 10 July.[80] All of Bristol's staple officials, the mayor, John le Spicer, and the constables, John de Wycombe and Walter de Frompton, were present at the July assembly, whilst two of York's staple officials, William Graa, mayor, and Hugh de Miton, a constable, were also in attendance. The debate about whether the policy of home staples was imposed from above or was the result of pressure from below misses the essential point that the introduction of the staple scheme in 1353 was based on negotiation and consultation between the crown and urban elites. If the crown stood to benefit financially from the higher rate of customs paid by alien merchants who were given control of the wool export trade, the interests of English merchants were also addressed.

Perhaps the most important aspect of the system of domestic staples – certainly the most enduring, the most novel and the most useful to the towns in which the staples were located – was the provision of new forms of mercantile justice in staple courts. The judicial aspects of the staples will be discussed shortly, but it is clear that royal concern with the regulation of the staples distinguished the staples established in 1353 from those set up in 1326.[81] In 1326 the staples had simply been towns at which wool for export was to be bought and sold; in 1353 separate jurisdictions were created for the staples within the towns in which they were located. In this sense, it is surely right to see the ordinance of the staple as a further example of the innovative legislation which characterised the mid-fourteenth century and which included the labour legislation, the reform of the coinage and the standardisation of the system of weights and measures.[82] The staple courts, with their new form of debt procedure under statute staple, in particular, were designed to facilitate mercantile credit and to promote trade by both English and foreign merchants, and were also a response to complaints in parliament in the mid-fourteenth century about the shortcomings of the system of debt

---

[78] *Dignity of a peer*, iv. 596–8, esp. pp. 596–7.

[79] Unwin, 'Estate of merchants', 229.

[80] *Dignity of a peer*, iv. 596–7; C 67/22, mem. 25.

[81] Lloyd, *English wool trade*, 115: the 1326 ordinance, 'unlike the legislation of 1353, did not prescribe the form the staple was to assume in each town'.

[82] The ordinance was confirmed as a statute in the parliament of 1354: *RP* ii. 254. For this other legislation see Ormrod, *Edward III*, 78–80.

recovery under statute merchant.[83] There were many factors determining the crown's decision to introduce home staples in 1353, but the main purpose was to channel commercial activity into certain urban centres such as Bristol and York, a need for which policy the merchants of these towns can only have impressed on the crown in their various meetings with the king in the early 1350s.

The 1353 ordinance of the staple created staple officials in the form of a mayor and two constables to govern the new jurisdictions. Their functions were fiscal and judicial. On the one hand, the mayor of the staple was given joint responsibility with the customs officials for the collection of the customs revenue. All wool intended for export had to be weighed and sealed by the mayor of the staple. In port towns like Bristol this was to be done in the presence of the customs staff, but in inland towns like York the wool weighed and sealed by the mayor of the staple was then to be taken to a customs port where it was weighed once more by the customs officials.[84] In the case of York's staple officials, moreover, the mayor and constables served as collectors of the cloth subsidy in the city between 1353 and 1358.[85] On the other hand, the staple officials were given far-reaching legal powers: the 1353 ordinance created separate jurisdictions within the staple towns and cities in which they had complete authority over people and goods associated with the staple, and all merchants coming to a staple had to swear an oath before the mayor and constables that they would submit to their jurisdiction and be ruled by law merchant rather than by the common law or by borough custom.[86] The staple officials were to hear all pleas of debt, contract and covenant between merchants and were also granted peacekeeping powers to hear and determine criminal cases involving merchants at the staple according to the common law.[87] To ensure that contracts made within the staple were honoured and to guarantee the speedy recovery of mercantile debts for merchants trading at the staple, the mayor of the staple, in the presence of the constables, had a seal to take recognizances of debt and was to imprison defaulting debtors in a staple gaol.[88]

In 1363,[89] when the staple was established at Calais, the home staples lost their economic function as the point at which all English wool exports had to be bought and sold, although wool still had to be weighed and registered at the home staples before it was exported to Calais. In 1369, with the resump-

---

[83] *RP* ii. 171; W. M. Ormrod, 'The origins of the *sub pena* writ', *HR* lxi (1988), 14 n. 22.

[84] *SR* i. 332–3.

[85] *CPR, 1350–4,* 536–7; H. L. Gray, 'The production and exportation of English woollens in the fourteenth century', *EHR* xxxix (1924), 19. The staple officials of Canterbury, Norwich and Lincoln were also appointed on 1 December 1353 to collect the cloth subsidy in their cities.

[86] *SR* i. 336, 341.

[87] *SR* i. 336.

[88] *SR* i. 336–7, 341.

[89] For what follows see Lloyd, *English wool trade*, 210–34.

tion of the Hundred Years War, Calais was abandoned and home staples regained, briefly, their economic importance, although York had its staple removed as did the other inland staples such as Lincoln.[90] A year later the staple returned to Calais and all the English staples lost their right to check wool ready for export. Thereafter the staple remained at Calais for commercial purposes except for brief periods when it was transferred to Middleburg in Zeeland in the 1380s and when home staples, including York, were restored with their economic privileges for one year in 1391. Throughout all these changes to their economic role, however, the home staples continued to operate as judicial franchises, and it is the legal dimension of the staples that is of particular interest here.

Two aspects of the legal machinery established in 1353 were of benefit to merchants. First, there was law merchant, according to which the staple officials were to judge all cases between merchants. Law merchant was not 'a definite code of laws, enacted and enforced by any sovereign body', but an internationally acknowledged 'composite corpus of the customs in general use among merchants', and its main advantage to merchants was summary justice.[91] It was predicated on the understanding that merchants were a transient group, so a court enforcing law merchant sat daily and offered justice more quickly than the more cumbersome procedures of the common law courts. In the words of the ordinance of the staple, law merchant was to be applied in the staple courts because, since 'Merchants may not often long tarry in one Place . . . We will and grant, that speedy Right be to them done from Day to Day, and from Hour to Hour.'[92] Secondly, there was the new debt procedure known as statute staple. M. M. Postan's work on credit instruments has done most to explain the importance of credit in medieval trade, while, among more recent scholarship on the subject, Maryanne Kowaleski has shown how improvements in the legal machinery enforcing contracts and obligations in late medieval Exeter 'made it much easier for creditors to compel debtors to pay up, thus reducing transaction costs'.[93] In 1353 the ordinance of the staple was significant in this respect because it empowered the mayor of the staple to seal recognizances of debts in order to guarantee the swift recovery of mercantile debts for merchants trading at the staple.

The practice of registering debts before an official was not new. Indeed, in the 1283 Statute of Acton Burnell and the 1285 Statute of Merchants Edward I had established statutory provision for the enforcement of the

---

[90] J. W. F. Hill, *Medieval Lincoln*, Cambridge 1948, 250.
[91] The main features of law merchant are explained in the editor's introduction to *The staple court books of Bristol*, ed. E. E. Rich (Bristol Record Society v, 1934), 31–8, quotation at p. 31.
[92] *SR* i. 340.
[93] M. M. Postan, 'Credit in medieval trade', *EcHR* i (1927–8), 234–61. The quotation is from Kowaleski, *Medieval Exeter*, 202.

payment of debts.[94] Debt registries were established in a number of towns and cities, including Bristol and York, and the mayors of the towns were given responsibility for enforcing statute merchant. The creditor and the debtor acknowledged the debt before the mayor and promised to repay the sum by a certain date before the recognizance was entered on a roll. One copy of the recognizance was given to the creditor and another was kept by the mayor, who was to seize the debtor and his goods if the terms of the contract were not upheld. In comparison with statute merchant the novelty of statute staple was two-fold. First, the cost of registering debts was cheaper;[95] secondly, the procedure for debt recovery under statute staple was much more efficient than statute merchant and allowed the creditor to secure repayment of his debts much more quickly.

Under statute merchant, if a debtor defaulted and his property was outside the mayor's jurisdiction, the creditor could deposit a certificate of his debt in chancery, which then ordered the local official in whose jurisdiction the debtor's property lay to imprison the debtor and to arrest and value his property by means of an inquest. The problem with this process was that the writ from chancery was returnable in the common law courts of common pleas and king's bench, where the legal machinery in cases of debt recovery was especially slow and delays in the enforcement of contracts common.[96] Under statute staple, if the debtor or his chattels and lands were not within the jurisdiction of the mayor of the staple, the creditor could inform chancery, which would then issue a writ to the official in question instructing him to seize the defaultor's goods that was returnable to chancery itself.[97] As W. M. Ormrod has demonstrated, this new debt procedure was intimately associated with the origin of the *sub pena* writ, a writ 'addressed and delivered directly to the defendant, thus avoiding the inefficiencies and delaying tactics of sheriffs and the immunities claimed by the bailiffs of liberties', by which the chancery could, if need be, summon the debtor in person on pain of a penalty usually of £100 in case of non-appearance.[98] At the same time, as the ordinance of the staple made explicit, under statute merchant, the debtor was given three months to sell his lands and tenements to pay his debt, whereas according to statute staple, the debtor's goods and his person were to be seized immediately and payment enforced.[99] It is little wonder that the mid-fourteenth century witnessed a dramatic fall in the number of recognizances enrolled under statute merchant

---

[94] *SR* i. 53–4, 98–100. For the operation of statute merchant see *The statute merchant roll of Coventry, 1392–1416*, ed. A. Beardwood (Dugdale Society xvii, 1939), pp. vii–xxvi.
[95] *SR* i. 337; *Select cases concerning the law merchant*, ed. C. Gross and H. Hall (Selden Society xxiii, xlvi, xlix, 1908–32), iii, pp. lxxxv.
[96] Kowaleski, *Medieval Exeter*, 215–16.
[97] *SR* i. 337.
[98] Ormrod, '*Sub pena* writ', 11, 14–15, quotation at p. 11.
[99] *SR* i. 337.

before the mayor of London, as the city's merchants turned instead to the new statutory provision available in Westminster's staple court.[100]

E. E. Rich has argued that the mayor and constables of the home staples had 'duties' which made them agents of the crown, but that they did not enforce royal policy, since they were elected by merchants in the staples rather than appointed by the crown.[101] None the less, inasmuch as the elections of the staple officials were officially ratified by the crown and, in 1390, a royal statute ordered the mayors and constables of the staples to swear an oath first to the king and then to their staple,[102] the operation of the staple system was dependent upon a partnership in government between the crown and the officials of the home staples. What was the nature of the relationship between the staple jurisdictions and the towns in which they were located? The question is important because the 1353 ordinance of the staple meant that the mayors of the staples were 'a new and important element in local government, and they ruled over mercantile communities which were now separated in many matters from the cities in which they lived', but it is not one that many historians have sought to answer.[103] The staples had a strong corporate character in the sense that all merchants, native and alien, who came to the staples for the purposes of trade, had to swear an oath of loyalty to the staple officials. Thus, in the same way in which individuals entering the civic franchise of Bristol and York had to swear an oath to the towns' mayors to maintain the liberties of the towns, so staple merchants swore to 'maintain . . . the Staple, and the Laws and Usages of the same, without Fraud or Deceit'.[104] The key difference between the staple and civic franchises lay, initially at least, in the 'extra-municipal' elements,[105] notably alien merchants and merchants from other towns, within the staple communities. In 1356 three foreign merchants, Peter de Striles, William Borel and Zanobius Forest, were among the electors of the officials of the Bristol staple, while Adam Pund, a burgess and merchant of Hull, was appointed a constable of the York staple in 1353 before his appointment as mayor of the Hull staple in March 1354 when a staple was established at the east-coast port.[106] In 1354 a disputed election at York came to the attention of the crown, in which the alien merchants elected William Graa while the English merchants chose Roger de Hovyngham. The king's council appointed Graa

---

100 Ormrod, '*Sub pena* writ', 14 n. 23; P. Nightingale, 'Monetary contraction and mercantile credit in later medieval England', *EcHR* 2nd ser. xliii (1990), 565.

101 E. E. Rich, 'The mayors of the staples', *CHJ* iv (1933), 123; *RP* ii. 250.

102 *SR* ii. 76.

103 The quotation is from Rich, 'Mayors of the staples', 125. The work of E. E. Rich is very much the exception.

104 For the civic oaths see *LRB* i. 51; YCA, D1, fo. 1r. For the staple oath see *SR* i. 341.

105 The expression belongs to Rich, 'Mayors of the staples', 129.

106 C 267/5/1; C 67/22, mems 25, 19. For Pund see the biography in Kermode, 'Merchants of York, Beverley and Hull', ii, appendix 4 (Hull).

to serve as mayor until Michaelmas and then appointed Roger de Normanvill to see out the remainder of the mayor's term of office.[107] Similarly, two Flemings from Bruges are known to have participated in the election of the mayor of the staple at Newcastle-upon-Tyne in 1354.[108]

It is clear, too, that the staple franchises overlapped with, and in some cases duplicated, the existing urban liberties. In the first place, at the request of the commons in parliament in 1354, the territorial boundaries of the staples were established within the walls of the towns and cities in which they were located.[109] At the same time, the mayor of the staple's jurisdiction in 1353 was so extensive as to include criminal jurisdiction and the right to hear and determine felonies committed within the bounds of the staple,[110] although this aspect of the staple franchise was removed in 1362 and the jurisdiction of the staple officials limited to the hearing of pleas of debt, covenant and contract between merchants and other cases involving merchandise.[111] Two other aspects of the staple jurisdiction were very similar to the existing civic legal provisions within Bristol and York. The first, as has already been explained, was the mayor's responsibility to enforce statute merchant and to supervise debt registration. Indeed, the way in which debt procedure under statute staple was made accessible to non-merchants as well as merchants after 1362 mirrored the development of recognizances under statute merchant, which were used increasingly for the enforcement of contracts rather than for the recording of mercantile debts.[112] Secondly, in Bristol, as in London, law merchant, the law of the staple court, was already enforced in one of the town's own courts, the Tolzey court, over which the town's bailiffs presided, and which had executed law merchant since the thirteenth century in cases of debt and breach of contract.[113]

Perhaps unsurprisingly, there are signs that serious tensions quickly developed between the staple franchises governed by the mayors of the staple and the urban liberties of Bristol and York ruled by the mayors of the towns. In Bristol conflict took the form of a personal attack on the mayor of the town by the mayor of the staple. In May 1354 a commission of oyer and terminer headed by Sir Thomas de Bradeston,[114] a Gloucestershire landowner and a king's banneret, was appointed to inquire into an incident in Bristol 'touching the evildoers who assaulted Richard le Spicer', the mayor of the town, who, 'as he was attending to the arrest of some disturbers of the peace in the town . . . prevented him from arresting them and doing justice on them

---

[107] C 267/8/83; C 67/22, mem. 18.
[108] *Staple court books*, 28.
[109] *RP* ii. 261–2.
[110] *SR* i. 336.
[111] *RP* ii. 271.
[112] *RP* ii. 270–1; *Statute merchant roll of Coventry*, pp. xx–xxii.
[113] For the history and jurisdiction of Bristol's Tolzey court see *GRB* iv. 6–14, 33–46. Law merchant was administered in London in the mayor's court: *Staple court books*, 37–8.
[114] For Bradeston see Saul, *Knights and esquires*, 76.

according to his office'. The malefactors had imprisoned the mayor and 'by duress compelled him to renounce his office', before electing John de Cobyndon in his place.[115] Cobyndon was elected mayor of the staple a few months later.[116] Judicial proceedings of the commission of oyer and terminer over which Bradeston presided commenced on 11 July 1354, continued until around 4 August 1354, before reopening on 3 March 1355 and terminating just over two weeks later.[117] John le Spicer, the mayor of the staple at the time of the assault on the mayor of Bristol and the first to have been appointed in Bristol when the system of home staples was introduced in 1353, was subsequently indicted before the justices of oyer and terminer for a series of offences: these included extortion and bribery, in addition to 'having confederated with others to expel Richard le Spicer, of Bristol, then mayor, from his office'.[118] The events in Bristol of the mid-1350s require further consideration in order to elucidate the precise causes of the internal disorder of which the expulsion of the town's mayor was one episode, but there are good grounds for thinking that it was in part a consequence of a jurisdictional dispute between the staple and urban liberties. First, Richard le Spicer was in the process of 'attaching malefactors against the peace' when he was beaten, forced to take refuge in his own home, and driven from office;[119] and secondly, after his imprisonment, Richard bound himself over 'by a writing obligatory' for £800.[120] It is possible that the mayor of the staple, John le Spicer, had forced the town's mayor to seal a recognizance under statute staple, thus abusing the responsibilities with which he had been entrusted by the crown.

In York, too, the home staple was, at least in the short term, a disruptive influence on the city's internal politics. Here tensions crystallised around the figures of John de Langton and John de Gysburn, who became involved in a long-running conflict. What was at stake in this factional dispute? The quarrel between Langton and Gysburn, as Edward Miller noted, was not just about personalities; it was also about 'competition for the control of the city government between the old ruling group, represented by Langton, and the new class of rich merchants', represented by Gysburn.[121] The Langton family were property-owners whose wealth and political importance in civic affairs were based on their landed estates within and without York rather than on

---

115 *CPR, 1354–8*, 69–70. Bristol deeds to which Cobyndon was a witness indicate that he was definitely mayor of Bristol between February and May 1354: J. Latimer, 'The maire of Bristowe is kalendar: its list of civic officers collated with contemporary legal MSS', *TBGAS* xxvi (1903), 125.
116 See appendix below.
117 The work of the commission in Bristol is in JUST 1/772/1–4.
118 *CPR, 1354–8*, 180.
119 *CPR, 1354–8*, 181.
120 *CPR, 1354–8*, 70.
121 Miller, 'Medieval York', 81.

participation in trade.[122] The Langtons were 'rural *rentiers*' rather than overseas merchants.[123] The roots of the rivalry between Langton and Gysburn lay
in the changing nature of the English economy, which saw the rise of a native
cloth-making industry and the dramatic expansion of foreign trade in wool
and cloth by English merchants. In York these economic developments, it
has been argued, transformed the complexion of the city's ruling elite after
1363.[124] Prior to this date the Langton family had been the dominant force in
York politics: John de Langton and his father, Nicholas, were elected to the
mayoralty of York twenty-nine times between 1322 and 1363, while John
alone held the office of mayor continuously from 1352 to 1363.[125] The
increasing prosperity of 'the new class of rich merchants' in the city, whose
wealth was derived from overseas trade in the export of wool and cloth
through the port of Hull, led first to political conflict in York and then to the
political ascendancy of these merchants in the city.[126] After 1363 a transformation took place in the 'nature and personnel of the city's ruling élite', and
when the dominance of the mayoralty by the Langton family came to an end,
'nearly every mayor of York', in the words of R. B. Dobson, 'can be proved to
have been heavily involved in overseas trade from Hull'.[127] There is much to
commend this economic interpretation, not least because it fits into a wider
pattern of urban development. Richard Britnell, for instance, found that the
growth of Colchester's cloth trade meant that the town's merchants
'increased in numbers and wealth to the point of taking the leading share in
government', with the result that the period after 1350 saw the 'establishment of a new urban élite' in the town.[128] The problem with this analysis is
that it ignores the means by which York's merchants assumed political
authority in the city. The reason for the growing ascendancy of the
merchants in York's civic government can be found in the crown's policy
towards the staple.

The first evidence of trouble between Langton and Gysburn was in
September 1357 when John de Langton, then mayor of York, rejected John
de Gysburn's election as bailiff on the grounds that he had recently subverted
the liberties, laws and customs of the city and acted against his oath as a
freeman.[129] Fourteen members of the original electoral panel of twenty-four
were dismissed so that a new election could take place with the remaining

---

[122] Ibid. 71.
[123] Dobson, 'Risings', 119.
[124] For the economic background see Nightingale, 'Capitalists, crafts and constitutional
change', 3–35, and Bartlett, 'Expansion and decline of York', 20–7. The political consequences are outlined in Miller, 'Medieval York', 84; Dobson, 'Risings', 119; and Kermode,
Medieval merchants, 25, 54, 56.
[125] YCA, D1, fos 4v–6r.
[126] Miller, 'Medieval York', 81.
[127] Dobson, 'Risings', 119.
[128] Britnell, *Colchester*, 114.
[129] YCA, D1, fo. 313v.

ten members. The exact nature of Gysburn's offence against the civic franchise was not made explicit in the city's record of the election, but it was
probably associated with the York staple, for he was one of its most prominent
merchants. In 1358, one year after his failed attempt to become bailiff of the
city, Gysburn was elected mayor of the staple, an office he held without interruption until 1363.[130] Moreover, of the fourteen dismissed members of the
electoral panel that had chosen Gysburn in 1357, half were past, present or
future officials of the York staple, including William Graa, Walter de
Kelstern, Hugh de Miton, Robert de Howom, William de Beverlay, John de
Rypon and Roger de Hovyngham, who was elected mayor of the York staple
in 1354 but replaced, on the crown's orders, by William Graa and then by
Roger de Normanvill. None of the ten remaining electors ever held staple
office.[131]

Initially a destabilising factor in York's internal politics, the staple helped
to transform the nature of the city's ruling elite. Specifically, the staple
allowed the city's merchants to exercise authority in York at a time when
John de Langton monopolised the mayoralty, and it is likely that they used
their newfound authority to pressure Langton. In 1363 the series of domestic
staples came to an end and a staple was established at Calais.[132] The sudden
loss of authority resulting from the closure of York's staple encouraged the
merchants to challenge Langton for the mayor's office. In February 1364 John
de Acastre, previously a constable of the staple for three consecutive years,
was elected mayor in what appears to have been a highly contested election:
in addition to the mayor's annual fee, he was granted a conditional bonus of
£20 'in return for his good behaviour'.[133] Doubts as to Acastre's suitability for
office might have arisen from the disorderly conduct of the mayoral candidates preceding the mayoral election. Subsequent entries in the mayoral
calendar recording similar conditional payments suggest that the next few
elections were equally fractious, probably as the merchants sought to thwart
Langton's attempts to recapture office. In 1365 Richard de Wateby, one of
the dismissed electors in 1357, was elected mayor, in 1366 Roger de
Hovyngham, another dismissed elector, was appointed mayor of the city, and
in 1367 William Graa was elected mayor only six months after his term as
mayor of the staple had finished in August 1366.[134] Staple office thus
provided a point of entry into the highest civic office in the city and experi-

---

130 See appendix below.
131 See YCA, D1, fo. 313v; C 67/22, passim.
132 *Staple court books*, 64.
133 C 67/22, mems 16–18; YCA, D1, fo. 6r: 'et in recessu officii sui communitas ei
concessit pro suo bono gestu xx li'.
134 YCA, D1, fo. 6v: Wateby, Hovyngham and Graa all received additional remuneration
on condition of their good behaviour. Wateby was given an extra £40 and there seems to
have been serious disturbances surrounding his election in February 1365, which was
delayed for a day and a half: CPR, 1364–7, 208.

ence in the staple allowed the merchants to undermine Langton's position and to gain control of civic government.

The conflict between Gysburn and Langton continued into the early 1370s and the two were mayoral candidates at the centre of the disturbances leading up to the February 1372 election. The unrest came to the attention of the king, who ordered the city's bailiffs to let neither Langton nor Gysburn 'be mayor nor meddle in such election'.[135] Despite the royal edict, Gysburn was elected to the mayoralty for the second year running, an indication perhaps of his standing among the merchants of the city. Only a week after his first election as mayor on 3 February 1371, and barely two years since the removal of York's status as a staple town, new civic ordinances were drawn up for the safekeeping of the rolls of statute merchant in the mayor's chamber on Ouse Bridge. In the past the rolls had remained in the private possession of the mayor of the city, even after his departure from public office, leading to loss and damage. Henceforth, all who had occupied the mayoralty were to bring – in person or, in the event of their death, represented by their heirs and executors – the rolls of statute merchant which they had in their possession for deposit in the mayor's chamber on Ouse Bridge, where they were to remain in the city's treasury in perpetuity. Meanwhile, all future mayors of the city, once their term of office had ended, were to leave their copies of the statutory bonds registered in their presence in the treasury.[136] Gysburn sought to ensure that the city's merchants would not suffer through the loss of statute staple by improving the city's existing facilities for debt enforcement in order to bring 'speedy remedy' to the parties concerned.

Were the tensions evident in Bristol and York arising from the introduction of home staples in 1353 peculiar to these two urban communities? Pamela Nightingale's detailed work on the tumultuous events in London of the later fourteenth century has shown how the city's internal politics in this period were largely the politics of the staple. In particular, the fate of the foreign staple after 1363 became one of the key issues dividing London's civic elite between the staplers, notably members of the grocers' company, who wanted the staple to remain at Calais at all costs, and those merchants whose commercial interests lay elsewhere.[137] In contrast, with the exception of the studies of E. E. Rich from the 1930s, the political impact of the system of home staples on the towns and cities in which they were fixed in 1353 has been neglected by historians, and there is considerable scope for further work on the subject.

In Bristol the organisation of the staple was absorbed into the town's governing structure in 1379, when the mayor of the town became *ex officio* mayor of the staple. According to Robert Ricart, Bristol's town clerk writing in the late fifteenth century, on the annual election of the town's mayor 'the olde

---

[135] CCR, 1369–74, 275.
[136] YMB i. 12–13.
[137] Nightingale, 'Capitalists, crafts and constitutional change', 3–35.

Maire' delivered to 'the new maire the kynges Swerde, and his hatte, and the casket with the seale of office, the seale of the Statute of the Staple, the seale of the Statute merchant', and on the third day after Michaelmas, the mayor received the commission of the staple on which he took his oath.[138] What occurred in 1379 was a redefinition and a simplification of the relationship between the staple franchise and the urban liberty of Bristol. While Rich is right to point out that Bristol's staple court continued to operate throughout the fourteenth and fifteenth centuries and into the early modern period administered by its own officials and procedures and with its own records,[139] civic authority was also extended, for the mayor of the town was now given formal control of the staple court and the accompanying valuable legal privilege of statute staple. To all intents and purposes, the staple court had become part of the judicial apparatus of civic government: hence the copying of a treatise on law merchant and the entering of the 'usages' of the staple court in the Little Red Book, the main record of civic government in the fourteenth century.[140]

Bristol was not exceptional in this regard because very quickly after 1353 the staple organisations came to be dominated by members of the civic elites of the towns and cities in which they were fixed. The mayors of the Westminster staple in the fourteenth century, for example, included the likes of Adam Fraunceys, John Pyel, Nicholas Brembre and John Hadley, all London aldermen, while William Walworth held the office continuously from 1369 until his death in 1385, during which time he was also twice mayor of the city of London.[141] Indeed, in Bristol and York it was fairly common for individuals to hold civic and staple office simultaneously.[142] In York William Frankissh, elected a constable of the staple in 1358 and 1359, was made a bailiff of the city in 1359, while John de Knapton, a constable in 1360 and 1361, was elected bailiff in 1361. In Bristol, even before 1379, Geoffrey Beauflour, a constable in 1357, was also elected bailiff in the same year, and William de Combe held the staple office of constable concurrently with the office of bailiff of the town in 1376. The same pattern was also true of the mayoral offices. Reginald le Frensshe held the two offices simultaneously in 1356 and 1358, and so did John de Stoke in 1365 and 1367, Walter de Derby in 1364 and 1368, and Walter de Frompton in 1374. The way in which the holding of staple office coincided with the holding of civic office suggests that there was a conscious attempt by the civic elites of Bristol and York to resolve potential jurisdictional conflicts by vesting similar judicial responsibilities in one

---

138 Ricart, *Maire of Bristowe is kalendar*, 74, 76.
139 The staple court books of Bristol, edited by Rich, are extant from 1509.
140 The Little Red Book, 1344–1574, BRO, 04718, fos 22r–30v (printed in *LRB* i. 57–85), 49r–50r (calendared in *LRB* i. 103).
141 Rich, 'Mayors of the staples', 126–7, 130, and his 'Lists of officials of the staple of Westminster', *CHJ* iv (1933), 192–3.
142 For what follows see appendix below.

person which, in the case of Bristol, was formally acknowledged from 1379 when the offices of mayor of the staple and mayor of the town were merged. In personal and practical terms the staple franchise and civic government were one and the same.

The main constitutional significance of the system of home staples, according to E. E. Rich, lay in the replacement of a single, national estate of merchants in the first half of the fourteenth century, by 'a series of municipal "Estates of Merchants"' composed of alien and English merchants.[143] The evidence from Bristol's returns to the crown notifying the chancellor of the annual election of its staple officials – important because, along with those of Newcastle-upon-Tyne, they are the only returns to provide the names of electors – suggests that alien merchants disappeared very quickly from the staples.[144] Indeed, the lists of the electors of the staple officials extant between 1356 and 1371 confirm that only in 1356, 1359 and 1362 was the participation of alien merchants in a staple election noted, and only in 1356 were the names of foreign merchants actually given.[145] The returns indicate, instead, that the electors were drawn essentially from the civic officeholding elite of Bristol and that the staple was dominated by a very small group of individuals. Richard le Spicer, Edmund Blanket, Walter de Frompton, John de Stoke, Richard de Brompton, Robert de Cheddre, Walter de Derby, Ellis Spelly, William de Somerwell, William Canynges and John Bathe were among the most frequent attenders of staple elections and all were mayors of Bristol.[146] In fact, between 1353 and 1403 forty-seven men were elected to a total of 144 offices. Twenty-six individuals were staple officials on one occasion, which means that only twenty-one men held 118 of the 144 offices. Forty-two of the forty-seven men occupied office in the staple prior to, or concurrently with, civic office-holding, while the office of mayor was monopolised by the likes of Walter de Frompton, Walter de Derby and John de Stoke, who, between them, were elected to the mayoralty of the staple every year between 1362 and 1380 without interruption.

In theory, foreign merchants should have benefited most from the establishment of home staples in 1353. First, they were given a monopoly of the wool export trade, and secondly, the staples were to be ruled by certain forms of mercantile justice that should have privileged them. These included law merchant and the right to have a jury composed entirely of foreign merchants if a case was between aliens, and one made up of half alien merchants and half English merchants in the event of legal action between alien and denizen.[147]

[143] *Staple court books*, 27.
[144] For these returns see C 267/5/1–11; SC 1/40/173. They are printed as an appendix in *Overseas trade of Bristol*, 297–302.
[145] C 267/5/1, 4, 6.
[146] For their experience of civic office see appendix below.
[147] SR i. 336.

Their wool monopoly, however, was lost within a few years,[148] and in the absence of the staple court records of Bristol and York, the electoral returns of the Bristol staple suggest that the legal position of alien merchants within the staples was greatly inferior to that of native merchants. As Alice Beardwood noted, the 1353 ordinance of the staple, while it gave certain legal privileges to alien merchants, did not actually create special courts for foreign merchants, and the legal facilities that were established were to be of benefit to English as well as alien traders.[149] In the case of Bristol the staple became part of the mayor's jurisdiction, while the staple and, in particular, the staple court presided over by the mayor and constables, provided a mechanism by which the civic government of Bristol could exercise authority over alien merchants, who were seen both as a transient group which needed to be contained and as a source of competition for Bristol merchants in the whole-sale and retail trades. In the same way in which the town's rulers sought to regulate the activities of foreign merchants coming to the town by imposing restrictions on the amount of time which they could spend there, and limiting their freedom of movement generally, the staple court extended the capacity of the town's civic officials to supervise the activities of these foreign merchants.[150]

Moreover, the staples in Bristol and York, dominated as they were by the merchants of the two towns, also provided local elites with further opportunities for officeholding. As Susan Reynolds suggested, the staple courts established in 1353 'seem to have become gradually integrated into local merchant life', giving 'leading townsmen further scope for work and influence'.[151] Francis Hill's work on medieval Lincoln has shown similarly how the occupation of the mayoralty of the Lincoln staple in the second half of the fourteenth century became part of a wider career pattern in royal service for the handful of the city's merchants who held the post.[152] In York, too, John de Gysburn and his contemporaries among the city's mercantile community readily seized the opportunities presented by the staple that were denied them within the existing civic hierarchy.

The home staples were also significant for the way in which they distinguished merchants as a discrete and privileged element within urban society. The facilities provided by the home staples were, at the outset, designed

---

[148] In 1357 English merchants were allowed to purchase licences to export wool, although they had to pay the alien rate of customs duties: Ormrod, *Edward III*, 193.

[149] A. Beardwood, *Alien merchants in England, 1350 to 1377: their legal and economic position*, Cambridge, Mass. 1931, 77.

[150] In the 1188 charter granted to Bristol, alien merchants were only to stay in the town for forty days, but in undated civic ordinances, probably of the fourteenth century, the time limit was reduced to three days: *Bristol charters, 1155–1373*, 10–11; *LRB* ii. 225–6. For the system of hosting alien merchants in English towns and cities see, for example, Beardwood, *Alien merchants*, 34.

[151] Reynolds, *English medieval towns*, 178.

[152] Hill, *Medieval Lincoln*, 249–50.

solely for the benefit of merchants, and the staples themselves were ruled according to mercantile forms of justice embodied in the set of customs known as law merchant, which was of particular use to those individuals engaged in long distance trade. Even after 1362, when staple justice became available to non-merchants as well as merchants, there persisted the idea that the staples were comprised of local communities of merchants and that membership of the staple was a valuable privilege.[153] The election returns of Bristol, for example, articulated this corporate mercantile identity. The 1364, 1365, 1367, 1368 and 1371 elections of staple officials, returned to chancery in the name of individual electors, were made 'by the common assent of us and of other merchants of the said staple' ('per communem assensum nostrum et aliorum dictae stapulae mercatorum').[154] The return of the 1372 election, the first in which the practice of recording the names of the individual merchants of the Bristol staple responsible for the election of the staple officials was abandoned, was simply addressed in the name of the 'mayor, constables and community of merchants' ('maior constabularii ac communitas mercatorum') of the staple.[155]

Some historians such as R. H. Hilton and Heather Swanson have seen class conflict between artisans and mercantile elites as a perennial feature of urban life in later medieval England, with merchants seeking to exploit craftsmen economically, financially and politically, while the members of the crafts struggled to resist this exploitation.[156] The discussion of York's internal politics in the previous chapter showed that, despite the unequal distribution of political power in the city, the exercise of government was, in practice, dependent on negotiation among those who had a stake in the city's governance, and that relations between the civic elite and the commons were not inherently antagonistic.[157] None the less, the system of home staples instituted in 1353 placed great emphasis on the importance of mercantile status, just as had been the case when domestic staples had been established in 1326. Indeed, as Pamela Nightingale has recently shown, many of the gentry wool producers of the south-west, as they took their wool to the port of Bristol for sale, began to describe themselves as merchants in certificates of debt sealed under statute merchant in the mayor's court of Bristol in the 1330s. 'Since the staple ordinances of 1326 referred to "the staple of merchants"', according to Nightingale, 'local knights and gentry had good reason to insist on their mercantile status in the face of likely hostility from the citizens of Bristol'.[158]

---

[153] Rich, 'Mayors of the staples', 130.
[154] C 267/5/7–8; SC 1/40/173; C 267/5/10–11.
[155] C 267/5/12.
[156] Hilton, *English and French towns*, ch. vi; Swanson, *Medieval artisans*, ch. ix.
[157] For a similar argument about the nature of Norwich's government see B. McRee, 'Peacemaking and its limits in late medieval Norwich', *EHR* cix (1994), 831–66.
[158] Nightingale, 'Knights and merchants', 43–5, quotation at p. 45.

One consequence was that in Bristol, as the staple organisation became absorbed into the government of the town, there were efforts to restrict membership of the civic franchise specifically to merchants. In 1367, under the mayoralty of John de Stoke, a prominent member of the Bristol staple who had just finished his second term as mayor of the staple in the previous year, new civic ordinances were issued concerning the types of people who could now be admitted into the freedom of the town.[159] From 1344 onwards no one was to be admitted to the liberty in future unless he was 'of free condition, good and honest report' and could 'produce two good and lawful burgesses to testify that his estate and condition are good and honest'.[160] At this date admission to the freedom seems to have been a prerequisite for membership of the town's crafts.[161] In 1367, however, it was decided that no one wishing to enter the freedom of the town by purchase could do so unless he was 'a merchant known as a man of good report and honest conversation' ('sil ne soit marchaund conu homme de bone fame et honeste conuersacion') and unless he paid at least £10. This ordinance was an extraordinarily explicit statement of the authority Bristol's merchants exercised over the town, setting merchants apart from craftsmen as a special and privileged group involved essentially in wholesale trade.[162] The mayor was made personally responsible for ensuring that the sum of £10 charged for the civic franchise was neither reduced nor cancelled, for in such an eventuality he had to make up the deficit from his own pocket, and the mayor's oath was amended to include such a provision.[163]

The fee of £10 was also a high charge compared to the cost of entering other urban franchises. For example, the usual fee in Hull in the fourteenth and fifteenth centuries was £2, while entry to Colchester's franchise was much cheaper to secure, varying from 2s. to 13s. 4d. in the fourteenth century. In London the cost of admission to the freedom by redemption was fixed at £3 in 1364, but this was seen as too prohibitive, forcing 'many to leave the City', so it was decided that people should pay what they could afford at the discretion of the aldermen and chamberlain.[164] Indeed, after 1367 Bristol's freedom organisation was made even more exclusive and expensive than that which operated in the city of Exeter in the second half of the fourteenth century. Maryanne Kowaleski has described that as 'highly selective' compared to other provin-

---

159 *LRB* ii. 47–9.
160 *LRB* i. 36–7.
161 See, for example, *LRB* ii. 4.
162 Here is evidence of the transition in the meaning of the word 'merchant', from an earlier period when it 'was used very widely to include even retail traders', to the later Middle Ages, when the word 'was usually restricted to those primarily engaged in wholesale trade': Reynolds, *English medieval towns*, 75.
163 *LRB* ii. 47–8; i. 46.
164 K. J. Allison, 'Medieval Hull', in VCH, *Yorkshire: East Riding: Hull*, Oxford 1969, 37; Britnell, *Colchester*, 36; *Letter-book G*, 180, 211–12.

cial urban franchises, and costing between £1 and £5 to enter.[165] In Bristol the distinction between freemen and others within the town was somewhat blurred by the existence of a group known as 'portmen' who belonged to an organisation called the 'portmanry' and who bridged the divide between fully enfranchised burgesses and non-freemen. In 1367 they were described as 'all those who are not burgesses and wish to trade or exercise their craft within the town and have not the means or will not pay the said sum of £10 in order to be enfranchised'.[166] They paid a fine according to what they could afford and according to the judgement of Bristol's mayor and stewards, but they remained a less privileged group within Bristol than the town's burgesses. In a 1449–50 ordinance of the town's common council the portmen were described as those who 'bi ne Selle in no wyse within the saide towne as a burgeys doth'.[167] Although the 1367 ordinance restricting the franchise to merchants and to those able to pay the £10 fine was subsequently erased, probably because it was deemed unenforceable in an urban environment which included many newly prosperous craftsmen, in its deliberate exclusion of artisans from economic and political power the ordinance is evidence of the development of a mercantile 'oligarchy' in the true sense of the word.[168] By the mid-1360s, then, the appearance of the staple in Bristol had sharpened distinctions between Bristol's merchants and their fellow townspeople sufficiently to encourage Bristol's rulers to equate burgess status solely with the occupation of merchant. In both Bristol and York the policy of home staples thus facilitated the process by which civic authority came to be concentrated in the hands of a relatively small mercantile elite.

Some of the merchants involved in the operation of the home staples in Bristol and York were also instrumental in the organisation of the Calais staple in 1363. In the later 1350s the king came under pressure to open the export trade to English as well as alien merchants. In 1357 native merchants were allowed to export wool in return for special licences and on condition that they paid the alien rate of customs; and in 1359 all wool exports had to pass through a new staple at Bruges.[169] In 1361 a merchant assembly composed of forty-five merchants from the home staples, including six from York and three from Bristol, was summoned to discuss the removal of the wool staple to Calais.[170] Further consultation took place in the 1362 parliament, when the proposal to fix the staple at Calais was presented to the

[165] Kowaleski, 'Exeter in the late fourteenth century', 186, and *Medieval Exeter*, 98 n. 82.
[166] *LRB* ii. 48. Other towns and cities such as Canterbury had a similar two-tier system based on the payment of a small fine in order to engage in trade: Goldberg, *Women, work, and life cycle*, 50.
[167] *GRB* ii. 133.
[168] *LRB* ii. 48. For evidence of the increasing wealth of Bristol's craftsmen in the post-plague economy see p. 197 below. For the debate see Reynolds, 'Medieval urban history', 14–23, and S. H. Rigby, 'Urban "oligarchy" ', 62–86.
[169] Ormrod, *Edward III*, 193.
[170] *CCR, 1360–4*, 267.

commons. It is clear from the parliamentary record that there were differences of opinion on the subject, for the knights of the shire said that they had spoken to several merchants about the proposal, some of whom had said that it was a good idea and 'others the opposite'. The shire knights asked that, since the matter was of special concern to merchants, the merchants should be consulted.[171] Neither the identity of these merchants nor what they said is known, but the staple was removed to Calais by royal ordinance and a 'new company of merchants' composed of twenty-six men was established to govern the town and the merchandise sold there on the king's behalf.[172] The twenty-six merchants comprised two mayors and twenty-four aldermen appointed by the king and council. A total of six came from London, and both mayors, John de Wroth and John de Wesenham, were London merchants. Two of the aldermen, Walter de Frompton and Reginald le Frensshe, were merchants from Bristol, and two, John de Gysburn and Roger de Hovyngham, were merchants from York: all had also been elected to office in their home staples.[173]

To George Unwin, the aim of the removal of the staple to Calais was to re-establish 'a system of monopolies' which could provide revenue to the crown in return for a monopoly of the wool trade.[174] In contrast, T. H. Lloyd argued that the company of twenty-six merchants was not in fact granted a monopoly of the wool trade and that its main purpose was to govern the town. Indeed, 'the principal motive' behind the creation of the 1363 company, according to Lloyd, was to make 'the town financially independent of the Crown' and to meet the town's expenses from a duty on wool coming to Calais.[175] There is much to be said for this argument, not least because it helps to explain the inclusion among the twenty-four aldermen of two Bristol merchants, whose trading interests lay essentially in cloth rather than wool. Moreover, Lloyd's thesis explains the crown's dissolution of the company in 1364 because of antagonism between the company and merchants trading at the staple.[176] The wool exporters were hostile to the monopolistic activities of the mayors and aldermen who were accused by the parliamentary commons of fixing wool prices and of imposing on each sack of wool coming to Calais a 40d. duty for their own profit.[177] A commission was appointed to

[171] RP ii. 269.
[172] The reference to the 'new company of merchants' is from a common petition of 1363: ibid. ii. 276. For the charter of liberties to the syndicate of merchants see Foedera (1816–69), iii/2, 690–1.
[173] See appendix below.
[174] Unwin, 'Estate of merchants', 244.
[175] Lloyd, English wool trade, 211.
[176] For what follows see R. L. Baker, 'The government of Calais in 1363', in W. C. Jordan and others (eds), Order and innovation in the Middle Ages: essays in honor of J. R. Strayer, Princeton 1976, 207–14.
[177] RP ii. 276.

investigate these claims and in 1365 separate provision was made for the governance of the town and of the staple of Calais.[178]

None the less, while Lloyd is right to point out that this new system of government at Calais 'was neither the company of 1363 nor the fifteenth-century fellowship of the staple',[179] it cannot be doubted that the long-term aim of the removal of the staple to Calais by the crown in 1363 was to return to the monopolistic practices of the 1330s and 1340s. Given what had happened in the past when the crown had fixed the staple overseas, it was inevitable that the Calais staple would become dominated by a small group of staple merchants.[180] In 1377 the merchants of the Calais staple, including a group of York merchants such as Robert and Thomas de Howom, lent £10,000 to the crown in return for a monopoly of the wool trade.[181] Ultimately, it was this shared fiscal interest in the wool trade between the crown, on the one hand, and the leading wool merchants from London and the east-coast provincial towns such as York, on the other, which explains the creation of the Calais staple.

Diplomacy

In the same way that the crown was reliant on urban elites to collect the king's taxes, both direct and indirect, to lend money and ships, and to implement its policies relating to the staple, the crown also turned to merchants to negotiate commercial treatises overseas. Although there is evidence of growing professionalism among English diplomats from the second half of the thirteenth century, permanent embassies overseas did not develop until the second half of the fifteenth century, so the crown relied, instead, on an *ad hoc* system in which embassies were sent abroad for a specific purpose and then returned to England on completion of their mission.[182] Thus, merchants were sometimes employed on diplomatic missions for their specialised knowledge and experience in commerce in order to 'negotiate trade agreements or to settle maritime disputes'.[183] In 1372 the Bristol merchant, John de Stoke, was appointed to royal embassies to negotiate with representatives of the count of Flanders and of the Flemish towns of Bruges, Ypres and Ghent. In 1388 Thomas Graa of York was entrusted with a diplomatic mission to negotiate

---

[178] *Foedera* (1816–69), iii/2, 768–9.
[179] Lloyd, *English wool trade*, 214.
[180] Ormrod, 'English crown and the customs', 38.
[181] Lloyd, *English wool trade*, 226; CCR, 1377–81, 30–1; CFR, 1377–83, 41–2. For Robert de Howom see also J. N. Bartlett, 'Robert Holme, citizen and merchant of York', *Journal of the Bradford Textile Society* xcvii (1952–3), 97–100.
[182] C. Allmand, *The Hundred Years War: England and France at war*, c. 1300–c. 1450, Cambridge 1988, 116–17. See also H. S. Lucas, 'The machinery of diplomatic intercourse', in Willard and others, *English government at work*, i. 300–31.
[183] C. Allmand, 'Diplomacy in late-medieval England', *HT* xvii (1967), 551.

for peace with representatives of the Hanse. The crown's commercial policies were, as the foregoing discussion of the operation of the customs system and the staple has shown, the product of interaction and negotiation between urban elites and the royal government. The embassies involving Stoke and Graa are instructive because they suggest that, while the merchants were appointed by the crown to act on its behalf, the royal government was also concerned with the economic interests of its urban and mercantile subjects overseas. Like the customs and the staple, however, they also reveal the extent to which royal commercial policies were influenced by the interplay of the crown's political, diplomatic and fiscal interests.

The ties between England and Flanders were both economic and diplomatic.[184] Economically, the three great Flemish weaving towns of Bruges, Ypres and Ghent were dependent on the supply of English wool for the production of cloth, while England's economy continued to be largely reliant on the export of wool to Flanders despite the crown's efforts to promote a domestic cloth industry. Flanders also had a political significance to the English crown as an ally in the Hundred Years War. Political loyalties could be forged on the strength of these economic ties, and it is for this reason that, at the beginning of the war against France in the 1330s, Edward III banned the export of English wool to the Flemish towns so as to force Flanders into an alliance with England.

The resumption of the Hundred Years War in 1369 placed enormous strains on Anglo-Flemish relations. Essentially, the English crown hoped to maintain Flemish neutrality and to prevent a Franco-Flemish alliance, a prospect which looked increasingly likely when the count of Flanders, Louis de Mâle, reneged on a promise to marry his daughter, Margaret, to Edward III's son, Edmund of Langley; Margaret was married to Philip duke of Burgundy, the brother of the French king, Charles V, in 1369.[185] At the same time, there was the problem of piracy between England and Flanders (a separate issue in itself), which threatened to undermine completely any attempts to secure Flemish neutrality.[186] Between 1369 and 1371 English attacks on Flemish shipping and Flemish reprisals on English vessels spiralled out of control to such an extent that the St Albans chronicler, Thomas Walsingham, was to describe 1372 as the year of a 'naval war between the English and Flemish' ('bellum navale inter Anglicos et Flandrenses').[187] English attacks might well have been triggered by the determination of the Flemish towns to continue to trade with France. Certainly, this is what Edward III's council claimed

---

[184] A good introduction to the subject of Anglo-Flemish relations is provided by C. M. Barron, 'Introduction: England and the Low Countries, 1327–1477', in C. M. Barron and N. Saul (eds), *England and the Low Countries in the late Middle Ages*, Stroud 1995, 1–28.
[185] Ibid. 4.
[186] D. Nicholas, 'The English trade at Bruges in the last years of Edward III', *JMH* v (1979), 34–5; Lloyd, *English wool trade*, 218–19.
[187] Thomas Walsingham, *Historia anglicana*, ed. H. T. Riley (RS, 1863–4), i. 313.

when it confirmed a peace treaty with the envoys of the count of Flanders and of the towns of Bruges, Ghent and Ypres in 1370.[188] Indeed, according to the terms of the treaty, Flemish merchants could only trade with France and Castile if the merchandise was not of a broadly military nature, such as armour, artillery or victuals.

Incidents of piracy continued, however, and attacks were made on English wine convoys.[189] In 1371 an English royal fleet attacked and destroyed twenty-two Flemish vessels in the Bay of Bourgneuf, and the crown ordered the mayors and bailiffs of Bristol, York, and several east-coast ports to arrest the Flemish merchants trading there and to seize their goods. The Flemish responded by confiscating English property at Sluys. It was in this context that, one year later, John de Stoke of Bristol was sent on two missions to Calais to treat for peace with the representatives of the count of Flanders and of the towns of Bruges, Ypres and Ghent.[190] The embassies were composed of Henry Lord Scrope, a knight banneret and former governor of Calais, Hugh Segrave, a knight, John Shepey, a clerk, and three merchants, John Pyel and Adam de Bury of London and John de Stoke of Bristol.[191] Stephen O'Connor, in his study of the royal service of two London merchants, John Pyel and Adam Frounceys, has suggested that 'Pyel's engagement in what were probably crucial talks with important allies during renewed conflict with the French was a sign of a closer alliance with members of the court party at this time',[192] though it is doubtful if this were also true of John de Stoke, who would have been familiar to the crown from his occupation of Bristol's mayoralty in 1365 and 1367 and his service in the Bristol customs from 1365 to 1375, but whose personal connections with the court are not known.[193]

In fact, Stoke's appointment owed much to his mercantile interests and those of his fellow merchants in Bristol. The avowed purpose of the diplomatic mission which left for Calais in February 1372 was to deal with breaches of the 1370 treaty between England and Flanders caused by the continuing problem of piracy,[194] and in April 1372 an agreement was reached in which the 1370 peace treaty was confirmed. Property seized by both sides was to be released immediately and a day in June was established for hearing individual piracy claims.[195] Stoke was also present at this second round of negotiations to examine the claims of Flemish and English merchants;[196] and

---

188 *Foedera* (1816–69), iii/2, 898.
189 For what follows see Nicholas, 'English trade at Bruges', 35.
190 For the financial account of Stoke's missions see E 364/5, rot. 8r.
191 *Foedera* (1816–69), iii/2, 932, 945; E 364/5, rot. 8r.
192 O'Connor, 'Finance, diplomacy and politics', 31.
193 See appendix below.
194 *Foedera* (1816–69), iii/2, 932.
195 Ibid. iii/2, 938–9, 945. For the terms of the agreement see *Letter-book* G, 282.
196 The claims and counter-claims of Flemish and English merchants are in E 30/1271; E 30/1635; E 30/1275–6; E 30/1665; E 30/1618; E 30/1226.

as a royal envoy, he was paid expenses and wages of £44 13s. 4d. for the total of eighty-four days which he spent away on royal business.[197] In short, Stoke was appointed by the crown to consider the claims of a large number of English merchants, including a group of Hull merchants who alleged losses amounting to nearly £9,000, but also several Bristol merchants whose ship had been attacked by Flemish pirates off the coast of Brittany carrying goods valued at over £600.[198] These merchants included the likes of Richard le Spicer, William de Somerwell, John Vyell and William Canynges, Stoke's colleagues in high-ranking civic office in Bristol and a powerful lobbying group in their own right.[199] Thus, there was a sense in which Stoke was acting as the representative of the commercial interests of Bristol's civic elite.

From the crown's point of view, the naval conflict with Flanders might not have been perceived solely in terms of a commercial dispute between English and Flemish merchants. The problem with piracy was that it endangered any attempt by the crown to ensure Flemish neutrality and threatened to force the Flemish into a French alliance. The agreement of April 1372, for instance, confirmed the peace treaty of 1370, whose main purpose had been to prevent Flemish assistance for the French war effort. Nevertheless, it is also true that the royal government was particularly aware at this time of the need to defend merchant shipping from enemy attack,[200] a concern that was impressed on the crown by the urban representatives in parliament. In June 1371, less than a year before Stoke's commission, a meeting of a great council at Winchester attended by certain knights of the shire and burgesses and citizens who had been present at the previous parliament in February 1371, granted a subsidy of tonnage and poundage for naval defence.[201] Stoke was also one of Bristol's MPs at the parliament of November 1372, barely four months after the conclusion of his diplomatic activity in Calais. Having been involved in important negotiations to settle claims relating to naval attacks on English shipping, Stoke was among the urban representatives who remained behind at the conclusion of the 1372 parliament to renew the subsidy of tonnage and poundage for one year to meet the costs of the protection of English merchant vessels at sea.[202] In this way, war and the diplomacy associated with it were seen not just as an expression of the king's own military needs, but also in terms of the defence of the economic interests of his urban and mercantile subjects.

In the fourteenth century the Hanse was essentially a confederation of German and Prussian towns whose trading interests stretched from England in the west to the Baltic in the east, but this association 'never became a

---

[197] E 364/5, rot. 8r; E 403/444, 5 Feb.; E 403/446, 11 June; E 403/447, 26 Oct.
[198] E 30/1271, no. 3 (Bristol), no. 28 (Hull).
[199] See appendix below.
[200] Sherborne, 'Battle of La Rochelle', 21.
[201] Roskell, 'Introductory survey', 123.
[202] See appendix below; RP ii. 310.

political federation', remaining instead 'a loose alliance . . . for the defence of common economic interests and exclusive privileges'.[203] Although the Hanse held a diet which became a forum for discussion of common interests, there could be divergent views within it, notably between the German and Prussian towns, since the latter also owed allegiance to the grand master of the Teutonic order, who was the ruler of Prussia-Livonia as well as a member of the Hanse in his own right.[204]

England's relations with the Hanse were based on two points of contact, which were also the source of friction between English and Hanseatic merchants.[205] First, there was a resident Hanse population within England, concentrated in London and Hull, which formed a privileged community. The Hanseatic merchants were free from the 1347 cloth custom payable by denizen and alien merchants on exports, and they were also allowed, through royal protection, to engage freely in the retail as well as wholesale trades.[206] Secondly, in the second half of the fourteenth century English merchants were increasingly trying to break into the Baltic trade and, in particular, into Prussia's internal markets. Anglo-Hanseatic relations were divided on the question of reciprocity because English merchants did not enjoy the same rights and immunities in Prussia that the Hanse merchants possessed in England. Specifically, English merchants were prevented from trading inland and were unable to enter the retail trade to sell their imports. The escalating conflict between English and Prussian merchants came to a climax in May 1385 when a royal squadron of ships attacked six Prussian vessels anchored in the estuary of the Zwin in the Low Countries. Since England was at war with Flanders at the time of the incident, the Prussians were trading with the king's enemy and the attack, from the point of view of the English crown, was excusable. The Prussians, however, viewed it as piracy, and two months later a diet of Prussian towns ordered the arrest of all English goods in Danzig and Elbing and prohibited trade with England.

Domestic and foreign policy towards the Hanse was initiated by merchants meeting in parliament. In the parliament of October 1385 a petition was presented to the king in the name of 'his liege merchants of England trading in Prussia' ('ses liges marchantz dengleterre repeirantz ouesqz lour marchandises en la terre de Pruyce'), who complained that goods to the value of £20,000 had been arrested in Prussia by Hanseatic merchants.[207] The English merchants demanded that goods, to the same value, of Hanseatic traders

---

[203] R. de Roover, 'The organization of trade', in Postan and others, *Cambridge economic history of Europe*, iii. 105–18, quotation at p. 111.

[204] T. H. Lloyd, *England and the German hanse, 1157–1611: a study of their trade and commercial diplomacy*, Cambridge 1991, 51.

[205] For what follows see ibid. 51–63.

[206] This privilege was of particular concern to both English merchants and town governments: Beardwood, *Alien merchants*, 56–7.

[207] SC 8/125/6213.

resident in England should be arrested until restitution was made of the goods taken in Prussia. They also requested the removal of Hanseatic privileges in England. It is impossible to identify the specific authors of this petition, and the exact role of York's MPs in the drafting of it is uncertain. What is clear is that York's merchants had suffered substantial losses in the seizure of English goods in Prussia in 1385. Thirty-three York merchants later claimed losses totalling more than £1,500, and only Lynn's merchants made greater claims, amounting to nearly £2,000.[208] There is no doubt that York's merchants had a specific interest in the breakdown of Anglo-Hanseatic relations in 1385. So, too, did the city's MPs, for when the crown ordered the arrest of Prussian goods in east-coast towns, four York men were appointed to oversee this detention between Boston and Newcastle, one of whom was Thomas de Howom, who had been an MP for York at the 1385 parliament and who himself had property valued at fifty-four marks seized in Prussia.[209]

Although the king did not suspend the Hanse's privileges in England, perhaps in recognition that the dispute was with Prussia rather than with the Hanse as a whole, the merchants' petition did result in the immediate arrest of all Prussian property in England, to the value of £20,000.[210] York's mayor and bailiffs then became involved in consultation with the king's council for the recovery of the goods lost by the city's merchants. Between June 1386 and March 1388 York's civic officials, as well as the officials of other English towns and cities, received repeated orders 'to give notice to all men within the city who have any goods arrested in Prussia, or feel otherwise aggrieved concerning extortions, damages . . . inflicted on them by subjects of that land' to appear before the king's council by a certain date. The information presented to the king's council was then to be used as the basis for talks between envoys of England and the Hanse so that the goods could be recovered.[211] The crown also wanted this information for financial reasons, for the civic officials were to send to the king's council a list of the names of merchants whose goods had been arrested in Prussia. The crown was aware that the decision to arrest Prussian property in England had been initiated by, and for, English merchants trading in Prussia, and tried to impress this point on the merchants and civic officials of York and other towns by making the diplomatic mission to Prussia self-financing. Specifically, the crown was prepared to fund the costs of sending one ambassador to Prussia, but the other diplomats were to be paid from the goods of English merchants arrested there.[212]

---

208 See Kermode, *Medieval merchants*, 248–52, for both York's claims and the importance of the Baltic trade to the city's merchants.
209 *CPR, 1385–9*, 61. For Howom see Kermode, 'Merchants of York, Beverley and Hull', ii, appendix 4 (York), and appendix below.
210 Lloyd, *England and the German hanse*, 63; *CPR, 1385–9*, 61.
211 *CCR, 1385–9*, 67–8, 163, 194–5, 481, quotation at pp. 67–8.
212 *CCR, 1385–9*, 163.

The appellants, who were in control of royal government between the Wonderful Parliament of 1386 and the Merciless Parliament of 1388,[213] continued the royal policy commenced before their assumption of power. The embassy which left England to negotiate for peace with the grand master of the Teutonic order in June 1388 consisted of Master Nicholas Stocket, a clerk, and two merchants, Walter Sibille of London and Thomas Graa of York. The ambassadors were appointed in the Merciless Parliament of 1388 'at the petition of certain lieges and of the commons in this parliament by advice of the council'.[214] Reasons for Thomas Graa's appointment are not hard to find. First, Graa had been one of York's MPs at the parliament of October 1385 at which the proposal of a diplomatic mission to Prussia had first been discussed.[215] Secondly, since York merchants suffered major losses in 1385, he was also their representative and, consequently, had a vested interest in the success of the mission. More intriguingly, it is possible that Graa was also seen by the appellants as a man of similar political persuasion to themselves, for he had been a member of a committee appointed to inquire into the reform of the royal household and the expenses of the royal government in the parliament of January 1380.[216]

Thomas Graa and the other envoys were instructed to present several demands to the grand master, the two most important of which were that all property of English merchants arrested in Prussia should be released immediately and that English merchants should enjoy the same freedom to trade in Prussia as Prussian merchants did in England. On 21 August 1388 an agreement was signed in which both key demands were met.[217] In particular, English merchants trading in Prussia secured the right of freedom of trade whereby they could conduct business in any port and in inland markets without restriction. The treaty of 1388 was valued so highly by York's merchants and civic government that it was copied verbatim into the York Memorandum Book.[218] Graa's diplomatic efforts raise the issue of reciprocity because the initiative did not come from the royal government. The crown responded to parliamentary pressure and acted as a facilitator of mercantile aspirations, since the reason that York's merchants and the city's MPs turned to the crown in the first place was because they sought royal protection and royal support for the recovery of their goods. Although ideas of economic nationalism did not develop properly until the fifteenth century, an underlying reason behind the appointment of the embassy in 1388 was the crown's recognition of its responsibility to promote the prosperity of its urban and

---

[213] For the political situation see Saul, *Richard II*, 161–6, 191–4.
[214] *CCR, 1385–9*, 403.
[215] See appendix below.
[216] *RP* iii. 73–4. The significance of this relationship between Graa and the appellants is discussed at pp. 151–2 below.
[217] Lloyd, *England and the German hanse*, 65–6; *CCR, 1385–9*, 654–5.
[218] YMB ii. 3–6.

mercantile subjects in the face of foreign competition.[219] In short, Thomas Graa of York was appointed by the crown to act on behalf of a powerful mercantile interest group meeting in parliament, which included merchants of York.

There were, however, specific political reasons for the crown's response to the demands of the merchants who had lost property in Prussia in 1385. English merchants had previously complained in parliament about the contradiction between Hanseatic privileges in England and the prohibition on English trade in the Baltic,[220] but no attempt had been made by the crown to send an embassy overseas to resolve these tensions. The parliament of October 1385 has been described as 'the stormiest that Richard and his ministers had yet faced', in which the commons presented a series of petitions demanding reform of the royal government.[221] In these circumstances it is likely that the king would have been acutely aware of, and sensitive to, the concerns of his subjects. Similarly, although neither Walter Sibille nor Thomas Graa was paid wages by the crown in 1388 for their service overseas, the king, 'of his own gift' ('de dono suo'), paid the two merchants £20 each in 1391 for the expenses incurred during their visit to Prussia three years earlier.[222] Could these payments by Richard II, relatively small though they were, have been a conciliatory gesture by a king who had only assumed personal control of the reins of government in May 1389 and who sought to restore harmonious relations with some of his leading subjects?[223]

There were differences in purpose between the diplomatic missions undertaken by Thomas Graa and John de Stoke. The embassies sent to Calais were concerned with diplomatic as well as economic objectives, while Graa's journey to Prussia aimed purely to establish a commercial treaty. Yet these diplomatic missions shared other similarities. First, in both cases, Graa and Stoke were involved in negotiations with urban representatives, whether of Prussian towns or of the towns of Bruges, Ghent and Ypres in Flanders. There was a sense in which they, too, were representing the commercial interests of their own towns as well as of the wider body of English overseas merchants. Secondly, in both cases the crown was responding to the concerns of its urban and mercantile subjects and acting as a mouthpiece for their sectional interests.

The king's duty to promote the economic well-being of his subjects was influenced by wider diplomatic, political and fiscal interests. One of the consequences was that the crown's actions were not always consistent and shifts occurred in royal policy, whether in the location of the staple or in the

---

[219] The best discussion of these economic ideas remains Miller, 'Economic policies of governments', 330–40, although see also Bolton, *Medieval English economy*, 322–30.
[220] For these petitions see Lloyd, *England and the German hanse*, 53–60.
[221] Saul, *Richard II*, 146.
[222] For Graa's payment see E 403/536, 9 Nov.
[223] For Richard's style of kingship in the early 1390s see Saul, *Richard II*, 201, 235–6.

collection of customs revenue. Charles Ross has written of Edward IV's concern to promote English commercial interests that 'it would be hard to find an occasion in the reign when he allowed commercial pressures to compete successfully with the demands of foreign policy and internal politics', and that 'Yorkist commercial policy' was the result of 'a series of pragmatic responses to conflicting and competing demands'.[224] The same could also be said of the commercial policies of Edward III and Richard II in the second half of the fourteenth century. The one constant, however, was the crown's consultation with, and reliance on, the ruling elites of major towns and cities such as Bristol and York in the formulation and implementation of its commercial policies. This collaboration was characteristic of 'a system of government' in later medieval England 'in which king and subjects shared responsibility',[225] and the focus of much of this negotiation and consultation was parliament.

[224] Ross, *Edward*, iv. 356.
[225] Harriss, 'Growth of government', 57.

4

Parliament

At the beginning of October 1377 Walter de Bixton and Peter de Alderford, two leading citizens of Norwich, were elected to represent their city at the first parliament of Richard II's reign. At Westminster they petitioned the king for the confirmation of the city's liberties, but without immediate success: two further embassies were sent to the capital, after the conclusion of parliament, to secure the confirmation of the city's charters, the second of which left in early January 1378. On their election, Walter de Bixton and Henry Lomynour, the two members chosen for this mission, were instructed specifically to go to London 'to prosecute the confirmation of our charter of liberty and the increase of our liberties as they may be able'.[1] This statement, drawn from the city's records, has been taken by several historians to epitomise the essential nature of urban expectations of the crown within parliament. They argue that such parliamentary representatives were more preoccupied with local issues – the presentation of petitions seeking the confirmation or extension of charters of corporate liberties, or the redress of local financial and judicial grievances – than with matters of wider, national policy.[2] Yet the explicit nature of the instructions to Norwich's representatives in January 1378 should not be divorced from the immediate context in which they were delivered: it was only six months since Richard II had succeeded to the throne on the death of Edward III, and it was customary for towns and cities to seek the confirmation of corporate charters on the accession of a new king.[3] The Norwich evidence needs to be treated with caution, not least because it fits all too comfortably into the prevailing paradigm of crown–town relations in later medieval England, based on the interplay of finance and chartered liberties, in which the crown was looked on by towns and cities as a source of favours and privileges.

How important was the role of parliament as a channel of communication and as a forum for political debate between the crown and its urban and

---

1   *Records of the city of Norwich*, i. 271; M. McKisack, *The parliamentary representation of the English boroughs during the Middle Ages*, Oxford 1932, 134.
2   M. McKisack, 'Borough representation in Richard II's reign', *EHR* xxxix (1924), 515, and her *Parliamentary representation*, 119; J. R. Maddicott, 'Parliament and the constituencies, 1272–1377', in R. G. Davies and J. H. Denton (eds), *The English parliament in the Middle Ages*, Manchester 1981, 70.
3   Moreover, as Ben McRee has shown, there were particular local reasons why the city's rulers viewed the journey of Bixton and Lomynour with urgency at this time: McRee, 'Peacemaking', 840–3.

mercantile subjects? Parliament's significance as a link between the centre and the localities in the later medieval period has been much debated. On the one hand, there is the view of J. R. Maddicott that, 'by the 1370s parliament had become the chief intermediary between the crown and its subjects'; on the other, Christine Carpenter has emphasised, instead, the 'infrequent' nature of 'parliamentary gatherings', suggesting that Maddicott's interpretation 'can only have been true for matters affecting the whole kingdom, not for everyday local issues, for which the nobility would have been the channel of communication'.[4] Similarly, John Watts has argued that it was the nobility rather than the parliamentary commons who were the most important mediators between the king and his subjects.[5] Opinion is divided for two reasons. First, building on the pioneering scholarship of K. B. McFarlane, the recent work of Carpenter and Watts on the nobility's representative role in the governance of later medieval England has provided a necessary corrective to an older view of the crown's major landowners, which saw them as overmighty subjects, whose violence, greed and personal ambition seriously weakened the power of the crown and led, ultimately, to civil war in the mid-fifteenth century.[6] Secondly, there can be little doubt that in the mid-fifteenth century, the period in which Carpenter and Watts have been most interested, parliament was becoming a less important – certainly less frequent – point of contact between the centre and the locality than it had been a century earlier. From 1350 to the end of Edward III's reign, nineteen parliaments were held, while there were twenty-five between 1377 and 1400, amounting to a total of forty-four parliaments in fifty years, an average of almost one a year. In contrast, while parliament was assembled on thirty-eight occasions from 1400 up to and including 1450, there were only eighteen parliaments in the remainder of the century.[7] In the late fourteenth century parliament was, in the words of G. L. Harriss, 'a regular event.[8] Previous chapters have explored a public morality of governance, based on the notion of the common good, which underpinned relations between the crown and the civic elites of Bristol and York. This political discourse – the language of government – also informed meetings of parliament, where the dialogue between the king and his subjects, represented by the parliamentary petition, was explicitly concerned with 'the necessities of the king and

---

4   Maddicott, 'Parliament and the constituencies', 86; Carpenter, 'Gentry and community', 364 n. 106.
5   Watts, *Henry VI*, 9, 74–80; but see the perceptive comments of S. J. Payling in his review of Watts's book in *PH* xvi (1997), 359–61.
6   This historiography is summarised briefly in C. Carpenter, *The Wars of the Roses: politics and the constitution in England, c. 1437–1509*, Cambridge 1997, 8–10.
7   Fryde and others, *Handbook of British chronology*, 566–72. For the growing infrequency of parliament in the second half of the fifteenth century see also McKisack, *Parliamentary representation*, 44.
8   Harriss, 'Dimensions of politics', 10.

kingdom . . . the obligations of subjects and rulers . . . the crown and the commonweal'.[9]

Significantly, both the role and importance of urban representatives within parliament and the extent of urban interest in meetings of parliament have tended to be minimised by historians. In part, this interpretation rests on the nature of the extant evidence, for the main parliamentary records, the rolls of parliament, 'have remarkably little to tell us of the activities of the burgesses', about whom May McKisack wrote, 'despite their numerical superiority the part played by them in parliament was, if not insignificant, at least inconspicuous'.[10] Yet the parliament rolls, as several historians have acknowledged,[11] are not by any means a complete record of everything that took place within parliament. Compiled by chancery clerks as a government record of parliamentary proceedings and written from the perspective of the government, they were concerned to record primarily the grant of taxation by the commons and the commons' petitions; the rolls, therefore, rarely recorded the debate leading up to the formal declaration of the grant of taxation or the successive stages involved in the drafting and presentation of commons' petitions. Furthermore, the clerks who enrolled the petitions edited their address, so that almost all were in the name of 'les Communes'.[12]

None the less, it is generally accepted that the invisibility of the urban representatives in the parliament rolls is not an illusion. First, historians have argued, on the basis of prosopographical research into the composition of the members of parliament, that the silence of the parliamentary records is a genuine reflection of the underlying reality of the internal dynamics of the commons, in which the will of the knights of the shire prevailed. In his introduction to the *History of parliament* volumes of biographies of members of parliament between 1386 and 1421, J. S. Roskell stated emphatically that 'the shire knights, by reason of their superior social status as gentry, their greater involvement in the regional administration of the county, and their more personal connexions with the King and members of the Upper House, discharged a more important role in the Commons than the townsmen, especially in the sphere of high politics'.[13] These qualifications meant that it was the representatives of the counties who dominated the agenda of the commons, an impression confirmed by the record of the Good Parliament in the *Anonimalle chronicle*, a chronicle written at the Benedictine abbey of St Mary's in York, in which only the speeches of the shire knights attacking the king's ministers were noted.[14]

Secondly, the limited role played by the urban representatives in parlia-

---

[9] Ibid. 15.

[10] McKisack, *Parliamentary representation*, 119.

[11] For example, A. L. Brown, 'Parliament, c. 1372–1422', in Davies and Denton, *English parliament*, 109–10.

[12] D. Rayner, 'The forms and machinery of the "*commune petition*" in the fourteenth century', *EHR* lvi (1941), 227.

[13] Roskell, 'Introductory survey', 48.

[14] *The anonimalle chronicle, 1333 to 1381*, ed. V. H. Galbraith, Manchester 1927, 79–94.

ment has been seen as further confirmation of the marginal position occupied by urban communities within the late medieval polity. If the commons were expected to speak for the common good through their common petition, parliamentary burgesses were entrusted specifically with 'the burden of local business', and it was this local dimension of their work, according to McKisack, which 'may help in large measure to account for the inconspicuous part played by them, as a class, in parliament'.[15] This local business included the presentation of petitions relating to the confirmation of charters, the removal of obstacles to local trade and the reduction of the *firma burgi*, but significantly, it also embraced other activities on behalf of the urban community that had little to do with their attendance at parliament. Indeed, Lorraine Attreed has suggested that, viewed from the town's perspective, 'a representative's most important duties . . . did not always lie within parliament itself', since many, for example, 'undertook private business for constituents in or near London'.[16] Parliament was, then, simply another, albeit direct, point of contact between urban communities and the crown, where, like other channels of communication such as aristocratic patronage and intercession, local issues were at the forefront of a town's concerns. Thus, of London's attitude to parliament in the first half of the fifteenth century, Caroline Barron has suggested that, due to the city's close geographical proximity to the organs of royal government, there were more opportunities for Londoners to speak to the king or seek redress of their local grievances through the central courts. Meetings of parliament, therefore, held less interest than they might have for other towns and cities. To London's rulers, 'meetings of Parliament were not so much opportunities for access but, rather, times when it was necessary to keep a watchful eye on other communities which might try to enlarge their own privileges by successful parliamentary lobbying'.[17] More attention needs to be paid to the role of parliament as a place for public debate and negotiation as well as the conduct of local, private business.

The following study is divided into three sections. The first, based on prosopographical research, explores the identity of the MPs for Bristol and York. What kinds of people were elected to represent Bristol and York, and how different were they from the representatives of the shires? The aim of this section is to provide a more nuanced understanding of the internal workings of the commons and of the place of the representatives of Bristol and York within parliament. Some historians have argued that the second half of the fourteenth century saw the growing corporate identity of the commons and 'a greater sense of solidarity' among its members,[18] while others have noted that the divisions that did exist within the commons were between the

15 M. McKisack, 'The parliamentary representation of King's Lynn before 1500', *EHR* xlii (1927), 584.
16 Attreed, *King's towns*, 59.
17 C. M. Barron, 'London and parliament in the Lancastrian period', *PH* ix (1990), 343.
18 For example, Ormrod, *Edward III*, 166–7, quotation at p. 166.

shire knights and the parliamentary burgesses.[19] But what happened when Bristol and York became counties in their own right in 1373 and 1396 respectively? Did their elevation to county status lead to a blurring of the distinctions between knights of the shire and urban representatives? The second section examines the evidence of the common petitions from Bristol and York, focusing on the role of their MPs as representatives of their local communities and from whom they received their wages. What did the MPs request of the crown? How useful is the dichotomy of 'local' and 'national' in seeking to understand the issues addressed in the common petitions? Moreover, to what extent did the common petitions express the collective interests of Bristol and York? How inclusive was the rhetoric of community? Although the commons could act together as a unified, corporate body at specific moments, particularly at times of political crisis, it may in fact be more useful to view the commons as composed of a range of a different interest groups – geographical, mercantile and urban – of which the representatives of Bristol and York were a part. Indeed, the third section considers the evidence and significance of parliamentary committees comprising Bristol and York merchants in order to argue that the rulers of Bristol and York belonged to a national estate of merchants that met in parliament in the second half of the fourteenth century.

Personnel

What calibre of people served as parliamentary representatives of Bristol and York in the second half of the fourteenth century? The identity of the MPs can help to explain the attitude of their electors to meetings of parliament. It is also important to consider J. S. Roskell's claim that the dominance of the shire knights within the commons was due to their superior political status, itself derived from a number of factors, including their close personal ties to the king and to members of the lords, their service as local officials of the crown within their counties and their parliamentary experience.[20] To what extent did these characteristics distinguish the knights of the shire from the representatives of Bristol and York in the period 1350 to 1400?

Essentially, there were two types of MP elected to represent Bristol and York. On the one hand, there were 'outsiders', that is, 'men with local interests who advised the town but played no direct part in its government'.[21] The second type belonged to the officeholding elite of their towns. The fifteenth century saw an increasing number of gentry and lawyers representing urban communities in parliament.[22] Although it used to be thought that the reason

---

[19] For example, Brown, 'Parliament', 120–1.
[20] Roskell, 'Introductory survey', 40, 48–9.
[21] Horrox, 'Urban patronage', 155.
[22] McKisack, *Parliamentary representation*, 60–4, 113–18.

for this phenomenon lay in the personal ambition of members of the nobility and gentry to gain representation in the commons, Rosemary Horrox has shown that parliamentary representation by lawyers and gentry was not forced on the towns and cities. Rather, urban communities sought 'the support of well connected lawyers and gentlemen' who possessed 'outside contacts' that their own burgesses might not have possessed.[23] In the election of outsiders to represent Bristol and York, is it possible to identify specific qualifications or connections that could be employed to the towns' advantage?

Bristol's outsiders were William Yonge, John Serjeant, Thomas Denbaud and Richard de Sydenham. They shared two characteristics. First, they each represented Bristol on only one occasion, an indication, perhaps, that they were elected to serve a specific purpose. Secondly, they were all elected in the 1360s, the significance of which will be considered shortly. William Yonge, MP for Bristol in 1361, John Serjeant, MP in 1363, and Thomas Denbaud, MP in 1366, seem to have been members of the local gentry. Yonge and Denbaud served the crown in local administration: the former, for instance, as a member of several royal commissions in the south-west in the late 1350s and early 1360s, including a commission of inquiry into the activities of the escheator and subescheator of Gloucestershire, Herefordshire and the Welsh marches in 1360 and a commission of oyer and terminer into the felling of trees in Queen Philippa's chase in the manor of Bedminster, just south of Bristol, in the same year;[24] the latter, who held property in the town of Bristol, as a tax collector in the county of Somerset in 1360 and also as a deputy controller of customs in the port of Bristol between 1363 and 1368.[25] The absence of the 1361 parliament roll means that it very difficult to determine what service Yonge might have performed for Bristol at this particular parliament, while the precise reasons for Denbaud's election in 1366 are equally difficult to fathom.

Far more is known about John Serjeant,[26] a landowner from Stone in Gloucestershire, who had previous parliamentary experience as MP for Gloucestershire in 1350. He was also appointed a justice of the peace in the same county in 1351, 1353 and 1359, and his appointments to royal office in the county continued after his election to represent Bristol in 1363. Perhaps more significantly, Serjeant was a retainer of the earl of Stafford between 1360 and 1372. Stafford, who owned a large amount of land in Gloucestershire through the inheritance of his wife, Margaret Audley, held the lordship of Thornbury, a manor ten miles north of Bristol, and was a 'royal confidant'

---

23 Horrox, 'Urban patronage', 158–9.
24 CPR, 1358–61, 409, 483.
25 LRB i. 5, 7; CPR, 1358–61, 345; CPR, 1361–4, 411; E 356/5, rot. 22r.
26 Return of the name of every member of the lower house of parliament . . . 1213–1874, London 1878, i. 148; CPR, 1350–4, 89, 508; CPR, 1358–61, 219; CFR, 1368–77, 192, 270; Saul, Knights and esquires, 288.

of Edward III who served the king in France in the 1340s and was a founding member of the king's Order of the Garter.[27] Although there is no direct evidence in the rolls of parliament of Serjeant's actions on behalf of Bristol, it is likely that the town's rulers recognised the value of representation by an individual who had access to, and was favoured by, a powerful lord within parliament. Indeed, Ralph earl of Stafford is known to have acted as a patron to members of Bristol's civic elite, petitioning the chancellor to release a ship belonging to Walter de Derby, five times bailiff and five times mayor of Bristol, which had been arrested for royal naval service but was unfit to serve.[28]

Bristol's fourth outsider, Richard de Sydenham, MP for the town in 1368, was a lawyer. Sydenham owned several landed estates throughout Somerset and was employed as a legal adviser by the Somerset town of Bridgwater between 1373 and 1375.[29] He was a justice of the peace in Somerset in 1374 and again in 1375, before being appointed to the central law courts, first as a king's serjeant in the court of common pleas in 1388 and then as a justice of common pleas a year later. Elected MP at the beginning of his legal career, Sydenham was probably valued by Bristol's political elite for the legal expertise that he could bring to parliament in the drafting of petitions. Bristol was not alone in seeking such legal skills, which were perceived as so useful because lawyers, as their critics complained to the crown, knew how to present petitions of a private nature in the name of 'les Communes', thereby securing the unofficial endorsement of the commons. In 1372, in response to a common petition, the crown prohibited the election of lawyers as knights of the shire on the grounds that they 'put forward several petitions in parliaments in the name of the commons, which do not concern them but only the individuals with whom they resided' ('les singulers persones ove queux ils sont demorez').[30]

York's outsiders were Roger de Normanvill, MP for the city in 1351 and 1355, and John de Selby, MP in 1363. As a king's yeoman, Normanvill was a member of the royal affinity, who served as keeper of the king's horses north of the river Trent between 1343 and 1350 and then as surveyor of the king's works in York. He owned property in the city and in 1350, a year before his

---

27 For Stafford's relations with Edward III see C. Given-Wilson, *The English nobility in the late Middle Ages: the fourteenth-century political community*, London 1987, repr. 1996, 40–1, and Ormrod, *Edward III*, 14, 18, 103, 109, quotation at p. 18.

28 SC 1/42/116; appendix below.

29 For what follows on Sydenham see *Pedes finium (commonly called feet of fines) for the county of Somerset, 1347–1399*, ed. E. Green (Somerset Record Society xvii, 1902), 72, 132, 156; *Bridgwater borough archives, 1200–1377*, ed. T. B. Dilks (Somerset Record Society xlviii, 1933), 221–2, 224–5; CPR, 1370–4, 478; CPR, 1374–7, 139; and *Select cases in the court of king's bench*, ed. G. O. Sayles (Selden Society lv, lvii, lviii, lxxiv, lxxvi, lxxxii, lxxxviii, 1936–71), vi, pp. ci, lxxvi–lxxvii.

30 RP ii. 310. For further comment see K. L. Wood-Legh, 'Sheriffs, lawyers, and belted knights in the parliaments of Edward III', EHR xlvi (1931), 372–88.

first election to parliament, he became a freeman of York.[31] It is interesting to speculate on the specific reasons for Normanvill's election in 1351 and 1355. That Normanvill was a trusted royal servant is confirmed by his appointment to the office of mayor of the York staple by the crown after the disputed election in 1354,[32] so it is likely that his electors valued him for his personal contact with the king. This connection was particularly useful to the city in the early 1350s because of the association with the wool monopoly companies of the 1340s of a number of York merchants, some of whom became involved in prolonged litigation with the king when these companies collapsed in the mid-fourteenth century.[33] At a time when relations between the crown and York's merchants were far from harmonious, perhaps Normanvill was viewed as a conciliatory figure who could work to resolve these tensions.

John de Selby was different from Normanvill in that, although he never held high-ranking civic office in the city, he was a York merchant and a founding member of the fraternity of Our Lord Jesus Christ and the Virgin Mary in 1357, which included several civic officials and which later became the Mercers' guild.[34] He was a wool exporter, like many of York's merchants, who died in Calais while on business,[35] and it was Selby's involvement in the Calais staple which probably explains his election as MP for the city in 1363. It was at this parliament that a common petition was presented on behalf of merchants trading at the staple which complained about the activities of the recently appointed governing body of the town, whose members were accused of imposing a duty of 40d. on each sack of wool coming to the staple and of fixing wool prices for their own personal profit.[36] Although it is impossible to determine Selby's role in the drafting of this petition, it can be no coincidence that he was elected to parliament in 1363. He was clearly there for a specific purpose, namely to voice the concerns of York's merchants about the new government of the town of Calais and its interference in the wool trade.

There is little doubt that the outsiders had particular skills, connections or interests, which ensured their election as parliamentary representatives. The precise circumstances of their election cannot be known with absolute certainty, however, because of the silence of the civic records on the conduct

---

31 *CPR, 1343–5*, 107; *CPR, 1348–50*, 470; *CCR, 1354–60*, 4; *Feet of fines for the county of York, from 1347 to 1377*, ed. W. P. Baildon (Yorkshire Archaeological Society Record Series lii, 1914), 42; *Register of freemen of York*, i. 42.

32 This episode is discussed at pp. 118–19 above.

33 Fryde, 'Business transactions', 3–5.

34 *The York mercers and merchant adventurers, 1356–1917*, ed. M. Sellers (Surtees Society cxxix, 1917), 1; L. R. Wheatley, 'The York mercers' guild, 1420–1502', unpubl. MA diss. York 1993, i. 35–7.

35 BIHR, probate register 1, fo. 10v.

36 *RP* ii. 276.

of parliamentary elections in Bristol and York in the period 1350 to 1400,[37] while the services performed by these men on behalf of Bristol and York at parliament can only be the subject of speculation. None the less, the timing of the election of outsiders as MPs for Bristol and York is suggestive of the attitude of the towns' rulers towards meetings of parliament. It is, for example, significant that, with the exception of Roger de Normanvill, the other MPs who did not belong to the governing elite of Bristol and York were all elected in the 1360s and represented the towns on only one occasion. The 1360s were marked by a nine-year truce between England and France, the longest period of peace since the beginning of the Hundred Years War, which meant that the commons did not grant direct taxation to the crown.[38] Whatever the concerns of Bristol and York during the parliaments of peacetime, their electors had different priorities, revolving around the issues of finance and trade, when war returned in 1369. From 1369, when the commons had to consider the crown's requests for grants of direct taxation for the war effort and of tonnage and poundage for the protection of overseas trade and shipping, the towns' MPs were merchants drawn from the ruling elites who either had parliamentary experience or would continue to represent the towns on several later occasions.[39] With the exception of William Frost, MP for York in 1399, who was, in the words of Carole Rawcliffe's biography, a member of 'the middle ranks of the Yorkshire gentry', and Thomas Beaupyne, MP for Bristol at six parliaments, who, although engaged in overseas trade, also owned extensive lands and properties in Somerset and who represented this county at parliament in 1390,[40] the MPs were part of 'the group of wealthy merchants drawn from the greater towns and united by their common interest in trade and national finance'.[41] They had a particular interest attending parliaments at which questions about royal finance and naval defence were at the top of the commons' agenda.

In the second half of the fourteenth century the absence of either parliamentary returns or writs *de expensis* means that the names of only thirty-four of Bristol's and twenty-five of York's MPs are known.[42] With the exception of William Yonge, Thomas Denbaud, John Serjeant and Richard de Sydenham, Bristol's other thirty MPs held high civic office in the town at some point in their careers, whether as mayor, sheriff, bailiff, steward and/or member of the

---

[37] It is only from 1407 that even the names of those participating in parliamentary elections in Bristol and York are known, thanks to the royal statute issued in the previous year: McKisack, *Parliamentary representation*, 47; Roskell and others, *House of Commons, 1386–1421*, i. 405 (Bristol), 750 (York).

[38] Ormrod, *Edward III*, table 1 at p. 204.

[39] See appendix below.

[40] Roskell and others, *House of Commons, 1386–1421*, ii. 164–6; iii. 139.

[41] McKisack, *Parliamentary representation*, 101.

[42] In the case of Bristol evidence has survived for thirty-one of the forty-four parliaments which met between 1350 and 1400, compared to thirty-three parliaments for York.

common council.[43] Twenty occupied the mayoralty, and the vast majority (twenty-six) belonged to the common council. Of York's twenty-five MPs, twenty-three occupied high civic office in the city as mayor, sheriff, bailiff, chamberlain and/or member of the inner councils of government. Sixteen were mayors of York, and from 1378 to the end of the fourteenth century twelve of the thirteen MPs representing the city were drawn from the ruling councils of twelve and twenty-four.

Apart from their dominance of civic government, what else characterised the parliamentary burgesses of Bristol and York? First, they all received appointments to royal office and/or served the royal government in a less formal capacity, for example lending money or ships to the war effort. It should be noted that what follows is not a description of the totality of their administrative experience, but rather, an attempt to indicate the kinds of connections which tied the MPs to the crown. Of Bristol's MPs, John de Stoke, Walter de Derby, Thomas Beaupyne, Ellis Spelly and William Canynges would perhaps have been the most familiar to the royal government.[44] All were involved in the administration of the poll taxes in Bristol and monopolised the collection of the customs in the port of Bristol from the mid-1360s to the end of the century, while Stoke, Canynges and Beaupyne farmed the cloth subsidy in Dorset, Somerset and Gloucestershire for over twenty years, Derby and Beaupyne made personal loans to the crown, and Stoke and Beaupyne were appointed to diplomatic missions abroad. Similarly, among York's MPs, William Graa and his son and heir, Thomas, John de Gysburn and William Frost were all extremely active in royal service. For instance, Thomas Graa and John de Gysburn administered the poll taxes in York; William Graa lent money to the crown and supplied goods for the war against the French; Thomas Graa and William Frost were escheators of Yorkshire and served on a total of more than thirty royal commissions in Yorkshire and the city of York; and Graa was appointed to a royal embassy to Prussia in 1388.[45] Apart from William Frost, to whom in the summer of 1404 Henry IV granted an annual payment for life of two tuns of wine as a reward for his support of the nascent Lancastrian regime, none of these MPs had the personal relationship with the king denoted by the receipt of a retaining fee or a royal annuity.[46] Equally, they were not 'insignificant townsfolk'.[47]

Similarly, if, as Anthony Tuck has argued, the shire knights were 'more active' in the commons because of the 'confidence that came from friendship,

---

[43] See appendix below for what follows.

[44] For employment on tax commissions see CFR, 1368–77, 390; CFR, 1377–83, 150, 164, 231. Otherwise see appendix below, and the biographies of Beaupyne, Canynges and Spelly in Roskell and others, House of Commons, 1386–1421, ii. 164–6, 476–8; iv. 414–17.

[45] For biographies of Frost and Thomas Graa see Roskell and others, House of Commons, 1386–1421, iii. 138–41, 218–20. For participation in the collection of the poll taxes see CFR, 1377–83, 150, 164.

[46] CPR, 1401–5, 406.

[47] McKisack, Parliamentary representation, 100.

blood ties, and neighbourly relations with members of the lords',[48] then it is important to acknowledge that some of the MPs for Bristol and York also had links to the nobility. For example, Walter de Derby, three times MP for Bristol, was a major wine merchant for John of Gaunt, duke of Lancaster, supplying wine worth at least £275 for consumption by the duke and his household between 1380 and 1383.[49] Robert de Howom, twice MP for York, lent £200 to John of Gaunt while the duke was at Bruges in 1375 engaged in talks with the French for the negotiation of a peace settlement.[50] Meanwhile, several of Bristol's MPs provided practical help to Gaunt in 1372 during the series of diplomatic negotiations which occupied the duke in this year, as he sought to build a number of Iberian alliances in order to remove from power the usurper Enrique of Trastamara, the king of Castile, who, since the summer of 1368, had been in alliance with Charles V of France.[51] John Bathe, one of Bristol's MPs in 1371, lent money to Juan Fernández Andeiro, a Castilian exile at Gaunt's court since 1371, who left Bristol for Portugal as the duke's envoy to conduct talks with the Portugese king, Fernando I.[52] Thomas Knappe, twice MP for Bristol, was paid by Gaunt for transporting a party of Castilian knights led by Sancho Ruiz de Quintana Redonda, another exile who had been with the duke since 1371, which left Bristol in May 1372 on its way first to Aquitaine and then to Barcelona for negotiations with the Aragonese king, Pere III.[53]

Linda Clark is quite right to warn that 'the resulting web of debt and credit, obligation and dependency, led to highly complex relations of a different order from the relatively straightforward bonds of lord and retainer',[54] and only John Serjeant, Bristol's MP in 1363, is known to have been retained by a magnate: in his case, the earl of Stafford.[55] The ties between Bristol's MPs and members of the nobility were not, however, simply commercial. A group of the town's parliamentary representatives – Ellis Spelly, John Vyell, William Canynges, Walter de Derby and Walter Tedistille – were joint members with their wives of the prestigious Holy Trinity guild in Coventry, which was founded in 1364 and which, by 1369, had absorbed the older guilds of St Mary, St John the Baptist and St Katherine.[56] In the later

---

[48] A. Tuck, *Richard II and the English nobility*, London 1973, 26–7.

[49] *Gaunt's register, 1379–1383*, i. 213, 228; ii. 268–9, 273.

[50] *John of Gaunt's register, 1372–1376*, ed. E. C. Lodge and R. Somerville (Camden 3rd ser. vi–lvii, 1937), ii. 343–4.

[51] For the diplomatic background see P. E. Russell, *The English intervention in Spain and Portugal in the time of Edward III and Richard II*, Oxford 1955, 138–95.

[52] *Gaunt's register, 1372–1376*, ii. 42. For Andeiro see Russell, *English intervention*, 181–2.

[53] *Gaunt's register, 1372–1376*, ii. 42.

[54] L. Clark, 'Magnates and their affinities in the parliaments of 1386–1421', in Britnell and Pollard, *McFarlane legacy*, 136.

[55] See pp. 145–6 above.

[56] *The register of the guild of the Holy Trinity, St Mary, St John the Baptist and St Katherine of Coventry*, ed. M. D. Harris (Dugdale Society xiii, 1935), 7, 27, 88.

fourteenth century the guild numbered among its members John of Gaunt and his brother, Thomas of Woodstock, later duke of Gloucester, and the 4th earl of Arundel, Richard Fitzalan.[57] There were well-established trading links between Bristol and Coventry, based on the export of Coventry cloth through the port of Bristol and the import of wine through Bristol to Coventry,[58] and it is fair to assume that the Bristol burgesses who joined the guild had commercial interests there too. John Vyell, for example, remembered both the Holy Trinity guild of Coventry and an unnamed guild of Lynn in his will, the wide geographical scope of these bequests suggesting that he traded through both towns.[59] However, if there were sound business reasons for entering the Coventry guild, which also included many local merchants,[60] attendance at the guild's large cycle of annual feasts offered additional attractions. As Gervase Rosser has shown, the wider social value of such gatherings, in establishing new ties and relationships, should not be underestimated.[61]

In the case of York several of the city's MPs had personal connections with the lords appellant between 1386 and 1388. In the Wonderful Parliament of 1386 the chancellor, Michael de la Pole, was impeached at the instigation of the parliamentary commons and a commission of government was appointed to rule for a year, to examine the state of royal finances and to implement the necessary fiscal reforms.[62] Two years later, in the Merciless Parliament of 1388, the appellants, with the support of the parliamentary commons, found the king's favourites, Robert de Vere, duke of Ireland, Robert Tresilian, chief justice of king's bench, Nicholas Brembre, a former mayor of London, and the archbishop of York, Alexander Neville, guilty of treason.[63] Whatever the motives of the lords appellant,[64] the hostility of the commons in 1386 and 1388 towards the king's ministers was essentially financial, for there was a growing resentment about the rising costs of the royal government, particularly the household, at a time when the realm faced serious threats of invasion from the French and the Scots. Indeed, the commission established in 1386 was very much a response to Michael de la Pole's failure to introduce the financial reforms which had been demanded by the commons in the parliament of 1385.[65] It has already been shown how this disquiet towards the

---

[57] Ibid. p. x.

[58] Penn, 'Fourteenth-century Bristol', 40–1; C. Phythian-Adams, *Desolation of a city: Coventry and the urban crisis of the late Middle Ages*, Cambridge 1979, 19–20.

[59] Wadley, *Great orphan book*, 57–8.

[60] *Register of the guild of the Holy Trinity*, p. xiii.

[61] G. Rosser, 'Going to the fraternity feast: commensality and social relations in late medieval England', *JBS* xxxiii (1994), 430–46.

[62] For the political background to the period 1386 to 1388 see Roskell, *Michael de la Pole*, 11–55.

[63] Ibid. 197–204.

[64] These motives are discussed in Saul, *Richard II*, 177–82.

[65] J. J. N. Palmer, 'The parliament of 1385 and the constitutional crisis of 1386', *Speculum* xlvi (1971), 477–90.

state of royal finances had echoes in York in the 1370s.[66] Thomas Graa's experience of local politics can only have helped to shape his outlook and to develop his sympathies towards the appellants' cause. It is surely no coincidence that Graa, who had been appointed to a parliamentary committee in January 1380 to examine the finances of the royal administration, was elected to represent York in the Wonderful Parliament of 1386 and was appointed by the appellants to a diplomatic mission to Prussia in the Merciless Parliament of 1388.[67] The continuity of parliamentary experience and appointments suggests that Graa supported the appellants and enjoyed their confidence.

Local issues certainly served to reinforce attachments between the appellants and some of York's MPs. For example, the royal grant to Robert de Vere of the wardship of the son and heir of Sir Thomas Roos of Helmsley in 1384 meant that the majority of York's fee farm was paid to the king's favourite.[68] Meanwhile, Archbishop Neville was a deeply unpopular figure within the city of York. Indeed, John de Rypon, an MP for York at the Cambridge parliament of 1388, was one of several York citizens who attacked the archbishop's palaces at York, Cawood and Bishopthorpe in early 1386, but who managed to avoid punishment.[69] In the words of Carole Rawcliffe, Rypon's 'election to the next Parliament, while the Appellants still remained in power, may not have been entirely unconnected with this incident, which clearly reflects where his political sympathies lay'.[70] In 1398 a number of prominent York citizens, including Thomas de Howom, one of York's MPs in the Merciless Parliament of 1388, John de Howeden, MP for York at both parliaments in 1388, and Robert Savage, MP in 1386, were forced to sue for letters of pardon or to seal 'letters obligatory' for large sums of money with no promise of repayment. Howom's pardon referred specifically to his relationship with the lords appellant between 1386 and 1388.[71] In this period, at least, there were ties of a personal nature between York's MPs and a group of magnates.

Many of the MPs for Bristol and York also had a wealth of parliamentary experience. The imperfect survival rate of the election returns and writs *de expensis* for Bristol and York makes it very difficult to determine the extent of repeated election to parliament, particularly re-election to successive parlia-

---

[66] See p. 98 above.
[67] For Graa see appendix below. The 1380 committee is discussed in greater detail at pp. 175–7 below.
[68] *CFR, 1383–91*, 42. The relationship between the Roos family of Helmsley in North Yorkshire and York's fee farm is examined at pp. 61–2 above.
[69] *CPR, 1385–9*, 172. For a complaint from the archbishop to the king about the trespasses and injuries committed against him 'by certain people of your city of York' see SC 8/249/12405. Neville's unpopularity as a diocesan is discussed in R. G. Davies, 'Alexander Neville, archbishop of York, 1374–1388', *YAJ* xlvii (1975), 87–101.
[70] Roskell and others, *House of Commons, 1386–1421*, iv. 214.
[71] *CCR, 1396–9*, 305, 416, 425; *CPR, 1396–9*, 368; C 67/31, mem. 12; Roskell and others, *House of Commons, 1386–1421*, iii. 402.

ments, but it is clear that the last three decades of the fourteenth century saw more frequent re-election.[72] William and Thomas Graa represented York at twenty-four parliaments between 1344 and 1397.[73] In fact, William attended seven successive parliaments between 1363 and 1372, while his son, Thomas, represented the city successively at three parliaments between 1378 and 1380, two parliaments in 1385 and 1386 and four parliaments between 1393 and 1397. The two Graas may have been unusual in the extent of their parliamentary attendance, but there were others who represented Bristol and York on repeated, and sometimes consecutive, occasions. For Bristol, these included Thomas Beaupyne, Ellis Spelly and William Frome, who, between them, represented the town a total of fifteen times; for York, John de Howeden, John de Acastre and William de Selby, who, between them, represented the city at parliament on a total of fourteen occasions. Like the knights of the shire, then, the parliamentary representatives of Bristol and York had experience that must have been valued highly by their electors.

Parliamentary burgesses, as May McKisack noted, 'were not a homogenous body'. Rather, they consisted of 'two distinct groups' within parliament, 'the smaller consisting of wealthy merchants . . . drawn mainly from London and such great cities as Bristol and York, the larger consisting of representatives of the lesser towns, men who had, perhaps, risen to importance in their borough council'.[74] The parliamentary representatives of Bristol and York were not just important men in local politics, but were also merchants who served the crown abroad on commercial diplomatic missions and who were involved in royal finance. In many ways these MPs had more in common with the leading merchants of other major towns and cities than with their fellow townsmen.[75] The Holy Trinity guild of Coventry, for example, to which several Bristol MPs belonged, also included among its membership in the late fourteenth and early fifteenth centuries Richard Whittington, the London merchant and royal financier of Richard II and Henry IV, MP for London on only one occasion but four times mayor of the city and a member of Henry IV's council between 1399 and 1400.[76] Another member was William Greville, a wool merchant from Chipping Campden in Gloucestershire, but also a non-resident London freeman, who was perhaps the most important English merchant in the expanding Cotswolds wool trade of the later fourteenth century, and whose memorial brass in his parish church in Campden unashamedly proclaimed him 'late a citizen of London and the flower of the

---

[72] See appendix below for what follows.

[73] For William Graa's two elections as MP for York before 1350 see *Return of members*, i. 140 (1344), 147 (1348).

[74] McKisack, *Parliamentary representation*, 100.

[75] This paraphrases S. H. Rigby's point about the nature of York's civic elite after 1350 in his *English society in the later Middle Ages: class, status and gender*, Basingstoke 1995, 154.

[76] For this and what follows see *Register of the guild of the Holy Trinity*, pp. xx–xxi. For Whittington see Barron, 'Richard Whittington', 197–248. The description of Greville is from Roskell and others, *House of Commons, 1386–1421*, iii. 240.

wool merchants of all of England' ('quondam civis Londonie et flos mercatorum lanarum totius Anglie'). Several Bristol MPs also had particularly strong personal ties to London, a pattern that was to become well established in the fifteenth century. William Canynges (1402–74), who was elected mayor of Bristol on five occasions and who joined the grocers' company in the capital and held the leading offices in London's civic hierarchy, first as alderman, then as sheriff, before election as mayor of London, is perhaps only the pre-eminent example of what was, by the mid-fifteenth century, an increasingly common tendency for Bristolians to gravitate towards London for business.[77] Indeed, his grandfather, William Canynges, three times MP for Bristol in the late fourteenth century, was described as a citizen of London in July 1371 in a petition concerning the theft of his cargo from a ship wrecked off the Kent coast, and it was presumably his trading connections with London which provided him with the contacts necessary to supply goods to the royal household.[78] John Canynges, probably William's son, who served as MP for Bristol on one occasion in 1383, was also a non-resident freeman of London who, like William Greville, was assessed in 1380 to contribute to London's parliamentary subsidy and civic taxes.[79] It is little wonder that the second half of the fourteenth century saw a growing acknowledgement, both by the shire knights and by the crown, of the distinction between the majority of the parliamentary burgesses and the leading merchants within the commons who had particular interests and expertise in questions of trade and national finance.[80]

Despite the personal qualifications of many of the MPs for Bristol and York, however, it was only when the town of Bristol was elevated to county status that the town's representatives became collectively more visible in the parliament rolls. When Bristol was made a separate county in 1373, Bristol's MPs were elevated to the joint status of 'Knights of the County of Bristol' and 'burgesses of the town and Borough of Bristol'.[81] Similarly, after 1396 York's parliamentary representatives were paid as knights of the shire, receiving 4s. per day rather than the daily wage of 2s. rendered to citizens and burgesses.[82] Bristol's representatives exerted a significantly greater influence on parliamentary proceedings after 1373. Before the charter there is no evidence that they authored any common petitions, but afterwards the parliament rolls record three common petitions from Bristol in 1376, one in 1377, two in

---

[77] For the strength of the 'personal links' between Bristol and London in the fifteenth century see C. Burgess, 'Educated parishioners in London and Bristol on the eve of the reformation', in C. M. Barron and J. Stratford (eds), *The Church and learning in later medieval society: essays in honour of R. B. Dobson*, Donington 2002, 286–9.

[78] *CPR, 1370–4*, 176. In 1365 Canynges was owed nearly £70 for the wax and hemp that he had supplied to the great wardrobe: E 101/395/3.

[79] *Letter-book H*, 146.

[80] For further discussion of this point see pp. 183–9 below.

[81] *Bristol charters, 1155–1373*, 136–7.

[82] *York city chamberlains' account rolls*, 16.

1378, one in 1390, one in 1393 and another in 1394.[83] It may, then, be true that it was the knights of the shire rather than the parliamentary burgesses who ordinarily dominated the agenda of the commons and decided which petitions would go forward in their name, but the political consequences of county status for the growing number of towns and cities that became counties in their own right in the course of the fifteenth century need greater consideration. From 1373, on each occasion that Bristol's sheriff made a parliamentary return to the crown informing the king's officials of the election of the town's MPs, the return stated that the representatives were elected to act in a dual capacity, as knights of the shire and as parliamentary burgesses.[84] When, in 1426, the parliamentary writ to Bristol's sheriff referred to the town's representatives 'by the name of burgesses only', neglecting to mention their status as knights of the shire, the sheriff was forced to return the writ in the same words. Thus, the parliamentary commons complained on Bristol's behalf at the 1426 parliament that the town's two elected representatives 'could not be received to appear and to answer in this present parliament as knights for the said county of Bristol as well as burgesses for the said town and borough', praying that the mistake be remedied and that henceforth the town's MPs enjoy their customary dual status, which the king duly agreed.[85] In the second half of the fourteenth century the increasing collective prominence of Bristol's representatives within parliament reflected the changing corporate identity of the town of Bristol, emphasising, in the process, that the grant of county status, far from conceding autonomy to the town, actually bound Bristol's ruling elite more closely into the apparatus of royal government.

Common petitions

There has been serious disagreement among historians over the meaning of the common petition ('commune petition'). To William Stubbs, common petitions were

> the result of deliberation and debate among the Commons themselves, whether they originated in the independent proposition of an individual member, adopted by the house as a subject of petition, or in the complaints of his constituents, or in the organized policy of a party, or in the unanimous wish of the whole house.[86]

Doris Rayner revised this view of the common petition, demonstrating instead that, while the commons as a corporate body could present petitions,

83 *RP* ii. 352–3, 372; iii. 45–6, 272, 308, 322.
84 McKisack, *Parliamentary representation*, 32.
85 *RP* iv. 315.
86 Stubbs, *Constitutional history of England*, iii. 478–9.

a common petition in the fourteenth century was not always a petition from the knights and burgesses in parliament. Rather, a common petition was one that was 'concerned with a common or public interest', in contrast to the private petition ('singulere petition') which referred 'only to one particular part of the country and the burdens consequent upon its geographical position'.[87] A. R. Myers made a similar point about the fifteenth-century common petition, arguing that 'the essential feature of a common petition should be, not that it was a petition of the Commons, but that it was one concerned with a common or public interest'.[88] In short, according to Rayner and Myers, it was the subject matter of a petition, not its origin, which determined its status as a common petition.

The work of Rayner and Myers is useful for two reasons. First, it raises the question of what constituted the common interest in the medieval parliament; and secondly, it draws attention to the problem of determining the relationship between a parliamentary petition and an MP for the simple reason that a petition was rarely presented in the name of an individual parliamentary representative.[89] In the cases of Bristol and York, moreover, the records of civic government in the second half of the fourteenth century do not provide evidence of either instructions or payments to MPs to present business at parliament, such as the £10 with which York's MPs were rewarded in 1478 'for the writing of a certain petition'.[90] Although the *plena potestas* clause in the parliamentary writ of summons empowered parliamentary representatives to act ' "in the name of the whole community" ' of their town or county, this clause was included for fiscal purposes so that the king could 'secure grants of taxation which should, through the consent of fully empowered representatives, be legally binding upon the communities of shire and borough which they represented'.[91] Far more is known about the theory than the practice of representation. That the common petitions from Bristol and York were, however, presented by their MPs is suggested by their status as 'group' petitions, that is, petitions which came from a particular region or from a particular economic interest group, and it is likely that, as J. S. Roskell has argued, 'if a common petition came to be presented for the mutual benefit of more than one county, the representatives involved would collaborate in the course of a session'.[92] This collaboration would certainly explain the existence of three

[87] Rayner, 'Forms and machinery of the "commune petition" ', 204.
[88] A. R. Myers, 'Parliamentary petitions in the fifteenth century', *EHR* lii (1937), 606.
[89] G. L. Haskins, 'The petitions of representatives in the parliaments of Edward I', *EHR* liii (1938), 1–20, esp. pp. 15–16.
[90] *York city chamberlains' account rolls*, 167. For the evidence from civic records generally see McKisack, *Parliamentary representation*, 134–5.
[91] J. G. Edwards, 'The *plena potestas* of English parliamentary representatives', in *Oxford essays in medieval history presented to Herbert Edward Salter*, Oxford 1934, 142, 147.
[92] The term was first used by H. L. Gray, *The influence of the commons on early legislation: a study of the fourteenth and fifteenth centuries*, Cambridge, Mass. 1932, ch. x, esp. pp. 337, 343. The quotation is from Roskell, 'Introductory survey', 79.

consecutive common petitions on the parliament roll of 1376 from Bristol and its neighbouring counties.[93] Perhaps the parliamentary representatives of Bristol and York came to parliament with instructions to present a petition about an issue that specifically affected their own towns, but the significant point is that that they recognised that their local interests were shared by representatives of other communities in parliament and were able to broaden their particular concerns into a much wider complaint.

The examples of Bristol and York indicate that, in the period 1350 to 1400, two factors, of shifting importance, determined the status of a common petition. In essence a common petition was one that sought more than judicial remedy or favours or privileges for individuals or individual groups. A common petition could address an issue such as the defence of the realm, but it could also, more generally, ask for legislation,[94] in the form of statutes or ordinances, which had some bearing on the realm as a whole. In this respect, the language of the common petition deserves particular attention since it has been claimed that 'on the whole each town looked to its own interests, and the business of its representatives was to seek the vindication of local rights in parliament'.[95] Whether the MPs for Bristol and York were simply paying lip-service to the morality of the common good is irrelevant: as John Watts has argued, albeit in a slightly different context, the significant fact is that 'people were aware of a broader politics beyond their own immediate relationships and interests'.[96]

Yet a common petition was increasingly the product of the influence and lobbying skills that particular MPs could exercise in the commons: hence the increasing visibility of Bristol in the parliament rolls when the town became a separate county and the political status of its MPs in parliament was enhanced. None the less, while common petitions were the result of debate and dialogue within the commons, the procedure by which petitions came to be presented in the name of the commons is unknown. Even in the *Anonimalle chronicle*'s account of the Good Parliament – the most detailed contemporary record of the late medieval parliament – 'we are not told how different opinions were reconciled or, if unreconciled, how the view of the majority was established'.[97] Common petitions, unlike private petitions, went directly to the king and council for discussion rather than to the auditors and triers of petitions.[98] It was, therefore, of obvious advantage to a petitioner to

---

[93] *RP* ii. 352–3.
[94] On this point see Roskell, 'Introductory survey', 78, and G. L. Harriss, 'The formation of parliament, 1272–1377', in Davies and Denton, *English parliament*, 49. Private petitions could be 'brought with great frequency to central courts, local courts and private courts of law': G. O. Sayles, *The functions of the medieval parliament of England*, London 1988, 50.
[95] McKisack, 'Borough representation', 519.
[96] J. Watts, 'Ideas, principles and politics', in A. J. Pollard (ed.), *The Wars of the Roses*, Basingstoke 1995, 117.
[97] Harriss, 'Formation of parliament', 39.
[98] Ibid.

gain the support of the commons if he wanted the king's immediate attention, and it is clear that the commons' procedures were susceptible to abuse. In 1372 the crown banned the election of lawyers as knights of the shire because they were drafting petitions in the name of the commons which only concerned private business and which had not been the subject of discussion in the commons.[99] Thus, it was not always possible for the commons as a corporate body to examine the petitions that were put forward in its name.

Although it was not until the end of the fourteenth century that individuals began to petition the commons to adopt private petitions and to present them to the king,[100] group petitions, whether from counties, towns or economic interests, were a different matter. A 1373 petition to the king from 'your liege burgesses of your town of Bristol' requesting the confirmation of both the recently granted county charter and the letters patent delineating the county's boundaries seems to have been sponsored by the commons, for the petition ended with the words, added in a different hand: 'and the commons pray that this petition is confirmed in this present parliament'.[101] Similarly, in the Good Parliament there was a petition from the commons on behalf of 'the citizens of York' who had freighted a Dutch ship at Hull with wool to take to Calais. The problem for the York citizens was that the shipowner, Peter Arnaldeson, had taken the wool, valued at £900, to Holland, where it was seized by the lord of Arkel and Gorinchem, who claimed it as compensation for Edward III's unpaid debts for his military service in France.[102] As the petition explained the damage was explicitly to the 'very great loss and impoverishment of the said citizens', and the citizens asked for a warrant to arrest the ships and merchandise belonging to the Dutch lordship in England and Calais. In fact, not only was the subject of this petition a private grievance, but it is also evident from another almost identical but undated petition that 'the citizens of York' were actually nine 'merchants of York and of Hull'.[103] York's MPs at the 1376 parliament are not known, but of the seven York merchants mentioned in the petition, four were former mayors of the city and four, John de Gysburn, Robert de Howom, Thomas de Howom and John de Rypon, served as MPs for York.[104] The petition was in

---

99   *RP* ii. 310. See also p. 146 above.

100   For this procedure see Gray, *Influence of the commons*, 354–5; J. G. Edwards, *The second century of the English parliament*, Oxford 1979, 55; and H. Cam, 'The legislators of medieval England', in her *Law-finders and law-makers in medieval England*, London 1962, 148. A good example of this later practice is the 1394 petition of John Banbury, a Bristol merchant, whose petition, concerning the theft of merchandise from his ship-wrecked vessel in the river Severn by a group of Welshmen, requested the intercession of the commons with the king: SC 8/96/4758.

101   For the original petition see SC 8/269/13401. It is also part of the parliament roll under the caption 'les petitions de communes et les respons d'ycelles': *RP* ii. 320.

102   *RP* ii. 353.

103   For this petition see SC 8/114/5653.

104   See appendix below.

the name of the communal interests of the city, but, in reality, it expressed the commercial concerns of a small number of individuals who dominated civic government in York.

The most striking feature of Bristol's common petitions was the frequency with which they addressed certain issues. The subjects were four-fold: first, the cloth trade in the south-west; second, relations with the Welsh; third, legislation on river traffic; and fourth, the jurisdiction of the court of admiralty. That the petitions articulated similar concerns, sometimes at nearly successive parliaments, suggests that Bristol's representatives were not only able to co-operate with the representatives of other communities to present petitions of mutual interest, but that they could also sustain a particular agenda.

In 1376 and 1390 Bristol's representatives petitioned the crown about the state of the cloth trade in the south-western counties. In 1376 the petition was in the name of 'the knights and merchants of Wiltshire, Bristol, Somerset, Gloucestershire and Dorset, and all the commons of the realm of England', who were concerned with the damage to the local manufacture and trade of cloth caused by the production of a woollen yarn, which was being exported illegally to Normandy and Lombardy, hidden in various containers.[105] In 1390 the petition from the parliamentary commons complained about the fraudulent manufacture and sale of cloth in the counties of Somerset, Dorset, Bristol and Gloucestershire. The problem was that cloth was being offered for sale in rolls, making it impossible for the buyer to know the condition of the cloth on the inside of the rolls, which was often of a poor quality and uneven colour and size. Merchants who bought the cloth for export then faced imprisonment, even death, from foreign buyers overseas when the rolls of cloth were opened.[106] In both cases, then, the petitions were specifically in the interests of Bristol's cloth merchants. While the 1390 petition was addressed in the name of 'les Communes', it was actually from 'the merchants who purchase the said cloths and take them out of the realm to sell'. The names of Bristol's MPs in 1376 are unknown, but in 1390 the representatives were William Frome and John Vyell,[107] both of whom exported cloth and perhaps co-authored the petition. They would no doubt have collaborated with Thomas Beaupyne of Bristol who was not only MP for Somerset in 1390, but was also the farmer of the cloth subsidy in the counties of Bristol, Somerset, Gloucestershire, Devon, Cornwall and Dorset.[108] In return for a fixed sum of money paid to the exchequer, Beaupyne was allowed to collect alnage, an internal tax on cloth exposed for sale, receiving 4d. for every cloth which he sealed. It was his responsibility, like that of other alnagers,

[105] *RP* ii. 353.
[106] *RP* iii. 272.
[107] See their biographies in Roskell and others, *House of Commons, 1386–1421*, iii. 135–6; iv. 721–2.
[108] See his biography ibid. ii. 164–6, esp. p. 164.

'to certify, for the benefit of the buyer, as to the true dimensions of the pieces of cloth submitted for scrutiny and sealing before being offered for sale'.[109] Beaupyne had probably detected the fraud in the first place.

On one level, such petitions reflected an awareness among Bristol's MPs and the representatives of the neighbouring counties of a shared interest in the cloth trade. Given that the area between Winchester and Bristol was the largest and most important cloth-producing area in the country in the late fourteenth century,[110] the perception of a common economic bond was hardly surprising. Indeed, the fact that the 1376 petition was in the name of the knights, as well as merchants of Bristol and its neighbouring shires, is of special interest, since it was from this period and from the 1380s, in partic-ular, that the price of wool fell and the south-western gentry became less interested in the Calais staple, turning instead to other profitable ventures including the sale of wool to cloth manufacturers in the region.[111] At the same time, the petitions expressed more than regional concerns. They were also conscious of the wider realm and of a wider politics, referring, for instance, to the 'very great loss of the king and of his people' caused by the smuggling of woollen yarn and to the way in which the illicit sale of cloth abroad was to the 'great slander of the realm'.[112] The 1376 petition appealed specifically to the financial interests of the crown, pointing out that the clan-destine export of the woollen yarn to Normandy and Lombardy not only deprived the knights and merchants of their cloth, but also resulted in the loss to the king of valuable revenue from the cloth and wool customs. At a time when the crown was desperately short of money for its foreign engage-ments, it is not surprising that the petition resulted in a ban on the export of the woollen yarn. The 1390 petition sought a royal ordinance to protect the cloth buyer from fraud. Cloths were not to be sold in rolls, but were to be open so that 'the purchasers could view and identify them, as was customary in the county of Essex', while weavers and fullers were to place their seal on the cloth guaranteeing its quality. The request for legislation to protect the interests of the buyer might have struck a chord with the royal government, since the control of markets for the benefit of the purchaser was one aspect of royal economic policy,[113] but it is more than likely that the crown recognised the need to placate an influential economic interest group within the commons, particularly since this was Richard II's first parliament after his resumption of power in 1389.[114] The petition's request was transformed into

---

[109] For the cloth subsidy see Gray, 'English woollens', 13–35, quotation at p. 14; A. R. Bridbury, *Medieval English clothmaking: an economic survey*, London 1982, 47–59, quotation at p. 47.

[110] Gray, 'English woollens', 31–2.

[111] Nightingale, 'Knights and merchants', 59.

[112] *RP* ii. 353; iii. 272.

[113] Miller, 'Economic policies of governments', 328.

[114] For the most recent discussion of Richard II's approach to parliament in the early 1390s see Saul, *Richard II*, 201–4, 235–6.

statutory legislation and the statute followed the wording of the petition almost verbatim.[115]

Another subject of Bristol's common petitions was the freedom of river traffic on the river Severn, which was hindered by the construction of weirs and other obstacles to river navigation. In 1377 a common petition, addressed in the name of 'the commons of the counties of Bristol, Gloucestershire, Worcestershire, Herefordshire, Shropshire and the other counties adjoining the river Severn between Worcester and Bristol', complained about the erection of fishing weirs in the river Severn which reduced the flow of the river so that boats could not travel on it except at great danger and which flooded the meadow and arable land bordering the river.[116] In the Gloucester parliament of 1378 a petition from the commons articulated 'a common grievance . . . in the counties of Gloucesterhire, Bristol, Worcestershire, Herefordshire and Shrewsbury [sic]' on the same subject as the previous year, namely the building of various fishing weirs and kiddles in the river Severn.[117] The petitions represented sustained parliamentary pressure from the Welsh border region in the 1370s about the state of the river Severn. An undated private petition from 'the community of the counties of Bristol, Gloucestershire, Worcestershire, Herefordshire, Shropshire and Staffordshire' concerning obstructions on the river Severn seems to have marked the beginning of this lobbying process.[118] It was very similar in wording to the 1377 common petition, referring, for instance, to 'the gorces' that were 'so tightly fixed' that 'the water could not flow easily', leading to the flooding of the meadow and arable land on either side of the river. The 1377 common petition differed from the earlier petition primarily in its emphasis on the dangers to 'women and their children' caused by the flooding, which seems to have been added to the petition almost as an afterthought, while the 1378 common petition went a stage further, making the threat to women and children the main interest of the petitioners.

The changing emphasis of the petitions is particularly interesting. Keeping rivers free from weirs and other obstructions was a key responsibility of a town's civic officials,[119] not least because of their concern about the sustenance of their communities and the provision of an adequate food supply.[120] The private petition, for instance, emphasised the fact that the vessels whose passage was blocked on the river Severn were carrying wine, fish, corn 'and other victuals' presumably to feed the inhabitants of the communities that bordered the river. Certainly, Bristol was reliant on the Severn valley trade to

[115] SR ii. 64.
[116] RP ii. 372.
[117] RP iii. 46.
[118] SC 8/14/659.
[119] Attreed, King's towns, 214–17.
[120] A. B. Hibbert, 'The economic policies of towns', in Postan and others, Cambridge economic history of Europe, iii. 157–229, esp. p. 161.

feed itself, with grain and corn and other foodstuffs coming down the river from towns such as Worcester and Tewkesbury.[121] Meanwhile, the 1377 petition highlighted the dangers to the ships and their crews who perished because of river obstructions, and the 1378 petition drew explicit attention to the serious hazard weirs and other fishgarths posed to the women and children of the counties bordering the river, perhaps as a result of the flooding of the river's banks. Despite the participation of many of Bristol's common councillors in regional trade in addition to overseas commerce and the role of the river Severn as a crucial artery in the inland distribution of wine and raw materials such as hides,[122] what was conspicuously absent from this inclusive view of the urban community presented in Bristol's petitions was a mercantile perspective. In the rhetorical strategy adopted by Bristol's MPs, the town's communal interests were given deliberate preference over the sectional concerns of its rulers, yet what the crown and the town's MPs knew, but did not say, was that the clearance of weirs from rivers was essential for the passage of merchandise, on which both the town's mercantile elite and the crown were dependent for financial reasons. According to the prevailing political morality in parliament, common petitions were meant to be concerned with the common good which, in this instance, meant the interest of the urban community as a whole, rather than the personal profit of a few merchants.[123]

At the same time, although the undated private petition and the 1377 common petition asked the king and council to provide a remedy to the particular grievance held by the border counties, the 1378 common petition requested legislative action. Not only were the existing statutes on the freedom of river traffic to be enforced, but this 'same ordinance was to be proclaimed throughout the realm'.[124] The petitioners recognised that their specific complaint about the river Severn was part of a wider, national concern about navigation on England's rivers and that the best way to secure a satisfactory response from the crown was to connect their problem with the wider concerns among the political community at parliament. The issue of river obstructions was one that was raised repeatedly by the commons in parliament and to which the crown responded in the second half of the fourteenth century either with new legislation or with confirmation of the existing laws. The crown's interest in fishing weirs was not a peculiarity of this period. Indeed, clause thirty-three of the 1215 Magna Carta (later clause twenty-three of the reissue of 1225) had ordered the complete removal of all kiddles from the Thames and the Medway 'and throughout all England',[125]

---

121 Penn, 'Fourteenth-century Bristol', 29.
122 Ibid. 201–4.
123 On this point see H. G. Richardson, 'The commons and medieval politics', in H. G. Richardson and G. O. Sayles, The English parliament in the Middle Ages, London 1981, 33.
124 RP iii. 46.
125 J. C. Holt, Magna carta, 2nd edn, Cambridge 1992, 459–61, 507.

while clause eighteen in the second Statute of Westminster (1285) limited the occasions on which certain rivers should 'be in defence' for salmon fishing.[126] None the less, it is also true that the crown was increasingly attentive to the severity of the problem of river navigation because of persistent parliamentary lobbying on the subject, which resulted in the submission of common petitions about the regulation of rivers in 1351, 1352, 1363, 1371, 1376, 1377, 1378, 1384, 1390, 1397 and 1399.[127] In 1351 the crown revised and updated the 1285 statute, ordering the removal of all fishing weirs and other obstructions which had been erected since the beginning of the reign of Edward I 'in the great rivers of England', namely the Thames, the Severn, the Ouse and the Trent.[128] In 1371, in response to a complaint that weirs and other fishing traps still remained in several places despite legislation, the crown declared that the existing statutes should be enforced and imposed a fine of 100 marks on those found guilty of not removing their traps within a certain time period.[129] Bristol's common petitions of 1377 and 1378, therefore, emphasised the integration of local and national issues within parliament.

A further subject of Bristol's common petitions was lawlessness in the Welsh border region. In the Good Parliament 'the counties of Worcestershire, Shropshire, Staffordshire, Herefordshire, Bristol and Gloucestershire' complained that the men of Wales, the Welsh March and Cheshire, with little provocation ('pur petit debate ou pur petit ire'), entered the Welsh border counties killing and burning the inhabitants, safe in the knowledge that, because of their judicial immunity, their goods and chattels could not be forfeited for felonies or trespasses committed in England. The petitioners asked that the offenders be subject to due legal process for their crimes in the particular county in which they had committed their offence and that their goods and lands be seized by their respective lords in Wales, the Welsh March and Cheshire as forfeiture.[130] In 1378 the 'liege citizens and burgesses of Bristol, Shrewsbury, Hereford, Gloucester, Worcester and the other marcher towns' petitioned the crown concerning their experiences in parts of Wales where they had gone to trade, informing the crown that they were reluctant to return to Wales for fear of being distrained for the debts of others in which 'they are neither debtors, pledges, nor trespassers' and seeking a solution in parliament to the problem.[131] Bristol merchants were especially prominent in Wales, particularly in the towns along the coast of south Wales.[132] Yet, as the

---

[126] SR i. 94–5.
[127] RP ii. 229, 240, 277, 305, 331, 333–4, 346, 366, 372; iii. 46, 201, 282, 371–2, 438–9.
[128] SR i. 315–16.
[129] SR i. 393.
[130] RP ii. 352–3.
[131] RP iii. 45.
[132] R. R. Davies, The revolt of Owain Glyn Dŵr, Oxford 1995, 5, 28; Penn, 'Fourteenth-century Bristol', 42–3.

1378 petition explained, they and their colleagues in the marcher towns entered Wales in order 'to victual the said cities and towns and to acquire merchandise for their sustenance'. Like the parliamentary campaign to keep the river Severn free from fishgarths, the commercial interests of Bristol's merchants, though clearly not too far beneath the surface of the petition, were purposely relegated to a position of secondary importance. Of primary concern was the general welfare of the English marcher towns and cities including Bristol, for whom the petition sought relief ('en relevation de voz Villes et Citees suis dites').

In 1393 the parliamentary commons addressed the crown on behalf of 'the counties of Gloucestershire, Worcestershire, Bristol, Shropshire, Hereford-shire, Staffordshire and other counties of the realm', joining the main elements of the two earlier petitions into a single complaint.[133] On the one hand, the men of Cheshire and the Welsh March had, so the petitioners alleged, committed a litany of crimes in the English counties including murder and robbery, as well as the theft of cattle, horses and sheep, with which they then returned to their own lands. Although they were outlawed in England for their offences, they remained outside English jurisdiction and those aggrieved parties who tried to pursue the malefactors in Cheshire and the Welsh March could secure no redress because 'the said malefactors do not wish, nor are they held, to answer for robbery or trespasses committed outside the jurisdiction of their marcher lords'. On the other hand, the men of Cheshire and the Welsh March continued to distrain, for the debts of their fellow merchants, 'all manner of merchants and others of the realm' who were engaged in trade in Cheshire and the Welsh March, which practice was 'to the great destruction and impoverishment of the commons aforesaid'. Thus, the petitioners asked that the injured parties, who could prove the legitimacy of their claim before the lord of the land in which the malefactors were resident, should be able to either reclaim their goods directly or receive damages awarded by the officials of the local lord.

These petitions from Bristol and the neighbouring counties were not the only parliamentary complaints issued to the crown about the Welsh border region in the second half of the fourteenth century. Indeed, almost identical common petitions were presented in the parliaments of April 1379, January 1380, October 1382, November 1384 and November 1390 about the actions of the people of Cheshire, who made armed raids into various neighbouring English counties, perpetrating a series of crimes including robbery, kidnap, rape and murder before returning to Cheshire and other liberties. Though they were indicted for their offences, nothing could be done to punish them because they belonged to semi-autonomous jurisdictions in which the king's writ did not run, which meant that they could not be held to account for offences committed outside their county.[134] These rather stereotyped

---

[133] *RP* iii. 308.
[134] *RP* iii. 62, 81, 139, 201, 280.

complaints have helped gain for the people of Cheshire a reputation for violence and lawlessness among historians of late medieval England, which has been difficult to cast off.[135] Paul Booth has viewed these petitions as crucial evidence of growing disorder in Cheshire in the late fourteenth century,[136] but the parliamentary petitions should be treated with more scepticism than they have hitherto. The Black Prince, as was by now customary for the king's eldest son, held the earldom of Chester from 1333 until his death in 1376. He also, significantly, enjoyed the title of prince of Wales which, in this period, was borne by the king's son and heir.[137] It is surely no coincidence that the parliamentary petitions about disorder on the Welsh border, which Booth and others have cited, date from the Good Parliament, for it was during this assembly, on 8 June 1376, that the Black Prince died.[138] The result was that both the earldom of Chester and the principality of Wales reverted to the crown. Furthermore, after the investiture of the future Richard II, the Black Prince's son, with his father's titles on 20 November 1376,[139] titles he never relinquished as king for default of a direct male heir, petitioners could appeal in parliament to the king's personal lordship for matters relating to Wales and Cheshire, which remained under his direct control. In short, there is reason to doubt whether the alleged lawlessness along the border was anything new in the second half of the fourteenth century, but was, instead, the result of carefully co-ordinated lobbying designed to take advantage of the availability of greater opportunities for redress at parliament.

The main problem for Bristol and for the entire Welsh border region in the period 1350 to 1400 was, what it had always been, namely the existence of separate judicial franchises in the principality of Wales, the Welsh March and Cheshire. In the principality and the Welsh March, as R. R. Davies has pointed out, neither could the English king's writ 'be served in most parts of the country', nor did 'royal justices or English sheriffs have any authority there'. Furthermore, 'there was no legal process available for the recovery of goods stolen from English merchants travelling through the country; and the Welsh seemed to take a delight in capturing and ransoming travellers, whether to recover debts owed to them by others or for the sheer devilry and profit of it'.[140] The Welsh March, in particular, was 'beyond the reach of royal justice and of the common law of England' and thus it was 'impossible to pursue an offender from England into the March or to compel a man from the

---

[135] See, for example, G. Barraclough, *The earldom and county palatine of Chester*, Oxford 1953, 24. For comment see T. Thornton, *Cheshire and the Tudor state, 1480–1560*, Woodbridge 2000, 8–9.

[136] P. H. W. Booth, 'Taxation and public order: Cheshire in 1353', *NH* xii (1976), 29–31.

[137] For the Black Prince's titles see R. Barber, *Edward, prince of Wales and Aquitaine: a biography of the Black Prince*, Woodbridge 1978, 16, 18, 20, 41.

[138] Saul, *Richard II*, 17.

[139] Ibid.

[140] Davies, *Revolt of Owain Glyn Dŵr*, 5.

March to answer for an offence committed in England or against an English-man'.[141] Instead, it was the Marcher lords who were supreme in the March, for writs were issued in their name and each lord was the final arbiter of justice within his lordship.[142] Similarly, the earldom of Chester was a palatinate and enjoyed a semi-independent position within the kingdom of England, with its own chancery, exchequer and judiciary separate from, but modelled on, those that operated from Westminster. Its lord, from 1254 usually the king's eldest son, had complete power of justice 'in life and limb' and its inhabitants were immune from trial outside the county.[143] The crown, nevertheless, retained the right of 'superior lordship' to hear cases concerning areas in which the king's writ did not operate, a right enshrined in the first Statute of Westminster (1275), according to which, if a crime was committed 'in the Marches of Wales, or in any other Place, where the King's Writs be not current, the King, which is Sovereign Lord over all, shall do Right there unto such as will complain'.[144] In the final quarter of the fourteenth century the MPs of the Welsh border region appealed to the king as a higher authority in cases where there were no local opportunities for the redress of grievances, but, more significantly, they also took advantage of the king's position as both earl of Chester and prince of Wales to address him repeatedly in parliament to correct the judicial and administrative anomalies represented by the principality of Wales, the Welsh March and the palatinate of Chester. To those living along the Welsh border, it was the very privileges and immunities of these powerful neighbouring franchises that were the main cause of the lawlessness, providing a direct incentive to commit crime in England with impunity.

Yet there remained a fundamental difference in the priorities of the representatives of the border region and the crown in the second half of the fourteenth century, a tension that was revealed in the non-committal answers given to Bristol's common petitions in 1376, 1378 and 1393, in which the crown stated that the existing laws should be enforced, that the king would be advised by his council and the Marcher lords, and, rather tersely, that 'the king shall be advised'.[145] The king sought generally to respect the liberties of the Welsh March, not least because many of their lords were powerful figures in English politics, numbering two dukes and seven earls in the mid-1390s.[146] As earl of Chester, Richard II was expected personally to uphold the special privileges of the palatinate, and his answers to common petitions in May 1382 and November 1390 seeking remedy to continuing armed incursions into the border counties were especially mindful to preserve palatinate rights

141 Idem, *Lordship and society in the march of Wales, 1282–1400*, Oxford 1978, 3.
142 Ibid. 3–4, 151–2.
143 Barraclough, *County palatine of Chester*, 20.
144 SR i. 31; Davies, *March of Wales*, 251.
145 RP ii. 352–3; iii. 45, 308.
146 Davies, *March of Wales*, 256–7, and *Owain Glyn Dŵr*, 37.

('sauvant la Franchise del Countee de Cestre'), avowing his sympathy for the petitioners' plight without seriously aiming to erode them.[147] Moreover, as is well known, Richard II's relationship with Cheshire was especially intimate:[148] the king was dependent on a large force from Cheshire at the battle of Radcot Bridge on 20 December 1387 between Robert de Vere, duke of Ireland, and the lords appellant; in the last two years of his reign, Richard had a permanent bodyguard consisting largely of Cheshire archers; and he raised the county to the status of a principality in September 1397 as a sign of his personal favour towards the liberty. All three aspects of his close association with Cheshire made it highly unlikely that the king would try to revoke palatinate privileges, a task that was left instead to his successor, Henry Bolingbroke, who, in the parliament of October 1399, his first as king, made a conciliatory gesture to appease a longstanding complaint from the border counties by ordering that the inhabitants of Cheshire could no longer claim immunity from appearing in courts held outside the county.[149]

Despite a perception in government circles that Wales represented 'a security-risk for the English government, be it from external attack or internal revolt',[150] it was only the beginning of Owain Glyn Dŵr's revolt in September 1400 that transformed the crown's perspective on the situation in the principality of Wales and the Welsh March, not least because it seemed to confirm what representatives of the border communities such as Bristol had been saying in parliament at various times throughout the later fourteenth century. In 1401 a series of common petitions about the rebellion was presented at parliament, demanding immediate legislative action against the Welsh.[151] The crown responded to some of the common petitions with statutory legislation: two of these statutes provided the legislative changes which had been implicit in Bristol's earlier requests to bring Wales into administrative and judicial compliance with the English legal system. Clause sixteen dealt with those who distrained the goods and chattels of the men of English counties for debts in which they were neither debtors nor pledges, stating that letters testimonial were to be sealed by the sheriff or mayor of the franchise in which the arrested lived and then delivered to the governor or steward of the appropriate lordship, who was to return the property.[152] Clause

---

[147] *RP* iii. 139, 280.
[148] For Richard II's special relationship with Cheshire see, for example, R. R. Davies, 'Richard II and the principality of Chester, 1397–9', in Du Boulay and Barron, *Reign of Richard II*, 256–79. An important reappraisal is T. Thornton, 'Cheshire: the inner citadel of Richard II's kingdom?', in G. Dodd (ed.), *The reign of Richard II*, Stroud 2000, 85–96.
[149] The common petition from the county of Shropshire prompting this action is in *RP* iii. 440.
[150] Davies, *Owain Glyn Dŵr*, 66–7.
[151] *RP* iii. 457, 472–4, 476. The petitions are also discussed in R. A. Griffiths, 'Wales and the Marches', in S. B. Chrimes and others (eds), *Fifteenth-century England, 1399–1509: studies in politics and society*, Manchester 1972, 148–9.
[152] *SR* ii. 128–9.

seventeen aimed to prevent the Welsh from committing felony and trespass in English counties and then claiming judicial immunity in Wales. In future, the records of such offences tried before the king's justices in England were to be delivered to the lords and royal officials of the franchises in Wales in which the offender was resident for punishment.[153]

Bristol's common petitions, then, demonstrated frequent co-operation and collaboration between the town's parliamentary representatives and the MPs for the neighbouring counties and towns: Bristol's MPs were part of a regional interest group in parliament based on strong geographical and economic ties. Pamela Nightingale's recent work on the certificates of debt registered under statute merchant in Bristol has shown that in the south west of England, especially, there were specific economic reasons for the increasingly active engagement of the region's gentry in the wool trade, not least because Bristol's merchants were interested primarily in the export of cloth rather than wool and did not dominate the inland wool trade. As a result of the gentry's mercantile connections, the commercial and political interests of the knights and merchants of the south-west region were closely related.[154] This relationship helps to explain an otherwise curious common petition presented at the Good Parliament: 'the counties of Worcestershire, Shropshire, Staffordshire, Herefordshire, Bristol and Gloucestershire' petitioned on behalf of 'several merchants and other people of the said counties' who 'travel to Calais with their merchandise to the profit of the said counties and of the whole realm' and who had been arrested at the staple for the debts of their fellow merchants, an arbitrary practice against which merchants had been formally protected by a statute of 1275.[155] The inclusion of Bristol as a co-author of the 1376 petition was probably the result of the emergence, from the mid-1360s, of the south-western gentry as 'middlemen between Bristol's merchants and London's exporters', purchasing wool from Bristol merchants on behalf of London staplers such as the grocer, William Venour.[156]

Yet if there was something distinctive about the economic structure of the south west in the fourteenth century, which helped to encourage Bristol's MPs to collaborate with the representatives of the region on issues of mutual concern, it is true that York's MPs also occasionally formed regional alliances within parliament. In 1382 'the commons of the counties of Yorkshire and Lincolnshire, with all the cities and towns' complained about the royal practice of granting licences to merchants to export grain, which led to scarcity and rising prices ('escharestee et chiertee') in the region.[157] The grain trade was lucrative for York's merchants,[158] who had been required to obtain special

---

153 *SR* ii. 129.
154 Nightingale, 'Knights and merchants', 61.
155 *RP* ii. 352. See clause twenty-three of the 1275 statute: *SR* i. 33.
156 Nightingale, 'Knights and merchants', 52–6.
157 *RP* iii. 141.
158 In January 1383, for example, two York merchants, William Richemond and Thomas

permission to export the foodstuff in the first place because of concern over high prices in England.[159] The crown's policy of issuing licences to export grain was evidently of serious concern to York's MPs who, in association with the other urban and rural representatives of Yorkshire and Lincolnshire, asked that it be prohibited altogether and that ships carrying corn for export should only be allowed to travel overseas to the English possessions of Calais and Bordeaux. Here, then, was evidence of tension between the private interests of individual merchants within York and the public duties of members of the urban elite, who were expected to govern on behalf of the common good of their community. The provision of an adequate and affordable food supply in the city's markets was an issue of critical importance to York's rulers, just as it was for the governors of other towns and cities.[160] The city was reliant on the grain produce of the counties of Yorkshire and Lincolnshire and the 1382 petition reflected the public interests of the city's rulers who wanted the grain from the surrounding countryside to enter the city's markets rather than to go abroad. In short, there was a regional dimension to the petition, in which York's need for a hinterland as a source of food helped to establish socio-economic ties that could be articulated by its representatives in parliament. At the same time, the petitioners were aware that theirs was not just a regional concern: they requested an ordinance to prevent all merchants from exporting grain, which the king issued, declaring a 'general ban' ('defens general') on the export of grain 'throughout the realm', although significantly he also reserved the right to grant licences in the future, stating that no licence would be issued contrary to this ordinance 'without the advice of his council and reasonable cause'.[161] The difference between Bristol and York lay less in the regional perspective of their parliamentary representatives and more in the former town's elevation to the status of a county in its own right in 1373. The relative paucity of common petitions relating specifically to York in the second half of the fourteenth century, compared to the more numerous petitions from Bristol's MPs, points towards the higher political status enjoyed by Bristol's representatives in parliament after the town attained county status.

On occasion, as Pamela Nightingale has suggested, 'regional interests were likely to be more important than social divisions' in parliament,[162] but if there was a regional view of parliament, it is also the case that there were some issues that were of specific concern to the representatives of urban

---

de Kilburn, were granted a licence to purchase 1,000 quarters of barley from the county of Lincolnshire and to export it to Scotland: *Rotuli Scotiae*, ed. D. Macpherson and others, London 1814–19, ii. 47.

159 For the practice of issuing licences see S. H. Rigby, *Medieval Grimsby*, Hull 1993, 53.
160 For contemporary civic ordinances regulating the victualling trade in the city of York see YMB i. 45–6. For discussion see Rees Jones, 'York's civic administration', 126–7.
161 *RP* iii. 141. The royal proclamation is in *CCR, 1381–5*, 236.
162 Nightingale, 'Knights and merchants', 61.

communities.[163] One of these issues was the jurisdiction of the court of admiralty. The court of admiralty evolved in the mid-fourteenth century in order
to keep the king's peace on the sea and to protect overseas trade involving
English and foreign merchants by settling piracy claims.[164] The problem was
that the court's jurisdiction was not properly defined, so that it began to
determine cases on land such as pleas of debt and contract, which had previously been tried in civic courts, as well as purely maritime disputes arising
from piracy and spoil of wreck. In January 1390 the parliamentary commons
petitioned the king about the growing jurisdiction of the admirals and their
deputies who were 'usurping to themselves greater power than belongs to
their office', to the prejudice of the king and the common law and to the
'great impairment of several various franchises'. The petition asked that the
extent of the jurisdiction of the court of admiralty be defined and the king
answered that, from henceforth, the court of admiralty could not hear cases
arising 'within the realm, but only of a thing done upon the sea' ('soulement
de chose faite sur le Meer'), as was customary in Edward III's reign. The king's
answer was then enshrined in statutory legislation.[165]

The issue of the admiralty court is important for four reasons: first, it was
part of an urban agenda in parliament that was maintained in successive
parliaments in the early 1390s; secondly, it was the subject of parliamentary
debate in which the MPs for both Bristol and York were involved; thirdly,
although the issue concerned urban liberties, it was not really so much about
the interests of civic subjects as much as the interests of civic rulers; and
fourthly, the common petitions demonstrate that the defence of urban liberties was not always a local, private matter to the particular town concerned,
but that it could become part of a wider, national agenda within parliament
through consultation and negotiation.

In November 1390, in response to the statute proclaimed at the previous
parliament, the 'commons of your cities and boroughs and sea ports' petitioned the king, claiming, both by charter and by custom, to have jurisdiction in all manner of pleas, contracts, covenants and trespasses 'as well by
land as by sea', the profits of which contributed to the payment of their
annual fee farm to the crown, a fiscal point which would not have been lost
on the king. The representatives of the urban and maritime communities
complained that the court of admiralty had heard cases which had arisen
within their civic franchises and which were 'to the disinheritance of the said
citizens and burgesses'. Once more they asked for a clarification of the jurisdiction of the admiralty court, and the king replied that the matter would be

---

[163] A point noted by McKisack, 'Borough representation', 519; Ormrod, *Edward III*,
195–6.
[164] For the origins and early history of the court see *Select pleas in the court of admiralty*, ed.
R. G. Marsden (Selden Society vi, xi, 1892, 1897), i, pp. xiii–xv; McKisack, *Fourteenth
century*, 245.
[165] *RP* iii. 269–70; *SR* ii. 62.

referred to his council for discussion.[166] In the following parliament, which met in November 1391, the commons petitioned again about the extent of the jurisdiction of the admirals and their deputies – on this occasion 'for the profit of the king and of the realm' – complaining that their actions encroached on the franchises of the cities and boroughs by hearing cases which did not properly belong to them. This time, they requested that the admirals place their jurisdictional claims before parliament so that the political community could know, once and for all, the limits of their jurisdiction. The king's response went further than the January 1390 statute in limiting the power of the admirals. In future, the court of admiralty would have no jurisdiction in cases of contracts and pleas 'and all other things done or arising within the bodies of the counties, as well by land as by water', including spoil of wreck.[167] The clock was turned back so that the powers of the admirals were what they had been in the early fourteenth century: essentially military and occasional. The admirals were to be responsible for the arrest of ships for royal fleets, with the power to maintain discipline on board among the crew while the vessels were away at sea in royal service. The 1391 statute, then, was the reaction of the royal government to concerted pressure from the parliamentary burgesses over a number of parliaments. However, the admiralty's jurisdiction had grown in the first instance neither at the will of the admiralty nor of the king, but as a response to the needs of litigants. In 1391 the clamour of the urban representatives in parliament for legislation against the court of admiralty encouraged the king to act in their interests.

The common petitions of 1390 and 1391 were part of a clearly defined urban agenda to combat the growing power of the court of admiralty. But what part did the MPs for Bristol and York play in the drafting of the petitions? Although direct evidence is lacking, there is strong circumstantial evidence to suggest that the petitions were drawn up, at least in part, at their request. Bristol's Little Red Book contains an abbreviated copy of the 1391 statute defining the admiralty's jurisdiction, closely followed by a summary of the main clauses of the statutes of 1390, 1391 and 1401, entitled 'Notes of the statutes against the admirals' ('Nota Statutum contra admirallos').[168] Of particular significance is the fact that Bristol's copy of the 1391 statute is actually a copy of the king's answer to the common petition on the parliament roll rather than the more detailed legislation on the statute roll,[169] which raises the question of how the town's parliamentary representatives managed to acquire a copy of the king's answer before the proclamation of the parliamentary statute. Answers to common petitions were usually read out at the end of parliament, but while it was customary for statutes to be officially dated the

---

166 *RP* iii. 282.
167 *RP* iii. 291; *SR* ii. 78–9.
168 BRO, 04718, fos 34r, 37v. Only the headings are printed in *LRB* i. 89, 101. The 1401 statute is in *SR* ii. 124.
169 See BRO, 04718, fo. 34r; *RP* iii. 291; *SR* ii. 78–9.

last day of parliament, their communication in the localities was not immediate.[170] Perhaps the authors of the 1391 petition received the endorsed common petition;[171] it is likely that Bristol's MPs were eager to return home with something to show from their labours before the statute was proclaimed formally in the town and in the kingdom as a whole.

At the same time, evidence from the York Memorandum Book suggests that the jurisdiction of the admiralty court was of particular concern to York's ruling elite in the early 1390s, for the civic register contains a copy of letters patent revoking a judgment made in the court of the northern admiralty and of the record and process of the case which took place between September 1390 and February 1391, concerning a plea of debt between Thomas de Howom, an alderman and former mayor of the city of York, and Richard Gell, a fishmonger of the city.[172] In 1390 Thomas de Howom sued Richard Gell before York's mayor and bailiffs in the city's court of pleas for a debt of £8, which Gell owed for merchandise that he had bought from him. The case was decided in Howom's favour, but Gell did not pay the debt, so the court ordered the arrest of a ship belonging to Gell in order to force him to pay. According to the custom of the city, the ship remained in custody for eight days to give Gell time to pay what he owed, but Gell still refused to honour the debt within the allotted time and the ship was delivered to Howom in payment.[173] Gell, aggrieved at the loss of his ship, took his case before John Lord Beaumont, admiral of the north, claiming that the case belonged to the court of admiralty: ships 'within the sea or arm of the sea', that is, on tidal waters, were only to be arrested by the admiral, and Gell's ship was arrested near Bishopthorpe on the river Ouse, 'which is an arm of the sea in the county of York and within the said admiralty, which water flows and reflows . . . as the sea holds its course'. To add insult to the injury of Thomas de Howom, Gell claimed damages for wrongful arrest of £40. Thomas de Howom was summoned to appear before the court of admiralty to answer a plea of trespass.[174]

The importance of the case lies in the way it both responded to and anticipated the parliamentary petitions and statutes of 1390 and 1391. On the one hand, the January 1390 statute restricting the jurisdiction of the admiralty to actions at sea ('chose fait sur la meer'),[175] formed the basis of both Gell's prosecution and Howom's defence. While Howom's attorney claimed in court that 'the ship was attached with anchors to dry land within the port of the

---

170 Harriss, 'Formation of parliament', 39; J. R. Maddicott, 'The county community and the making of public opinion in fourteenth-century England', *TRHS* 5th ser. xxviii (1978), 35.

171 For the suggestion that the authors of common petitions were returned their petitions with the king's endorsement see Rayner, 'Forms and machinery of the "*commune petition*" ', 232–3.

172 For what follows see *YMB* i. 224–35, translated by M. Sellers ibid. i, pp. lxxvi–lxxxvi.

173 *YMB* i, p. lxxxi.

174 *YMB* i, pp. lxxix–lxxx.

175 *SR* ii. 62.

said city', Gell was adamant that the ship was in the Ouse 'fixed with anchors and other fastenings belonging to the abovesaid ship in the abovesaid water, the fastenings and anchors . . . being always covered by the aforesaid water'.[176] On the other hand, it is clear that the case informed wider griev-ances expressed in the common petitions of the parliaments of November 1390 and 1391. At the first of these parliaments Thomas de Howom peti-tioned the king's council about the overturning of the verdict in York's court of pleas by the admiral of the north, exactly the complaint which was made more generally in the common petition about the interference of the admi-rals in cases which belonged to the rulers of urban franchises.[177] In early 1391 Howom petitioned the king's council once more, and the council annulled the judgment against him and ruled that such pleas would no longer be heard by the court of admiralty.[178] In November 1391 the king, as was mentioned earlier, prohibited the court of admiralty from hearing cases of contract and covenant, arising both on land and sea. Can it be a coincidence that the extension of the 1390 statute in 1391 to cover maritime cases was made just after the resolution of the York case which had revolved so much around the question of whether the ship had been arrested on sea or land? The names of York's MPs in the November 1390 parliament are unknown, but Howom was an influential York citizen who had already represented the city twice in parliament, so it is very possible that he was an MP again in 1390.[179] More-over, there can be no doubt that York's MPs in 1391, William de Selby and John de Howeden, as former bailiffs and mayors themselves, would have recognised that, while the king's council had settled Howom's specific griev-ance, only a fundamental change in the law would prevent a similar situation arising again.

R. G. Marsden argued that it was specifically the appointment of John Holand, earl of Huntingdon, as admiral of the south and west, which led directly to the common petitions and statutes of 1390 and 1391 because 'great irregularities appear to have been committed by the judge of his court'.[180] It is certainly true that there were specific reasons for complaint about the court of the southern admiralty, and in 1394 a common petition from the king's 'poor liege burgesses of the towns of Bristol, Bridgwater, Exeter, Barnstaple and Wells' complained about 'several incorrect judge-ments' ('plusours erroignes juggementz') which had been returned in the court against several inhabitants of the towns in cases involving burglary, theft, battery and other trespasses, but which, according to the 1391 statute,

---

176 *YMB* i, pp. lxxxi–lxxxii.
177 *YMB* i, p. lxxvi; *RP* iii. 282.
178 *YMB* i, p. lxxxv.
179 For this and what follows see appendix below.
180 See *Select pleas in the court of admiralty*, i. 1, 1–26, for two cases which, according to Marsden, 'were amongst the immediate causes of the restriction which was then placed upon the admiral's jurisdiction'.

should not have been heard by the court in the first place.[181] Yet the issue of admiralty jurisdiction involved more than individual judicial grievances. Indeed, it was not even primarily about the interests of the urban subjects whom the MPs for Bristol and York represented. It is very revealing that, in the York case, the dispute was between an alderman and former mayor of the city and a fishmonger, since the real issue was the ability of the civic governments of Bristol and York to rule their towns without the interference of other royal officials.

In this respect, the conflict over the court of admiralty was part of a wider contemporary debate between civic rulers and the crown. In particular, the later fourteenth century witnessed a series of complaints from the parliamentary commons about the special jurisdiction enjoyed by certain royal household officials, namely the steward, the marshal and the clerk of the market, who were responsible for household purveyance as the king travelled through his kingdom. Hostility centred on the court of the steward and marshal of the household, otherwise known as the marshalsea court, and its right to hear pleas of trespass in the towns within the verge (an area covering a twelve-mile radius around the person of the king). The right of the clerk of the market to hold assizes of victuals within the verge, which involved the setting of prices and the examination of weights and measures, also interfered with the privileges claimed by the existing borough courts of Bristol, York and other urban communities.[182] Bristol, for instance, was certainly visited more frequently by Richard II than his royal predecessor, receiving the king at fairly regular intervals, in 1382, 1386, 1391 and 1398, compared to a single visit in fifty years by Edward III at the beginning of January 1358.[183] The difference between this dispute and the conflict over the court of admiralty was that the civic officials of Bristol and York sought to limit the jurisdiction of the royal household officials through chartered grants. In April 1396, in response to a petition from 'the mayor, sheriff and all the commonalty of the town of Bristol', the crown granted Bristol a charter which prohibited the steward, marshal and clerk of the market from exercising jurisdiction in the town; one month later, and just after Richard II's two-week stay in the city, York received a charter elevating the city to county status which contained an identical grant.[184]

[181] *RP* iii. 322.

[182] For the evidence of parliamentary complaints about the court see Given-Wilson, *Royal household*, 49–53. For the operation of the court see W. R. Jones, 'The court of the verge: the jurisdiction of the steward and marshal of the household in the later Middle Ages', *JBS* x (1970), 1–29.

[183] Saul, *Richard II*, appendix at pp. 469, 471, 472, 473. The evidence of Edward III's visit to Bristol in 1358 is discussed at pp. 65–7 above. A more detailed examination of Edward III's itinerary currently being undertaken by W. M. Ormrod may reveal other periods of royal residence in the town, but the place-name dating of royal letters patent and close has provided a useful indicator.

[184] For Bristol see SC 8/225/11246; LRB i. 173; and CChR, *1341–1417*, 353. For York see CChR, *1341–1417*, 355, and Saul, *Richard II*, appendix at p. 473.

Finally, the significance of the issue of the jurisdiction of the admiralty court lies in the way that a local problem, namely the infringement of a town's liberties, could be transformed by parliamentary debate into a general complaint by the parliamentary burgesses and into a request for legislation. Through this process, local matters became issues of wider, common interest. From the perspective of the parliamentary representatives of Bristol and York, who spoke ostensibly on behalf of the common good of the urban communities whom they represented, but whose petitions, in reality, voiced the concerns, mercantile or otherwise, of the towns' civic elites, the crown was not simply a source of favours and privileges.

Parliamentary committees

The final section of this chapter examines the role of MPs for Bristol and York on several parliamentary committees that were held between 1380 and 1382 to discuss fiscal and mercantile affairs. 'Rarely', wrote May McKisack, 'do we find burgesses among those appointed to serve on parliamentary committees or to perform any other special public service', a fact which has been taken as further evidence not only of the dominance of the commons by the knights of the shire, but of the local rather than national preoccupations of urban representatives.[185] The presence of MPs for Bristol and York on the committees suggests that they were not at parliament merely to petition, but also to consider issues of national interest and to advise the crown on the direction of royal fiscal and commercial policy. The committees raise a number of other important issues, including their composition, for there were merchants among their membership who were not at parliament as MPs, whose presence has significant implications for our understanding of the fate of the estate of merchants after the mid-fourteenth century when, it has been assumed, this separate estate disintegrated and was absorbed into the commons, who emerged 'as the mouthpiece of the business classes'.[186] What is clear is that the governing elites of Bristol and York saw parliament as a forum for political debate and discussion about, and criticism of, royal policy.

In January 1380, as English fortunes in the Hundred Years War continued to decline, the parliamentary commons, through their speaker, Sir John de Gildesburgh, expressed their concern about the state of the royal finances.[187] The speaker began his address by stating that, if the king had been 'well and reasonably governed in his expenses', then he would not have needed to burden the parliamentary commons with increasing financial demands. To reduce costs, he asked both for the removal of the system of continual councils which had been governing the realm since Richard II's accession to the

185 McKisack, *Parliamentary representation*, 120.
186 Ormrod, *Edward III*, 196.
187 For what follows see *RP* iii. 73.

throne in 1377 and for the appointment instead of a council composed of the five main officers of state, namely, the chancellor, the treasurer, the keeper of the privy seal, the chamberlain and the steward of the royal household. Furthermore, the speaker requested the appointment of a committee with wide-ranging powers 'to remedy the faults of the said government', that is, to inquire into the financial state of the royal household and of royal expenses in general from the beginning of Richard II's reign. The committee was then to report back to the king with its findings so that he could be 'more honorably governed within his realm' as was appropriate to his office, and, in particular, so that he could use his own resources to meet the costs of the 'defence of the realm'. The king, with the advice of the lords, appointed to the committee three bishops, three earls, three bannerets, three knights of the shire and three parliamentary burgesses, William Walworth and John Philipot of London and Thomas Graa, MP for York.

There is no evidence that the committee actually met,[188] but this does not minimise its significance. The committee's appointment reflected the growing concern of the parliamentary commons in the later 1370s and early 1380s about the rising costs of government and their suspicion that royal revenue, particularly taxation, was being mismanaged by the king's advisers and not spent on the purpose for which it was intended, namely the defence of the realm.[189] The issue of the royal finances was one that was of interest to parliament as a whole, and the 1380 committee reflected this fact, with the bishops, earls and bannerets representing the lords, and the shire knights and parliamentary burgesses representing the commons. Thomas Graa, the MP for York, was already an experienced parliamentary performer, having attended three previous parliaments on behalf of the city,[190] so in one sense his appointment owed much to his personal standing within the commons. It is, however, difficult to ignore the local context of Graa's commission.

Their experience of civic politics throughout the 1370s, as they struggled to fulfil their obligations to the crown in the face of severe financial and political strain,[191] can only have made York's rulers particularly sensitive to the use or misuse of royal revenue. They sought remedial action; and Graa was their representative. G. L. Harriss has written of parliamentary opposition that it was 'occasional and corrective, the intention being to restore good government, not to abrogate it',[192] and this was true of the 1380 committee. York's leading citizens paid taxes to, and collected taxes for, the king, and contributed to the building and maintenance of barges for the defence of the realm. What they wanted from the crown, in return, was not

---

188 Tuck, *Richard II*, 43; Roskell, *Michael de la Pole*, 25–6.
189 Tuck, *Richard II*, 43–5; Roskell, *Michael de la Pole*, 15–35; M. Prestwich, 'An estimate by the commons of royal revenue in England under Richard II', *PH* iii (1984), 148–51.
190 See appendix below.
191 See p. 43 above.
192 Harriss, 'Formation of parliament', 54.

the confirmation or extension of the city's liberties, but an assurance that it would use their fiscal contributions prudently.

Other committees appointed in the early years of Richard II's reign containing a significant urban element were specifically concerned with mercantile issues, notably the state of the currency. In the parliament of 1379, the commons, at the request of the mint officials at the Tower of London, addressed the crown about a perceived bullion shortage.[193] According to the commons' petition, they had been informed by officers of the Tower of London mint that 'for lack of good governance' there was a massive shortage of money. Neither gold nor silver was coming into the kingdom, while the existing gold and silver coinage in England was either exported or clipped so that the currency was losing its value and the price of goods was falling. The mint officials, the commons told the king, wanted a royal ordinance to attract bullion into England and to prevent its export, so that the coinage would be 'kept good and strong'. The commons asked that the crown take the advice of the mint officials, for an ordinance would be to the common profit ('the profit of the king and of all his realm'), as well as to the advantage of merchants who sold their wool at Calais, of English merchants who bought merchandise in Flanders to import into England, and of 'all those who distribute the said merchandise', Despite the rhetoric of the common good and the deleterious impact of a reduction in the money supply on local, retail trade,[194] the petition was explicitly in the sectional interests of overseas merchants involved in the import and export trade and of other wholesalers engaged as distributors of merchandise to internal markets, for whom a 'strong and stable coinage' was essential.[195] Indeed, in his answer to the petition, the king declared that he would provide a suitable remedy after first taking the advice of the officers of the mint and 'the merchants and others more learned on this matter'. Depositions of five London mint officials and of two London merchants – the grocers, John Hoo and Richard Aylesbury – were taken, in which they were charged to answer five articles about the currency crisis with suggestions for possible remedies. These depositions were then presented to the king, lords and commons in parliament.[196] The recommendations of the Tower of London officials amounted to a policy of bullionism, that is, of increasing the country's money supply by regulating overseas trade through the restriction of the export of gold and silver

---

[193] RP iii. 64. The original Tower of London petition is SC 8/19/932.

[194] R. H. Britnell, The commercialisation of English society, 1000–1500, 2nd edn, Manchester 1996, 181–2.

[195] The quotation is from J. H. A. Munro, Wool, cloth, and gold: the struggle for bullion in Anglo-Burgundian trade, 1340–1478, Brussels 1972, 28.

[196] The reports have been printed in RP iii. 126–7. W. M. Ormrod, 'The peasants' revolt and the government of England', JBS xxix (1990), 27–8, was the first to date these depositions correctly, although he thought that the commons' petition followed from the testimonials, when in fact it preceded them.

bullion.[197] There is no evidence, however, that Richard II's government acted on the recommendations to issue the necessary ordinance.[198]

Action was, moreover, urgently required, for the 1370s saw the output of the English mints fall sharply after the renewal of the Hundred Years War in 1369, while the period 1377 to 1381, in particular, was one of severe monetary contraction in England as a result of the crown's military ventures overseas.[199] First, the crown's financial demands to fund its military campaigns led to the grant of high and regular tax levies, as well as the extension of substantial loans, which greatly reduced the amount of money in circulation for trade. Secondly, the crown's operations in France were dependent on the export of large quantities of English coin to finance troops, build alliances and pay for other war-related expenditure. The shortage of coinage in the first four years of Richard II's reign led to a decline in prices and contemporaries were acutely aware of the problem of deflation:[200] with less money in circulation, people had less to spend, which reduced demand for goods and resulted in lower prices. When mercantile credit could not compensate for the shortage of money, the consequence was a slump in commercial activity.

In 1381 the issue of the coinage was debated again in parliament, on this occasion in the context of the aftermath of the Peasants' Revolt. Discussion was prompted by the submission of a petition, addressed to the king and council in parliament, from the officers of the mint at the Tower of London, the main royal mint, who complained that their business had declined to such an extent that they had stopped minting altogether. They requested that the king and his councillors take 'good and wise counsel' and provide a swift remedy to the crisis. The endorsed petition declared that the warden, master and others involved in the mint should be summoned before the lords in parliament to give their opinions on the subject and to name 'others most knowledgeable of this matter' ('mieultz sachantz de ceste matire'), presumably from whom further advice would be sought.[201] A parliamentary committee consisting of thirteen individuals was eventually appointed to advise the crown on the currency crisis, the parliamentary attendance of two of its members, Sir Richard Waldegrave of Suffolk and Sir John Kentwood of

---

[197] For a definition of the idea of bullionism see Bolton, *Medieval English economy*, 298.

[198] On the crown's failure to take decisive action see the wording of the endorsement to the original petition from the London mint officials: SC 8/19/932.

[199] For what follows see Nightingale, *Medieval mercantile company*, 241, and Britnell, *Commercialisation*, 182–3.

[200] Although economic historians are divided on the issue of whether price changes were affected more by demographic change or by changes in the volume and quality of coinage in circulation, in the period 1377 to 1381, contemporaries rightly attributed the problem to the shortage of money. A summary of this debate is provided in T. H. Lloyd, 'Overseas trade and the English money supply in the fourteenth century', in N. J. Mayhew (ed.), *Edwardian monetary affairs (1279–1344)* (British Archaeological Reports xxxvi, 1977), 96–124.

[201] SC 8/125/6230, which has been included mistakenly in the printed rolls of parliament among the 'petitiones in parliamento' under the regnal year 5 Richard II: *RP* iii. 126.

Cornwall, providing conclusive evidence that the committee met in the 1381 parliament.[202]

Several aristocratic members of the committee were drawn from an intercommuning committee which had already been appointed at the request of the commons to discuss the charges which the chancellor had set before them, one of which was to consider the causes of the revolt and to suggest remedies to prevent a future uprising.[203] William Wykeham, bishop of Winchester, Thomas Brantingham, bishop of Exeter, Thomas Beauchamp, earl of Warwick, Henry Percy, earl of Northumberland, Sir John Cobham and Guy Lord Brian all belonged to the delegation of the lords that met with a delegation of the commons. Similarly, although the names of the members of the commons' delegation are not known, it is highly likely that both Sir Richard Waldegrave, who was the commons' speaker in 1381, and Sir John Kentwood, a relatively experienced parliamentary performer, were delegates. Since the intercommuning committee concluded that misgovernment was one of the factors in the outbreak of the revolt and was seeking reforms in the government of the kingdom,[204] it would appear that the crown decided that certain members of this committee should also be involved in the reform of royal monetary policy.

The other five individuals who completed the coinage committee, John de Wesenham, John Hadley, Henry Spelly of Bristol, John de Gysburn of York and Adam de Bury, were presumably the 'others' whom the London mint officials had recommended to the crown. Only John Hadley, a London merchant, was present at parliament as an MP.[205] Moreover, of the other four, only John de Gysburn had ever been elected to parliament before and that had been in 1373.[206] Three – Wesenham, Hadley and Bury – were Londoners, while Spelly was from Bristol and Gysburn from York. The crown valued the five merchants primarily for their specific financial and mercantile interests and expertise. Two can be linked with certainty to the royal mint and exchange in London. John de Wesenham, originally of Lynn, was a citizen of London who, after having farmed the customs in the mid-1340s, became warden of the king's exchanges in 1351 and continued his involvement with the Tower of London mint in the 1360s, acting as mainpernor for Henry Brusele and John Chichester, assayers of the royal coinage in the Tower

---

[202] The names of the members of the committee are in SC 8/146/7275. The document was originally attached to the petition of the mint officials (SC 8/125/6230). Kentwood and Waldegrave were present at the parliaments of 1376, October 1377, 1378, 1381 and January 1390, but only at the 1381 parliament was a petition presented by the officers of the London mint. For their biographies see Roskell and others, *House of Commons, 1386–1421*, iii. 517–19; iv. 735–9.

[203] *RP* iii. 100. The best discussion of the parliamentary procedure of intercommuning remains J. G. Edwards, *The commons in medieval English parliaments*, London 1958.

[204] *RP* iii. 100.

[205] Roskell and others, *House of Commons, 1386–1421*, iii. 260–4.

[206] See appendix below.

mint.[207] Likewise, Adam de Bury seems to have been associated with the London mint, for in the Good Parliament he was charged with corruption, having 'destroyed the king's exchange in London for his own profit and made bullion in his own house'.[208]

The evidence is less clear in respect to the remaining three merchants, and is largely circumstantial. For example, very little is known about Henry Spelly, a parishioner of St Werburgh's in Bristol, who was elected to the town's common council in 1381, and who only later received a royal commission, serving as a collector of the subsidy of tonnage and poundage in the port of Bristol between 1382 and 1383; he was probably a relation of his much more prominent namesake, Ellis Spelly, five times MP for Bristol and mayor of the town on four occasions.[209] The singular nature of his appointment in 1381 suggests that he was a specialist in monetary affairs. Meanwhile, although the royal mint at York was not active in this period,[210] if the allegations against him made by a presentment jury before a commission of the peace in the summer of 1381 are to be believed, John de Gysburn seems to have had considerable expertise in the financial field. One of the key charges against Gysburn was that, aided by Scottish moneyers he had employed, he had overseen an unofficial recoinage for four years from October 1369, converting £10,000 of English coin into Scottish money.[211]

Under pressure from the intercommuning committee to make certain reforms in government, the crown first took advice from the officers of the mint and then appointed a parliamentary committee that included the five specialists to implement changes in its monetary policy. What these changes were, however, remains unknown, as the committee's work was rendered superfluous by the appointment, shortly afterwards, of another committee to consider the issue of the money supply and other related subjects. When the intercommuning committee reported to the king that there were several faults in the governance of the kingdom which had forced the king's subjects into severe poverty and were responsible for the recent revolt, the king appointed a committee of lords and gave it a wide brief to examine, in consultation with the commons, the defects in the royal government, starting with the king's household.[212] The commons seized the opportunity to present several petitions to the committee concerning the reform of the institutions

---

[207] For Wesenham's involvement in royal finance in the 1340s see Fryde, 'English farmers of the customs'. For a short biographical note on Wesenham see *A calendar of the cartularies of John Pyel and Adam Fraunceys*, ed. S. O'Connor (Camden 5th ser. ii, 1993), 26–7 n. 127. According to O'Connor, Wesenham 'probably' died in the mid-1360s, but that he was still alive in Richard II's reign is indicated by a series of payments made to him in 1380 'for good service to the late king': *CCR, 1377–81*, 404–5, 421.

[208] *CPR, 1374–7*, 453; Holmes, *Good Parliament*, 112.

[209] *GRB* ii. 212; appendix below; Wadley, *Great orphan book*, 27.

[210] Miller, 'Medieval York', 67.

[211] KB 27/482, mem. 35r.

[212] This paragraph draws on *RP* iii. 100–2. The complaint about poverty is at iii. 102.

of royal government, namely the household, the chancery, the exchequer and the judiciary. The subject of one petition was the 'great poverty' within the kingdom, which was now 'empty of riches and of all other wealth' ('voide de tresor et de tout autre bien') for two reasons: first, the state of the coinage, which had either been exported or clipped, and secondly, the costs of war, including losses at sea and on land caused by the inadequate defence of the coast. As a result, the price of merchandise such as wool, tin and lead was much lower than it should have been. The commons asked for a remedy and the crown answered that 'the merchants should for their part . . . be charged to consider among themselves the current troubles within the realm', namely the economic problems of deflation, the increasing expense of imports, the ruinous state of the country's shipping, and the export and debasement of the coinage. The merchants were instructed to put their advice in writing so that the lords and commons could learn how to restore this aspect of good governance from those most knowledgeable on the subject.

Who were the merchants to whom the crown referred? A clue to their identity is provided towards the end of the parliament roll, where the individuals in question are described as 'certain merchants of all the good towns and boroughs of the realm', who were 'charged and ordered on their oaths and their allegiance to inform our lords and commons . . . how the realm of England might best then be relieved of poverty through the increase of commodities produced in the realm and of the merchandise coming in'.[213] The fortunate survival, among the class of ancient petitions in the Public Record Office, of a list of twenty-one individuals below the main heading 'the merchants charged for the profit of the realm', followed by the names of four knights of the shire below a sub-heading 'the knights assigned to them', suggests that the individuals belonged to a parliamentary committee.[214] In the right-hand column, written in a different hand, are the names of a further six merchants, an indication perhaps that the original committee was extended in size at a later date. The document is undated, but a comparison with the known parliamentary attendance of the thirty-one members of the committee dates it to 1381: all four named as knights were knights of the shire at this parliament and fifteen of the twenty-seven merchants attended the 1381 parliament as MPs.[215] The document appears, therefore, to be a list of members of the 1381 parliamentary committee to propose changes to royal commercial policy. Its larger size in comparison with the coinage committee can be explained by the fact that the specific issue of the currency had been absorbed into a broader critique of several aspects of the crown's policy towards trade.

The 1381 committee included Thomas Graa of York, one of the city's MPs in 1381, Ellis Spelly, MP for Bristol in 1381, and Thomas Beaupyne of

[213] *RP* iii. 119.
[214] SC 8/125/6224.
[215] *Return of members*, i. 207–9.

Bristol, who had already represented the town at parliament on three occa-sions, but who was not, on this occasion, one of the town's parliamentary representatives.[216] There was only the smallest overlap between the two committees of merchants in 1381 in the person of John Hadley, the London grocer. The merchants were drawn from twelve towns and cities; London dominated the list with twelve merchants, while there were two each from Bristol, Winchester and Exeter, and one each from York, Norwich, Lincoln, Newcastle-upon-Tyne, Gloucester, Ipswich, Lynn and Salisbury.[217] All four of London's MPs, Sir John Philipot, John Hadley, William Barrett and Hugh Fastolf, were on the committee, but there was a contingent of eight London merchants who were at parliament primarily as merchants rather than as parliamentary burgesses and who were in attendance without parliamentary election. The same was also true of Thomas Beaupyne of Bristol, Stephen Haym of Winchester, Henry Mulsho of Northamptonshire and William Heyberer of Gloucester.[218]

If twelve of the twenty-seven merchants were not elected to parliament as MPs, it is important to ask how it was that they, like four of the five merchants on the coinage committee, happened to be at parliament in 1381. It is possible that, at least in the case of the larger committee of merchants, the presence of so many unelected merchants was the result of the adjourn-ment of parliament for Christmas.[219] In mid-December the commons asked that, since many of the important issues discussed in parliament had still not been resolved, parliament be adjourned so that each member could consider individually 'for his part a good remedy'. The king granted the request and ordered the MPs to examine, amongst other things, the related subjects of 'merchandise' and 'money' before their return to Westminster. It is tempting to think that the elected representatives then discussed these subjects with their fellow merchants in their respective towns and cities, some of whom then came to parliament after Christmas and were added to the committee. However, although the list of twenty-seven merchants suggests that the committee was formed in two stages, with twenty-one merchants as the orig-inal members, eleven of these twenty-one individuals were not MPs, while

---

[216] See appendix below.

[217] Identification has been based on evidence of parliamentary attendance in *Return of members*, i, passim. The exceptions are Robert Warbulton, a London mercer and alderman, and Henry Mulsho, a Northamptonshire wool merchant: *Letter-book H*, 88–9; Lloyd, *English wool trade*, 251.

[218] In my article, 'The estate of merchants in the parliament of 1381', *HR* lxxiv (2001), 337, I mistakenly identified Hugh Crane as another merchant who was in attendance in a non-parliamentary capacity, but he was actually one of the MPs for Winchester in 1381 (*Return of members*, i. 209). The absence of an extant parliamentary return for Gloucester is inconvenient, but it is also true that, from November 1380 until February 1388, William Heyberer was elected knight of the shire five times for Gloucestershire, for which he was definitely not an MP in 1381: Roskell and others, *House of Commons, 1386–1421*, iii. 370.

[219] For what follows see *RP* iii. 104, 113.

five of the six additions, Robert de Wilford and Richard Bossun of Exeter, Geoffrey Sterlyng of Ipswich, John Keep of Lynn and Robert Bont of Salisbury, were parliamentary burgesses. Furthermore, the *sub pena* clause below the names of these six merchants was not a personal summons to parliament, but an order to each of them on pain of a fine of £100 to appear daily before the committee and treat with its other members.[220] There is no evidence that the unelected merchants of either committee were summoned to parliament in 1381 by a royal writ, in contrast, for example, to the 1354 parliament, for which the issue rolls of the royal exchequer record a summons to 'certain un-named merchants' to attend 'for the King's "secret business" '.[221] Both committees in the 1381 parliament were drawn from merchants who neither were elected to parliament nor received an individual summons to attend and who presumably were already at parliament before their formal appointment.

From the mid-1330s to the mid-1350s the crown regularly summoned assemblies of merchants that were distinct from parliament to discuss issues such as loans, the wool subsidy and the location of the staple. As first George Unwin and more recently W. M. Ormrod have shown, however, the practices of the wool monopoly companies of the 1340s alienated a large number of merchants, who turned to the commons in parliament to express and protect their interests.[222] In other words, the orthodox interpretation is that in the mid-fourteenth century the estate of merchants disintegrated and was absorbed into the commons. The evidence of the two parliamentary committees in 1381 suggests that this decline was not complete by the early 1380s and that the merchants were still perceived as a separate estate within parliament, whose membership overlapped with, but was not necessarily identical to, that of the parliamentary burgesses. Occasional references in the parliament rolls to the presence of unnamed merchants point towards a similar conclusion, perhaps the best-known of which is from 1362, when Edward III approached parliament with a proposal to establish the wool staple at Calais: the knights of the shire told the lords that they had spoken to 'several merchants' who were divided on the matter, and asked to be excused from making a decision since knowledge of this issue resided with the 'merchants more than anyone else' ('Marchantz pluis qe en nul autre').[223] In 1373 a body calling itself 'the commonalty of merchants' petitioned the crown. This petition was among the common petitions on the unpublished parliament roll, but was excised from the late eighteenth-century printed edition, perhaps because it highlighted the disjointed nature of the commons.[224] The presence

---

220 Ormrod, '*Sub pena* writ', 11–20. The fine of £100 threatened in default of appearance in 1381 was not unusual.

221 There is no evidence of a writ of summons in E 403/487. For 1354 see Ormrod, 'English crown and the customs', 31 n. 24, citing E 403/374, 22 Apr.

222 Unwin, 'Estate of merchants', 179–255; Ormrod, *Edward III*, 187–96.

223 *RP* ii. 269.

224 C 65/29, mem. 3.

on the two 1381 committees, of London merchant financiers such as Sir William Walworth, Sir John Philipot, Sir Nicholas Brembre and John Hadley can be seen as a logical conclusion to the scaling-down of the estate of merchants from well over one hundred in the 1330s, drawn from a number of lesser towns and cities as well as larger ones such as Bristol, York and London, to 'the handful of capitalists' responsible for 'the royal finances' in the 1340s.[225]

However, the events of the May 1382 parliament examined in chapter 1 demonstrate that there were crucial differences between the estate of merchants in the early 1380s and the merchant assemblies of the 1330s and 1340s in size, composition and purpose. The crown's attempt in 1382 to reconstitute a separate estate of merchants representing a wide cross-section of the mercantile community from London and 'each city, borough, and good town within the realm' in order to agree to a substantial loan to the crown failed because the merchants declared that only parliament could provide the necessary safeguards for the repayment of so large a sum of money.[226] Parliament was, therefore, summoned and the crown turned to the parliamentary commons for the loan of £60,000. The commons, however, argued that 'the merchants now present in this parliament' should bear the charge because they knew more about this subject than 'any other estate of the realm'. Among the fourteen merchants who were appointed by the lords to consider the loan of £60,000 to finance the king's expedition to France, seven were London merchants, one, Thomas Beaupyne, MP in 1382, was from Bristol and one, John de Gysburn, was from York.[227] It has been argued that in 1382 'the term "merchants" was applied not to some other group present in the assembly, but to a sub-section of the burgesses in the commons',[228] yet although only three merchants, Thomas Beaupyne of Bristol, John Polymond of Southampton and Robert de Sutton of Lincoln, are known definitely to have been MPs, given that it was customary for London to elect four representatives, the presence of seven Londoners on the committee suggests that this was not the case.[229] Moreover, the merchants did not agree to the loan in 1382, referring to the experiences of William de la Pole and other prominent

---

[225] On the role of the London financiers in the late 1370s see, for example, Nightingale, *Medieval mercantile community*, 253–4. The quotation is from Unwin, 'Estate of merchants', 220

[226] For this and what follows see *RP* iii. 122–3.

[227] The members of the parliamentary committee are listed in *RP* iii. 123.

[228] Ormrod, *Edward III*, 252 n. 166.

[229] *RP* iii. 123; *Return of members*, i. 210–11. Unfortunately, there are no extant returns for London or York. Of the remaining non-London merchants, Stephen Haym of Winchester was not an MP for the town in 1381, while it is very unlikely that either William Greville of Chipping Campden or William Spaigne of Boston was present in May 1382 as a parliamentary representative. Greville appears to have had no prior experience as an MP, while Spaigne represented Lincolnshire twice (in November 1380 and October 1382), for which he was not an MP in May 1382: *Return of members*, i. 206, 212.

merchants in Edward III's credit arrangements in the 1340s, who, having made loans to the crown for profit, had then been impeached. It was one thing to advise the crown on matters of trade and finance, but quite another to lend the amount of money which it now demanded.

May McKisack 'inferred' that, with the demise of the assemblies of merchants, 'the main responsibility for directing the fiscal and mercantile policy of the country devolved upon the borough members of parliament in consultation with other merchants of the realm'.[230] The evidence of the two 1381 parliamentary committees confirms this supposition, but with one qualification. The 'merchants of the realm' McKisack had in mind were specifically Londoners, whom she imagined 'were in the habit of attending parliament without a summons'; but London was not the 'exception' in this respect.[231] The estate of merchants in parliament in the early 1380s was a small but coherent group, drawn predominantly from London, but also from a number of large and wealthy provincial towns and cities such as Bristol and York.[232] Valued individually by the crown, its members also formed a wider, national mercantile constituency. That they were a powerful lobbying group in parliament is suggested by the recommendations of the 1381 committee including twenty-seven merchants, which provided reforms to issues for which the merchants had been pressing for several years.

The avowed aim of this committee was to relieve the country's poverty, and its appointment can be viewed as a serious attempt by the commons to examine the causes of the revolt. Anthony Tuck has argued that the attitude of the parliamentary commons to the Peasants' Revolt 'was shaped by a desire to avoid provoking another rising, and to remedy the grievances which they believed underlay the 1381 rebellion', and that this attitude was translated into a campaign in the 1380s for the enforcement of the labour legislation.[233] The appointment of the committee of twenty-seven merchants suggests that there was a parliamentary debate about the economy as well as one about law and order after the revolt and that there was an important economic dimension to the commons' programme of legislative reform.

Although the members of the committee were instructed to act 'for the profit of the realm' and, in particular, to remedy poverty – according to the parliamentary commons one of the contributing factors to the revolt which had forced the 'humble commons' ('menues Communes') to rebel to escape their oppression – [234] the committee's vision of the common good was essentially mercantile. The committee's recommendations, namely that the export

---

[230] McKisack, *Parliamentary representation*, 133.
[231] Idem, 'Borough representation', 524.
[232] Compare the towns and cities represented in 1381 with the league tables ranking towns by population and wealth in the fourteenth century: Dyer, *English towns, 1400–1640*, 56–7, 62–3.
[233] A. Tuck, 'Nobles, commons and the great revolt of 1381', in Hilton and Aston, *English rising*, 209–10.
[234] *RP* iii. 100.

of gold and silver coinage and bullion be prohibited to increase the value of trade, that foreign merchants be encouraged to trade in England in order to expand the volume of commerce, that the king's subjects transport both their exports and imports only in vessels owing allegiance to the English king to promote English shipping, and that the import of foreign wine be strictly controlled in order to reduce the price of wine in England, were all designed to improve the fortunes of English trade.[235]

On the one hand, the committee's suggestions for economic reform were forward-looking, expressing, albeit in embryonic form, ideas of bullionism, the balance of trade and mercantilism: that is, of maintaining the money supply by preventing the export of English coin and bullion, of ensuring a balance of trade by restricting certain foreign imports and promoting English overseas trade and, ultimately, of increasing the country's wealth through trade.[236] Such ideas were increasingly influential in the fifteenth century and were expressed in parliament in anti-alien legislation and navigation acts, which sought to maintain the English merchant fleet by channelling English overseas trade through English vessels,[237] and conveyed in polemical treatises such as *The libelle of Englyshe polycye*.[238] While the poem was a product of the particular circumstances in which it was written, namely the aftermath of the collapse of the Anglo-Burgundian alliance in the mid-1430s,[239] its most interesting aspect lay in its underlying mercantile vision of English politics.[240] Although the *Libelle* professed to speak for the kingdom as a whole, it actually expressed a more longstanding mercantile agenda, perfectly encapsulating the mercantile concept of the 'national' interest that was emerging in the second half of the fourteenth century and that was articulated most cogently in the parliament of 1381. Among these mercantile ideas was the need to control the seas, which was essential both for England's defence and for the unimpeded passage of trade, on which the kingdom's entire economic health was dependent. Indeed, just as the committee of merchants in 1381 believed that the best way to reduce poverty within England was to increase the volume and value of trade, so the poem emphasised the importance of commerce and merchants to the whole realm (ll. 482–5).

On the other hand, the recommendations of the mercantile members of

---

235 *RP* iii. 119–21.
236 Bolton, *Medieval English economy*, 298, 329–30.
237 Ibid. 330; Ross, *Edward IV*, 359–61.
238 The modern edition of this poem is *The libelle of Englyshe polycye: a poem on the use of sea-power, 1436*, ed. G. Warner, Oxford 1926.
239 The historical context of the poem is provided by G. Holmes, 'The "libel of English policy" ', *EHR* lxxvi (1961), 193–216. Briefly, England was at war with both France and Burgundy, threatening the safety of Calais and the passage of wool and cloth exports to the Low Countries.
240 J. Scattergood, 'The libelle of Englyshe polycye: the nation and its place', in H. Cooney (ed.), *Nation, court and culture: new essays on fifteenth-century English poetry*, Dublin 2001, 28–49.

the 1381 committee looked backwards and were a response to recent pressure from a powerful commercial interest group in parliament which had complained about the state of the coinage and the fortunes of English trade and shipping over a number of years and of which they themselves were a part. Thomas Graa of York, for example, had been an MP for York at the parliaments of January 1377, 1378, 1379 and January 1380, while Thomas Beaupyne of Bristol had already represented his town in 1373, January 1377 and 1378, and Ellis Spelly had served as Bristol's MP in January 1377.[241] Other members of this committee, such as Walter Bixton of Norwich and William Heyberer of Gloucester, also possessed a wealth of parliamentary experience, representing their communities prior to 1381 on four and eight occasions respectively.[242] The 1370s had seen a concerted parliamentary campaign by the commons warning the crown of the harmful effect of aspects of royal naval service on England's merchant fleet, yet also reminding the king of the importance of naval defence and of the control of the seas.[243] The warning issued by the merchants in 1381, that if the state of English shipping was not improved the kingdom would be lost ('la soverein cause par quoi le Roialme serroit doutez ou serra perduz'),[244] was simply the most explicit, and deliberately alarming, prognosis of the baleful consequences of the neglect of English maritime interests by the crown. As the repeated complaints about shipping throughout the 1370s suggest, the royal government did not provide decisive action, just as it also failed to act on the issue of the coinage which the commons had brought to its attention in 1379. It has been noted that in 1381 the commons 'decided to take advantage of the king's precarious financial situation and to press for certain reforms that had been on the political agenda for much of the previous decade'.[245] The merchants in parliament had their own agenda which the crown had not implemented in the 1370s and it was this perceived failure, rather than the problem of poverty specifically, that the committee of merchants in 1381 sought to remedy. In other words, the economic reforms proposed by the merchants were a response to what they, and the commons in general,[246] saw as the major problem of the period and the underlying cause of the Peasants' Revolt: the lack of good governance. The crown responded positively, and the main force of the merchants' proposals became statutory legislation.[247]

That the evidence of parliamentary committees involving Bristol and York MPs and merchants dates from the period 1380 to 1382 may not be a coincidence, for these were years, marked by heavy taxation, which led to

---

[241] See appendix below.
[242] Roskell and others, *House of Commons, 1386–1421*, ii. 244; iii. 370.
[243] See pp. 52–3 above.
[244] *RP* iii. 120.
[245] Ormrod, 'Peasants' revolt', 23.
[246] *RP* iii. 100–1.
[247] *RP* iii. 119–21; *SR* ii. 17–20.

serious monetary and commercial problems.[248] Moreover, given that the revolt was 'arguably the most serious threat ever posed to the stability of English government in the course of the Middle Ages',[249] it could be argued that the circumstances in which the 1381 parliament met were so unusual as to explain both the attendance of so many unelected merchants, also present without an individual summons, and the crown's willingness to consult those merchants. It is possible that the estate of merchants was more visible as a separate grouping within parliament in 1381 than was normally the case because of the crown's recognition, under pressure, of the need to consult directly, and as widely as possible, with the most appropriate interest group. Yet while it would perhaps be a mistake to claim too much importance for the committees of 1380, 1381 and 1382 for these reasons, it is also evident that this interest group was not present in only these years. The monetary and commercial reforms proposed in 1381 by the large committee of merchants implemented the mercantile agenda of the commons in the 1370s.

The evidence of the parliamentary committees containing Bristol and York MPs and merchants also lends weight to the broader theme of this chapter, namely that in the second half of the fourteenth century parliament was a dynamic institution and an important point of contact and interaction between the crown and the rulers of major towns and cities such as Bristol and York. This might not have been true of smaller towns such as Grimsby, for whom S. H. Rigby has argued that the town's MPs 'performed useful although hardly vital tasks for the borough' and that 'the burgesses of late medieval Grimsby perhaps saw the expense of sending men to parliament as a rather unwelcome burden'.[250] Those historians who emphasise the increasingly corporate character of the parliamentary commons in the second half of the fourteenth century risk neglecting the importance of the range of interest groups of which this body consisted.[251] The composition and internal workings of the commons were much more fluid than has been hitherto appreciated. Bristol's MPs collaborated, on occasion, with the representatives of neighbouring towns and counties to present petitions of regional interest, while there were some issues, such as royal finance and trade, in which a small group of parliamentary burgesses and merchants from Bristol, York, London and other prominent towns and cities were seen both by the shire knights and the crown to have a particular interest and expertise. Although recent work by Gwilym Dodd has provided an important reminder that the mercantile community was itself divided over certain issues,[252] the merchants

---

[248] Britnell, *Commercialisation*, 182–3.
[249] Ormrod, 'Peasants' revolt', 1.
[250] Rigby, *Medieval Grimsby*, 100–1.
[251] For example, Ormrod, *Edward III*, 166–7.
[252] G. Dodd, 'The Calais staple and the parliament of May 1382', *EHR* cxvii (2002), 94–104.

drawn from such large urban centres as London, Bristol and York formed an influential interest group.

Analysis of the language of the common petitions from Bristol and York and of the role of Bristol and York MPs and merchants on parliamentary committees advising the crown on fiscal and mercantile issues has also demonstrated that, among these individuals drawn from the civic elites of the two towns, there was a strong interest in wider regional and national affairs. Perhaps most significantly, while the representatives of Bristol and York often spoke in the name of the civic body and there were some issues which were of relevance to the community as a whole, the subjects of their common petitions and their work on parliamentary committees expressed, essentially, the sectional interests of the civic rulers, which did not necessarily coincide with those of their civic subjects. From the perspective of the rulers of Bristol and York, the crown's role in parliament lay not so much in the remedying of private grievances and the granting of privileges and favours, but in the framing of legislation on issues such as the regulation and promotion of internal and overseas commerce, law and order and the jurisdiction of the court of admiralty. It was this wider, legislative interest in meetings of parliament that helps to explain why the York Memorandum Book contains copies of complete parliamentary statute rolls from thirteen of the twenty parliaments that met between 1381 and 1399, all of which were glossed by York's common clerk for ease of reference.[253]

---

[253] The statutes were from the parliaments of Nov. 1381, May and Oct. 1382, Oct. 1386, Feb. and Sept. 1388, Jan. and Nov. 1390, Nov. 1391, Jan. 1393, Jan. 1394, Jan. 1397 and Oct. 1399: YCA, York Memorandum Book, A/Y, fos 93r–98v, 101r–102v, 99v–107v, 108r–125r, 83r–84v, 125r–126r, 135r–140r. For the wider practice of copying statutes into civic records see McKisack, *Parliamentary representation*, 144–5. The name of Roger de Burton, York's common clerk between 1405 and 1436, appears, on one occasion, in the margin: YCA, A/Y, fo. 138v. For Burton himself see Rees Jones, 'York's civic administration', 108–9.

5

Urban Charters

'Charters, the privileges they conferred, and the local officers they empowered to exercise them, formed the foundation of a town's relations with the
royal government.'[1] The degree of significance attached to royal charters to
towns, however, depends on the story that we wish to tell. In the early twentieth century the 'progress' of urban liberties underpinned the scholarship of
Adolphus Ballard, James Tait and Martin Weinbaum on the constitutional
development of the medieval English town.[2] To a more recent generation of
historians, concerned with exploring the collective character of the medieval
English town, charters have not entirely lost their importance, although they
are now seen as but one element in the process of self-definition and urban
growth.[3] Yet charters do not make sense in an administrative vacuum,
divorced from the political circumstances in which they were granted, while
the corporate identity of the medieval town is also problematic. As the
previous chapter showed, petitions in the name of the urban community were
largely in the interests of the discrete ruling groups within Bristol and York. It
is, therefore, vital to ask again why charters mattered to towns and whose
concerns they articulated.

This chapter focuses on three charters, which urban historians have
perceived as marking major milestones in the development of urban
self-government in late medieval England, namely Bristol's charter of 1373
and York's charters of 1393 and 1396, and addresses two seemingly straightforward questions. First, why did Bristol and York seek these charters, and in
particular, why did they solicit the charters when they did? Second, why was
the crown willing to grant the charters to Bristol and York? The constitutional significance of the three charters cannot be doubted. In essence, they
granted two new urban privileges: the appointment of the civic officials of
Bristol and York *ex officio* as justices of the peace, and the formal separation of
the two towns from the counties in which they were located and their elevation
to the status of counties in their own right. The charters of 1373, 1393 and 1396
freed Bristol and York from the interference of royal officials in the neighbouring
counties and gave their civic officials greater powers of self-government than
they had hitherto exercised. Since the early twelfth century the city of London

1   Attreed, *King's towns*, 33.
2   *British borough charters, 1042–1216*; *British borough charters, 1216–1307*; Tait, *Medieval
English borough*; Weinbaum, *Incorporation of boroughs*, The quotation is from *British borough
charters, 1307–1660*, p. xx.
3   Reynolds, *Kingdoms and communities*, ch. vi; Attreed, *King's towns*, ch. ii.

had been a county in all but name, ruled by sheriffs who also administered the adjoining shire of Middlesex,[4] but the charters to Bristol and York were novel. From the early fifteenth century several other major towns and cities, beginning with Newcastle-upon-Tyne, Norwich and Lincoln, followed suit, receiving charters granting the two associated privileges of county status and permanent justices of the peace.[5]

The six-hundredth anniversary of York's 1396 charter prompted renewed interest in all three charters and resulted in the publication of a collection of essays.[6] On several issues, however, questions remain and opinion is divided, particularly about the timing of the charters. On the one hand, there are those historians who emphasise the particular local context in which the charters of 1373, 1393 and 1396 should be located. Thus, it has been argued that in the case of Bristol the charter of 1373 was entirely the product of the problems attendant on the town's peculiar constitutional position, situated as it was on the border of two counties, Gloucestershire and Somerset, formed by the river Avon which ran through the town. In the words of David Palliser, Bristol was 'a special case'.[7] There is much to be said for this interpretation. Indeed, the author of the Wigmore chronicle, probably written at the Augustinian house at Wigmore in Herefordshire during the 1360s and 1370s, was acutely aware of Bristol's anomalous position, even though his sense of geography was a little confused. Under the year 1373 the chronicler noted that a parliament was held at London at which 'a new county was made by ordinance in the city of Bristol in which there was no county before, but a certain part of the city was in the county of Gloucestershire and a certain part in the county of Wiltshire'.[8] Yet it is also interesting to note that, what both Bristol's petition claimed and the crown acknowledged in 1373, was not a constitutional problem resulting from the town's division by two counties, but the hindrance to Bristol's trade.[9] In the case of York, the charters of 1393 and 1396 have been viewed within the context of a purportedly special relationship between Richard II and the city. According to John H. Harvey, writing in the early 1970s, the charters were the result of special royal favour to a city which the king seriously considered establishing as his capital on a permanent basis: in the summer of 1392 Richard II first transferred the central offices of royal government – the chancery, exchequer and the courts of king's bench and common pleas – from Westminster to York, then confiscated London's liberties, while residing for several months in the northern

4   Reynolds, *English medieval towns*, 113.
5   Rigby, 'Urban "oligarchy" ', 80.
6   Rees Jones, *Government of medieval York*.
7   Ormrod, 'York and the crown', 32; Dobson, 'The crown, the charter and the city', 38. The quotation is from Palliser, 'Towns and the English state', 133.
8   J. Taylor, *English historical literature in the fourteenth century*, Oxford 1987, appendix ii, 'A Wigmore chronicle, 1355–1377', 298 (my translation).
9   See pp. 194–5 below.

city.[10] However, the significance of this relocation of the royal government to the north has been the subject of recent debate, and Nigel Saul, in a careful analysis of royal diplomatic practice, has demonstrated that this 'alternative capital' thesis, based heavily on the evidence of Richard's visits to the city, cannot be sustained since the king did not visit the city any more than he did other towns and cities. In the critical year of 1392, for example, the king, far from staying in York 'from early June to late November, with only occasional absence', as Harvey contended, spent only ten days there in June.[11] It is hard to disagree with Saul's conclusion that, from the perspective of the crown at least, the relationship between Richard II and York was not especially close.

On the other hand, to Martin Weinbaum, the charters marked a crucial stage in the larger process of urban incorporation, which reached a climax in the second half of the fifteenth century in the granting of charters formally conferring on towns the privileges of perpetual succession, the authority to sue and be sued as a corporate body at law, the power to hold lands, the possession of a common seal and the right to decree by-laws.[12] Weinbaum touched briefly on the particular local reasons why the town of Bristol sought and received its charter of 1373 and suggested in passing that the 1391 statute extending the statute of mortmain to towns and cities as corporate bodies provided an 'impetus' to the wave of grants of county corporate status in the late fourteenth and early fifteenth centuries, since urban communities now needed royal licence to hold land.[13] None the less, the overriding impression from Weinbaum's work is that, in this evolutionary and remorseless process towards formal incorporation – 'the terminal point of municipal history' between the fourteenth and seventeenth centuries – the desire for further corporate privileges and greater autonomy embodied in the charters of 1373, 1393 and 1396 was entirely natural and inevitable.[14]

Susan Reynolds has done much to debunk the idea of incorporation, pointing out that many towns and cities already possessed the rights associated with this privilege before charters of formal incorporation began to be issued by the crown from the second half of the fifteenth century and that the emerging concept of incorporation itself was the product of legal niceties rather than the reality on the ground.[15] Yet in recent work on the subject of urban liberties in late medieval England, the idea of the corporate personality

---

[10] J. H. Harvey, 'Richard II and York', in Du Boulay and Barron, *Reign of Richard II*, 202–17.

[11] Saul, 'Richard II and the city of York', 1–13, esp. p. 5; Harvey, 'Richard II and York', 206–7.

[12] Weinbaum, *Incorporation of boroughs*, 54–8. For the five points see *British borough charters, 1307–1660*, pp. xxiii–xxv.

[13] Weinbaum, *Incorporation of boroughs*, 54–8. The statute is in *SR* ii. 80.

[14] The quotation is from *British borough charters, 1307–1660*, p. xxiii.

[15] S. Reynolds, 'The history of the idea of incorporation or legal personality: a case of fallacious teleology', in her *Ideas and solidarities of the medieval laity: England and western Europe*, Aldershot 1995.

of the town as an autonomous agent persists. The starting point of Lorraine Attreed's study of relations between the civic and ecclesiastical franchises within the cities of Exeter, York and Norwich, for example, was 'these boroughs' concept of themselves as unique entities in both a physical and legal sense', in which, moreover, the ambition for urban growth in constitutional and geographical terms was both 'natural' and 'basic'.[16] The late medieval English town was not a monolithic entity with a mind of its own. The aim of this chapter, therefore, is to examine what Brigitte Bedos-Rezak has referred to as the 'dialectic between group identity and individual experience' in order to consider the question of 'townspeople's personal experience of urban identity'.[17]

Urban aspirations

The charters of 1373, 1393 and 1396 were the product of local initiative, that is, they were all preceded by urban requests. A formal copy of Bristol's petition was entered in the Little Red Book, while York's MPs formally petitioned Richard II in the Winchester parliament of January 1393 after earlier negotiations had presumably been conducted during the period of government residence in York.[18] At the end of May 1392 the offices of chancery and exchequer as well as the courts of common pleas and king's bench were instructed to move to York by 25 June and, although the order for their return to Westminster was given on 25 October, it is clear that several organs of state, including the exchequer and common pleas, were still located in York after Christmas and were only operational again in Westminster by the middle of January 1393.[19] It can hardly be doubted that it was during Richard's albeit brief visit to York in June 1392 that the subject of the city's new charter was first broached and that, in his absence, discussions continued with members of his administration still present in the city. Although there is no extant petition from York in 1396, it would appear that the city's rulers again took advantage of the king's presence in the city to begin negotiations for another charter, which then continued for over a month in London with chancery clerks. The 1396–7 accounts of the city's chamberlains show that a delegation from the city, including the mayor and two chamberlains, stayed in London for more than five weeks immediately prior to the grant of the

---

16 Attreed, 'Arbitration', 205–35, quotation at pp. 207, 212.
17 B. Bedos-Rezak, 'Civic liturgies and urban records in northern France, 1100–1400', in Hanawalt and Reyerson, *City and spectacle*, 34–55, quotation at pp. 37, 34.
18 *LRB* i. 115–26; SC 8/103/5147. Although undated, the petition can be dated with confidence to 1393 from its request for permanent justices of the peace, which was the main concession in the charter. For the parliamentary context see *CChR, 1341–1417*, 337.
19 *CCR, 1389–92*, 466–7, 565; *CPR, 1391–6*, 65; *CCR, 1392–6*, 21, 76; Tout, *Chapters*, iii. 482.

charter, during which period they were engaged in talks concerning the precise terms of the charter.[20]

There were certainly important practical reasons why the rulers of Bristol and York sought the extension of the towns' corporate liberties. The way in which Bristol's 1373 charter and York's 1393 and 1396 charters were copied verbatim into the main civic registers of their respective towns, where they were annotated with appropriate marginal headings for future reference, is highly suggestive of the seriousness with which their rulers took their new powers.[21] In the case of Bristol, there were problems of governance resulting from its location 'partly in the county of Gloucester and partly in the county of Somerset'.[22] In 1326, for instance, 'the mayor and commonalty of the town of Bristol' complained of the trouble which had arisen when the king instructed the sheriff of Gloucestershire to execute his orders in the town and 'the people of the town of Bristol' removed their goods and chattels to Temple Street, south of the river Avon, in the county of Somerset, beyond the reach of both Gloucestershire's sheriff and Bristol's bailiffs.[23] The fact that the charter of 8 August 1373 separating Bristol from Gloucestershire and Somerset was followed by the royal appointment of ten justices to oversee the perambulation of the boundaries of the new county is instructive. Lorraine Attreed has shown how the 'failure' of Norwich's 1404 charter (raising the city to county status) 'to specify the exact geographic range of the city's liberties caused decades of frustration in Norwich's disputes with rival jurisdictions'.[24] There was no such uncertainty in the case of Bristol, and the order to the justices to establish the respective boundaries of Bristol, Gloucestershire and Somerset expressed a determination that they 'shall be set in certainty' and 'that upon the metes and divisions of the said three Counties there shall be no ambiguity in the future'.[25]

However, the constitutional issue, namely the juridical relationship between the civic authorities and the adjoining counties, needs to be kept in perspective. Bristol's anomalous location served as a convenient justification for the charter. Significantly, when they petitioned in 1373, the town's rulers drew attention to the deleterious economic rather than political consequences of Bristol's position. Since the town's burgesses were obliged to attend judicial sessions, including meetings of the county court, in the county towns of Gloucestershire and Somerset (depending on which side of the river they lived), which were a great distance from Bristol, they were 'constrained

[20] *York city chamberlains' account rolls*, 6–7. For payments to chancery clerks see ibid. 7.
[21] Rees Jones, 'York's civic administration', 115; BRO, 04718, fo. 38r ff. Rather than the original royal charter, it was the parliamentary grant of 20 December 1373 confirming the town's county status and the bounds of the new shire which was copied into Bristol's Little Red Book.
[22] *LRB* i. 115.
[23] *RP* i. 434.
[24] Attreed, *King's towns*, 40, 260–4.
[25] *Bristol charters, 1155–1373*, 142–3.

to travel painfully daily to the great disturbance of their trade and impoverishment of their estate'. Therefore, the petition asked that the town of
Bristol, along with its suburbs, 'be severed and exempt, in all points, from the
said two counties for ever'.[26] This sort of economic rhetoric was a fairly standard ploy adopted by towns and cities to secure the attention of the crown
and there is reason to doubt its sincerity, although not its effectiveness. In
Lorraine Attreed's words, urban dwellers 'rarely hesitated to point out to
kings the ways in which timely charters and grants could advantage their
markets and tame the physical elements that impeded trade'.[27] Yet this is not
to deny the power of this language, and what made it so resonant in 1373 was
that it chimed in with contemporary royal fears in the early 1370s of the
danger to trade arising from the resumption of the Hundred Years War and
from French and Flemish attacks on English merchant shipping: these were
concerns which had been impressed on the crown by mercantile and maritime interest groups in parliament.[28] If, as James Sherborne has argued, 'the
defence of merchant shipping was . . . the Crown's main consideration in the
limited [naval] action of early 1372', the 1373 parliamentary writs of
summons instructing citizens and burgesses to be knowledgeable of shipping
and trade suggest that it remained a priority a year later.[29] Certainly, it would
explain the wording of the preamble to Bristol's 1373 charter, in which the
crown acknowledged that the need to travel to judicial sessions outside of
Bristol on a regular basis meant that the town's burgesses 'are sometimes
prevented from paying attention to the management of their shipping and
merchandise'.[30] Bristol's 'exceptional constitutional features' do not, therefore, adequately explain the 1373 charter.[31]

In the cases of both Bristol and York, the main practical value attached to
their charters was the grant to their rulers of the powers of justices of the
peace on a permanent basis. Indeed, it is revealing of their priorities that
York's civic elite requested and secured this right in 1393, three years before
the concession of county status to the city. The 1373 petition from Bristol's
mayor, bailiffs and commonalty asked that the burgesses of the town 'have
power to punish evil doers and disturbers of the peace, labourers, workmen
and artificers trespassing against the statutes, by amercements, fines, imprisonment . . . before the said Mayor and Bailiffs within the same town for
ever'.[32] Similarly, the first request of the citizens of York in their 1393 petition was that the mayor and citizens be granted the right to have justices of
the peace 'by provision of charter'. Specifically, they asked that each year, on

[26] LRB i. 115–16.
[27] Attreed, King's towns, 8.
[28] See pp. 51–3 above.
[29] Sherborne, 'Battle of La Rochelle', 21; Dignity of a peer, iv. 661.
[30] Bristol charters, 1155–1373, 118–19.
[31] Dobson, 'The crown, the charter and the city', 38.
[32] LRB i. 117–18.

the day of the mayor's election, they be allowed to elect 'certain persons' – presumably the mayor and aldermen in the council of twelve who were annually elected officeholders – to be justices of the peace within the city, with complete authority to act 'by the same charter without previous commission or writ of oyer and terminer'.[33] In other words, the burgesses of Bristol and the citizens of York wanted the civic officials of the two towns to exercise the powers of justices of the peace *ex officio*: that is, to act as justices continuously as a regular function of civic government.

The emergence of the office of justice of the peace was the most important development in local government in the late medieval period. The early fourteenth century saw the crown alternate between granting and withdrawing the judicial powers of the keepers of the peace to determine as well as to hear cases of felony and trespass. Although the reasons for changing royal policy in this period have been the subject of much historical debate,[34] the Black Death had a crucial impact on the judicial powers of the justices.[35] In 1350 and 1351 the peacekeeping powers of the justices were extended to the enforcement of the 1349 Ordinance of Labourers and the 1351 Statute of Labourers, economic legislation which sought to restrict wage and price increases and to control the greater mobility of labourers resulting from labour shortages after the plague. Between 1352 and 1359 there were separate commissions of the peace and of labourers, but these were then replaced by single commissions which, from 1361, were given statutory authority to hear and determine felonies and trespasses, with full jurisdiction over the labour legislation. In 1362, according to royal statute, justices of the peace were expected to hold their sessions quarterly, and in 1368 the 1361–2 legislation was confirmed. Further additions were made to the powers of the justices of the peace in the later fourteenth century, including the enforcement of the 1388 legislation requiring servants and labourers to secure written licences in order to leave their place of work and the 1390 legislation allowing justices to fix wages according to local conditions rather than to a predetermined national wage structure.[36]

There was, from the beginning, an important urban dimension to the parliamentary labour laws. This fact has tended to be ignored by political and legal historians, who have focused largely on the relations between the

---

[33] SC 8/103/5147.

[34] The key studies here are B. H. Putnam, 'The transformation of the keepers of the peace into the justices of the peace, 1327–1380', *TRHS* 4th ser. xii (1929), 19–48; A. Verduyn, 'The politics of law and order during the early years of Edward III', *EHR* cviii (1993), 842–67; A. Musson, *Public order and law enforcement: the local administration of criminal justice, 1294–1350*, Woodbridge 1996, 49–82. See also A. Musson and W. M. Ormrod, *The evolution of English justice: law, politics and society in the fourteenth century*, Basingstoke 1999, 86–9.

[35] For what follows on the evolution of the powers of the justices of the peace see Musson and Ormrod, *Evolution of English justice*, 50–3.

[36] For the 1388 and 1390 statutes see *SR* ii. 56, 63.

county gentry and the royal government after the Black Death not only in parliament, but also in the enforcement of the labour legislation in the localities.[37] Above all, there was a strong urban, and specifically London, influence on the 1351 Statute of Labourers, which reflected the concerns of the parliamentary burgesses about the social and economic consequences of the shortage of labour after the plague. In the case of Bristol, in particular, these concerns should come as no surprise, for though there is some disagreement among the chroniclers about the port through which plague first entered England in the summer of 1348, Bristol seems a probable conduit.[38] It was certainly one of the first English towns to be seriously affected. According to Henry Knighton, 'almost the whole population of the town perished, snatched away, as it were, by sudden death, for there were few who kept their beds for more than two or three days, or even half a day', while the author of the *Eulogium historiarum*, writing at Malmesbury abbey in Wiltshire in the mid-fourteenth century, noted that when plague arrived in Bristol 'very few were left alive'.[39] A comparison of the two membership lists of Bristol's common council from 1349 and *c.* 1350 suggests that about half of Bristol's common councillors, drawn from the town's civic elite, might have perished within a year or two of the first appearance of plague.[40] One of the consequences of declining population was a scarcity of labour, which also had an impact on the level of wages that workers could now demand. The subsequent amendments to the 1346 ordinances of the fullers' craft in Bristol, for example, demonstrate the daily wage increases experienced in the second half of the fourteenth century by those engaged in this aspect of the cloth industry.[41] There can be little doubt that civic elites, both in their public and private lives, viewed such developments with alarm, for they undermined their corporate vision of the social hierarchy in which everyone knew his place and his duties, while also threatening their status as employers of labour.[42]

The 1349 Ordinance of Labourers was issued by the king and council after discussion with prelates, nobles and royal justices,[43] but the Statute of Labourers was negotiated in parliament following the submission of a

---

[37] See, for example, Harriss, *King, parliament, and public finance,* 516–17; E. Powell, *Kingship, law, and society: criminal justice in the reign of Henry V,* Oxford 1989, 16; and R. C. Palmer, *English law in the age of the Black Death, 1348–1381: a transformation of governance and law,* Chapel Hill 1993, 14–27.

[38] The evidence is surveyed briefly in *The Black Death,* ed. and trans. R. Horrox, Manchester 1994, 9–10, 62–3.

[39] *Knighton's chronicle 1337–1396,* ed. and trans. G. H. Martin, Oxford 1995, 98–9; *Black Death,* 63.

[40] Twenty-three members of the 1349 council do not appear a year later: *LRB* i. 20–1

[41] *LRB* i. 12. Compare these revisions with the wage-levels set out in the craft's 1381 ordinances: ibid. ii. 15.

[42] Britnell, *Commercialisation,* 173.

[43] *SR* i. 307, discussed in B. H. Putnam, *The place in legal history of Sir William Shareshull, chief justice of the king's bench, 1350–61,* Cambridge 1950, 51.

common petition.[44] This drew attention to the ineffectiveness of the earlier Ordinance of Labourers, stating that labourers did not want to work according to the terms set out by the king and council in 1349 and that they ignored the fines imposed upon them. Thus, the parliamentary commons asked for the introduction of corporal punishment for those who refused to accept the wages they had received before the plague. The resulting statute incorporated not only the demand for corporal punishment, but also a list of specific rates of pay for agricultural and urban workers.[45] B. H. Putnam placed the responsibility for the statute firmly upon the shoulders of the chief justice of king's bench, Sir William Shareshull,[46] but the Statute of Labourers was certainly not created by the crown in a political vacuum and then imposed by the centre on the localities. As the statute roll indicates, it was the product of consultation between the commons and the lords.[47] Specifically, the royal government found the model for the urban aspects of the statute in London, where a long tradition of labour regulation existed.[48]

London letter-book F contains a civic ordinance issued by London's mayor and aldermen establishing the wages of craftsmen in the city and the prices to be charged by victuallers.[49] The ordinance is dated 1350 and thus falls between the 1349 ordinance and the 1351 Statute of Labourers. In contrast to the 1349 ordinance, which stated simply that labourers should be paid the wages that they were accustomed to receive in 1346, London's ordinance established a wage structure for certain types of craftsmen and labourers 'who take immeasurably more than they have been wont to take'.[50] The London ordinance can be seen both as a local response to the 1349 ordinance and, more significantly, as a model for the 1351 statute. The similarities between the London ordinance and the 1351 statute are striking. Although the 1351 statute first regulated the wages of rural workers such as carters, ploughmen and shepherds who, unsurprisingly, were not mentioned in the London ordinance,[51] the royal statute then followed the civic ordinance in its concern with the wages of members of the building crafts such as carpenters, masons

---

[44] RP ii. 227.

[45] SR i. 311–12.

[46] Putnam, William Shareshull, 53–4.

[47] SR i. 311

[48] For this tradition see S. Rees Jones, 'Household, work and the problem of mobile labour: the regulation of labour in medieval English towns', in J. Bothwell and others (eds), The problem of labour in fourteenth-century England, Woodbridge 2000, 133–53.

[49] Letter-book F, 212, translated in full in Memorials of London and London life in the XIIIth, XIVth and XVth centuries, 1276–1419, ed. and trans. H. T. Riley, London 1868, 253–8. Although Putnam was aware of this ordinance, she did not draw any firm conclusions from it: The enforcement of the statutes of labourers during the first decade after the Black Death, 1349–1359, New York 1908, 156.

[50] SR i. 307; Memorials, 253.

[51] SR i. 311–12.

and tilers.[52] The next group of craftsmen to receive royal attention consisted of those who carried goods by land and by water, exactly the same order as in the London ordinance.[53] The last group referred to by name in the 1351 Statute of Labourers comprised leather, cloth and metal workers including cordwainers, horsesmiths and spurriers: also the final group of workers regulated in the London ordinance.[54] In short, while there were differences between the 1351 Statute of Labourers and the 1350 civic ordinance, notably in the regulation of agricultural as well as urban workers, the urban aspects of the royal statute were provided by the London legislation. Although it is impossible to prove conclusively, it is certainly plausible that the crown, under pressure from the parliamentary commons, acquired a copy of the London legislation and generalised the London experience for all of England's urban communities. The national labour legislation arose, in part, then, from local, urban initiative.

The 1349 Ordinance of Labourers empowered the mayors and bailiffs of towns and cities to inquire into offences against the labour legislation; two years later, in the 1351 Statute of Labourers, civic officials were instructed specifically to co-operate with the justices of the peace in the enforcement of the labour legislation by informing the justices of the names of offenders during sessions of the peace.[55] Crucially, though, separate commissions of the peace to urban jurisdictions 'were issued where and when they were thought to be needed, the reasons for them often being obscure'.[56] Prior to 1373 Bristol only received one commission of the peace, in 1332, whereas York was subject to fifteen commissions between 1334 and 1391.[57] Government policy towards peacekeeping in urban jurisdictions was 'experimental and opportunistic', and commissions were issued on 'an individual basis'.[58] In normal circumstances, when separate provision was not made for an urban liberty, the town became part of the county (or counties) in which it was located for the purposes of criminal justice and urban cases came before justices of the peace on shire commissions based on the sworn testimony of jurors drawn from the individual hundreds of the county.[59] Thus, while these county commissions tended to contain figures from the governing elites of the towns and cities, such as the 1338 Gloucestershire commission of the peace, which

---

[52] *SR* i. 312; *Memorials*, 253–4.

[53] *SR* i. 312; *Memorials*, 254.

[54] *SR* i. 312; *Memorials*, 256–7.

[55] *SR* i. 308, 312.

[56] E. G. Kimball, 'Commissions of the peace for urban jurisdictions in England, 1327–1485', *Proceedings of the American Philosophical Society* cxxi (1977), 467.

[57] For the commissions see ibid. appendix 2 at pp. 472, 474.

[58] Ibid. 467, 460.

[59] In the case of Bristol see, for example, *Rolls of the Gloucestershire sessions of the peace, 1361–1398*, ed. E. G. Kimball (Bristol and Gloucestershire Archaeological Society lxii, 1940), 18, 74–5, 78–9.

included Bristol's mayor, Eborard le Frensshe,[60] they still enjoyed jurisdiction over urban communities.

Civic rulers perceived these county commissions as an intrusive and alien force in urban life, infringing on their rights of self-government. Simon Walker's study of Yorkshire justices of the peace in the late fourteenth and early fifteenth centuries has highlighted the tensions between the ruling elite of Beverley and the justices on the East Riding commission, concluding that it was the 'burgesses' consistent ambition throughout this period . . . to gain the right to have the town's own officers act as justices of the peace within the liberty . . . without interference from the East Riding bench'.[61] Meanwhile, in the case of Colchester, as Richard Britnell has demonstrated, friction between the town's civic officials and county justices developed into a full-blown 'constitutional crisis' in 1352, when Colchester's bailiffs, charged with collecting fines from those found guilty of certain offences against the 1351 Statute of Labourers before the commission of the peace in Essex, 'refused to collect and pay over the full sum' due from the town.[62] Although the city of York received several commissions of the peace prior to 1393, the city's ruling elite was dependent on royal commissions which could be withdrawn at any moment according to royal whim and which seem to have been terminated in any case when new county commissions were appointed and resumed jurisdiction within the towns and cities.[63] A dispute between the citizens of Lincoln and the dean and chapter of Lincoln cathedral provided the background to the appointment of the city's mayor and bailiffs as justices of the peace in 1380: the commission then aroused the hostility of the dean and chapter of the cathedral who, presumably fearing that Lincoln's civic officials would abuse their judicial powers, alleged in parliament that the commission had been bought by the civic officials. As a result of the petition, all the peace commissions issued to urban communities throughout England were withdrawn.[64] It is hardly surprising that York's citizens, in their 1393 petition, placed great emphasis on their intention to have their own justices of the peace 'by point of charter' without the necessity of waiting for a royal commission or a writ of oyer and terminer and free from the incursion of justices 'from the three ridings of the same county'.[65]

Yet the ambition for increased autonomy and for permanent justices of the peace, in particular, was much more than an articulation of a collective urban identity. The pursuit of urban liberties was bound up with private, vested interests. Indeed, the longstanding conflict between the city of York and the

---

[60] A. Verduyn, 'The selection and appointment of justices of the peace in 1338', *HR* lxviii (1995), 15–16.

[61] S. Walker, 'Yorkshire justices of the peace, 1389–1413', *EHR* cviii (1993), 296–7.

[62] Britnell, *Colchester*, 136–7.

[63] Kimball, 'Commissions of the peace', 458–9.

[64] A. Verduyn, 'The revocation of urban peace commissions in 1381: the Lincoln petition', *HR* lxv (1992), 108–11.

[65] SC 8/103/5147.

Benedictine abbey of St Mary's, which came to a dramatic climax in the mid-fourteenth century, demonstrates the way in which what was ostensibly a quarrel over the issue of their respective rights of jurisdiction in Bootham, which lay just outside the city walls to the north-west of the city and which the abbot claimed 'as his free borough' and the mayor maintained was 'a suburb of the city',[66] also revolved around questions of personal authority and status. The dispute came to the crown's attention in the 1260s and 1270s with reports that the citizens of York had attacked the abbey and its property in Bootham, and in 1275 Edward I declared that Bootham belonged to the abbey as 'the abbot's borough', whose inhabitants were exempt from civic tallages and from tolls and murage, and in which the mayor and bailiffs of York had no jurisdiction.[67] It is clear, however, that York's civic officials did not accept the 1275 settlement, and in 1312 and 1317, in response to complaints from the abbot of St Mary's, commissions of oyer and terminer were appointed to investigate claims that the mayor of York had assessed tallages, tolls and other taxes in Bootham.[68] In 1343, prompted by physical threats to the abbot and monks of St Mary's by 'several malefactors' of the city, the king went so far as to threaten to seize the city's liberties if the violence against the abbey continued.[69] In 1350, probably as a result of another petition from the abbot, Edward III decided to take the contested territory of Bootham into his hands, to reserve the case for the arbitration of the king's council and to place the abbey under royal protection.[70]

The mayor and bailiffs of York and the abbot of St Mary's were summoned to appear at Westminster before the king's council, whose members were commissioned 'to survey all charters, writings, records and other evidences herein produced by either party, to hear their arguments . . . and to finally determine the whole business'.[71] A council memorandum detailing the abbey's complaints about the criminal behaviour of York's civic officials, who were accused of orchestrating the violence, reveals that the only York citizen to be named individually was John de Gysburn, who was charged with forcibly arresting and imprisoning the abbey's officials.[72] The significant point is that it is unclear upon what authority Gysburn was acting, as he did not then occupy civic office and his position within the civic hierarchy was ambiguous. Philippa Maddern's study of the disorder which affected East Anglia in

---

66 CPR, 1348–50, 584.
67 Miller, 'Medieval York', 39–40; CPR, 1350–4, 393–4, which repeats the 1275 settlement.
68 CPR, 1307–13, 470–1; CPR, 1313–17, 692–3.
69 CCR, 1343–6, 96–7.
70 Although undated, the petition from the abbey asked that, in relation to the dispute over Bootham, 'final discussioun soit faite de la dite bosoigne': SC 8/176/8780. See also CPR, 1348–50, 496–7, 530, 584; CPR, 1350–4, 292, 471.
71 CPR, 1348–50, 530, 584. This last clause of the commission echoed the abbey's petition: SC 8/176/8780.
72 C 49/7/25.

the first half of the fifteenth century has shown how violence, and in particular the threat of violence, could actually have a particular purpose in justi-
fying authority.[73] In the conflict between the Benedictine priory and the city
of Norwich, for example, Maddern argued that 'the rivals attempted to
demonstrate their authority over disputed areas by much-publicized arrests
and imprisonments'.[74] In September 1357 John de Gysburn's nomination as a
bailiff was rejected by the mayor, John de Langton, and it is evident that
Gysburn was part of a mercantile elite within the city trying to secure control
of civic government in the 1350s and 1360s.[75] It is certainly possible that he
was exploiting the long-established enmity between the city and the abbey to
pursue his own agenda and to establish his own authority within York at a
time when the Langton family dominated civic government.

The charters of 1373, 1393 and 1396 extended the authority of the civic
elites of Bristol and York, establishing new financial, judicial and administrative offices. Bristol's 1373 charter separated the town from Gloucestershire
and Somerset so that it became 'a County by itself . . . called the County of
Bristol', while York's 1396 charter removed the city from the county of Yorkshire, elevating it to the status of 'a county by itself . . . called the county of
York'.[76] With their transformation into counties in 1373 and 1396 Bristol
and York gained the offices of sheriff and escheator with all the powers that
the sheriff and escheator in other counties exercised.[77] Similarly, the office of
justice of the peace already operational in the counties on a permanent basis
was grafted on to the existing system of civic government in Bristol and York.
According to its 1373 charter Bristol's mayor and sheriff were to inquire into,
hear and determine less serious criminal offences known as trespasses and
cases 'concerning victuallers, workers, labourers and artificers within the
same town, suburbs and precinct, as often as they shall see it right to be done',
but were only given powers of inquiry and arrest into felonies which had to
await gaol delivery and sentencing by a quorum of justices, of which the
mayor was to be a member.[78] In this respect, Bristol's charter brought the
town completely into line with the judicial arrangements in the counties
where, since 1368, a quorum composed of justices of assize was required for
the determining of felonies.[79] York's 1393 charter also kept the city in tune

[73] P. C. Maddern, *Violence and social order: East Anglia, 1422–1442*, Oxford 1992, 230.
[74] Ibid. 229.
[75] See pp. 121–2 above.
[76] *Bristol charters, 1155–1373*, 120–1; *CChR, 1341–1417*, 354.
[77] *Bristol charters, 1155–1373*, 120–3; *CChR, 1341–1417*, 354–5. Note the insistence in
Bristol's petition that the town should have its own sheriff and escheator with 'such power,
jurisdiction and liberty . . . as the other Sheriffs and Escheators in other counties have': *LRB*
i. 116.
[78] *Bristol charters, 1155–1373*, 124–5.
[79] E. Powell, 'The administration of criminal justice in late-medieval England: peace
sessions and assizes', in R. Eales and D. Sullivan (eds), *The political context of law*, London
1987, 54.

with the changing system of criminal justice in the shires, granting the city's mayor and twelve aldermen, 'or at least two of them with the said mayor', the power 'to correct, punish, enquire, hear and determine all matters as well of all felonies, trespasses, misprisions and extorsions, as of all other causes and plaints whatsoever' arising within the city and suburbs.[80] The new justices, like the justices on the county benches, were to be supervised by a quorum of assize justices.[81]

It is widely acknowledged by historians of the late medieval gentry that appointment to certain offices of local government played an important role in the acquisition of gentility, reflecting and reinforcing an individual's social standing in the shire.[82] Michael Braddick's work on local officeholding in the sixteenth and seventeenth centuries has argued for a similar dynamic in the process of state formation, pointing out that 'office not only reflected social status but also confirmed it' and suggesting that 'this was a motive, sometimes perhaps the chief one, for seeking office'.[83] It is certainly clear, for instance, from the way in which the size of the county peace and tax commissions began to expand from the late fourteenth and early fifteenth centuries to incorporate members of the lesser gentry, that officeholding was an integral part of the process of gentrification.[84] Nigel Saul's study of the gentry of Gloucestershire has demonstrated that the late fourteenth-century tax commissions in the shire were filled not by knights and wealthy esquires, but 'by men below the gentry in rank' who 'sought to gain admission to the ranks of the office-holders'.[85] In the sense that 'service in local government could and did bring a man respect and status',[86] there is no reason to believe that rural and urban elites were any different.

R. B. Dobson has described York's ruling group in the 1390s as 'the most dynamic overseas mercantile élite recorded in the history of medieval or indeed post-medieval York', a group which included the likes of the brothers, Thomas and Robert de Howom, Thomas Graa and his good friend, William de Selby, John de Howeden, Robert Savage and William Frost.[87] The same can be said of prominent members of Bristol's civic elite in the years around 1373, among whom were merchants such as Walter de Derby, John de Stoke, Richard le Spicer, Walter de Frompton, John Vyell, Ellis Spelly and Thomas Knappe. Thanks to the extraordinary topographical survey of Bristol

---

80 CChR, 1341–1417, 336.
81 For the operation of the assize justices in York in 1395 see YMB i. 146–8.
82 This work is summarised briefly in Harriss, 'Growth of government', 33–4.
83 Braddick, State formation, 35, and, more generally, ch. i.
84 Saul, Knights and esquires, 133–5, 145–6.
85 Ibid. For a similar pattern elsewhere see Acheson, Gentry community, 112–16.
86 Kermode, Medieval merchants, 68.
87 Dobson, 'The crown, the charter and the city', 42. Their biographies are in Roskell and others, The House of Commons, 1386–1421, iii. 138–41 (William Frost), 218–20 (Thomas Graa), 401–3 (Thomas de Howom), 433–4 (John de Howeden), and iv. 311–12 (Robert Savage), 332–4 (William de Selby).

compiled in the last quarter of the fifteenth century by William Worcestre, a native Bristolian,[88] it is possible to gain some impression of the way in which these figures were perceived within the town of Bristol. Unquestionably, they made a considerable impact on not only the civic landscape, but also the collective civic memory of Bristol. Richard le Spicer, three times mayor of Bristol in the third quarter of the fourteenth century, was remembered as a 'famous merchant and burgess (*famosum mercatorem et burgensem*) of the said town' and the founder of a chapel dedicated to St George in the town's guild-hall.[89] Walter de Frompton, three times mayor of Bristol, was variously 'a worthy merchant (*nobilem mercatorem*) of the town of Bristol' and 'a famous merchant, burgess of the aforesaid town', who paid for the rebuilding of the parish church of St John's along with the gateway into the walled town which it incorporated.[90] William Worcestre also described the stained glass window in the chapel of the Assumption of the Blessed Virgin on Bristol Bridge, below which was a crypt used for meetings of the common councillors and civic officials of the town, that depicted Ellis Spelly, four times mayor of Bristol between 1370 and his death in office in January 1391, along with other unnamed leading burgesses and their wives, the major benefactors of the chapel.[91] Meanwhile, Worcestre was suitably impressed by the imposing residence of John Vyell, the first sheriff of Bristol, which lay on The Key, the quay formed in the mid-thirteenth century specifically for overseas trade, and which had been constructed along the town wall. By the last quarter of the fifteenth century the property was commonly known as 'Vyell's Place', and, for William Worcestre at least, the dwelling remained a 'most splendid tower', notable for its masonry 'of huge stones' ('de lapidibus magnis').[92] The sight on The Back, the wharf designed for inland and coastal trade, of the 'fine chapel' dedicated to St John the Evangelist, whose two chaplains were to say mass every morning at 5 o'clock 'for the merchants, seamen, craftsmen and servants' of the town, reminded Worcestre of its founder, Thomas Knappe, five times mayor of Bristol in the later fourteenth and early fifteenth centuries. Worcestre described him both as 'a great man (*magnificum virum*), a merchant and burgess of Bristol' and as 'a respected merchant' ('venerabilem Mercatorem'), whose chapel he knew simply as 'Thomas Knapp's chapel'.[93]

Bristol's civic elite in the 1370s had much in common with that of York in the 1390s, most obviously in their extraordinary wealth. Using the evidence

---

[88] K. B. McFarlane, 'William Worcester: a preliminary survey', in Davies, *Studies presented to Sir Hilary Jenkinson*, 196–221.

[89] *William Worcestre: the topography of medieval Bristol*, ed. F. Neale (Bristol Record Society li, 2000), 210–11. See also appendix below.

[90] *William Worcestre*, 102–3, 200–1. See also appendix below.

[91] *William Worcestre*, 142–3: the editor notes that this window 'must have been particularly spectacular; it is the only stained glass in Bristol of which Worcestre gives any details'. For Spelly see appendix below.

[92] *William Worcestre*, 204–5, 214–15. See also appendix below.

[93] *William Worcestre*, 146–7, 150–1, 126–7. See also appendix below.

of the cash estates recorded in their wills as a guide to the relative wealth of York merchants, Jennifer Kermode has shown that 'several sizeable fortunes were left in the late fourteenth century, the largest belonging to York staplers', most notably Robert de Howom, twice MP for York, a member of the council of twelve, and a former chamberlain and bailiff of the city, who bequeathed close to £2,500 in his will, a fortune 'unsurpassed' in late medieval York.[94] Meanwhile, Robert de Cheddre, twice mayor of Bristol in the 1360s and a member of the town's common council from the mid-fourteenth century,[95] was remembered a hundred years later as the wealthiest ever burgess of Bristol. In August 1464 William Canynges, five times mayor of Bristol, whom William Worcestre described as 'a very rich and very wise merchant (*ditissimus ac sapientissimus mercator*) of the aforesaid town of Bristol',[96] was party to the arrangement of the marriage of his son and heir, John Canynges, to the daughter of a local gentry family. After the marriage, and to the consternation of his new in-laws, William began to divert his great wealth into the patronage of ecclesiastical foundations. The father of William's new daughter-in-law responded to this turn of events by petitioning chancery, seeking legal assistance to ensure that William kept to the terms of the pre-nuptial agreement, according to which, it was alleged, he had promised 'that he wold leve his seid son after his decese as well at ease in goodez as any man left his son in Bristowe within a hundred yere next before the seid accorde savynge only Robert Chedder'.[97]

There is little evidence that members of the civic elites of Bristol and York in the later fourteenth century aspired to gentility through the accumulation of a large landed estate in the countryside, though they did invest in landed property outside Bristol and York. Recent research has uncovered many examples of Bristol's merchants acquiring land in the neighbouring counties, especially in the areas from which they had originally migrated, but with the exception of the family of Thomas Norton, elected to the mayoralty of Bristol in 1413, 'landed property acquisition was aimed at securing a safe capital reserve for the town's merchants, rather than helping them attain rural retirement'.[98] Bristol merchants acquired land piecemeal in order to generate further wealth. With the notable exception of William Frost, the same is true of York's civic elite, about whom Jennifer Kermode has argued that 'there is little evidence of many merchants accumulating sufficient land or rents to achieve "gentrification" '.[99] Indeed, although he was dead by 1390,

94 Kermode, *Medieval merchants*, 296; BIHR, probate register 1, fos 100v–103v. See also appendix below.
95 See appendix below.
96 *William Worcestre*, 260–1.
97 *Overseas trade*, 141–2.
98 Penn, 'Fourteenth-century Bristol', 211.
99 Roskell and others, *House of Commons, 1386–1421*, iii. 138–41; Kermode, *Medieval merchants*, 288. For the nature and extent of investment in land by York merchants in the fourteenth and fifteenth centuries see ibid. 276–91.

John de Gysburn's investment in property was entirely characteristic of York's merchants in the last decade of the fourteenth century. Although both of his daughters married into the county gentry – Isabel to William Frost, and Alice to Sir William Plumpton, a member of 'one of the leading gentry families of Yorkshire' who was executed in 1405 for his involvement in the rebellion of his uncle, Richard Scrope of Masham, archbishop of York – Gysburn purchased only a small amount of rural property, and this was a financial investment rather than an attempt to gain landed gentry status.[100] His main residence was south of the river Ouse in the city of York,[101] and his interests lay firmly in overseas trade, civic office and royal service.

In many ways, the careers of Bristol and York merchants in the later fourteenth century had much in common with that of the London merchant, Richard Whittington, who also had no interest in becoming a country gentleman, but whose social ambitions were fulfilled by engagement in officeholding and less formal kinds of royal service.[102] Similarly, in Exeter, though the urban elite did own property outside the town, 'there is no evidence that members of the Exeter oligarchy either worked for or desired the life of a country gentleman'.[103] In this sense these figures could be seen as precursors of what Rosemary Horrox, for the fifteenth century, has termed 'an explicitly urban gentry', for whom gentility was not sought through the ownership of a country estate, but through several avenues, 'perhaps the most effective' of which 'lay through service to the crown'.[104] Largely as a result of Bristol's increasing importance to the crown in the Hundred Years War, there were, in the early 1370s, several burgesses, such as Walter de Derby, John de Stoke, Walter de Frompton and Richard le Spicer, at the pinnacle of Bristol society, who monopolised civic office and were especially active in royal service, lending money and ships to the crown and even, in one case, serving on royal diplomatic missions overseas.[105] Walter de Frompton, a mayor of Bristol, a member of the town's common council from the mid- fourteenth century and twice MP for Bristol, was a regular servant of the crown, performing *ad hoc* services as a lender of money and ships, but also securing repeated employment as a tax collector and a staple and customs official in the port of Bristol in the third quarter of the fourteenth century.[106] He was also armigerous, bequeathing to his son, Walter, his gold signet ring ('quo solebam sigillare'), and remembered a century after his death by the inclusion of a

---

[100] Roskell and others, *House of Commons, 1386–1421*, iii. 138–41; Miller, 'Medieval York, 112.

[101] YMB iii. 73.

[102] Barron, 'Richard Whittington', 210, 221–4.

[103] Kowaleski, 'Exeter in the late fourteenth century', 212.

[104] R. Horrox, 'The urban gentry in the fifteenth century', in Thomson, *Towns and townspeople*, 22–44, quotation at pp. 22, 29.

[105] See appendix below.

[106] Ibid. For his employment on tax commissions see CFR, 1347–56, 270; CFR, 1368–77, 390; CFR, 1377–83, 164, 189.

drawing of his arms alongside the record of his first election to the mayoralty in Robert Ricart's *Kalendar*.[107] His claims to gentility seem to have derived from his wealth of experience in royal service. To Bristol's civic elite the 1373 charter was, ultimately, a formal confirmation of the social and political status that its members already enjoyed through local officeholding and informal ties with the crown.

In the 1390s York's civic elite included individuals with long records of service to civic and royal government, such as Thomas and Robert de Howom, John de Barden and Thomas Graa, who held royal office as tax collectors and justices of the peace, and lent money to the crown; Graa also served on a royal embassy abroad and acted as a parliamentary adviser on commercial and fiscal policy.[108] At the centre of what R. B. Dobson has described as a 'remarkable galaxy of overseas merchants at York during the decades immediately before and after 1396' was William Frost, seven times mayor of the city in the last decade of the fourteenth and first decade of the fifteenth centuries.[109] Frost had a different background from other leading citizens of York, belonging 'to the middle ranks of the Yorkshire gentry' on his admission to the freedom of the city in 1395. Despite the fact that he was, by this date, married to one of the daughters of John de Gysburn, four times mayor of York, and the owner of Gysburn's large house in Micklegate, his urban status could not have been secure, least of all because of the recent notoriety surrounding his father-in-law.[110] The 1396 charter was perhaps crucial in establishing Frost's civic credentials. Certainly, he was closely associated with its acquisition. On his re-election as mayor on 3 February 1397 Frost was rewarded by the city for his efforts with a payment of the unusually large sum of £100 'for his fee and for his remuneration for this past year'.[111]

In the last quarter of the fourteenth century York's rulers became increasingly status-conscious, preoccupied with the city's standing in relation to other urban communities. In 1372 and again in 1377 the crown instructed certain towns and cities, including York, to build a vessel for service at sea at their own expense.[112] In 1378 the city's rulers petitioned Richard II, at great pains to remind the king that the city had built three ships 'all at sea at greater expense than any other city in the kingdom with the exception of London'.[113] At Winchester in January 1393 the 'fellow-citizens of your city and chamber of York' petitioned the king to request that the city be given

107 Wadley, *Great orphan book*, 19–21; Ricart's kalendar, BRO, 04720(1)a, fo. 96r.
108 See appendix below. For service as tax collectors see CFR, *1377–83*, 150, 164; for employment as JPs in the city of York see CPR, *1374–7*, 490; CPR, *1377–81*, 45, 515, 572, 631; CPR, *1385–9*, 81, 254; CPR, *1388–92*, 139, 343, 524.
109 Dobson, 'The crown, the charter and the city', 42 n. 23.
110 Roskell and others, *House of Commons, 1386–1421*, iii. 138–41.
111 YCA, D1, fo. 9v.
112 See p. 44 above.
113 SC 8/216/10758.

permanent justices of the peace.[114] The rhetoric of the chamber challenged explicitly the pretensions of London's rulers, who until now had claimed exclusively that their city was the 'king's chamber'.[115] It was against London that York's ruling elite measured themselves, and their appropriation of the metaphor of the chamber in 1393 was a rhetorical device, employed to impress on the king their own self-importance and prestige. York's 1393 and 1396 charters were part of the same self-imaging. Thus, around 1400, when the commons of York presented a petition to the mayor and council of twelve aldermen seeking a more selective policy of admission into the civic franchise, they supported their argument by tapping into the acute sense of rivalry and competition for status felt so keenly by the city's rulers and so evident in the city's 1378 and 1393 petitions. The commons asked for a change in the cost of entering the freedom of the city, requesting that, from henceforth, no one was to be admitted as a freeman for less than 60s. Why did the commons choose this figure as the franchise threshold? Well, the commons continued, 'honourable cities of the realm such as London and Bristol do not receive anyone into their franchise for less than 60s. . . . whereas in lesser towns such as Lynn and Hull, entrants to the freedom only pay 40s'.[116] Further, since the city of York 'is and always has been . . . a city of great reputation and always named the second city of the realm and the king's chamber', it was not appropriate for dishonest men to be received into the freedom to enjoy the privileges of such an honourable city.

Royal interests

Why was the crown willing to grant the charters of 1373, 1393 and 1396? In particular, how is the timing of the charters to be explained? R. B. Dobson has described the process by which York received the 1396 charter as ' "horse-trading" ' between the crown and the mayor and aldermen of the city, so that 'one party (the city) gained what the other party (the Crown) had no particular objection to giving away'.[117] David Palliser has argued, more generally, from the way in which petition and charter followed practically verbatim, that towns and cities knew what they were to receive beforehand.[118] The petitions and charters of 1373 and 1393 reveal a broad congruence in what was requested and what was granted by the crown. One notable difference between York's 1393 petition and subsequent charter was the issue of to whom fines generated by the sessions of the peace in the city should be paid. Although the civic elite of York asked that the profits of

---

114 SC 8/103/5147; CChR, 1341–1417, 336–7.
115 For the meaning of this rhetoric see p. 64 above.
116 The petition was one of several presented at this time: YCA, D1, fo. 348r–v.
117 Dobson, 'The crown, the charter and the city', 39–40.
118 Palliser, 'Towns and the English state', 129.

justice be reserved to the city 'in maintenance and support of its own great expenses' ('en relevement et subportacion de grantz chargez dycelle'), the charter stated that such income was to be paid to the crown instead.[119] Three years later, however, Richard II granted to the citizens of York 'all fines, forfeited issues and amercements belonging to justices of the peace within the liberty of the said city and suburbs', which were to be used for the maintenance of Foss Bridge and Ouse Bridge 'and other daily charges'.[120] The concession was part of an older royal policy of allowing the profits of the king's courts to benefit the local community rather than the royal government. In 1349, 1351 and 1352 the crown had agreed that the profits of justice from those convicted of offences under the Ordinance and Statute of Labourers should help to subsidise the payment of the lay subsidy, and in 1357 fines from the escapes of felons and fugitives indicted before the justices of the peace were used for the same purpose.[121] Indeed, in 1357, although a struggle developed between the citizens of York and the sheriff of Yorkshire over the collection of the tax rebate, financial penalties eventually contributed £10 towards York's tax quota of £162, thus providing relief to the city's taxpayers.[122] By allowing financial penalties from the sessions of the mayor and aldermen to contribute towards the city's own corporate income in 1396, the city's ruling elite was given a direct financial interest in the enforcement of royal justice.

Bristol's 1373 charter was given 'in consideration of the good behaviour of the said burgesses towards us and of their good service given us in times past by their shipping and other things and for six hundred marks which they have paid to us ourselves into our Chamber'.[123] Similarly, York's 1396 charter was granted by the king 'out of affection for the city of York and in consideration of the good service done by the citizens'.[124] Given this rhetoric it is scarcely surprising that historians have tended to see patronage (involving a reciprocal exchange of goods and services) as the essential glue binding urban communities and the crown together.[125] Of course, the grants of 1373, 1393 and 1396 did represent the exercise of royal patronage and, in such circumstances, it was entirely to be expected that the crown would use the rhetoric of patronage, namely the distribution of favour and privilege in return for

---

[119] SC 8/103/5147; CChR, 1341–1417, 336. In the case of Bristol, the town's 1373 petition was ambiguous on this issue, but the crown was much more transparent, granting the burgesses justices of the peace, 'saving always to us and our heirs the said fines and amercements and other things belonging to us thereupon': LRB i. 117–18; Bristol charters, 1155–1373, 124–5.

[120] CChR, 1341–1417, 355.

[121] Harriss, King, parliament, and public finance, 340–3.

[122] E 359/14, rot. 48d. For York's complaint to the king and council see SC 8/205/10240.

[123] Bristol charters, 1155–1373, 118–21.

[124] CChR, 1341–1417, 354.

[125] See pp. 2–3, 17 above. For this aspect of patronage see Powell, 'After "after McFarlane" ', 5.

service. It is also the case that the rulers of Bristol and York oiled the machinery of patronage to secure their charters. The payment of 600 marks to the king's chamberlain, William Lord Latimer, helped to secure access to the king for Bristol's burgesses,[126] while in the 1390s York's ruling elite capitalised on the visits to the city of the royal administration, the king and Thomas Arundel, archbishop of York and king's chancellor, to petition for the charters and to court Richard and his government with gifts and entertainment.[127]

The underlying reason for the timing of the charters lay in the existence of small groups of men within Bristol and York, dominant in civic office and vastly experienced in royal service, on whom the crown was already dependent in the exercise of government not only locally, but also at Westminster and abroad. This relationship meant that there were individuals within Bristol and York in whom the crown had confidence such that the towns could carry out their new responsibilities. The importance of this trust is demonstrated by the crown's decision to withdraw all urban peace commissions in 1381 in response to a single complaint from the dean and chapter of Lincoln cathedral alleging the abuse of power by the mayor and bailiffs of the city in their capacity as justices of the peace.[128] Powers were not given away lightly by the crown or bought easily for money: urban elites were expected to maintain the king's peace. A group of York notables, composed of William de Selby, Thomas Graa, Thomas de Howom, Thomas Thurkyll, John de Barden, Robert Savage, John de Rypon, Thomas Smyth, Thomas de Staynlay and William de Tykhill, seven of whom had been mayors of the city, acted as justices of the peace in York on a continual basis from 1385. First commissioned in December 1385, they were reappointed in January 1387, November 1389, July 1390 and November 1391.[129] In 1393, as a result of the terms of the city's charter, the justices appointed in 1385 were freed from their responsibility to send the records of their sessions to the exchequer for royal inspection; this concession was duly noted in the York Memorandum Book.[130] Although it is likely that York received its own justices of the peace primarily because of continuing unrest in the city, which the general pardon issued by the king to the city of York in 1382 had done little to resolve,[131] the years from 1385 can also be seen as a trial period in the exercise of these judicial powers for York's ruling elite. This perspective makes it possible to understand why the crown was willing to delegate these powers to the city's mayor

---

[126] See pp. 33–4 above.

[127] Saul, 'Richard II and the city of York', 7, 9–10; Dobson, 'The crown, the charter and the city', 43.

[128] Verduyn, 'Revocation', 108–11, and p. 200 above.

[129] CPR, 1385–9, 81, 254; CPR, 1388–92, 139, 343, 524. The only extant record of York's justices dates from 1389 to 1391: JUST 1/1145, mem. 6.

[130] YMB i. 215

[131] See, for example, KB 27/483, mem. 7r.

and aldermen permanently in 1393. Furthermore, in 1396 there is no doubt that the city's mayor, William Frost, who had held the escheatorship of Yorkshire between 1388 and 1390 and had served on a number of other royal administrative and judicial commissions in the county, was a critical figure in the negotiations preceding the grant of the charter.[132] Like his father-in-law, John de Gysburn, Frost was seen by his contemporaries in the councils of twelve and twenty-four to have valuable connections which could mediate relations between the city and the crown. Despite a February 1393 civic ordinance designed to prevent re-election to the mayoralty until all members of the council of twelve had first held the office,[133] Frost enjoyed an almost uninterrupted occupation of the mayor's office from 1396 to 1405, the years which saw first York's elevation to county status in 1396 and then the deposition of Richard II in 1399.[134]

The co-operative structure of government was extended by the charters of 1373, 1393 and 1396, since these royal grants did not concede to Bristol and York autonomy from the crown; rather they increased the financial, administrative and judicial responsibilities of their rulers to the royal government and made them directly accountable to the crown. With their own offices of sheriff, escheator and justice of the peace, the towns were freed from the interference of officials from the counties in which they had hitherto been located.[135] Indeed, in the case of Bristol, the crown used the opportunity presented by the town's ambition for a new charter to reduce the membership of the common council (from which the mayor and sheriff were drawn) from forty-eight to forty, and changed the electoral procedure of the council so that the power of election lay, in the first instance, with the mayor and sheriff of the town rather than through 'common assent' as had previously been the case.[136] The crown also reserved the power to choose Bristol's sheriff annually from three candidates submitted by the burgesses to the royal chancery,[137] thereby maintaining a permanent influence on the composition of the town's ruling elite and a direct link with civic government.

The charters of 1373, 1393 and 1396 were the product of local initiative. In the case of York, the presence in the city of the king and, in 1392, of his administration, would probably of themselves have generated petitions for

132 Frost's importance in 1396 is noted also in Dobson, 'The crown, the charter and the city', 41–2; Rees Jones, 'York's civic administration', 134; Roskell and others, *House of Commons, 1386–1421*, iii. 138–41.

133 YCA, D1, fo. 9v.

134 Roskell and others, *House of Commons, 1386–1421*, iii. 138–41.

135 This point about the nature of urban autonomy was true of all royal charters to towns and cities: Palliser, 'Towns and the English state', 135–7.

136 *Bristol charters, 1155–1373*, 136–7. The quotation comes from the first election of the common council in 1344: *LRB* i. 25.

137 *Bristol charters, 1155–1373*, 120–1. This may be the earliest example of 'pricking': Ormrod, *Edward III*, 243 n. 58. For an example of this practice from 1422, albeit in the somewhat unusual circumstances created by the sheriff's death in office, see *LRB* i. 142–9.

the confirmation and/or extension of charters of corporate liberties.[138] In the case of Bristol, the dispute with the crown over the town's fee farm occasioned by the renewal of the Hundred Years War in 1369 raised serious questions about the powers of self-government exercised by the town's rulers, which needed to be placed on a firmer constitutional footing.[139] Yet the charters also marked the beginning of a trend, which saw several major towns and cities such as Newcastle-upon-Tyne, Norwich, Lincoln, Hull and Southampton follow the lead of Bristol and York in securing the privileges of county status and permanent justices of the peace.[140] In order to understand why these charters were conferred, attention needs to be paid to the individual circumstances surrounding each grant. None the less, the pattern of urban constitutional development cannot be ignored: the charters reflected a wider change in the financial and political role of provincial towns and cities in national affairs in the later fourteenth and early fifteenth centuries resulting from the Hundred Years War and the failure of Italian credit. Their increasingly important role in national finance and politics helps to explain both why the royal government was willing to extend the powers of urban elites as crown agents and why leading townsmen sought a more formal acknowledgement of their growing prominence within the kingdom.

[138] See, for example, Saul, 'Richard II and the city of York', 7, for discussion of the relationship between charters and royal visits.
[139] See pp. 79–80 above.
[140] Rigby, 'Urban "oligarchy" ', 80.

Conclusion

In wealth, size and constitutional status Bristol and York were more exceptional than typical of the wide spectrum of late medieval English towns and
cities. Around 1500 an Italian visitor to England wrote that, apart from
London, 'there are scarcely any towns of importance in the kingdom,
excepting these two: Bristol, a seaport to the west, and Boraco (Eboracum)
otherwise York, which is on the borders of Scotland'.[1] Notwithstanding the
brief and rather predictable reference to York's Roman past, few clues were
provided as to the precise criteria by which the significance of Bristol and
York was measured. If such a ranking could be assigned in a period of severe
economic decline for both Bristol and York,[2] however, there can be little
doubt that similar conclusions would have been drawn in the second half of
the fourteenth century. And yet, in questioning the special corporate and
autonomous character of the late medieval town, which has hitherto
hindered attempts to integrate English urban communities into a wider political narrative, the conclusions of this study of relations between the crown
and Bristol and York may have wider relevance. Political historians have
tended to assume that it was only the gentry and nobility who really mattered
in politics and that towns, because of their privileged constitutional status,
were only interested in augmenting their chartered liberties, while urban
historians have generally neglected the broader political context in which
towns operated.

If we shift our focus from towns to townspeople – specifically, the urban
elite comprising civic officeholders and town councillors – a more profitable
avenue of inquiry is opened up. There is much to be said for the view that late
medieval England saw an increasing trend towards oligarchic control in
English towns and cities.[3] 'Oligarchic' specifically in the sense that civic
government came to be dominated by a small mercantile elite whose
sectional interests, both locally and nationally, were in tension with, and
frequently overrode, a notion of the public good to which their urban
subjects subscribed. This study has shown how the very concept of 'oligarchy'
was the stuff of political debate in this period, in which questions were asked
about the extent to which urban government was conducted by the

---

1   *A relation, or rather a true account, of the island of England . . . about the year 1500*, ed. and
trans. C. A. Sneyd (Camden xxxvii, 1847), 41.
2   Sacks, *Widening gate*, 24–8; Palliser, *Tudor York*, 201–11.
3   For a recent discussion of the subject see S. H. Rigby and E. Ewan, 'Government, power
and authority, 1300–1540', in D. M. Palliser (ed.), *The Cambridge urban history of Britain*,
600–1540, Cambridge 2000, 291–312.

self-interested few or by the 'better sort' for the common good.[4] But this political debate, vigorous as it was, also reminds us of the essentially co-operative
nature of civic government in late medieval England, in which, though the
balance of power between elite and commons might shift, the exercise of
political power was dependent ultimately upon negotiation and consultation
and the distinction between public interest and sectional interest was often
blurred.[5]

By the end of the fourteenth century the civic elites of Bristol and York
had become an integral part of what G. L. Harriss has described as the emergence in late medieval England of 'a political society deeply versed in government, and a system of government in which crown and subjects shared
responsibility'.[6] The desire for royal favour and privilege was not central to
the workings of crown – town relations. Rather, this relationship, like that
between town rulers and their subjects, was founded upon an underlying
belief that government should be broadly collaborative and consensual. In
the mid-1370s, only two years after the granting of county status to their
town, Bristol's rulers refused a request for a loan, probably because of the
perceived dominance of the royal government by a court faction which was
widely seen to be acting in its own private interests.[7] In 1399, only three years
after York received the charter making the city a county in its own right, the
city's rulers responded to Richard II's oppressive fiscal demands on members
of the civic elite in the last few years of his reign by lending money to his
successor, Henry Bolingbroke, prior to his accession to the throne. It was a
brave decision and it is little wonder that York's common clerk noted eagerly,
in the margin of the city's copy of the statutes of Henry IV's first parliament,
the immunity from prosecution granted by Henry to those of his subjects who
had pledged their support to the new king before his coronation. According
to the statute, no one, either lord temporal or spiritual or 'other Person, of
what Estate or Condition that he be', who 'came with our Sovereign Lord the
King that now is into the Realm of England' or who, within the kingdom,
'came to the King in Aid of him to pursue them that were against the good
Intent of our Sovereign Lord the King and the Common Profit of the Realm',
was to 'be impeached, grieved nor vexed'.[8] Alongside the city's copy of this
statute, the clerk made a special note – 'concerning those who came to the
king immediately with armed might and aid to him' ('de ceux qe viendre au
Roy a son primer venir en force et eide de luy')[9] – and he can only have been

4 Ibid. 291, 308.
5 McRee, 'Peacemaking', 831–66. For a different perspective on this last point see
Britnell, *Commercialisation*, 176–7.
6 Harriss, 'Growth of government', 57.
7 See pp. 30–1 above.
8 SR ii. 111–12.
9 YCA, A/Y, fo. 135r.

thinking about the 500 marks lent by York to Henry 'in his necessity before he undertook the governance of the realm' in the summer of 1399.[10]

By the second half of the fifteenth century, in the context of economic decline and political crisis, it is likely that this interdependence between civic and royal government had become one of increasing dependence, as towns and cities lavished gifts on, and offered other forms of hospitality to, local nobles and royal dignitaries, and looked upon the crown as a source of salvation.[11] Yet, there is reason to doubt whether, as has been argued,[12] the ruling elites of major towns and cities sought neutrality in the Wars of the Roses, anxious about supporting the wrong side at the cost of losing valuable urban privileges. Their ties with the crown were too strong and they were too important in national finance, trade and politics to detach themselves from the wider affairs of the kingdom in this way.

---

10 CPR, 1399–1401, 354.
11 See, for example, Dobson, 'The crown, the charter and the city', 55.
12 For example idem, 'General survey', in Palliser, Cambridge urban history of Britain, 281, and Rigby and Ewan, 'Government, power and authority', 293.

APPENDIX

Urban Elites and the Crown

The purpose of this book was to examine relations between the crown and Bristol and York in the second half of the fourteenth century from the perspective of the individuals directly involved in mediating these relations. For this reason the methodology informing the research was prosopographical. Prosopography aims at a *histoire totale* of the individuals who form the subject of study; one of the problems of this kind of research is knowing where to stop.[1] In this case, the prosopographical research undertaken was designed to address a series of discrete questions about those individuals in Bristol and York who lent money or ships to the crown, served in the customs, acted as officials in the domestic staples, participated in diplomatic missions overseas or were elected as parliamentary representatives of the two towns, with particular reference to their wider experience in royal service and their position within the civic hierarchy. The answers to such questions informed the last chapter, in which it was argued that the charters of 1373, 1393 and 1396 could be best understood from the perspective of the civic elites of Bristol and York in light of their formal appointment to royal office or performance of other *ad hoc* services to the crown. Although the book examines various aspects of their public and private lives, notably their mercantile interests, the appendix presents in tabular form the basic evidence relating to each individual's political career upon which the chapters were based.

Dates

The names of creditors are drawn from the period 1347 to 1401, since 1347 marked the end of the dominance of the merchant syndicates in the crown's credit arrangements and the beginning of a new fiscal policy by Edward III's government to 'appeal both to individual merchants and to town governments for loans'.[2] For the collection of customs, the period is 1351 to 1401, since 1351 saw the crown assume direct responsibility for the administration of the customs after the collapse of the wool monopoly companies.[3] The names of York's staple officials cover the years 1353 to 1369, the year in which York's staple was removed, and 1391, when it was reinstated briefly for

---

1 Powell, 'After "after McFarlane" ', 7.
2 Ormrod, *Reign of Edward III*, 184.
3 Idem, 'The English crown and the customs', 27.

a single year. The list of Bristol's staple officials spans the period 1353 to 1403 in order to provide a fifty-year sample. The evidence of civic officeholding represents the totality of the individual's political career in high-ranking civic office within Bristol and York both before 1350 and after 1400.[4]

The dates provided for the civic officials of Bristol and York are generally the years in which they were elected to civic office, although the names of members of York's inner councils are taken not from the record of formal elections, but from meetings of the city council in February 1378, 1379 and 1392, noted in the York Memorandum Book.[5] The list of York's councillors is also supplemented by the names of the city's *probi homines* recorded in the 1359 exchequer receipt roll.[6] The dates given for service as a staple official in Bristol or York or as a royal diplomat are the years in which the individuals received their royal commission or were elected to office, but the customs field covers the entire period in which individuals undertook their commission, since these tended not to be yearly or occasional appointments.

Sources

In the case of Bristol, the names of the mayors, sheriffs, bailiffs and stewards have been extracted from the record of civic officials provided by the Bristol antiquary, John Latimer, in the early twentieth century, who used the evidence of witness lists of Bristol deeds,[7] while York's civic officials have been compiled from the contemporary lists of civic officeholders contained in the Freemen's Roll.[8] The lists of Bristol's common councillors who were elected in 1344, 1349, *c.* 1350, 1381 and 1409–10 have been invaluable.[9] The identity of the creditors has been established from the exchequer receipt and issue rolls (E 401; E 403), while the names of shipowners whose vessels were employed by the crown have been compiled from a sample of the extant royal naval accounts.[10] The officials of the domestic staples are derived from C 67/22–3 and C 267/5/1–31 (Bristol), and C 267/8/83–90 (York), while those occupying positions in the various offices of the customs have been identified from the record of their appointment in the *Calendar of fine rolls*. The names of the individuals employed on diplomatic missions overseas are drawn from the record of their formal appointment in the *Calendar of close rolls* and/or their accounts for payment submitted to the exchequer.[11] The names of the parlia-

[4]   For the structure of civic office in Bristol and York see pp. 11–12 above.
[5]   YMB i. 30 (1378), 31–2 (1379), 32 (1379), 173 (1392).
[6]   E 401/447, 29 Aug.
[7]   Latimer, 'Maire of Bristowe', 108–37.
[8]   YCA, D1, fos 5r–11v (mayors), 290v–294v (bailiffs/sheriffs), 321v–331r (chamberlains).
[9]   LRB i. 25–6 (1344), 20–1 (1349, 1350), 114–15 (1381), 137–8 (1409–10).
[10] E 101/32/7 (1372); BL, MS Add. 37494 (1373); E 101/33/31 (1374–5); E 101/42/22 (pre-1375); E 101/40/21 (1386); E 101/41/31 (1394); E 101/42/5 (1400).
[11] CCR, 1385–9, 403 (Thomas Graa of York); E 364/5, rot. 8r (John de Stoke of Bristol).

mentary representatives of Bristol and York are in the two-volume *Return of the members*.

Key to abbreviations and symbols

The headings of several columns have been abbreviated:

Loan = Royal creditor
Ship = Shipowner
Cust. = Customs collector
Staple = Staple official
Dipl. = Diplomat
MP = Member of parliament

Within the main body of the tables there are further abbreviations and symbols:

[1] = the first parliament of the year
[2] = the second parliament of the year
w = collector of the wool and petty customs
t = collector of the subsidy of tonnage and poundage
m = mayor of the staple
c = constable of the staple

Table 1

Royal service and civic office: Bristol

Name	Loan	Ship	Cust.	Staple	Dipl.	MP	Mayor	Sheriff	Bailiff	Steward	Council
Appurleye, Walter				1366c							
Armes, Richard des			1391–5 w/t								
Babbecary, Thomas	1351					1360				1348	1344, 1349, 1350
Badecok, William	1347										
Banbury, John	1400	1400		1397m		1397	1397	1391	1389		
Barbour, Robert		1373									
Barstaple, John	1396			1395m, 1401m			1395, 1401, 1404–5	1389	1379		1381, 1409–10
Barugh, Peter atte	1396							1386			1381
Bath, Robert de	1347								1383	1347	1344
Bathe, John						1371	1369, 1371		1365		
Baxter, Robert	1400							1398			
Beauflour, Geoffrey				1357c		1360			1357		1349, 1350
Beauflour, Robert	1347								1346		1344
Beaupyne, Thomas	1394, 1400		1371–2t, 1373–5t, 1375–6w, 1387–91w, 1395w/t	1383m	1388	1373, 1377, 1378, 1382, 1388, 1393	1377, 1383	1374	1371		1381
Blanket, Edmund	1356		1361–3w	1357m		1362, 1369	1352		1349		1349, 1350
Blanket, John	1347	pre-1375								1355	1344, 1349

				1402-3c		1407, 1416	1399	1393		1409-10
Blount, Thomas										
Bord, John		1373, pre-1375								
Brompton, Richard de	1351		1361–2w, 1364–70w	1356c, 1359–60m	1358	1362		1357	1352	1349, 1350
Candever, John			1387–90w/t, 1391t	1382–1403c	1383[1]		1381			1381
Candever, William			1390–1t							
Canynges, John	1400			1386–8c, 1392m, 1398m	1383[2]	1392, 1398	1382	1380		1381
Canynges, Simon		1394								
Canynges, William		pre-1375	1390–1w	1381m, 1385m, 1389m	1383[1], 1384[1], 1386	1373, 1375, 1381, 1385, 1389		1362, 1370		1381
Castelacre, John	1351			1354c				1349, 1353	1352	1349, 1350
Castell, John		1373, 1374–5, pre-1375, 1394, 1400						1394		1381
Chaumberleyn, Richard					1368			1367		
Chaumpeneys, John		pre-1375								
Cheddre, John				1369–70c						
Cheddre, Robert de (*alias* Seward)	1351, 1356		1363–5w	1355c, 1371–5c	1369	1361, 1363		1352		1349, 1350, 1381
Cheddre, William de			1370–5w							

Name	Loan	Ship	Cust.	Staple	Dipl.	MP	Mayor	Sheriff	Bailiff	Steward	Council
Chepman, Nicholas				1364c							1350
Clerk, Edward		1400									
Clerk, Thomas		1400									1381
Clerk, William		1400									
Clyve, John								1408	1405		1409–10
Cobyndon, John de	1347, 1351, 1356		1354–61w	1354m			1353		1348, 1351, 1355		1344, 1349, 1350
Cobyndon, Richard		pre-1375									
Colston, Thomas de	1347									1345	1344
Colston, Thomas	1400	1394		1390–9c					1387		
Colyngton, John de						1351			1341	1343	1344, 1349, 1350
Combe, William de			1375–6w, 1382–7w, 1386–8t	1359–60c, 1376–7c				1378	1350, 1376	1354	1349, 1350, 1381
Cornekey, John		1400									
Coventre, Thomas de	1351								1353	1351	1349, 1350
Dale, Henry de			1362–4w								
Danham, John		1400									
Davy, John		1373									
Denbaud, Thomas						1366					
Dene, Richard de				1361c					1354		1350

Derby, Walter de	1370	1372, 1373, pre-1375	1371–2t, 1373–5t, 1376–87w, 1382t, 1386–7t	1355c, 1359–60c, 1364m, 1368m, 1369–75c, 1380m, 1384m	1372, 1373, 1382[2]	1364, 1368, 1376, 1380, 1384		1352, 1356, 1359–60, 1362		1349, 1350, 1381
Dodyng, John		1373, 1374–5, pre-1375								
Draycot, John		1394								
Dudbrook, Robert		1394				1404	1400	1390, 1395		1381
Erlyngham, William		1374–5		1365c				1378	1365	
Farewey, John			1382–3t							
Felter, William le	1347									1344
Fishewer, John	1347									1344
Fraunceys, Hugh		1373								
Frensshe, Eborard le	1347					1337, 1339, 1341		1323, 1326–7	1332	1344
Frensshe, Reginald le	1351			1355–6m, 1358m	1355 1358 1361	1356, 1358		1350		1349, 1350
Frere, Thomas		1394, 1400								
Frome, William				1389c	1383[2], 1390[1], 1391, 1397	1394, 1400	1387	1386		1381, 1409–10
Frompton, Henry de	1347									1344

Name	Loan	Ship	Cust.	Staple	Dipl.	MP	Mayor	Sheriff	Bailiff	Steward	Council
Frompton, Nicholas	1347										
Frompton, Roger de		pre-1375									
Frompton, Walter de	1351, 1356	1373, 1374–5	1351–3w, 1354–61w, 1371–2t, 1376w	1353c, 1366m, 1369–75m		1362, 1378	1357, 1366, 1374		1375	1350	1349, 1350, 1381
Fulbroke, John						1382², 1388²					1381
Gardener, Robert			1391t			1388²					1381
Glastyngbury, Thomas				1367c							
Godeman, Henry		pre-1375									
Gournay, Roger		1373									
Gyen, Robert	1347, 1351						1345, 1347, 1349		1326–7, 1331, 1334		1344, 1349
Hakeston, John		1374–5		1361m					1360		1350
Hamme, William		1394, 1400									1409–10
Hantesford, Richard		1394, 1400							1391		1409–10
Hardewyk, John		1373, 1394							1396		1381
Hattere, Edward le	1347										1344
Haukere, John le				1354c, 1358c							
Haveryng, John		1394						1393	1389		1409–10
Hayl, William	1351			1364c					1365	1350	1349, 1350

Name									
Hertham, John (*alias* Pokelchurche)		1392–5 w/t, 1397–9 w/t							
Horncastel, John de	1347								1344
Horslisle, John		1400							
Inhyne, Richard			1362c				1355		1350
Inhyne, Thomas			1358c, 1367c				1356	1359	1350
Kernesdale, William		pre-1375							
Knappe, Thomas	1396, 1400	1373, 1374–5, pre-1375, 1394, 1400	1386m, 1391m, 1396m, 1399m, 1403m	1385, 1388[1]	1386, 1391, 1396, 1399, 1403*	1379	1376		1381
Lemman, John		1391t					1398		1381
Mare, Piers de la		1400							
Martyn, Geoffrey		1353–4w							1349
Mawardyn, Richard		1395–7 w/t							
Michell, Robert	1400								
Michell, William	1374–5								
Mois, Alex			1365c					1365	
More, Thomas	1400								
Mulleward, Walter			1368c					1368	
Neel, John	1347						1345		1344

* In June 1404 Thomas Knappe, Bristol's mayor, died in office, and was replaced by John Barstaple.

Name	Loan	Ship	Cust.	Staple	Dipl.	MP	Mayor	Sheriff	Bailiff	Steward	Council
Norton, Richard de			1351–3w								
Norton, Thomas		1394, 1400				1399	1413	1401	1392		1409–10
Panys, Richard						1399			1401		
Peper, John			1391t								
Phelpes, Nicholas		1373									
Pichmaker, Simon		1373									
Piers, John		1373, 1374–5									
Pilk, William	1347										
Plummer, Hugh		1400									
Pochyn, John			1399–1401w								
Pounde, William		1400									
Prentys, Robert				1362					1348		1349, 1350
Preston, John				1400c					1372, 1381		1381, 1409–10
Preston, William de			1378–9t							1362	
Ropere, Nicholas		1400									
Ropere, Robert		1394									
Russel, John	1351										
Sampson, John	1347									1353	1349, 1350
Sannsom, John	1351										
Saundres, Richard de	1347										
Serjeant, John						1363					

Name										
Seward, William	1347									1349
Seymor, John de					1351					
Shepherd, William		1400								
Sloo, John	1373, 1374–5, pre-1375							1366		
Somerwell, John de		1400		1393m		1393	1385	1383	1369	1381
Somerwell, William de		pre-1375		1378–81c, 1387m	1366, 1384[1]	1387	1376, 1380	1361, 1367		1350, 1381
Spelly, Ellis		1386	1388–91t	1357c, 1382m, 1390m	1377[1], 1381, 1384[1], 1385, 1386	1370, 1378, 1382, 1390**		1361, 1363	1356	1350, 1381
Spelly, Henry			1382–3t							1381
Spelly, John		1373								
Spert, Roger	1351									1349
Spicer, John le (alias Goterest)	1347			1353m		1348, 1351		1339		1344, 1349, 1350
Spicer, Richard le	1351, 1356, 1370	1374–5			1355	1354, 1360, 1372				1350
Stevenes, John	1400	1394	1395–8 w/t	1402m	1391, 1393	1402	1394	1388		1381, 1409–10
Stoke, John de			1365–75w, 1376–82w	1361c, 1362m, 1365m, 1367m, 1376–9m	1363, 1372, 1381	1365, 1367, 1379		1354, 1359, 1375		1349, 1350, 1381

** In January 1391 Ellis Spelly died during his mayoralty and Thomas Knappe was elected in his place.

Name	Loan	Ship	Cust.	Staple	Dipl.	MP	Mayor	Sheriff	Bailiff	Steward	Council
Stowe, Stephen de	1347										1344, 1349
Sydenham, Richard de						1368					
Taillour, Reginald	1396										1381
Taillour, Walter		1400									
Tanner, Thomas		1394									
Tedistille, Walter				1382–5c		1384[2]		1377			1381
Thorp, John			1398–1401w								
Toryton, Philip de	1347									1336, 1345	1344, 1349
Vyell, Edmund	1351										
Vyell, Henry				1376c				1375	1358, 1371		1349, 1350
Vyell, John		pre-1375		1377–81c, 1388m		1382[1], 1390[1]	1388	1373	1369–70		1381
Walshe, Walter		pre-1375									
Warde, Adam		pre-1375									
Welde, Richard		1374–5									
Wermynstre, Geoffrey				1368c						1368	
Wermynstre, William	1396, 1400							1396	1382		1381, 1409–10
White, Edmund		1400									
Wilcokes, Walter				1366c							

Name										
Wilkins, John	pre-1375									
William, John	pre-1375									
William, Mark (*alias* Spaynell)	1394, 1400					1422	1405	1400		1409–10
Wryngton, Alan de	1351									1349, 1350
Wryngton, John de	1351								1349	1349, 1350
Wryngton, Robert de	1347					1343		1334, 1336, 1339		1344
Wycombe, John de	1347, 1356	1353–4w	1353c			1346, 1350			1343	1344, 1349, 1350
Wygen, John	1373									
Yonge, William					1361					

Table 2
Royal service and civic office: York

Name	Loan	Ship	Cust.	Staple	Dipl.	MP	Mayor	Sheriff	Bailiff	Chamberlain	Council
Acastre, John de				1360–2c 1367m		1366, 1368, 1369, 1373, 1378	1364, 1379*		1357		1378, 1379
Allerton, John de	1359			1356m		1362			1353		1359
Barden, John de			1390–1w			1379 1381	1378		1372	1368	1379 1392
Benteslowe, Peter de	1351										
Beverlay, William de				1358–9c, 1364–5c					1353	1352	1378, 1379
Bolton, Jr., John de						1399	1410		1386	1384	1392
Bossal, Andrew	1347								1324	1321	
Bowere, Andrew le	1347									1330	
Brigenhale, Richard de	1347								1329	1328	
Bristoll, John de	1347								1334		
Buk, William	1351										
Cawod, William de	1351	pre-1375								1350	
Cottyngham, John de				1368c							

* In November 1379 John de Acastre, York's mayor, died in office and John de Gysburn was elected mayor.

Coupmanthorp, George de			1367c				1364	1366
Creyk, John de	1351				1352		1340	
Crome, John de							1360	1355
Dalby, Robert de	1347						1331	1324
Essheton, John de					1377[l]		1367	1364
Estryngton, William de	1347						1332	1328
Fouk, Nicholas de	1347, 1351					1342	1322	
Frankissh, William			1358–9c		1399		1359	
Frost, William						1396–7, 1400–4, 1406		
Fyssh, William		pre-1375						1366
Gare, Robert del			1364–5c, 1368c				1362	
Goldbeter, Thomas			1355–7c					
Gouk, Simon			1367c				1362	
Graa, Thomas			1391m	1388	1377[l], 1378, 1379, 1380[l], 1381, 1384[l], 1385, 1386, 1393, 1394, 1395, 1397	1375, 1397		1378, 1379, 1392
Graa, William	1347, 1359		1353–4m, 1365m		1355, 1358, 1361, 1363, 1365, 1366, 1368, 1369, 1371, 1372	1367	1345	1359, 1378

Name	Loan	Ship	Cust.	Staple	Dipl.	MP	Mayor	Sheriff	Bailiff	Chamberlain	Council
Grantham, Stephen	1347										
Grantham, William de	1347								1339	1334	
Gysburn, John de	1351, 1359	pre-1375		1358–62m, 1366m		1360, 1361, 1373	1371–2, 1379–80				1359, 1378, 1379
Harome, Robert de	1377								1370		
Hathington, William de	1347								1347	1338	
Haunsard, John	1347								1339		
Helmeslay, William de						1393	1394		1375	1373	1378, 1379
Holme, William									1338	1336	
Horneby, Ralph de	1347			1366c 1368m			1376		1359	1356	1378
Hosiere, Alan de	1347									1341	
Hovyngham, Roger de	1359					1358, 1360	1366				1359
Howeden, John de						1384[2], 1388[1], 1388[2], 1391	1386		1374		1378, 1392
Howom, Robert de	1351, 1377, 1385			1364m		1365, 1372	1368		1353	1352	1378, 1379
Howom, Thomas de	1377, 1385					1385, 1388[1]	1374		1366		1378, 1379
Kelstern, Walter de	1351			1355–6c, 1357m		1351			1335	1333	
Knapton, John de				1360–1c					1361	1358	

Name							
Ladychapeman, William	1351						
Langton, John de	1347, 1351			1352–63	1346	1351	
Lutton, Robert de	1351				1364	1351	
Lyddeyate, Robert	1347				1346		
Miton, Hugh de	1359	1353c	1352		1351	1348	1359
Moreton, Roger de	1377			1373	1365	1363	1378, 1379
Moreton, Jr., Roger de			1380[1]		1367		1378, 1379
Normanvill, Roger de		1354–5m	1351, 1355				
Pund, Adam		1353c					
Quixlay, Simon de	1377		1384[2]	1381–3	1375		1378
Rypon, John de		1357c, 1362c			1356	1355	
Rypon, John de			1388[2]				1378, 1379
Santon, Nicholas de	1347, 1351				1350		
Santon, Richard de	1347						
Santon, William de	1347, 1351					1349	
Savage, Robert	1377		1383[1], 1386	1384, 1391–2	1374	1370	1378, 1379
Selby, John de			1363				
Selby, Robert de	1347				1344		
Selby, Roger de			1362	1369–70	1358		

Name	Loan	Ship	Cust.	Staple	Dipl.	MP	Mayor	Sheriff	Bailiff	Chamberlain	Council
Selby, William de						1383[1], 1384[1], 1391, 1395, 1397	1385, 1387–8		1373		1378, 1379, 1392
Sevenhous, John de				1366c					1364		
Skelton, Robert de	1347								1337	1335, 1354	
Skelton, William de	1351								1347		
Skorby, Henry de	1347, 1351, 1359						1347–51		1331	1326	1359
Skorby, Nicholas de	1351								1326	1325	
Skorby, William de	1347										
Smyth, Thomas		pre-1375		1391c			1389–90		1377	1372	1379
Sporier, William	1347										
Swanland, William de	1351								1352		
Syggeston, Thomas de	1347, 1351								1349	1338	
Thurkyll, Thomas				1391c							1378, 1379
Warde, Robert	1377								1379	1376	1392
Wateby, Richard de	1359						1365		1356	1351	
Womme, John	1347								1326		
Wystowe, Robert de				1354c							

Bibliography

Unpublished primary sources

Bristol, Bristol Record Office
01208, 01209, 01210 Royal charters and letters patent
04718 The Little Red Book, 1344–1574
04720(1)a Ricart's kalendar

London, British Library
MS Add. 37494

London, The National Archives
Public Record Office
Chancery
C 47 Chancery miscellanea
C 49 Parliament and council proceedings
C 65 Parliament rolls
C 67 Supplementary patent rolls
C 267 Tower and rolls chapel series: certificates of election

Exchequer
E 30 Treasury of the receipt: diplomatic documents
E 34 Treasury of the receipt: loans to the crown
E 36 Treasury of the receipt: miscellaneous books
E 101 King's remembrancer: accounts, various
E 122 King's remembrancer: customers' accounts
E 163 King's remembrancer: miscellanea
E 179 King's remembrancer: particulars of account and other records relating to
    lay and clerical taxation
E 356 Pipe office: customs accounts rolls
E 359 Pipe office: accounts rolls of subsidies and aids
E 364 Pipe office: foreign accounts rolls
E 368 Lord treasurer's remembrancer: memoranda rolls
E 372 Pipe office: pipe rolls
E 401 Exchequer of receipt: receipt rolls and registers
E 403 Exchequer of receipt: issue rolls and registers

Justices Itinerant
JUST 1/772 General oyer and terminer, inquiry into felonies and trespasses in
    Bristol (1–4) and nearby, 1354–5: rolls of presentments and plaints, files of
    writs/precepts, names of jurors etc.
JUST 1/1138 General oyer and terminer, inquiry into treasons and felonies,
    1382: roll of plaints and attorneys

JUST 1/1145 Peace rolls, East, West and North Ridings, 4, 6, 7, 9, 13–16 Richard II

King's Bench
KB 27/482 *Coram rege* roll: 5 Richard II Michaelmas term
KB 27/483 *Coram rege* roll: 5 Richard II Hilary term

Special Collections
SC 1 Ancient correspondence of the chancery and the exchequer
SC 6 Ministers' and receivers' accounts
SC 8 Ancient petitions

Manchester, John Rylands University Library
MS Latin 236: account of William de Feriby, Queen Philippa's cofferer, 1357–8

York, Borthwick Institute of Historical Research
Probate registers, exchequer court: probate register 1

York, York City Archives
The York Memorandum Book, A/Y
Freemen's roll, D1

Published primary sources

The anonimalle chronicle, 1333 to 1381, ed. V. H. Galbraith, Manchester 1927, repr. 1970

Beresford, M. W. and H. P. R. Finberg, *English medieval boroughs: a handlist*, Newton Abbot 1973

The black book of the admiralty, ed. T. Twiss (RS, 1871–6)

The Black Death, ed. and trans. R. Horrox, Manchester 1994

Bond E. A., 'Chaucer as page in the household of the countess of Ulster', in *Life-records of Chaucer*, ed. W. D. Selby and others (Chaucer Society 2nd ser. xxi, 1886), 97–113

Borough customs, i, ed. M. Bateson (Selden Society xviii, 1904)

Borough customs, ii, ed. M. Bateson (Selden Society xxi, 1906)

Bridgwater borough archives, 1200–1377, ed. T. B. Dilks (Somerset Record Society xlviii, 1933)

Bristol charters, 1155–1373, ed. N. Dermott Harding (Bristol Record Society i, 1930)

Bristol charters, 1378–1499, ed. H. A. Cronne (Bristol Record Society xi, 1945)

British borough charters, 1042–1216, ed. A. Ballard, Cambridge 1913

British borough charters, 1216–1307, ed. A. Ballard and J. Tait, Cambridge 1923

British borough charters, 1307–1660, ed. M. Weinbaum, Cambridge 1943

A calendar of the cartularies of John Pyel and Adam Fraunceys, ed. S. O'Connor (Camden 5th ser. ii, 1993)

Calendar of letter-books . . . of the city of London, ed. R. R. Sharpe, London 1899–1912

Calendar of plea and memoranda rolls of the city of London, 1323–1482, ed. A. H. Thomas and P. E. Jones, Cambridge 1926–61

Chronicon Angliae, 1328–1388, ed. E. M. Thompson (RS, 1874)

City chamberlains' accounts in the sixteenth and seventeenth centuries, ed. D. M. Livock (Bristol Record Society xxiv, 1965)

The Coventry leet book, ed. M. D. Harris (Early English Text Society o.s. cxxxiv, cxxxv, cxxxviii, cxlvi, 1907–13)

Dialogus de scaccario: the course of the exchequer by Richard, son of Nigel, ed. and trans. C. Johnson, London 1950

Eulogium historiarum sive temporis, ed. F. S. Haydon (RS, 1858–63)

Feet of fines for the county of York, from 1347 to 1377, ed. W. P. Baildon (Yorkshire Archaeological Society Record Series lii, 1914)

Foedera, conventiones, literae, et . . . acta publica, ed. T. Rymer, The Hague 1745, republ. 1967

Foedera, conventiones, litterae et . . . acta publica, ed. T. Rymer, London 1816–69

Fortescue, John, *The governance of England*, ed. C. Plummer, London 1885

Froissart, John, *Chronicles*, trans. T. Johnes, London 1839

Fryde, E. B. and others (eds), *Handbook of British chronology*, 3rd edn, London 1986

Fuller, E. A., 'The tallage of 6 Edward II (December 16, 1312) and the Bristol rebellion', *TBGAS* xix (1894–5), 171–278

Gesta Stephani, ed. and trans. K. R. Potter, Oxford 1976

The great red book of Bristol, ed. E. W. W. Veale (Bristol Record Society ii, iv, viii, xvi, xviii, 1931–53)

Issue roll of Thomas de Brantingham . . . 44 Edward III, ed. and trans. F. Devon, London 1835

John of Gaunt's register, 1372–1376, ed. S. Armitage-Smith (Camden 3rd ser. xx–xxi, 1911)

John of Gaunt's register, 1379–1383, ed. E. C. Lodge and R. Somerville (Camden 3rd ser. lvi–lvii, 1937)

Knighton's chronicle, 1337–1396, ed. and trans. G. H. Martin, Oxford 1995

Latimer, J., 'The maire of Bristowe is kalendar: its list of civic officers collated with contemporary legal MSS.', *TBGAS* xxvi (1903), 108–37

'The lay poll tax returns for the city of York in 1381', ed. J. N. Bartlett, *Transactions of the East Riding Antiquarian Society* xxx (1953), 1–91

The lay subsidy of 1334, ed. R. E. Glasscock (British Academy Records of Social and Economic History n.s. ii, 1975)

The libelle of Englyshe polycye: a poem on the use of sea-power, 1436, ed. G. Warner, Oxford 1926

The little red book of Bristol, ed. F. B. Bickley, Bristol 1900

Memorials of London and London life in the XIIIth, XIVth and XVth centuries, 1276–1419, ed. and trans. H. T. Riley, London 1868

Middle English dictionary, Ann Arbor 1956–

The overseas trade of Bristol in the later Middle Ages, ed. E. M. Carus-Wilson (Bristol Record Society vii, 1937)

Owen, D. M., *The making of King's Lynn: a documentary survey* (British Academy Records of Social and Economic History n.s. ix, 1984)

The peasants' revolt of 1381, ed. R. B. Dobson, London 1970

Pedes finium (commonly called feet of fines) for the county of Somerset, 1347–1399, ed. E. Green (Somerset Record Society xvii, 1902)

The poll taxes of 1377, 1379 and 1381, ed. C. C. Fenwick (British Academy Social and Economic n.s. xxvii, 1997)

The records of the city of Norwich, ed. W. Hudson and J. C. Tingey, Norwich 1906–10

Register of the freemen of the city of York, ed. F. Collins (Surtees Society xcvi, cii, 1896–9)

The register of the guild of the Holy Trinity, St Mary, St John the Baptist and St Katherine of Coventry, ed. M. D. Harris (Dugdale Society xiii, 1935)

A relation, or rather a true account, of the island of England . . . about the year 1500, ed. and trans. C. A. Sneyd (Camden xxxvii, 1847)

Ricart, Robert, *The maire of Bristowe is kalendar*, ed. L. T. Smith (Camden n.s. v, 1872)

Rollason, D. W., *Sources for York history to AD 1100*, York 1998

Rolls of the Gloucestershire sessions of the peace, 1361–1398, ed. E. G. Kimball (Bristol and Gloucestershire Archaeological Society lxii, 1940)

Rotuli parliamentorum Anglie hactenus inediti, ed. H. G. Richardson and G. O. Sayles (Camden 3rd ser. li, 1935)

Select cases concerning the law merchant, ed. C. Gross and H. Hall (Selden Society xxiii, xlvi, xlix, 1908–32)

Select cases in the court of king's bench under Edward III, ed. G. O. Sayles (Selden Society lv, lvii, lviii, lxxiv, lxxvi, lxxxii, lxxxviii, 1936–71)

Select pleas in the court of admiralty, ed. R. G. Marsden (Selden Society vi, xi, 1892, 1897)

The staple court books of Bristol, ed. E. E. Rich (Bristol Record Society v, 1934)

The statute merchant roll of Coventry, 1392–1416, ed. A. Beardwood (Dugdale Society xvii, 1939)

'The 1377 poll tax return for the city of York', ed. J. I. Leggett, YAJ xliii (1971), 128–46

Wadley, T. P., *Notes or abstracts of the wills contained in . . . the great orphan book and book of wills* (Bristol and Gloucestershire Archaeological Society, 1886)

Walsingham, Thomas, *Historia anglicana*, ed. H.T. Riley (RS, 1863–4)

The Westminster chronicle, 1381–1394, trans. and ed. L. C. Hector and B. F. Harvey, Oxford 1982

William Worcestre: the topography of medieval Bristol, ed. F. Neale (Bristol Record Society li, 2000)

York city chamberlains' account rolls, 1396–1500, ed. R. B. Dobson (Surtees Society cxcii, 1978–9)

York memorandum book, ed. M. Sellers and J. W. Percy (Surtees Society cxx, cxxv, clxxxvi, 1912–69)

The York mercers and merchant adventurers, 1356–1917, ed. M. Sellers (Surtees Society cxxix, 1917)

Official publications

Calendar of charter rolls
Calendar of close rolls
Calendar of fine rolls
Calendar of patent rolls
Jurkowski, M. and others, *Lay taxes in England and Wales, 1188–1688*, Kew 1998
Letters and papers, foreign and domestic, of the reign of Henry VIII, 2nd edn, London 1864–1932
Proceedings and ordinances of the privy council of England, ed. N. H. Nicolas, London 1834–7
Report from the lords' committees . . . for all matters touching the dignity of a peer, London 1820–9
Return of the name of every member of the lower house of parliament . . . 1213–1874, London 1878
Rotuli parliamentorum, London 1783
Rotuli Scotiae, ed. D. Macpherson and others, London 1814–19
Statutes of the realm, London 1810–28

Secondary sources

Acheson, E., *A gentry community: Leicestershire in the fifteenth century, c. 1422–c. 1485*, Cambridge 1992
Allison, K. J., 'Medieval Hull', in VCH, *Yorkshire: East Riding, Hull*, Oxford 1969, 11–89
Allmand, C., 'Diplomacy in late-medieval England', *HT* xvii (1967), 546–53
———— *The Hundred Years War: England and France at war, c. 1300–c. 1450*, Cambridge 1988
Attreed, L., 'The king's interest: York's fee farm and the central government, 1482–92', *NH* xvii (1981), 24–43
———— 'Arbitration and the growth of urban liberties in late medieval England', *JBS* xxxi (1992), 205–35
———— 'The politics of welcome: ceremonies and constitutional development in later medieval English towns', in Hanawalt and Reyerson, *City and spectacle*, 208–31
———— 'Poverty, payments, and fiscal policies in English provincial towns', in S. K. Cohn Jr and S. A. Epstein (eds), *Portraits of medieval and renaissance living: essays in memory of David Herlihy*, Michigan 1996, 325–48
———— *The king's towns: identity and survival in late medieval English boroughs*, New York 2001
Baker, R. L., *The English customs service, 1307–1343: a study of medieval administration* (Transactions of the American Philosophical Society n.s. li, 1961)
———— 'The government of Calais in 1363', in W. C. Jordan and others (eds), *Order and innovation in the Middle Ages: essays in honor of J. R. Strayer*, Princeton 1976, 205–14
Barber, R., *Edward, prince of Wales and Aquitaine: a biography of the Black Prince*, Woodbridge 1978

———— and J. Barker, *Tournaments: jousts, chivalry and pageants in the Middle Ages*, Woodbridge 1989

Barnes, F. R., 'The taxation of wool, 1327–1348', in Unwin, *Finance and trade*, 137–77

Barraclough, G., *The earldom and county palatine of Chester*, Oxford 1953

Barron, C. M., 'The tyranny of Richard II', *BIHR* xli (1968), 1–18

———— 'Richard Whittington: the man behind the myth', in Hollaender and Kellaway, *Studies in London history*, 197–248

———— 'The quarrel of Richard II with London, 1392–7', in Du Boulay and Barron, *Reign of Richard II*, 173–201

———— 'London and the crown, 1451–61', in Highfield and Jeffs, *Crown and local communities*, Gloucester 1981, 88–109

———— *Revolt in London 11th to 15th June 1381*, London 1981

———— 'London: the later Middle Ages: 1270–1520', in Lobel, *Atlas of historic towns*, iii. 42–56

———— 'The deposition of Richard II', in Taylor and Childs, *Politics and crisis*, 132–49

———— 'London and parliament in the Lancastrian period', *PH* ix (1990), 343–67

———— 'Introduction: England and the Low Countries, 1327–1477', in C. M. Barron and N. Saul (eds), *England and the Low Countries in the late Middle Ages*, Stroud 1995, 1–28

———— 'Richard II and London', in Goodman and Gillespie, *Richard II*, 129–54

Bartlett, J. N., 'Robert Holme, citizen and merchant of York', *Journal of the Bradford Textile Society* xcvii (1952–3), 97–100

———— 'The expansion and decline of York in the later Middle Ages', *EcHR* 2nd ser. xii (1959), 17–33

Beardwood, A., *Alien merchants in England, 1350 to 1377: their legal and economic position*, Cambridge, Mass. 1931

Bedos-Rezak, B., 'Civic liturgies and urban records in northern France, 1100–1400', in Hanawalt and Reyerson, *City and spectacle*, 34–55

Bennett, M., *Community, class and careerism: Cheshire and Lancashire society in the age of Gawain and the green knight*, Cambridge 1983

———— 'Isabelle of France, Anglo-French diplomacy and cultural exchange in the late 1350s', in J. S. Bothwell (ed.), *The age of Edward III*, York 2001, 215–25

Black, A., *Political thought in Europe, 1250–1450*, Cambridge 1992

Bolton, J. L., *The medieval English economy, 1150–1500*, London 1980

———— 'The city and the crown, 1456–61', *London Journal* xii (1986), 11–24

———— 'Commerce and credit: the grocers' company and the growth of medieval London', *The Ricardian* xi (1997), 25–30

Booth, P. H. W., 'Taxation and public order: Cheshire in 1353', *NH* xii (1976), 16–31

Braddick, M., 'State formation and social change in early modern England: a problem stated and approaches suggested', *Social History* xvi (1991), 1–17

———— *State formation in early modern England c. 1550–1700*, Cambridge 2000

Bridbury, A. R., 'The Hundred Years' War: costs and profits', in D. C. Coleman and A. H. John (eds), *Trade, government and economy in pre-industrial England: essays presented to F. J. Fisher*, London 1976, 80–95

—— *Medieval English clothmaking: an economic survey*, London 1982

Britnell, R. H., *Growth and decline in Colchester, 1300–1525*, Cambridge 1986

—— *The commercialisation of English society, 1000–1500*, Cambridge 1993

—— and A. J. Pollard (eds), *The McFarlane legacy: studies in late medieval politics and society*, Stroud 1995

Broome, D. M., 'Exchequer migrations to York in the thirteenth and fourteenth centuries', in A. G. Little and F. M. Powicke (eds), *Essays in medieval history presented to T. F. Tout*, Manchester 1925, 291–300

Brown, A. L., 'Parliament, c. 1377–1422', in Davies and Denton, *English parliament*, 109–40

Bryant, W. N., 'The financial dealings of Edward III with the county communities, 1330–1360', *EHR* lxxxiii (1968), 760–71

Burgess, C., ' "For the increase of divine service": chantries in the parish in late medieval Bristol', *JEH* xxxvi (1985), 46–65

—— ' "By quick and by dead": wills and pious provision in late medieval Bristol', *EHR* cii (1987), 837–58

—— 'Educated parishioners in London and Bristol on the eve of the reformation', in C. M. Barron and J. Stratford (eds), *The Church and learning in later medieval society: essays in honour of R. B. Dobson*, Donington 2002, 286–304

Burwash, D., *English merchant shipping, 1460–1540*, Newton Abbot 1969

Butcher, A. F., 'English urban history and the revolt of 1381', in Hilton and Aston, *English rising*, 84–111

Cam, H., 'The legislators of medieval England', in H. Cam, *Law-finders and law-makers in medieval England*, London 1962, 132–58

Carpenter, C., *Locality and polity: a study of Warwickshire landed society, 1401–1499*, Cambridge 1992

—— 'Gentry and community in medieval England', *JBS* xxxiii (1994), 340–80

—— 'Political and constitutional history: before and after McFarlane', in Britnell and Pollard, *McFarlane legacy*, 175–206

—— *The Wars of the Roses: politics and the constitution in England, c. 1437–1509*, Cambridge 1997

Carus-Wilson, E. M., *Medieval merchant venturers: collected studies*, 2nd edn, London 1967

—— 'The overseas trade of Bristol in the fifteenth century', in Carus-Wilson, *Medieval merchant venturers*, 1–97

—— 'Trends in the export of English woollens in the fourteenth century', in Carus-Wilson, *Medieval merchant venturers*, 239–64

—— and O. Coleman, *England's export trade, 1275–1547*, Oxford 1963

Castor, H., *The king, the crown, and the duchy of Lancaster: public authority and private power, 1399–1461*, Oxford 2000

Childs, W. R., *The trade and shipping of Hull, 1300–1500* (East Yorkshire Local History Society xliii, 1990)

Clark, L., 'Magnates and their affinities in the parliaments of 1386–1421', in Britnell and Pollard, *McFarlane legacy*, 127–53

Coleman, O., 'The collectors of customs in London under Richard II', in Hollaender and Kellaway, *Studies in London history*, 181–94

Danbury, E., 'English and French artistic propaganda during the period of the Hundred Years War: some evidence from royal charters', in C. Allmand (ed.),

Power, culture, and religion in France, c. 1350–c. 1550, Woodbridge 1989, 75–97

Davies, J. C. (ed.), *Studies presented to Sir Hilary Jenkinson*, London 1957

Davies, R. G., 'Alexander Neville, archbishop of York, 1374–1388', *YAJ* xlvii (1975), 87–101

—— and J. H. Denton (eds), *The English parliament in the Middle Ages*, Manchester 1981

Davies, R. R., 'Richard II and the principality of Chester, 1397–9', in Du Boulay and Barron, *Reign of Richard II*, 256–79

—— *Lordship and society in the march of Wales, 1282–1400*, Oxford 1978

—— *The revolt of Owain Glyn Dŵr*, Oxford 1995

Davis, E. J., and M. I. Peake, 'Loans from the city of London to Henry VI, 1431–49', *BIHR* iv (1926), 166–72

Dobson, R. B., 'Admissions to the freedom of the city of York in the later Middle Ages', *EcHR* 2nd ser. xxvi (1973), 1–22

—— 'The risings in York, Beverley and Scarborough, 1380–1381', in Hilton and Aston , *English rising*, 112–42

—— 'The crown, the charter and the city, 1396–1461', in Rees Jones, *Government of medieval York*, 34–55

—— 'General survey', in Palliser, *Cambridge urban history of Britain*, 273–90

Dodd, G., 'The Calais staple and the parliament of May 1382', *EHR* cxvii (2002), 94–104

Du Boulay, F. R. H. and C. M. Barron (eds), *The reign of Richard II: essays in honour of May McKisack*, London 1971

Dyer, A., *Decline and growth in English towns, 1400–1640*, Cambridge 1995

Dyer, C., *Standards of living in the later Middle Ages: social change in England, c. 1200–1520*, Cambridge 1989

—— 'Taxation and communities in late medieval England', in R. H. Britnell and J. Hatcher (eds), *Progress and problems in medieval England: essays in honour of Edward Miller*, Cambridge 1996, 168–90

Edwards, J. G., 'The *plena potestas* of English parliamentary representatives', in *Oxford essays in medieval history presented to Herbert Edward Salter*, Oxford 1934, 141–54

—— *The commons in medieval English parliaments*, London 1958

—— *The second century of the English parliament*, Oxford 1979

Everitt, A., *The local community and the great rebellion* (Historical Association, gen. ser. lxx, 1969)

—— *Ways and means in local history*, London 1971

Ford, C. J., 'Piracy or policy: the crisis in the Channel, 1400–1403', *TRHS* 5th ser. xxix (1979), 163–78

Friel, I., 'Winds of change? Ships and the Hundred Years War', in A. Curry and M. Hughes (eds), *Arms, armies and fortifications in the Hundred Years War*, Woodbridge 1994, 183–93

Fryde, E. B., *Studies in medieval trade and finance*, London 1983

—— 'The English farmers of the customs, 1343–51', in Fryde, *Studies in medieval trade and finance*

—— 'Parliament and the French war, 1336–40', in Fryde, *Studies in medieval trade and finance*

—— 'Some business transactions of York merchants: John Goldbeter, William

Acastre and partners, 1336–1349', in Fryde, *Studies in medieval trade and finance*

Given-Wilson, C., 'The merger of Edward III's and Queen Philippa's households, 1360–9', *BIHR* li (1978), 183–7

––––––– *The royal household and the king's affinity: service, politics and finance in England, 1360–1413*, New Haven 1986

––––––– *The English nobility in the late Middle Ages: the fourteenth-century political community*, London 1987, repr. 1996

––––––– 'Wealth and credit, public and private: the earls of Arundel, 1306–1397', *EHR* cvi (1991), 1–26

Goldberg, P. J. P., 'Urban identity and the poll taxes of 1377, 1379, and 1381', *EcHR* 2nd ser. xliii (1990), 194–216

––––––– *Women, work, and life cycle in a medieval economy: women in York and Yorkshire, c. 1300–1520*, Oxford 1992

Goodman, A., *John of Gaunt: the exercise of princely power in fourteenth-century Europe*, London 1992

––––––– and J. L. Gillespie (eds), *Richard II: the art of kingship*, Oxford 1999

Gray, H. L., 'The production and exportation of English woollens in the four-teenth century', *EHR* xxxix (1924), 13–35

––––––– *The influence of the commons on early legislation: a study of the fourteenth and fifteenth centuries*, Cambridge, Mass. 1932

Green, A. S., *Town life in the fifteenth century*, London 1894

Griffiths, R. A., 'Wales and the Marches', in S. B. Chrimes and others (eds), *Fifteenth-century England, 1399–1509: studies in politics and society*, Manchester 1972, 145–72

Gross, C., *The gild merchant*, Oxford 1890

Guth, D. J., 'Richard III, Henry VII and the city: London politics and the "Dun Cowe"', in R. A. Griffiths and J. W. Sherborne (eds), *Kings and nobles in the later Middle Ages: a tribute to Charles Ross*, Gloucester 1986, 185–204

Hadwin, J. F., 'The medieval lay subsidies and economic history', *EcHR* 2nd ser. xxxvi (1983), 200–17

Hanawalt, B. A. and K. L. Reyerson (eds), *City and spectacle in medieval Europe*, Minneapolis 1994

Harriss, G. L., 'Preference at the medieval exchequer', *BIHR* xxx (1957), 17–40

––––––– 'The struggle for Calais: an aspect of the rivalry between Lancaster and York', *EHR* lxxv (1960), 30–53

––––––– 'Aids, loans and benevolences', *HJ* vi (1963), 1–19

––––––– *King, parliament, and public finance in medieval England to 1369*, Oxford 1975

––––––– 'The formation of parliament, 1272–1377', in Davies and Denton, *English parliament*, 29–60

––––––– 'Theory and practice in royal taxation: some observations', *EHR* xcvii (1982), 811–19

––––––– *Cardinal Beaufort: a study of Lancastrian ascendancy and decline*, Oxford 1988

––––––– 'Political society and the growth of government in late medieval England', *P&P* cxxxviii (1993), 28–57

––––––– 'The dimensions of politics', in Britnell and Pollard, *McFarlane legacy*, 1–20

Harrod, H., *Report on the deeds and records of the borough of King's Lynn*, King's Lynn 1874

Harvey, J. H., 'Richard II and York', in Du Boulay and Barron, *Reign of Richard II*, 202–17

Harvey, P. D. A. and A. McGuinness, *A guide to British medieval seals*, London 1996

Haskins, G. L., 'The petitions of representatives in the parliaments of Edward I', *EHR* liii (1938), 1–20

Hibbert, A. B., 'The economic policies of towns', in Postan and others, *Cambridge economic history of Europe*, iii. 157–229

Highfield, J. R. L. and R. Jeffs (eds), *The crown and local communities in England and France in the fifteenth century*, Gloucester 1981

Hill, J. W. F., *Medieval Lincoln*, Cambridge 1948

Hilton, R. H., *English and French towns in feudal society: a comparative study*, Cambridge 1992

——— and T. H. Aston (eds), *The English rising of 1381*, Cambridge 1984

Hollaender, A. E. J. and W. Kellaway (eds), *Studies in London history presented to Philip Edmund Jones*, London 1969

Holmes, C., 'The county community in Stuart historiography', *JBS* xix (1980), 54–73

Holmes, G., 'The "libel of English policy" ', *EHR* lxxvi (1961), 193–216

——— *The Good Parliament*, Oxford 1975

Holt, J. C., *Magna carta*, 2nd edn, Cambridge 1992

Horrox, R., 'Urban patronage and patrons in the fifteenth century', in R. A. Griffiths (ed.), *Patronage, the crown and the provinces in later medieval England*, Gloucester 1981, 145–66

——— 'The urban gentry in the fifteenth century', in Thomson, *Towns and townspeople*, 22–44

——— 'Local and national politics in fifteenth-century England', *JMH* xviii (1992), 391–403

Horton, M., 'Bristol and its international position', in Keen, '*Almost the richest city*', 9–17

Howell, R., *Newcastle upon Tyne and the Puritan revolution: a study of the civil war in north England*, Oxford 1967

Hoyle, R. W., 'Urban decay and civic lobbying: the crisis in York's finances, 1525–1536', *NH* xxxiv (1998), 83–108

James, M. K., 'The fluctuations of the Anglo-Gascon wine trade during the fourteenth century', in M. K. James, *Studies in the medieval wine trade*, ed. E. M. Veale, Oxford 1971, 1–37

Johnson, C., 'The collectors of lay taxes', in Willard and others, *English government at work*, ii. 201–26

Johnstone, H., 'The queen's household', in Tout, *Chapters*, v. 231–89

——— 'The queen's household', in Willard and others, *English government at work*, i. 250–99

Jones, W. R., 'The court of the verge: the jurisdiction of the steward and marshal of the household in the later Middle Ages', *JBS* x (1970), 1–29

Justice, S., *Writing and rebellion: England in 1381*, Berkeley 1994

Kaeuper, R. W., *War, justice, and public order: England and France in the later Middle Ages*, Oxford 1988

Kan, F. J. W. van, 'Elite and government in medieval Leiden', *JMH* xxi (1995), 51–75

Keen, L. (ed.), *'Almost the richest city': Bristol in the Middle Ages* (British Archaeological Association Conference Transactions xix, 1997)

Kermode, J., *Medieval merchants: York, Beverley and Hull in the later Middle Ages*, Cambridge 1998

Kimball, E. G., 'Commissions of the peace for urban jurisdictions in England, 1327–1485', *Proceedings of the American Philosophical Society* cxxxi (1977), 448–74

Kleineke, H., 'The commission *de mutuo faciendo* in the reign of Henry VI', *EHR* cxvi (2001), 1–30

Kowaleski, M., 'The commercial dominance of a medieval provincial oligarchy: Exeter in the late fourteenth century', in R. Holt and G. Rosser (eds), *The English medieval town: a reader in English urban history, 1200–1540*, London 1990, 184–215

—— *Local markets and regional trade in medieval Exeter*, Cambridge 1995

Lapsley, G. T., *The county palatine of Durham: a study in constitutional history*, London 1900

Leech, R. H., 'The medieval defences of Bristol revisited', in Keen, *'Almost the richest city'*, 18–30

Liddy, C. D., 'The estate of merchants in the parliament of 1381', *HR* lxxiv (2001), 331–45

—— 'The rhetoric of the royal chamber in late medieval London, York and Coventry', *UH* xxix (2002), 323–49

—— 'Urban conflict in late fourteenth-century England: the case of York in 1380–1', *EHR* cxviii (2003), 1–32

Lloyd, T. H., *The English wool trade in the Middle Ages*, Cambridge 1977

—— 'Overseas trade and the English money supply in the fourteenth century', in N. J. Mayhew (ed.), *Edwardian monetary affairs (1279–1344)* (British Archaeological Reports xxxvi, 1977), 96–124

—— *England and the German hanse, 1157–1611: a study of their trade and commercial diplomacy*, Cambridge 1991

Lobel, M. D. (ed.), *The atlas of historic towns*, London–Oxford 1969–89

—— and E. M. Carus-Wilson, 'Bristol', in Lobel, *Atlas of historic towns*, ii. 1–27

Lucas, H. S., 'The machinery of diplomatic intercourse', in Willard and others, *English government at work*, i. 300–31

McFarlane, K. B., 'William Worcester: a preliminary survey', in Davies, *Studies presented to Sir Hilary Jenkinson*, 196–221

—— 'War, the economy and social change: England and the Hundred Years War', *P&P* xxii (1962), 3–13

—— *The nobility of later medieval England*, Oxford 1973

—— 'Loans to the Lancastrian kings: the problem of inducement', in K. B. McFarlane, *England in the fifteenth century: collected essays*, London 1981, 55–78

McIntosh, M. K., *Autonomy and community: the royal manor of Havering, 1200–1500*, Cambridge 1986

McKisack, M., 'Borough representation in Richard II's reign', *EHR* xxxix (1924), 511–25

——— 'The parliamentary representation of King's Lynn before 1500', *EHR* xlii (1927), 583–9

——— *The parliamentary representation of the English boroughs during the Middle Ages*, Oxford 1932

——— *The fourteenth century, 1307–1399*, Oxford 1959

McRee, B., 'Peacemaking and its limits in late medieval Norwich', *EHR* cix (1994), 831–66

Maddern, P. C., *Violence and social order: East Anglia, 1422–1442*, Oxford 1992

Maddicott, J. R., 'The county community and the making of public opinion in fourteenth-century England', *TRHS* 5th ser. xxviii (1978), 27–43

——— 'Parliament and the constituencies, 1272–1377', in Davies and Denton, *English parliament*, 61–87

Madox, T., *Firma burgi*, London 1726

Maitland, F. W., *Township and borough*, Cambridge 1898

Maxwell-Lyte, H. C., *Historical notes on the use of the great seal of England*, London 1926

Miller, E., 'Medieval York', in VCH, *Yorkshire: York*, 25–116

——— 'The economic policies of governments', in Postan and others, *Cambridge economic history of Europe*, iii. 281–340

Mills, M. H., 'The collectors of customs', in Willard and others, *English government at work*, ii. 168–200

Munro, J. H. A., *Wool, cloth, and gold: the struggle for bullion in Anglo-Burgundian trade, 1340–1478*, Brussels 1972

Musson, A., *Public order and law enforcement: the local administration of criminal justice, 1294–1350*, Woodbridge 1996

——— and W. M. Ormrod, *The evolution of English justice: law, politics and society in the fourteenth century*, Basingstoke 1999

Myers, A. R., 'Parliamentary petitions in the fifteenth century', *EHR* lii (1937), 385–404, 590–613

Nicholas, D., 'The English trade at Bruges in the last years of Edward III', *JMH* v (1979), 23–61

Nightingale, P., 'Capitalists, crafts and constitutional change in late fourteenth-century London', *P&P* cxxiv (1989), 3–35

——— 'Monetary contraction and mercantile credit in later medieval England', *EcHR* 2nd ser. xliii (1990), 560–75

——— *A medieval mercantile company: the grocers' company and the politics and trade of medieval London, 1000–1485*, London 1995

——— 'Knights and merchants: trade, politics and the gentry in late medieval England', *P&P* clxix (2000), 36–62

O'Connor, S., 'Finance, diplomacy and politics: royal service by two London merchants in the reign of Edward III', *HR* lxvii (1994), 18–39

Ormrod, W. M., 'The English crown and the customs, 1349–63', *EcHR* 2nd ser. xl (1987), 27–40

——— 'The origins of the *sub pena* writ', *HR* lxi (1988), 11–20

——— 'The peasants' revolt and the government of England', *JBS* xxix (1990), 1–30

——— *The reign of Edward III: Crown and political society in England, 1327–1377*, New Haven 1990

——— *Political life in medieval England, 1300–1450*, Basingstoke 1995

——— 'The west European monarchies in the later Middle Ages', in R. Bonney (ed.), *Economic systems and state finance*, Oxford 1995, 123–60

——— 'The politics of pestilence: government in England after the Black Death', in W. M. Ormrod and P. G. Lindley (eds.), *The Black Death in England*, Stamford 1996, 147–81

——— 'York and the crown under the first three Edwards', in Rees Jones, *Government of medieval York*, 14–33

——— 'Finance and trade under Richard II', in Goodman and Gillespie, *Richard II*, 155–86

Palliser, D. M., *Tudor York*, Oxford 1979

——— 'Urban decay revisited', in Thomson, *Towns and townspeople*, 1–21

——— 'The birth of York's civic liberties, c. 1200–1354', in Rees Jones, *Government of medieval York*, 88–107

——— 'Towns and the English state, 1066–1500', in J. R. Maddicott and D. M. Palliser (eds), *The medieval state: essays presented to James Campbell*, London 2000, 127–45

——— (ed.), *The Cambridge urban history of Britain, 600–1540*, Cambridge 2000

Palmer, J. J. N., 'The impeachment of Michael de la Pole in 1386', *BIHR* xlii (1969), 96–101

——— 'The parliament of 1385 and the constitutional crisis of 1386', *Speculum* xlvi (1971), 477–90

Palmer, R. C., *English law in the age of the Black Death, 1348–1381: a transformation of governance and law*, Chapel Hill 1993

Parsons, J. C., 'Eleanor of Castile (1241–1290): legend and reality through seven centuries', in D. Parsons (ed.), *Eleanor of Castile, 1290–1990*, Stamford 1991, 23–54

Patterson, C. F., *Urban patronage in early modern England: corporate boroughs, the landed elite, and the crown, 1580–1640*, Stanford 1999

Payling, S. J., *Political society in Lancastrian England: the greater gentry of Nottinghamshire*, Oxford 1991

——— review of J. Watts, *Henry VI and the politics of kingship*, Cambridge 1996, in *PH* xvi (1997), 359–61

Phythian-Adams, C., *Desolation of a city: Coventry and the urban crisis of the late Middle Ages*, Cambridge 1979

Platt, C., *Medieval Southampton: the port and trading community, A.D. 1000–1600*, London 1973

Pollock, F. and F. W. Maitland, *The history of English law*, 2nd edn, Cambridge 1968

Postan, M. M., 'Credit in medieval trade', *EcHR* i (1927–8), 234–61

——— 'Some social consequences of the Hundred Years' War', *EcHR* xii (1942), 1–12

——— 'The costs of the Hundred Years' War', *P&P* xxvii (1964), 34–53

——— and others (eds), *The Cambridge economic history of Europe*, Cambridge 1963

Powell, E., 'The administration of criminal justice in late-medieval England: peace sessions and assizes', in R. Eales and D. Sullivan (eds), *The political context of law*, London 1987, 49–59

——— *Kingship, law, and society: criminal justice in the reign of Henry V*, Oxford 1989

—— 'After "after McFarlane": the poverty of patronage and the case for constitutional history', in D. J. Clayton and others (eds), *Trade, devotion and governance: papers in later medieval history*, Stroud 1994, 1–16

Prestwich, M., *War, politics and finance under Edward I*, London 1972

—— 'An estimate by the commons of royal revenue in England under Richard II', *PH* iii (1984), 147–65

Prince, A. E., 'The army and navy', in Willard and others, *English government at work*, i. 332–93

Prynne, W., *Aurum reginae*, London 1668

Pugh, R. B., 'Prisons and gallows', in VCH, *Yorkshire: York*, 491–8

—— 'The seals, insignia, plate, and officers of the city', in VCH, *Yorkshire: York*, 544–6

Putnam, B. H., *The enforcement of the statutes of labourers during the first decade after the Black Death, 1349–1359*, New York 1908

—— 'The transformation of the keepers of the peace into the justices of the peace, 1327–1380', *TRHS* 4th ser. xii (1929), 19–48

—— *The place in legal history of Sir William Shareshull, chief justice of the king's bench, 1350–61*, Cambridge 1950

Raine, A., *Mediaeval York*, London 1955

Ralph, E., 'Bristol *circa* 1480', in R. A. Skelton and P. D. A. Harvey (eds), *Local maps and plans from medieval England*, Oxford 1988, 309–16

Rayner, D., 'The forms and machinery of the "*commune petition*" in the fourteenth century', *EHR* lvi (1941), 198–233, 549–70

Rees Jones, S., 'York's civic administration, 1354–1464', in Rees Jones, *Government of medieval York*, 108–40

—— 'Household, work and the problem of mobile labour: the regulation of labour in medieval English towns', in J. Bothwell and others (eds), *The problem of labour in fourteenth-century England*, Woodbridge 2000, 133–53

—— (ed.), *The government of medieval York: essays in commemoration of the 1396 royal charter* (Borthwick Studies in History iii, 1997)

Reynolds, S., *An introduction to the history of English medieval towns*, Oxford 1977

—— 'Medieval urban history and the history of political thought', *Urban History Yearbook* (1982), 14–23

—— 'The history of the idea of incorporation or legal personality: a case of fallacious teleology', in S. Reynolds, *Ideas and solidarities of the medieval laity: England and western Europe*, Aldershot 1995

—— *Kingdoms and communities in western Europe, 900–1300*, 2nd edn, Oxford 1997

Rich, E. E., 'Lists of officials of the staple of Westminster', *CHJ* iv (1933), 192–3

—— 'The mayors of the staples', *CHJ* iv (1933), 120–42

Richardson, H. G., 'The commons and medieval politics', in H. G. Richardson and G. O. Sayles, *The English parliament in the Middle Ages*, London 1981

Rigby, S. H., 'The customs administration at Boston in the reign of Richard II', *BIHR* lviii (1985), 12–24

—— 'Urban "oligarchy" in late medieval England', in Thomson, *Towns and townspeople*, 62–86

—— *Medieval Grimsby*, Hull 1993

—— *English society in the later Middle Ages: class, status and gender*, Basingstoke 1995

———— and E. Ewan, 'Government, power and authority, 1300–1540', in Palliser, *Cambridge urban history of Britain*, 291–312.

Roover, R. de, 'The organization of trade', in Postan and others, *Cambridge economic history of Europe*, 42–118

Roskell, J. S., *The impeachment of Michael de la Pole, earl of Suffolk, in 1386*, Manchester 1984

———— 'Introductory survey', in Roskell and others, *House of Commons, 1386–1421*, i. 1–160

———— and others (eds), *The history of parliament: the House of Commons, 1386–1421*, Stroud 1993

Ross, C., *Edward IV*, London 1974

Rosser, G., 'Going to the fraternity feast: commensality and social relations in late medieval England', *JBS* xxxiii (1994), 430–46

Runyan, T. J., 'Ships and fleets in Anglo-French warfare, 1337–1360', *American Neptune* xlvi (1986), 91–9

Russell, P. E., *The English intervention in Spain and Portugal in the time of Edward III and Richard II*, Oxford 1955

Sacks, D. H., *Trade, society and politics in Bristol, 1500–1640*, New York 1985

———— 'The corporate town and the English state: Bristol's "little businesses", 1625–1641', *P&P* cx (1986), 69–105

———— 'Celebrating authority in Bristol, 1475–1640', in S. Zimmerman and R. F. E. Weissman (eds), *Urban life in the renaissance*, Newark, NJ 1989, 187–223

———— *The widening gate: Bristol and the Atlantic economy, 1450–1700*, Berkeley 1991

Sargeant, F., 'The wine trade with Gascony', in Unwin, *Finance and trade*, 257–311

Saul, A., 'Great Yarmouth and the Hundred Years War in the fourteenth century', *BIHR* lii (1979), 105–15

———— 'Local politics and the Good Parliament', in A. J. Pollard (ed.), *Property and politics: essays in later medieval English history*, Gloucester 1984, 156–71

Saul, N., *Knights and esquires: the Gloucestershire gentry in the fourteenth century*, Oxford 1981

———— *Richard II*, New Haven 1997

———— 'Richard II and the city of York', in Rees Jones, *Government of medieval York*, 1–13

Sayles, G. O., *The functions of the medieval parliament of England*, London 1988

Scammell, G. V., 'Shipowning in England, c. 1450–1550', *TRHS* 5th ser. xii (1962), 105–22

Scattergood, J., 'The *libelle of Englyshe polycye*: the nation and its place', in H. Cooney (ed.), *Nation, court and culture: new essays on fifteenth-century English poetry*, Dublin 2001, 28–49

Schildhauer, J., *The Hansa: history and culture*, trans. K. Vanovitch, Leipzig 1985

Sherborne, J. W., *The port of Bristol in the Middle Ages* (Bristol Branch of the Historical Association, 1965)

———— 'The Hundred Years' War, the English navy: shipping and manpower, 1369–1389', *P&P* xxxvii (1967), 163–75

———— 'The battle of La Rochelle and the war at sea, 1372–5', *BIHR* xlii (1969), 17–29

———— 'The cost of English warfare with France in the later fourteenth century', *BIHR* l (1977), 135–50

———— 'English barges and balingers of the late fourteenth century', *Mariner's Mirror* lxiii (1977), 109–14

———— 'Charles VI and Richard II', in J. J. N. Palmer (ed.), *Froissart: historian*, Woodbridge 1981, 50–63

———— 'The defence of the realm and the impeachment of Michael de la Pole in 1386', in Taylor and Childs, *Politics and crisis*, 97–116

Steel, A., 'The practice of assignment in the later fourteenth century', *EHR* xliii (1928), 172–80

———— 'English government finance, 1377–1413', *EHR* li (1936), 29–51, 577–97

———— *The receipt of the exchequer, 1377–1485*, Cambridge 1954

———— 'The collectors of the customs at Newcastle upon Tyne in the reign of Richard II', in Davies, *Studies presented to Sir Hilary Jenkinson*, 390–413

———— 'The collectors of customs in the reign of Richard II', in H. Hearder and H. R. Loyn (eds), *British government and administration: studies presented to S. B. Chrimes*, Cardiff 1974, 27–39

Stone, L., 'Prosopography', in L. Stone, *The past and the present revisited*, London 1987, 45–73

Stubbs, W., *The constitutional history of England in its origin and development*, 4th edn, Oxford 1906

Swanson, H., *Medieval artisans: an urban class in late medieval England*, Oxford 1989

Tait, J., *The medieval English borough: studies on its origins and constitutional history*, Manchester 1936

Taylor, J., *English historical literature in the fourteenth century*, Oxford 1987

———— 'The Good Parliament and its sources', in Taylor and Childs, *Politics and crisis*, 81–96

———— and W. Childs (eds), *Politics and crisis in fourteenth-century England*, Gloucester 1990

Thomson, J. A. F. (ed.), *Towns and townspeople in the fifteenth century*, Gloucester 1988

Thornton, T., 'Cheshire: the inner citadel of Richard II's kingdom?', in G. Dodd (ed.), *The reign of Richard II*, Stroud 2000, 85–96

———— *Cheshire and the Tudor state, 1480–1560*, Woodbridge 2000

Thrupp, S. L., *The merchant class of medieval London, 1300–1500*, Ann Arbor 1948

Tittler, R., review of Attreed, *King's towns*, in *Speculum* lxxvii (2002), 1229–30

Tönnies, F., *Community and society: Gemeinschaft und Gesellschaft*, ed. and trans. C. P. Loomis, New York 1963

Tout, T. F., *Chapters in the administrative history of mediaeval England*, Manchester 1920–37

Tuck, A., *Richard II and the English nobility*, London 1973

———— 'Nobles, commons and the great revolt of 1381', in Hilton and Aston, *English rising*, 194–212

Unwin, G., 'The estate of merchants, 1336–1365', in Unwin, *Finance and trade*, 179–255

———— (ed.), *Finance and trade under Edward III*, Manchester 1918, repr. 1962

Vale, J., *Edward III and chivalry: chivalric society and its context, 1270–1350*, Woodbridge 1982

VCH, *Yorkshire: York*, Oxford 1961

Verduyn, A., 'The revocation of urban peace commissions in 1381: the Lincoln petition', *HR* lxv (1992), 108–11

—— 'The politics of law and order during the early years of Edward III', *EHR* cviii (1993), 842–67

—— 'The selection and appointment of justices of the peace in 1338', *HR* lxviii (1995), 1–25

Walker, S., 'Yorkshire justices of the peace, 1389–1413', *EHR* cviii (1993), 281–311

Watts, J., 'Ideas, principles and politics', in A. J. Pollard (ed.), *The Wars of the Roses*, Basingstoke 1995, 110–33

—— *Henry VI and the politics of kingship*, Cambridge 1996

Weber, M., *The theory of social and economic organization*, trans. A. M. Henderson and T. Parsons, ed. T. Parsons, New York 1964

Weinbaum, M., *The incorporation of boroughs*, Manchester 1937

White, A. B., *Self-government at the king's command: a study in the beginnings of English democracy*, Minneapolis 1933

Willard, J. F., *Parliamentary taxes on personal property, 1290 to 1334: a study in mediaeval English financial administration*, Cambridge, Mass. 1934

—— and others (eds), *The English government at work, 1327–1336*, Cambridge, Mass. 1940–50

Withington, P. and A. Shephard, 'Introduction: communities in early modern England', in P. Withington and A. Shephard (eds), *Communities in early modern England*, Manchester 2000, 1–15

Wolffe, B. P., *The royal demesne in English history: the crown estate in the governance of the realm from the conquest to 1509*, London 1971

Wood-Legh, K. L., 'Sheriffs, lawyers, and belted knights in the parliaments of Edward III', *EHR* xlvi (1931), 372–88

Wright, S. M., *The Derbyshire gentry in the fifteenth century* (Derbyshire Record Society viii, 1983)

Unpublished theses

Barron, C. M., 'The government of London and its relations with the crown, 1400–1450', PhD diss. London 1970

Bartlett, J. N., 'Some aspects of the economy of York in the later Middle Ages, 1300–1550', PhD diss. London 1958

Crouch, D. J. F., 'A medieval paying audience: the stationholders on the route of the York Corpus Christi play in the fifteenth century', MA diss. York 1990

Kermode, J. I., 'The merchants of York, Beverley and Hull in the fourteenth and fifteenth centuries', PhD diss. Sheffield 1990

Penn, S. A. C., 'Social and economic aspects of fourteenth-century Bristol', PhD diss. Birmingham 1989

Wheatley, L. R., 'The York mercers' guild, 1420–1502', MA diss. York 1993

Wright, A. P. M., 'The relations between the king's government and the English cities and boroughs in the fifteenth century', DPhil. diss. Oxford 1965

Index

Ricart, Robert, 56 n. 210, 63, 123–4, 206–7
Richard I, king of England, 60
Richard II, king of England: accession, 140, 175–6; and continual councils, 175–6; and customs administration, 106; deposition, 4, 37–8, 211, 214–15; family, 65, 165; household, 29, 98, 108, 137, 174, 175–6, 180–1; naval affairs, 54, 207; and parliament, 22–3, 42, 108–9, 110, 138, 141, 151, 160–1, 166–7, 193; pattern of urban lending, 41–2; proposed expedition to France, 22; relations with Cheshire, 165–7; relations with Ireland, 36–7, 46, 65; relations with London, 1, 30, 64; relations with Scotland, 24, 26, 35, 43; relations with Wales, 165–6; and trade, 51–2, 57, 139; tyranny, 29–30, 33, 37–8, 152, 214; visits to towns, 34, 64, 65, 174, 191–2, 193, 210–12; weight of royal taxation under, 92
Richard III, king of England, 2, 4
Richemond, William, 168–9 n. 158
Rievaulx (N. Yorks.), 28
river traffic, 161–3
Roos, Sir Thomas de, 61–2, 152
Roos family, of Helmsley (N. Yorks.), 61–2, 152
Rufford, John de, 86–7, 89
Rypon, John de, 122
Rypon, John de (d. c. 1398), 94, 152, 158, 210

Salisbury (Wilts.), 81 n. 124, 182
Sandwich (Kent), 46
Santon, John de, 94, 96
Savage, Robert, 37–8, 152, 203, 210
Savage, William, 37–8
Scotland, Scottish, 61, 180, 213, 168–9 n. 158; threatened invasions of England, 34–5, 43, 151; wars and relations with, 20, 24, 26, 34–5, 37, 45–6, 65–6
Scrope, Henry Lord, of Masham, 133
Scrope, Richard Lord, of Bolton, treasurer, chancellor of England (d. 1403), 22, 78
Scrope, Richard, of Masham, archbishop of York, 206
Segrave, Sir Hugh, 133
Selby (N. Yorks.), 48, 101
Selby, John de, 146–7
Selby, Robert de, 109
Selby, William de, 153, 173, 203, 210

self-government at the king's command, 13–14, 76, 102
Serjeant, John, 145–6, 148–9, 150
Sevenhous, John de, 37
Severn, river, 10, 101, 158 n. 100, 161–3
Severn Estuary, 10–11
Shareshull, Sir William, chief justice of king's bench, 112, 198
Shepey, John, 133
sheriffs, 14, 117, 165, 167; appointment, 108; of counties, 28, 58, 70, 107, 194, 202, 209; of towns, 190–1, 202, 211. See also Bristol, civic government; York, civic government
ships, shipping: barges and balingers, 30, 40 n. 116, 44, 46–8, 53–5, 79–80, 80–2, 85, 92–3; protection of, 34, 44–5, 49–50, 51–4, 186–7, 195; shipmasters, 47–8, 50; shipowners, 47–51, 52–3, 77, 107–8, 158, 206; ships to the crown, 19, 43–57, 77, 79–80, 146, 149, 171, 209 (see also barges and balingers); and trade, 8, 10–11
Shrewsbury (Salop), 113, 163–4
Shropshire, 161, 163, 164, 167 n. 149, 168
Sibille, Walter, 137, 138
Skelton, William de, 42
Sluys (Belgium), 133
Smithfield (London), 65–6
Smyth, Thomas, 48–9, 210
Somerset, 55–6, 79, 145, 146, 148, 149, 159, 191, 194–5, 202
Somerwell, William de, 49, 72–5, 125, 134
Soureby, Richard de, 94
Southampton (Hants.), merchants of, 13, 14 n. 71, 23, 44, 110, 184, 212
Spaigne, William, 23, 184 n. 229
Spain, 45–6
Spelly, Ellis, 150, 180, 203–4; civic officeholder, 49, 103, 125, 180, 204; customs collector, 103, 109 n. 52; member of parliament, 52–3, 149–50, 153, 180, 181–2, 187; poll tax collector, 149; shipmaster, 50; shipowner, 49, 52–3; staple official, 125
Spelly, Henry, 179–80
Spicer, John le, 114, 120
Spicer, Richard le, 38, 49, 50, 119–20, 125, 134, 203–4, 206
Stafford, Ralph, earl of (d. 1372), see Audley
Staffordshire, 161, 163, 164
staple, domestic: alien merchants, 118–19, 125–6; corporate character, 118,

126–7; denizen merchants, 115, 116, 118–19, 122, 125–6; jurisdiction, 114–20, 123–6; officials (mayor and constables), 114, 115, 116–27, 128, 130; ordinance of the staple (1353), 110–15, 116, 117, 125–6; relations with towns, 115, 119–29; staple gaol, 115

staple, overseas: Bruges, 111, 129; Calais, 31, 115–16, 122, 158, 160, 168, 183, 186 n. 239; merchants of Calais staple, 4, 22, 30, 35, 54, 87, 110–11, 123, 129–31, 147; Middleburg, 116

statute merchant, *see* debt

statute staple, *see* debt

Staynlay, Thomas, 210

Sterlyng, Geoffrey, 182–3

Stevenes, John, 49, 55, 107, 109 n. 52

steward of the royal household, 174, 175–6

Stocket, Master Nicholas, 137

Stoke, John de, 106; civic officeholder, 103, 124, 125, 128, 134, 203, 206; cloth subsidy, farmer of, 149; customs collector, 103–4, 149; diplomat, 104, 131–4, 138, 149, 206; member of parliament, 134, 149; poll tax collector, 149; staple official, 124, 125, 128

Stone (Gloucs.), 145

Striles, Peter de, 118

Suffolk, 178–9

Suffolk, Michael, earl of (d. 1389), *see* de la Pole

Sutton, Robert de, 23, 184

Swylington, Robert de, 61

Sydenham, Richard de, 145, 146, 148–9

taxation, civic, 79, 81–2, 84–5, 88–9, 91–2

taxation, royal, direct: fifteenths and tenths, collectors of, 48–9, 50, 67–8, 84, 87, 145, 203, 207; fifteenths and tenths, in counties, 39, 203; fifteenths and tenths, grants of, 22–3, 58, 67–70, 71, 99, 148, 156, 178; fifteenths and tenths, in towns, 11, 19, 29, 39, 40, 59, 67–71, 81–5, 154, 176, 209; poll taxes, collectors of, 36–7, 48–9, 50, 87, 92, 93–6, 149; poll taxes, grants of, 58, 89–90, 92; poll taxes, in towns, 11, 29, 36–7, 58, 83–4, 90, 92, 93–6, 149

taxation, royal, indirect: cloth subsidy, collectors of, 115, 149, 159–60; tonnage and poundage, collectors of, 53, 77, 102–4, 107, 109–10, 180; tonnage and poundage, grants of, 53,

102, 109–10, 134, 148; wool custom and subsidy, 22, 25, 183; wool custom and subsidy, collectors of, 103; wool and petty customs, collectors of, 77, 101–9. *See also* wool monopoly schemes

Tedistille, Walter, 150

Teutonic knights, grandmaster of the order of, 135, 137

Tewkesbury (Gloucs.), 161–2; abbey, 72 n. 85, 73

Thames, river, 162–3

Thomas of Woodstock, duke of Gloucester (d. 1397), 66, 150–1

Thornbury (Gloucs.), 63, 145–6

Thurkyll, Thomas, 210

Tothe, Robert, 94

tournaments, 65–6

Tower of London, 84, 177–80

treasurer, king's, 61–2, 72, 78, 175–6

Trent, river, 101, 163

Tresilian, Robert, chief justice of king's bench, 151

Trewman, Jack, 96 n. 205

Tudor dynasty, 2

Turtle, Roger, 28, 68

Tykhill, William de, 210

Ulster, Elizabeth, countess of, 66

Venour, William, 168

Vere, Robert de, marquess of Dublin, duke of Ireland (d. 1392), 65, 152, 167

Vyell, John, 134, 150–1, 159, 203–4

Waldegrave, Sir Richard, 178–9

Wales, Welsh, 34–5, 110, 113, 158 n. 100, 163–8. *See also* Wales, marches of

Wales, marches of, 145, 163–8

Wales, prince of, *see* Edward, prince of Wales, eldest son of Edward III

Walsingham, Thomas, chronicler, 31, 47, 132

Walworth, Sir William, 110, 124, 176, 183–4

Warbulton, Robert, 182 n. 217

Warde, Robert, 37–8

Wark-on-Tweed (Northumberland), 61

Wars of the Roses, 2–3, 4–5, 7, 64, 141, 215

Warwick, Thomas, earl of (d. 1401), *see* Beauchamp

Wateby, Richard de, 122

weights and measures, 114, 115, 174